AF478144

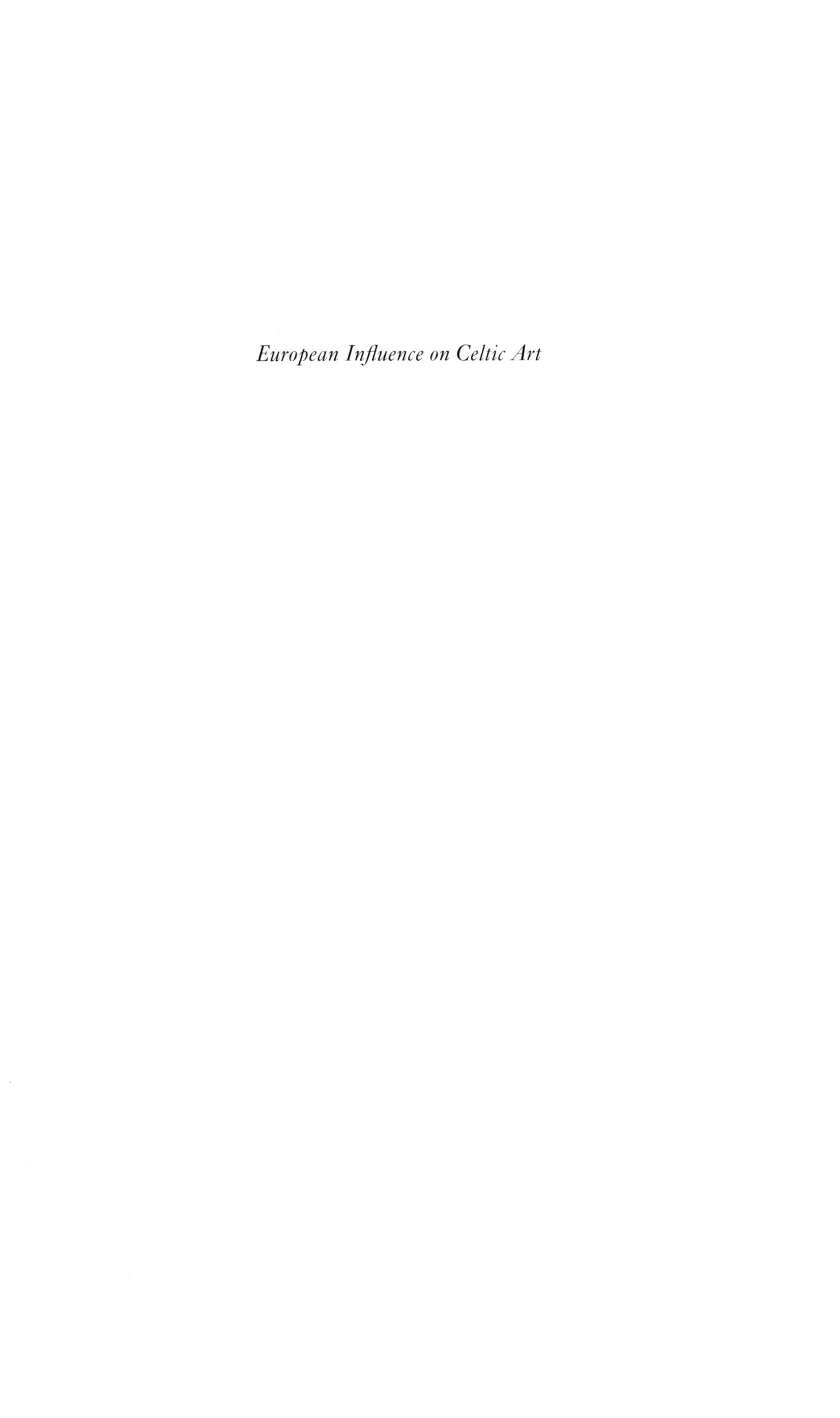

European Influence on Celtic Art

European Influence on Celtic Art

Patrons and Artists

Lloyd Laing

FOUR COURTS PRESS

Typeset in 11pt on 13pt EhrhardtMT
by Carrigboy Typesetting Services for
FOUR COURTS PRESS LTD
7 Malpas Street, Dublin 8, Ireland
www.fourcourtspress.ie
and in North America for
FOUR COURTS PRESS
c/o ISBS, 920 N.E. 58th Avenue, Suite 300, Portland, OR 97213.

A catalogue record for this title is available
from the British Library.

ISBN 978–1–84682–175–2

Printed in England
by MPG Books, Bodmin, Cornwall.

Contents

Illustrations

Abbreviations

Antiq. J.	*Antiquaries Journal*
Archaeol. J.	*Archaeological Journal*
BAR	British Archaeological Reports
CBA	Council for British Archaeology
JIA	*Journal of Irish Archaeology*
JCHAS	*Journal of the Cork Historical and Archaeological Society*
JRSAI	*Journal of the Royal Society of Antiquaries of Ireland*
Med. Arch.	*Medieval Archaeology*
PSAS	*Proceedings of the Society of Antiquaries of Scotland*
PRIA	*Proceedings of the Royal Irish Academy*
PPS	*Proceedings of the Prehistoric Society*
r.	reigned
RCAHMS	Royal Commission on the Ancient and Historical Monuments of Scotland
Repr.	Reprint/reprinted
UJA	*Ulster Journal of Archaeology*

Introduction

The term 'Celts' has been used fairly indiscriminately for people in various parts of western Europe from the seventh century BC to the present day. For the period after *c.*AD350, the term has been used especially in Ireland, the south-west peninsula of England, Wales and Scotland including the Hebrides and Northern Isles. These areas have retained or renewed Celtic identities that are distinct from those in areas settled initially by the Romans and then the Anglo-Saxons. Study of the Celts has given rise to particular challenges in art, history and archaeology, on which numerous books and papers have been produced.

This book is chiefly concerned with the period between *c.*AD350 and *c.*1200, in which the majority of surviving works of Celtic art in Britain and Ireland were produced. The period coincides with the adoption of Christianity and the resultant changes in patronage of the arts. It traces the development of Celtic art from its perceived beginnings in Iron Age Europe, through its amalgamation into Romano-British art and its absorption of iconography and images from the Anglo-Saxon world, the Continent and the Mediterranean in the fifth to eighth centuries AD.

From the ninth century, Celtic art further evolved with the acquisition of new ornament from the Scandinavian world via the Norse settlements, particularly in Ireland. By the twelfth century, Celtic art effectively ceased to develop due to the impact of the Normans. A few elements, such as interlace, re-appeared in later Insular (the term generally used in connection with the islands north of the English Channel) art, but they were not natural revivals. The Celtic Revival of the later nineteenth century, for example, was a deliberate creation which consciously imitated the motifs and designs of a previous age to serve the political and cultural aspirations of the day (Sheehy, 1980). As a result, from the nineteenth to the late twentieth century it was not acceptable to discuss Celtic art in terms of outside influences – the overwhelming aim was to prove that Celtic art was 'pure'. Art historical studies were thus at the centre of contemporaneous political and social thought, an uneasy situation that led to many false starts and, it must be suspected, deliberate confusions.

One of the many questions debated was whether Celtic art was art or craft in the modern sense, since apart from sculpture, the majority would in modern terms come under the category of decorative arts. However, the Celts were concerned with re-affirming fundamental, commonly-held values. The producers of the material, whether they are called artists, craftspeople or artisans, used the existing artistic vocabulary in ways which re-asserted these values and showed new aspects of them. Pagan Celtic art was concerned with helping the patrons represent their social standing as the continuation of the values shared by their predecessors. Christian Celtic art was concerned with how the fundamental truths of faith could be revealed and asserted in different ways through using the accepted symbols. In this sense, what was produced was undoubtedly art expressed through craft.

The diversity and strength of outside influences is so noticeable, especially when collected together in a volume such as this, that without seeing the artworks themselves, the reader might be forgiven for coming to the conclusion that Celtic art is simply an amalgam of other art styles. Certainly, no ornamental device was specifically a Celtic invention, but it is what was done with the devices that gives the art its unique essence. Geometrical principles were applied, interlace was developed in a bewildering variety of ways, and simple ornamental devices such as triskeles and scrolls were combined in ways not attempted by other artists. In figural art, the compositions were borrowed or the animals and figures directly inspired by imported models, but Celtic artists chose to combine the borrowed elements into composite wholes in a totally distinctive manner that is recognizable over several millennia. The ingredients were to be found in other recipes, but what reached the table was unique.

This book has been written with the needs of students in mind, and to that end some background information is given where it was felt necessary to provide a context for the discussion that followed, or some explanation of terms used and identification of people to whom reference is made. No attempt has been made, however, to give descriptions of individual key works: for this the reader is referred to the author's *Archaeology of Celtic Britain and Ireland, c.AD400–1200* (Cambridge, 2006) or Lloyd and Jennifer Laing's *Art of the Celts* (London, 1992), where this information can be found.

The book has benefitted considerably from the input and advice of Jennifer Laing.

CHAPTER I

The study of Celtic art

The ancient Celts were originally identified as distinct from non-Celts through references in Classical writings, linguistics and surviving material culture. The concept of a distinct Celtic art began in the nineteenth century when race and ethnicity were being examined. Having identified the existence of Celts from historical sources, scholars sought out a cultural assemblage with which to associate them and significantly, they grouped together all the types of ornament that were thought to have been produced by the Celts. In art historical studies, the term 'Celtic art' was therefore perceived to be associated with the archaeological Iron Age culture known as La Tène from a site in Switzerland where there was activity from the fifth century BC (Jacobsthal, 1944; Harding, 2007, 2). In the climate of thought that prevailed through much of the twentieth century, La Tène art was seen to have been brought to Britain by invaders from the Continent (James, 1999, 92).

DEFINING CELTIC ART IN BRITAIN AND IRELAND

The first person to speak of pre-Roman Iron Age Celtic art was Sir Wollaston Franks, Keeper in the British Museum, 1866–96. Franks published John Kemble's *Horae Ferales* (Kemble, Franks & Latham, 1863), describing a number of major pieces of Iron Age art including the Witham Shield and the enamelled horse trappings from the hoard from Polden Hills, Somerset. These were described as 'Late Celtic', a term that persisted into the twentieth century to distinguish the works of the Iron Age from that of the preceding Bronze Age, which was, however, also seen as Celtic.

Recognition of Celtic Christian art preceded the recognition of a Celtic Iron Age art, since it was clearly an attribute of known Celtic-speaking peoples. The process of identifying Celtic Christian art therefore began almost as early as the identification of the Celts themselves. It was certainly attracting the attention of antiquaries in Scotland and Ireland in the later eighteenth century, though the term 'Celtic' was not used to describe it, and the art was simply seen as early Christian.

The use of the term 'Celtic art' to embrace all the art produced in Britain and Ireland in the early medieval period (that is, after the collapse of the Roman province of Britannia in AD409) by Celtic-speaking peoples seems to have been first widely applied by J. Romilly Allen. He used the term 'Celtic Christian art in Wales' in his review of the sculptures published at the end of the nineteenth century (1899), and although the term had not been used in Allen and Anderson's *Early Christian Monuments of Scotland* in 1903, it was employed quite firmly in Allen's classic review *Celtic Art* (1904), which embraced both the Iron Age and medieval periods. Allen made it clear, however, that in his view there was no connection between the two traditions (1904, xvi). In the same period, George Coffey used the term 'Celtic ornament' to embrace both pre-Christian and Christian art in Ireland, in his *Guide to Celtic Antiquities of the Christian Period Preserved in the National Museum, Dublin* (1909, chap. 1).

The linking of Iron Age and early medieval Celtic art as a continuing phenomenon was largely due to E.T. Leeds in Britain, and Joseph Raftery and Adolf Mahr in Ireland. While acknowledging that there was an 'almost complete cessation of artistic production on the part of the native' in the early centuries AD (1933, 138), Leeds asserted that in the post-Roman period 'the Celt was coming into his own again … True it is, he was taking some new models, but it is none the less a renaissance, a renaissance not of a mere system of ornament, but of the life-force which informed that ornament' (1933, 153). For Leeds, one fact seems to have clinched the idea of revival – 'the Celt casts aside the formal quadripartite arrangement of the design and returns to his beloved tripartite scheme' (1933, 154). In this, Leeds seems to be thinking of the triskele, which is by no means universal as a motif in early medieval Celtic art, in which just as many examples of 'formal quadripartite arrangements' can be found.

In Ireland, the idea of renaissance was furthered by Mahr and Raftery's *Christian Art in Ancient Ireland*. 'It is in this period [the fifth century AD] that a sudden revival of the old Keltic style becomes apparent' (1932, xxi). Mahr and Raftery argued that the revival happened in Ireland due to the extinction of Celtic art in southern Britain. They posed the question 'Are we, then, to assume that the La Tène tradition of Celtic Christian art is entirely Gaelic in character?' (1932, xxii), which they went on to answer in the affirmative. This statement contains an underlying assumption that Iron Age Celtic art is to be equated with La Tène culture. From this the assumption followed that only in Ireland could it have been kept alive since it was further assumed to have been extinguished in Britain through Roman and subsequently Anglo-Saxon conquest. Once established, the ideas were perpetuated in Ireland by Françoise Henry, first in *Irish Art*

(1940, 1), then in the influential *Irish Art in the Early Christian Period to AD800*, in which she asserted that 'A remarkable continuity is one of the most striking aspects of Irish art' (1965, 1). Subsequent writers have followed this now-established view that Celtic Christian art was not a new phenomenon (at least in the form of its ornament if not its iconography), but a revival of that found in the La Tène cultural tradition. In turn, links have been sought, but those that have been found have been both sparse and unconvincing (for example, Finlay, 1973, 104–9; Megaw & Megaw, 1989, 243–4; Laing & Laing, 1992, 138).

Virtually no artworks survived from the areas outside Roman control, which was argued as being the result of impoverishment or possibly due to accident of survival of the materials used. Roman provincial art was largely ignored by Celtic researchers as irrelevant to their purposes and interests and, furthermore, regarded as inferior to Classical art by Romanists. Vital links in the chain of Celtic artistic development were therefore largely discounted. As a result, it was argued that the (apparent) re-emergence of identifiably Celtic ornament in the post-Roman period was 'pure' Celtic art that had been uncontaminated by Roman or other outside influence. This view was emphasized to prove the endurance of Celtic spirit and ethnicity, particularly in Ireland, through the years of external suppression under the Romans in Britain. Ireland's physical isolation from mainland Britain allowed the argument to flourish.

These factors had far-reaching results in Celtic studies in general and were persuasive in arguing that there was a separate Celtic cultural identity which was virtually untouched by outside influences. An influential factor in the endurance of this academic argument was the abundance of sumptuous artworks that survive from the seventh century onwards in Celtic areas, most notably in Ireland. Manuscripts, stone carvings, and metalwork were apparently suddenly produced in distinctive Celtic style, mostly as a result of patronage by the Church immediately after the formal conversion of people in the Celtic lands to Christianity.

Many modern approaches now consider that this is probably too simple a picture, since many of the motifs discernible in Iron Age and post-Roman Celtic areas were also common in Classical art of the time. To a certain extent, all areas possessed a common repertoire and influence between areas was highly complex. Although the Celtic areas lie geographically on the north-west fringe of Europe, they were never as isolated as originally thought and maintained considerable contact with their immediate neighbours and with the Mediterranean. The sea and rivers as a means of rapid and cost-effective transport have been underestimated by many historians.

THE LIMITS OF INFERENCE FOR CELTIC ART

The study of Celtic Christian art is limited by the fact that most works are without a fixed chronological context or association, either having been found by chance in non-scientific excavations, or having been stored in monasteries without written evidence of their origins. Only a few pieces of twelfth-century metalwork and a few sculptures of the ninth and tenth centuries have been (tenuously) dated – through the identification of the people named on them. A handful of items has come from archaeological contexts, where dating has been provided by associated finds or scientific methods such as radiocarbon. Unfortunately, archaeological finds of artwork are few and generally of no major significance. In a few cases, groups of objects have been found in hoards (such as those from Ardagh, Derrynaflan and Donore in Ireland and from Norrie's Law, Gaulcross and St Ninian's Isle in Scotland), but some of the objects could have been much older than the date of deposition or than the other items in the collections. The same can be said for the many Celtic art objects that have been found in Scandinavian graves of the Viking period, and which are presumed to have originated as loot from raids on Celtic areas.

In the absence of a firm fixed chronology, the study of the art has been largely dependent on art historical methodology. This approach compares motifs and iconography with those from other areas, periods or cultures. Dangerous and misleading though the tendency is, it has often been to assume that similar art must be of similar date.

Art history has also relied on the theory that art must be seen to evolve from simple beginnings, passing through a phase of elaboration followed by a period of degeneration. However, it is evident that there was a considerable degree of conservatism in Celtic (particularly Christian period) art; ancient designs were deliberately chosen out of a respect for the past. The ornament of such major works as the manuscript of *c.*AD800, the Book of Kells, did not so much evolve as form a legacy that was felt throughout the Celtic world and lasted down to the twelfth century (Lang, 1991). It notably contains elements found some 500 years earlier in Roman art (see below, chapter 2).

WRITTEN SOURCES

One of the basic sources for art historical studies is usually the written word. For the Celtic areas before *c.*AD1200, however, there are few direct historical sources and those that remain are rarely reliable and usually highly biased. Among British sources, the works of the Anglo-Saxon historian, the Venerable Bede (*c*.673–735); the colourful and highly controversial St Gildas (*c*.485–570) and the *Historia Brittonum* (a compilation of texts of different dates, originally attributed to a ninth-century monk, Nennius) are the most outstanding narrative histories. For the sixth century onwards, there are annals, genealogies Lives (biographies) of saints and law tracts, all of which have considerable deficiencies for study of the Celts and are even less helpful in studying Celtic art. A few useful insights can be gained from such Christian writings as Adomnán's *Life of Columba*, Cogitosus' *Life of Brigit*, Muirchú's *Life of Patrick* and Tirechán's *Collectanea* (which relates to St Patrick and a supposed journey he made in northern Ireland).

Documentary sources for Celtic art, artists or methods of manufacture are virtually non-existent in Britain, though more is known about early medieval Ireland from documentary sources than probably from anywhere else in Europe. The material is particularly difficult to evaluate, especially for the mid-seventh to mid-ninth centuries (Ó Cróinín, 1995, 8), although Irish law codes have proved a valuable source for understanding the way in which workshops and patronage operated (see chapters 5 and 6). Some useful data is found in the Lives of saints and occasionally in later sources such as Gerald of Wales (1146–1223), who provides occasional comments on how the artisans and their work were viewed.

THE IDENTITY OF THE CELTS

The word 'Celt' first appears in Greek sources – in the writings of Hecataeus and Herodotus in the sixth to fifth centuries BC – in which it is clear that the Celts were seen as an ethnic group located in central and western Europe. It is difficult to determine whether they spoke a language that would today be recognized as Celtic, or whether they had a geographical spread that coincided with the use of that language. Use of Celtic languages has been repeatedly claimed as the definitive feature in defining the Celts, with artistic motifs often being used to corroborate theories.

Celtic languages developed from a parent Indo-European root that was probably introduced to Europe at the end of the Neolithic or the beginning of the Bronze Age and it is generally held that Celtic was being spoken in Britain and Ireland as well as on the Continent at least as early as the Iron Age.

Language is usually seen as a binding factor between peoples, and it is clear that during the period under review people in the Celtic areas spoke

Celtic languages rather than Latin or Germanic, such as Anglo-Saxon, even though some inscriptions of the fifth and sixth centuries show vestigial knowledge of debased Latin. Languages from two main Celtic language families were spoken in the period and region covered by this book – Brittonic/Brythonic (notably Welsh) and Goidelic/Gaelic (notably Irish) (Ball & Fife, 1993).

By the post-Roman/early medieval period, the Celtic populations in Wales, Scotland, Ireland and the south-west peninsula of England, had not simply language, but cultural attributes in common with each other that differed from those of their neighbours. They are associated with distinct settlement and artefact types, burial practices and religious monuments, for example. The term 'Celt' was not used either by them or by their neighbours to describe them. While they clearly did not have a formal collective identity, they apparently thought of themselves in terms of regional groups such as Irish, Welsh or what are now known as Picts (a confederation of tribes in eastern and northern Scotland from Roman times until the ninth century). It is therefore probable that they recognized differences between themselves and non-Celtic people.

THE CELTS IN THE IRON AGE TO THE POST-ROMAN PERIOD

Iron Age people were tribal. They often operated within a radius of about thirty miles and rarely had loyalties or allegiances except to the immediate tribe. Society depended on warring with neighbours. The population had slaves, bartered for goods, owed kinship debts and was non-literate. They were highly disorganized outside the individual tribe, which partly accounts for the successful expansion of the Roman world during the first centuries BC and AD, through a mixture of diplomacy, bribery, military strength and two-way economic necessity. It is clear that from the start even the most remote Celtic populations were aware of and responded to the Roman presence in the new province of Britannia (for example, embassies were sent from the Orkneys to the emperor Claudius at time of the Roman conquest of AD43, and complex diplomatic relationships existed between Rome and some Celts in southern Britain). A two-way process of borrowing and adapting is apparent in many aspects of life, including art. Traditionally, art historians have regarded Romano-Celtic art disparagingly as inferior provincial work, but most commentators currently view it as an intriguing reflection of cultural change.

Roman domination was established during the late first century AD and continued, especially south of Hadrian's Wall, until from the mid-third- to late-fifth century there was considerable civil unrest and population movement in the Roman world. The period is often referred to as Late Antiquity (when viewed from the standpoint of the Roman civilization) or the age of the Great Migrations (when viewed from the standpoint of the Huns, Goths, Vandals and Anglo-Saxons who gradually encroached on or were integrated into Roman culture in Europe).

In 330, civil and external pressures led Constantine the Great to move the capital of the Roman Empire to Constantinople (later Byzantium) and the empire was split into two with different emperors. The last emperor in the West was deposed in 476 and replaced by the Ostrogothic leader, Theodoric. The eastern half continued as the Byzantine Empire until its fall to the Turks in 1453.

With the decline of Roman influence in Europe, new units gradually grew up, which became influential on the Celtic areas. Franks were settled by Treaty within the Roman province of Gaul from the third century onwards. In 481, Clovis (466–511), the first king of the Franks, effected the conquest of much of south and central Gaul. From this the dynasties of the Merovingians (fifth century to 751) and the Carolingians (*c*.751–987) grew into remarkable amalgamations of barbarian and Classical cultures. The traditional 'Golden Age' of the Carolingians began in 800 when Pope Leo III crowned Charlemagne (Charles the Great) Holy Roman Emperor.

EARLY MEDIEVAL BRITAIN AND IRELAND

The province of Britannia was abandoned by the Roman Empire (formally in 409, but effectively some years before). Literacy declined rapidly and historical records effectively ceased. Initially, Romano-British kingdoms grew up in the former province, the leaders of which seem to have succeeded the Roman city administrators. It is clear that there was considerable immigration of Angles, Saxons, Jutes and other Germanic groups from northern Europe. The incomers were pagans, with a pantheon of diverse nature gods, and by the seventh century they had formed distinctive kingdoms that took over from the short-lived Romano-British kingdoms. The Anglo-Saxon world was undoubtedly the most important external contributor to the development of Celtic art from the later sixth century onwards, transmitting in particular, new metalworking techniques and types of ornament, including animals and interlace. The Anglian kingdom of Northumbria (which extended across north-east England from the Humber to the Tyne), was of paramount importance in the transmission of artistic ideas, artisans and objects, especially in the Christian period. Mercia (in the English Midlands) was also influential from the later eighth-century onwards.

The Celts outside the former province of Britannia also developed kingdoms. Genealogies (set down in the ninth century and later) show that kings in Wales and southern Scotland traced their ancestry back to men with Roman names and titles. Fifth-century memorial inscriptions in Wales make it clear that leaders saw themselves as continuing Roman traditions.

Ireland was never totally isolated from contact with the Roman world, but after the collapse of Britannia, slave raiding and (probably) buy-offs seem to have increased the power and wealth of the Irish kings who then gained control of the Atlantic seaboard. Irish colonists moved into north-west Scotland, the Isle of Man, Wales and Cornwall and rapidly adopted a vestigial Roman-style material culture. During the sixth and seventh centuries, as elsewhere, smaller political units coalesced into larger groups, and kings and nobility acquired increasing wealth and power.

THE ADOPTION OF CHRISTIANITY

The adoption of Christianity in the Roman world affected virtually all aspects of life, including art. For historians, perhaps the most important aspect was that written sources were produced, albeit with strong religious biases. The faith was slow to become popular for a number of reasons, and was first adopted by women and the very poor who had no money to spend on artworks, objects or buildings. It was seen by the Roman authorities as subversive, since it taught that obedience to a higher authority than the state was overriding. Persecutions were carried out against Christians under several emperors, such as Septimius Severus and Diocletian.

In 313, the belief was adopted largely for political reasons by the Emperor Constantine and subsequently became the official state religion. This is of particular significance, since it meant that rich and influential patrons began to employ artists and craftspeople to produce works that were relevant to both secular and religious needs and aspirations.

Christianity was unofficially introduced into Britannia, c.200. The first English martyr, St Alban, probably died sometime between 251 and 259. Before the end of the Roman period, Christianity spread to the region north of Hadrian's Wall and westward into parts of Wales. There is some evidence to suggest that Christianity was already established in Ireland in the mid-fifth century, since the Romano-Briton Patrick (later St Patrick), was abducted into slavery to Ireland where he was converted by practising Christians. Prosper of Aquitaine (*c*.390–455) noted that Palladius (b. *c*.400) was sent by Pope Celestine to Ireland in 431 as the first bishop.

In Scotland, the spread of Christianity was (according to Bede), initiated by St Ninian (St Nynia) who was active among the Picts. Ninian's dates and historicity have been debated, though it is likely that he lived in the mid-fifth century.

No debate surrounds the arrival from Ireland of St Columba in 563, and his foundation of the monastery at Iona in Dál Riata (a Celtic over-kingdom which held land on both sides of the Irish Sea in Scotland and Northern Ireland in the late sixth and early seventh centuries). From this base, missionary activity was conducted among the northern Picts (Smith, 1996, 21). In Wales, the spread of the belief is associated with St Dubricius and St Illtud, who were active in the south-east around 475, and with St David in the later sixth century. South-west England (Dumnonia) had St Samson, also in the sixth century.

Outside the Celtic areas, the conversion of the Anglo-Saxon kingdoms began in 597 when St Augustine was sent by Pope Gregory to lead a mission to Britain to convert the pagan king Ethelbert of Kent. The Celtic, later Anglo-Saxon monastery at Lindisfarne, founded in 635, became highly influential to Celtic art.

PATRONAGE AND NEW ARTISTIC IDEAS

Christianity was particularly significant for the Celtic areas, since for the first time they began to look to the Mediterranean for guidance, with the result that ecclesiastical organization, liturgical and artistic models were non-Celtic in origin. The establishment of Christianity in Celtic lands exposed both patrons and artists to a wide array of fresh artistic models and impulses through direct contact with continental Europe. Unlike Celtic pagan art for example, Christian art stemmed from the humanism of the Classical tradition in which the human figure was paramount. The mixture of cultures and ideas is illustrated by the fact that the same models for individual images can be found throughout the Classical world, appearing as far apart as Ireland in the seventh to eighth centuries and Armenia and Georgia in the preceding centuries (Richardson, 1987 a&b; 1995).

Influences from southern Gaul and Italy were felt in Celtic areas – books in particular were acquired by early monastic libraries through gifts and trade. Early ecclesiastics travelled extensively throughout the Christian world – influences, ideas and objects reached remote parts of Scotland, Wales and Ireland from Byzantium and Armenia; possibly from Coptic Egypt and Visigothic Spain and certainly from Anglo-Saxon England and the Germanic world. Monasteries were industrious in copying manuscripts and other items. Techniques of manufacture were exchanged and adapted. Anglo-Saxon England, for example, provided expertise and techniques for the production of art, and continued to be an important influence into the Viking Age. The essence of art of the period was eclecticism, with a vast exchange of people, ideas and expertise with much borrowing and acquisition by gift as well as commerce.

In the late eighth to tenth centuries, a Classical revivalist art was developed in the Merovingian and Carolingian worlds, and this eventually transmitted new concepts of secular patronage, and an array of iconography that was new to the Celts.

CHAPTER 2

Pre-Christian Insular Celtic art

IRON AGE CELTIC ART IN BRITAIN AND IRELAND

The earliest Celtic art (La Tène) evolved in later prehistoric western and central Europe from the fifth century BC. It was seen on a range of objects such as personal adornments, weaponry, horse gear and the equipment for the feast which was produced for leaders and their immediate families in order to increase their prestige in society (Jacobsthal, 1944; Duval, 1977; Megaw & Megaw, 1989; Harding, 2007).

From the outset, Celtic art on the Continent employed compass ornament and designs which incorporated human masks and highly stylized animals alongside elements inspired by Classical foliage motifs of which the palmette and lotus-bud were the most prominent. This 'Early' phase was succeeded by the mature 'Waldalgesheim' (named after a site in Germany which produced classic examples of the style), which employed swirly plant-derived designs with swollen-tipped tendrils. In a later development, engraved ornament was used in the decoration in particular of scabbards (the Sword Style), while elsewhere high relief modelling and grotesque human and animal faces (the Plastic Style) enjoyed a vogue. This art is now seen not as a successive series of styles, but as regional expressions of a general trend to employ ornament.

In Britain, Iron Age art currently tends to be seen as an independent manifestation of the same ornamental trends. There are few obvious imports, though some pieces show a close resemblance to both 'Early Style' and 'Waldalgesheim' ornament on the Continent, suggesting that Britain was a participant in wider ornamental trends. A distinctive style did not evolve in Britain before the third century BC, when early engraved ornament appeared (often on military gear), which displays a fairly close similarity to what has been termed the 'Hungarian Sword Style', though close links are impossible to prove (Megaw & Megaw, 2008). This style (often termed Style IV), employed assymetrical plant-derived ornament, and had a relief-modelled counterpart. Sometimes both relief modelling and engraving in this style appear on the same object, notably on the Wandsworth Round shield boss from the Thames in London and the Witham Shield from Lincolnshire. The designs in Style IV are strongly reminiscent of foliage, but stylized birds and animals can sometimes be discerned in the patterning. It was succeeded by Style V, in which there was a greater degree of symmetry, and basketry patterns were used for infilling. It is found in both engraved and relief work, the finest of the products in the latter tradition being the series of torcs (neck-rings) in gold or electrum associated particularly with the Iceni tribe in East Anglia (Fox, 1958; Stead, 1985a, 1985b; Jope, 2000; Harding, 2007).

The corpus of surviving 'Celtic' art in Iron Age Britain and Ireland is small. A recent database has been compiled of everything that might be considered to constitute Iron Age Celtic art. It amounts to 2,582 items (Garrow, 2008, 19). However, when pieces are excluded that have no clear ornament beyond their shape, and attention is focused on pieces ornamented with 'swirly designs' (the term currently used to define it), the list is radically reduced. It has been suggested that there are fewer than a hundred such items from Britain and Ireland (Garrow, Gosden & Hill, 2008, 6). Even allowing for the possibility that a large percentage of what was made has perished, Celtic art was probably not produced in great quantities in Iron Age Britain, though distribution maps suggest that its use was fairly widespread (Garrow, 2008, figs 2.5 and 2.6).

Most of the surviving works of art from Iron Age Britain displaying Celtic style decoration were made between Julius Caesar's invasions (55 and 54BC) and the invasion of Claudius in AD43. It was a period when there were major developments in the political structure of the local tribes as well as increasing diplomatic and economic ties with Rome and Gaul. This was notably a period when some southern tribal leaders (for example of the Trinovantes, Catuvellauni and Atrebates) built up formidable power bases and wealth.

Particularly noteworthy among the works produced between *c.*55BC and *c.*AD43 are mirrors with richly engraved backs, sword scabbards and terrets (rein rings), bits and other horse gear. Roman and Gallo-Roman pottery arrived in south-eastern Britain, as well as imported bronze vessels, silverwork and figurines (MacReady & Thompson, 1981; Foster, 1977; 1986), which introduced new types of figural art and plant ornament to Romano-Celtic artists.

FEATURES COMMON TO ROMAN AND CELTIC ART

Some motifs, especially peltas and triskeles, were current in the Roman world as well as that of the Iron Age Celts. Some metalworking techniques too, were prevalent in both cultures and some survived into the post-

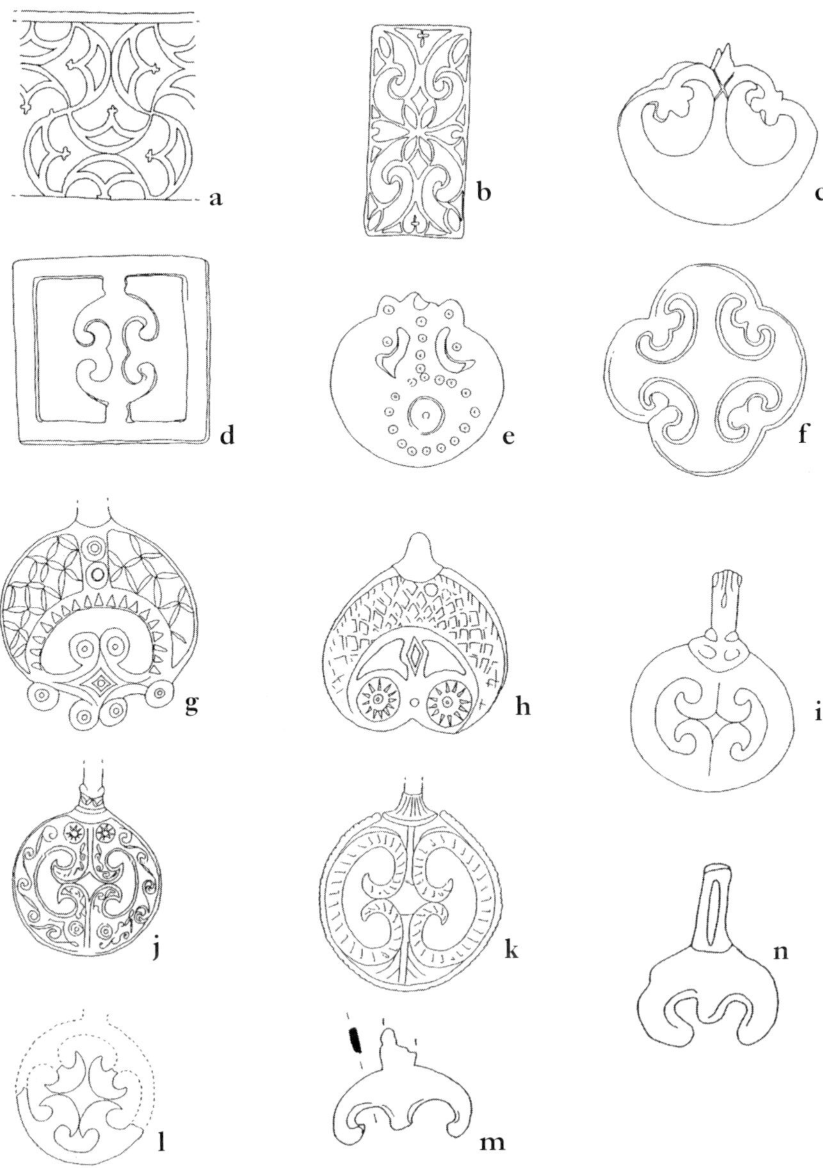

2.1 Peltas, Roman and post-Roman in Britain. a: Fullerton, Hants; b: London; c, e, f: Richborough, Kent; d: Caerleon, Monmouth; g: Sutton Hoo, Suffolk; h: Eastry, Kent; i: Castle Tioram, Inverness; j: Baginton, Warks; k: Hildersham, Cambs; l: Tummel Bridge, Perths; m: Colchester, Essex; n: Buiston, Ayrs (not to scale).

Roman period. The most prominent of these is the production of enamel (an opaque glaze fused to metal by heat). Paradoxically, it had been introduced to the Romans by the Iron Age Celts in Europe.

Peltas

The pelta (a mushroom-shaped motif that is often described as a mushroom pattern), originated in the Classical world as a profile view of a shield carried by Thracian warriors in the Greek army, and appears on Greek vases of the fourth century BC. By the Roman period, it was frequently used to form an element in a repeat pattern (Thompson, 1968, 48–9). Furnished with animal heads on the terminals, it was used as a finial motif on Roman inscriptions, for example from Hadrian's Wall where it was current particularly in the second century (Thompson, 1968). It survived, complete with griffin terminals, to the end of the fourth century, for example on a harness pendant from Margidunum, Nottinghamshire (Laing, 2005b). In Roman metalwork, particularly military, the pelta is ubiquitous, appearing on scabbard chapes, buckles, buckle plates and as border designs. Peltas also appear in Romano-British mosaics, and give the shape to enamelled plate brooches (Laing, 2005a, 151–5) (fig. 2.1). Peltas or mushroom patterns appear in many guises in Iron Age Celtic art.

Triskeles

The triskele (a three-limbed design), is a decorative motif that is sometimes seen in die-stamped work produced around the time of the Claudian invasion and which enjoyed a continuing currency among the post-Roman Celts. The design was not confined to Celtic art, occurring in many different cultures including that of the Roman world, so its perpetuation in the art of Roman Britain cannot be solely attributed to the influence of the Celts. In many societies, the number three was seen to have symbolic importance. It appeared intermittently in Iron Age art, and was widely used in Roman Britain (fig. 2.2). It was sometimes composed of trumpets. The simple triskele was fairly widespread in earlier Iron Age art in Britain (cf. Jope, 2000, patterns 582, 646, 685, 690, 693–7). The more sophisticated versions employing trumpets seem to have been developed in the creation of stamped mounts for caskets in the first century AD, and two dies are known from East Anglia that were for producing this type of design (Laing, 2005a, 149; fig. 2.3). Triskeles were employed in Roman Britain on two types of disc brooch: those with a fairly simple triskele in reserve against an enamelled ground, and those that have die-stamped plates (presumably derived from casket ornament traditions). They were still apparently around in the fourth century AD (Laing, 2005a, 147).

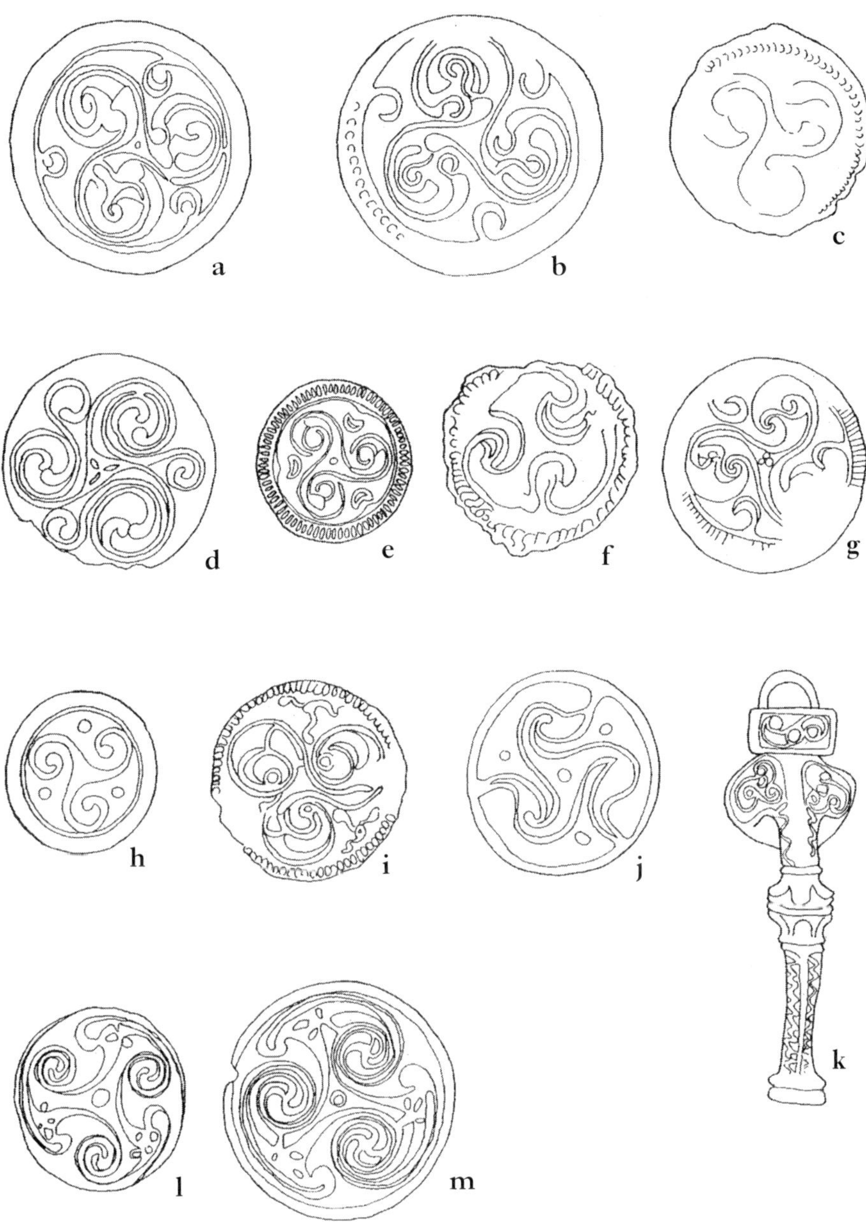

2.2 Triskeles, Roman to medieval. a: Silchester, Hants; b, g: Victoria Cave, Settle, Yorks; c: Caerleon, Monmouth; d: Barham, Suffolk; e: Brough, Cumbria; f: *Verulamium*, Herts; h: Manchester, Lancs; i: South Shields, Tyne & Wear; j: Colchester, Essex; k: Rudston, Yorks; l: Barrington, Cambs; m: Oving, Bucks (not to scale).

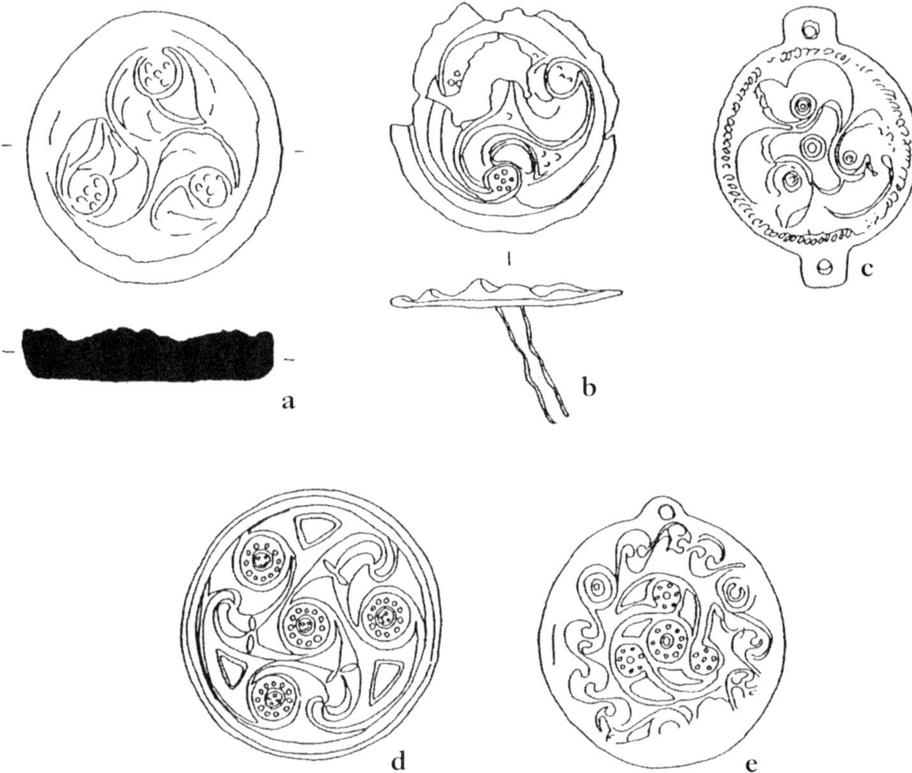

2.3 Iron Age and Roman triskeles. a: North Creake, Norfolk; b: Caistor, Norfolk; c: Hamworth, Norfolk; d: Loveden Hill, Lincs; e: 'Newcastle', Tyne and Wear (not to scale).

CELTIC ART IN EARLY ROMAN BRITAIN

After the Roman conquest, a large number of objects that are conventionally regarded as Celtic art were buried, significantly, often in hoards associated with Roman items. The vast majority of lesser artworks seem to have been deposited after AD65 (Garrow, 2008, 30). Some of these were types of item that had been used by Iron Age societies – horse gear, weaponry, jewellery. Others were Roman types of object decorated in a Celtic style – brooches, metal vessels, seal boxes, military belt fittings (Hunter, 2008, 133). In some cases it is clear that native artisans had been responding to new Roman technology, employing recycled Roman material such as brass in the creation of the items (Dungworth, 1996; Davis & Gwilt, 2008).

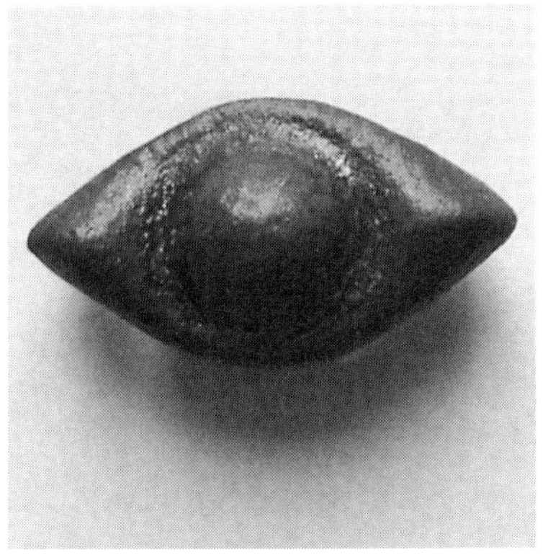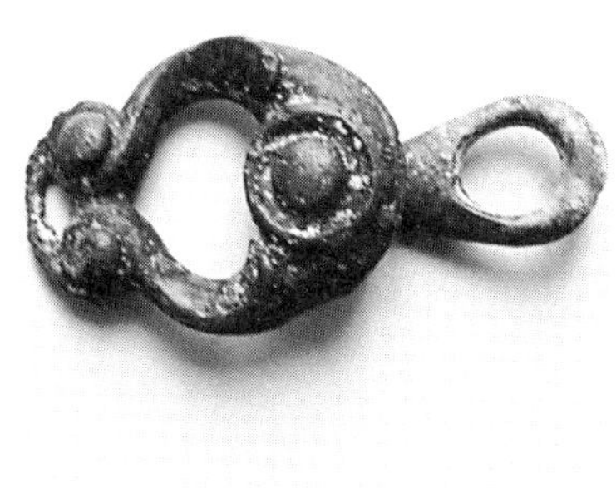

2.4 Leaf-and-pellet and their derivatives. a: leaf and pellet belt mount, Yorks;
b: leaf and pellet button and loop fastener from Gosbeck's, Colchester, Essex.

The northern frontiers of Roman Britain fluctuated over the four centuries of Roman administration between Hadrian's Wall and the Antonine Wall (between the Forth and the Clyde), the final frontier defence being established as Hadrian's Wall. Immediately after the Roman conquest there is some evidence from Roman forts for artistic activity, from which it has been suggested that the adoption by the Romans of objects in local designs may have been part of the process of integration (Hunter, 2008).

The arts of the smith in particular were well advanced, with regional differences. Differences in artistic traditions related to the technology used; casting being used to the north of the Humber, die-stamping to the south of it. Especially north of the Humber, a number of objects were decorated with polychrome enamelling, usually restricted to small areas and simple patterns, and relief-modelled confronted trumpets were also popular. South of the Humber, other ornamental devices are found: the 'Swash-N', berried rosettes, broken-backed scrolls and strongly flared trumpets. These ornamental devices were particularly used in the decoration of die-stamped plates for boxes and are known collectively as casket ornament.

Elements of this art (especially confronted trumpet patterns, triskeles and petal-and-boss) were taken up in Roman workshops and subsequently continued to enjoy popularity into the post-Roman period in Britain and Ireland.

Petal-and-boss ornament
The 'petal-and-boss' motif evolved from much earlier, Iron Age, origins but in the first two centuries AD the modelling was more pronounced (fig. 2.4). It survived into the post-Roman period in a very much altered

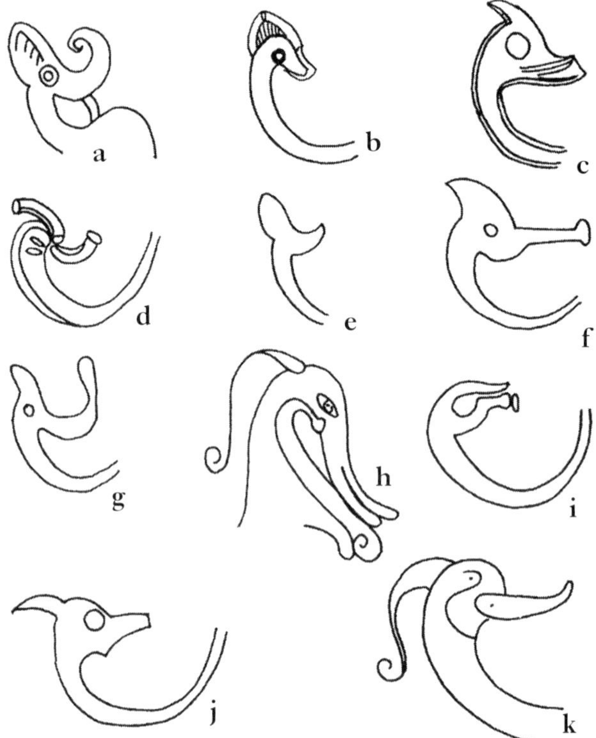

2.5 Dragonesque brooch animals and their relatives in the post-Roman period. a: dragonesque brooch, Cirencester, Glos; b, c: the Petrie Crown; d: the Bann Disc; e: detail on bronze ball, Walston, Lanarks; f: unprovenanced latchet, Ireland; g: unprovenanced hand-pin, Ireland; h: Pictish symbol-stone; i: hanging bowl escutcheon detail, Sutton Hoo, Suffolk; j: hanging bowl escutcheon detail, River Bann, Ireland; k: Hunterston Brooch, Ayrshire (not to scale).

form. In Roman Britain it was seen as a head with an eye, and was used to form the head of an animal on a series of brooches that are known as 'dragonesque', since they have an S-shaped profile with a crested head at each end (Feachem, 1951; Hunter, 2008). The type of head seen on these brooches seems to have been copied in Ireland, where it appears on the Cork Horns and the Petrie Crown (see below, p. 55); the 'head' motif may have inspired the so-called Pictish beast found in post-Roman sculpture in Scotland and the heads that end some whorls on post-Roman hanging bowls (Laing & Laing, 1990, 193–7; fig. 2.5). A variant motif, sometimes termed the 'dodo head', continued to be popular in post-Roman centuries. Although it lost many of the features of petal-and-boss ornament, it seems to have developed out of its use on Iron Age enamelled horse gear (fig. 2.6).

Confronted trumpet patterns
The confronted trumpet pattern gained wide currency through its use in *trompetenmuster* (openwork objects with trumpets and confronted

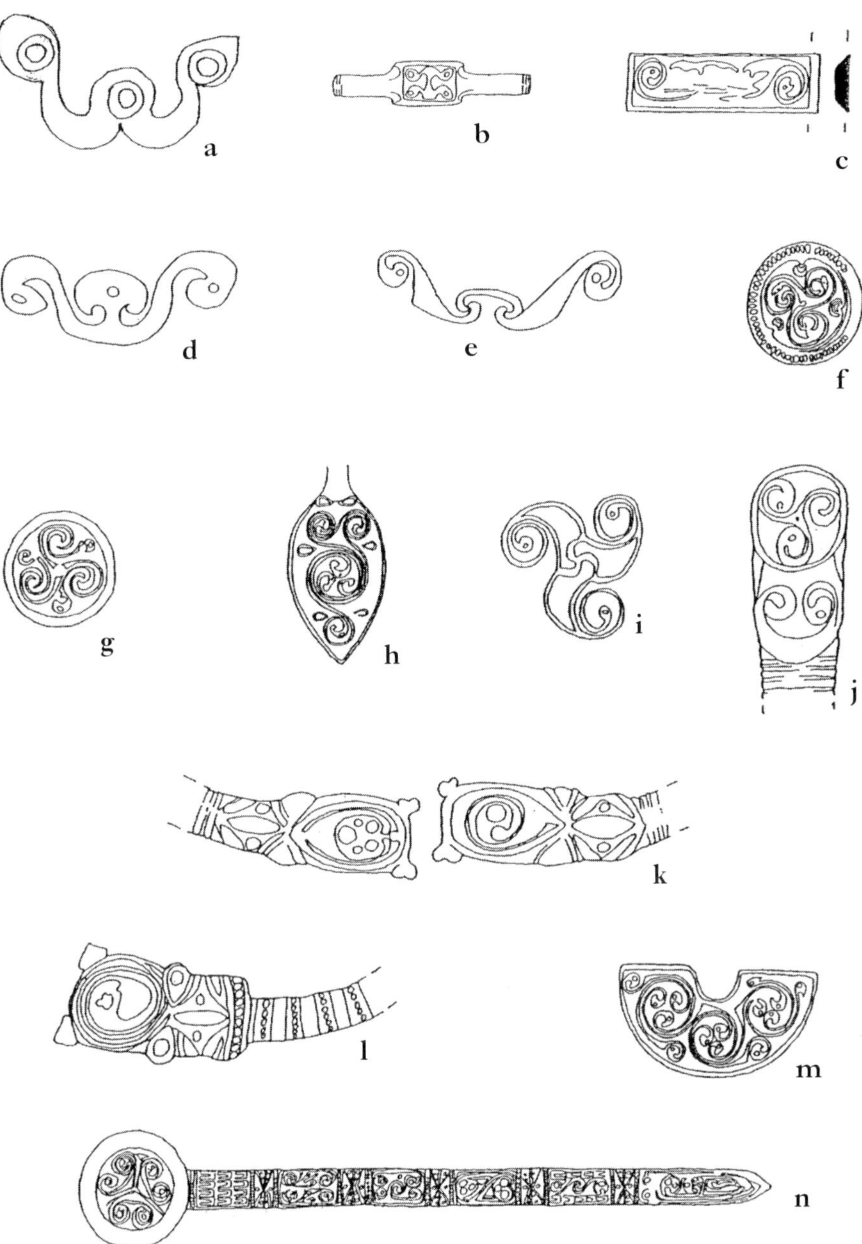

2.6 'Dodo heads' and their origins. a: London; b: Woden Eckford, Roxburgh; c: Trarain Law, E. Lothian; d: Oldcroft, Gloucs; e: Atworth, Wilts; f: Brough, Cumbria; g: near Coventry, Warks; h: Faversham, Kent; i: Attymon, Co. Galway; j: Ickham, Kent; k: Calne, Wilts; l: 'Ireland'; m: Norrie's Law, Fife; n: 'Ireland' (not to scale).

     European Influence on Celtic Art

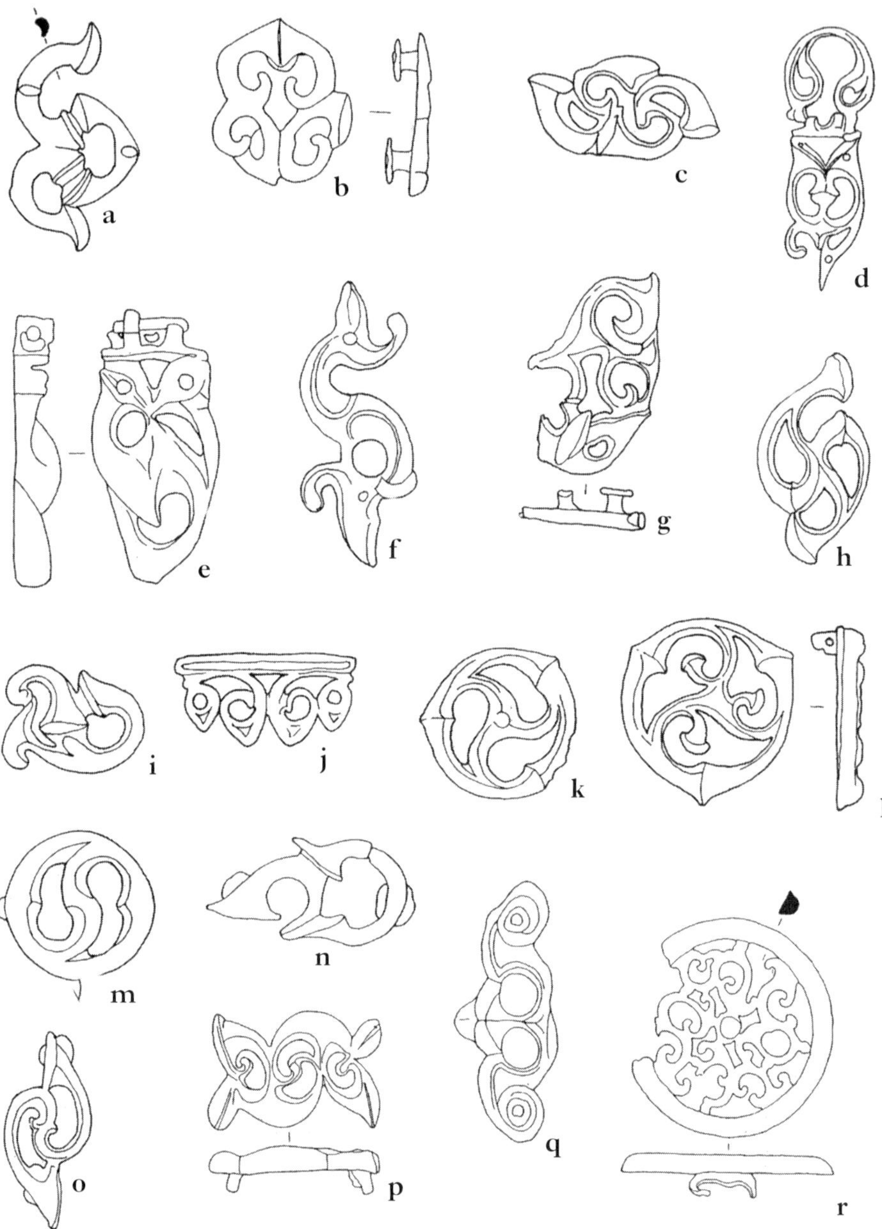

2.7 *Trompetenmuster* ornaments. a: Clatchard Craig, Fife; b: Cirencester, Glos; c, f, h, k, l, o: Corbridge, Northumberland; d: Newstead, Roxburgh; e: Maryport, Cumbria; g: Traprain Law, E. Lothian; i: Castlelaw, Midlothian; j: Brough, Cumbria; m: nr. Grantham, Lincs; n: Caerleon, Monmouth; p: *Vindolanda*, Northumberland; q: Langford, Notts; r: Chesters, Northumberland (not to scale).

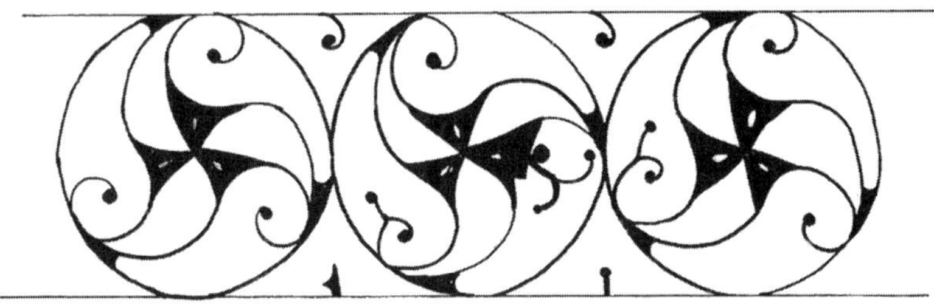

a

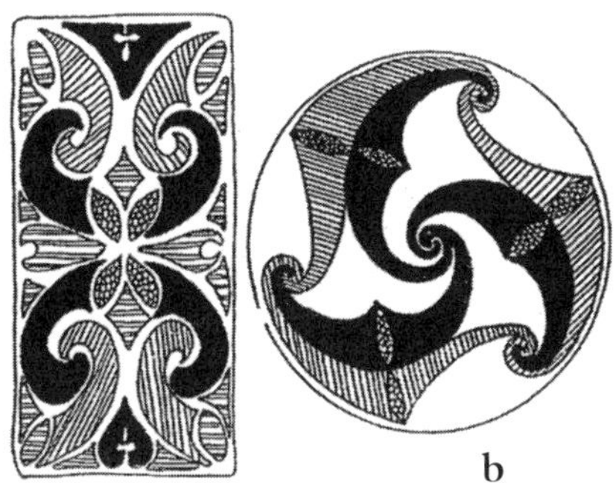

b

2.8 a: Staffordshire Moorlands pan (drawing: Dayanna Knight); b: ornament on enamelled patera handle from London, and the design elements re-arranged to form a hanging bowl design (after Kendrick, 1932).

trumpets in relief), which were employed widely in the Roman Empire probably because the Roman army became familiar with them in the northern military zones. The name of one factory operator, Gemellianus, is known from a second-century find in Switzerland (Berger, 1956, 24–39; Brogan, 1953, 152–3). *Trompetenmuster* ornaments have been found particularly in Upper Germany, but also in Gaul, Italy, Rhaetia and Noricum, with outliers as far afield as Dura-Europos on the Euphrates and Volubilis in north Africa. The main date range for *trompetenmuster* ornament on the Continent is the mid-second to early third century (Oldenstein, 1976, 203–7), but examples in Britain have been found in the late Roman period, one even surviving in a post-Roman context on the Early Christian period metalworking site at Clatchard Craig, Fife (Close-Brooks, 1986, 169–70; fig. 2.7).

Combined trumpet, pelta and triskele ornament
A number of enamelled items produced in Roman Britain are notable for their use of pelta, trumpet and triskele patterns. They include the paterae (pans) for drinking sets, of which the most notable is the Staffordshire Moorlands pan (named because it was found in this area), which bears the names of forts on Hadrian's Wall. The Staffordshire pan is enamelled in

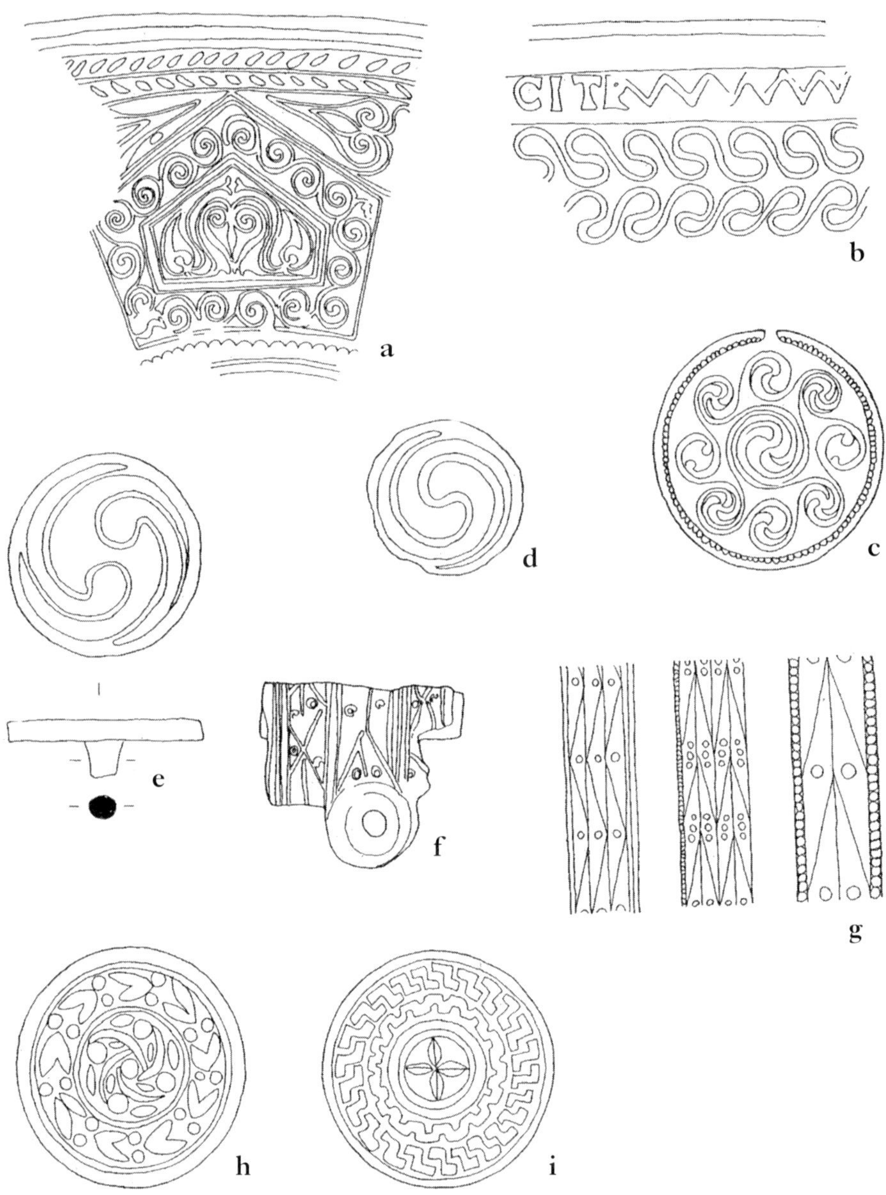

2.9 Miscellaneous Roman motifs and their early medieval versions. a: Bradley Hill, Somt; b: Beadlam, Yorks; c: Faversham, Kent; d: Corbridge, Northumberland; e: Kirby Thore (?), Cumbria; f: Nettleton, Wilts; g: Norrie's Law, Fife; h: Dover, Kent; i: Mildenhall, Suffolk (not to scale).

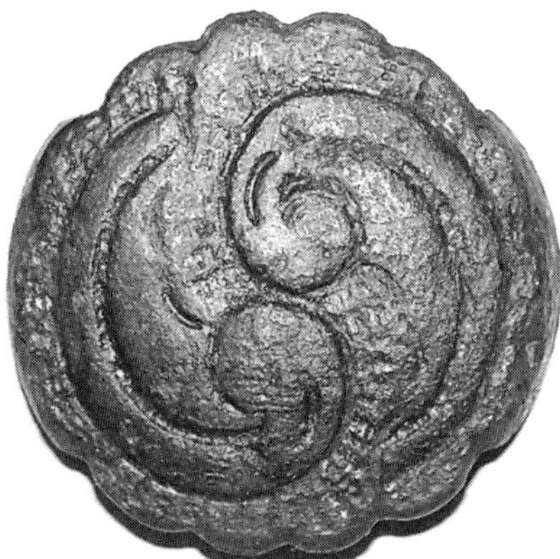

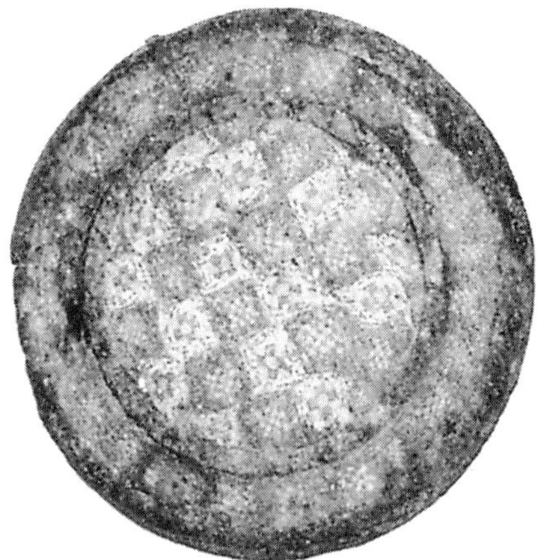

2.10 Romano-British mount with yin-yang, North Yorks.

2.11 Roman millefiori, Colchester, Essex.

red, blue, green and yellow, and has a sophisticated design of trumpet pattern triskeles (Kunzl, 2008; fig. 2.8a).

The same elements were employed on an enamelled patera handle from London. Thomas Kendrick re-arranged the decorative elements found on this to create an escutcheon for a post-Roman hanging bowl (Kendrick, 1932; fig. 2.8b). A recent discovery at Castleford, Yorkshire, of moulds for making enamelled spoons and flasks, clearly indicates that Britain was one of the main producers of enamelwork in the Roman Empire. Items that were probably produced at Castleford have been found near the Black Sea and in Sicily (Kunzl, 2008, 24).

Other Romano-British ornamental devices
A range of other ornamental devices can be found in Roman Britain that continued in popularity later. Laurel-leaf wreath patterns, which were commonly used on items such as enamelled paterae and probably originated with the victor's wreath in Classical art, comprised one type of border device that survived. Marigolds and rosettes were other long-lasting motifs, as were ring-and-dot, trellis patterns (widely used on Roman pottery) and swastikas (which had origins as far back as the Etruscans in pre-Roman Italy and were also found in ancient Greece). C-scrolls, broken scrolls and various step- and key-patterns were all survivors. Less common in Romano-British art, but of major importance later, were yin-yangs and so-called Durrow spirals (Laing, 2005a, 161–5; figs 2.9 & 2.10).

CELTIC AND ROMAN BRITAIN – SHARED METALWORKING TECHNIQUES

After *c.*AD350, surviving artworks were generally made of metal or stone and typically denote the high status of the owner. The metal objects include hanging bowls, stick pins, brooches and torcs. The earliest stone monuments are simple, inscribed Pictish standing stones. Growing evidence suggests that there was a strong late Roman tradition of metalworking in south-west England (Laing, 2005, 170), the Midlands and the north, with particularly rich finds of metalwork in parts of Lincolnshire, Yorkshire (Laing, 2005, 170) and Wales (Youngs, 2007).

Many of the techniques and motifs, as well as the types of objects themselves, were based on Roman antecedents, placing them firmly in the European traditions of the time.

The techniques available to the artisan clearly dictated what could be produced. Many techniques employed by smiths from the fourth to seventh centuries were traditional, and can be found in Iron Age societies throughout Europe. However, some techniques – for example, millefiori, the use of stamps, brass alloy and complex enamel work – were introduced in the Roman period, and continued in use through the sixth century and later.

Millefiori

Millefiori (literally a thousand flowers) is a decorative device in which different colours of glass rods are fused together and then sliced thinly so a pattern is revealed. The slivers are then inlaid in enamel or metal. Two main types of millefiori are found in the Roman and post-Roman periods. A third type with sections fused together into patterned panels is found only in the post-Roman period. Although it is found almost entirely in Ireland and Scandinavia, it was probably inspired by millefiori work produced in the Anglo-Saxon world (Carroll, 1995; Laing, 1999).

Notable Roman objects displaying millefiori are a series of hexagonal vessels (probably inkpots), one of which was found at Elsenham, Essex. These were certainly also produced on the Continent, and have turned up as far afield as the Black Sea. The Elsenham vessel may have been made in Germany, and was dated to the mid-second century from associated finds, including coins. The type of millefiori (with chequer-pattern arrangements) represented on it is also found on a series of Romano-British enamelled studs, and some belt fittings (Bateson, 1981). It is likely that some were imported (there may have been production at Namur, Gaul) but some were also made in Britain (fig. 2.11).

Millefiori continued in use in the post-Roman Celtic world, initially on the mounts from which hanging bowls were suspended. In early medieval Ireland millefiori is found on brooches and pins.

Stamps
The Roman technique of using stamps to make up designs (usually for borders), can be seen in a range of penannular brooches, such as a group from Wales and the Marches (Youngs, 2007, 91–5). It is also found on silver brooches from the Tummel Bridge Hoard, Perths (Laing, 1993a, nos 3–4). The same technique employing rings rather than square punches appears on the pins from Tripontium, Warwickshire (where it is from a Roman context); from Gaulcross, Banff and from Norrie's Law, Fife. It is also found in Ireland on some brooches and pins. In Roman Britain, the use of punched ornament was quite widespread, and was employed in the fifth century in south-east England on Quoit Brooch Style metalwork (named after a particular style of brooch on which it is typical), which is mostly known from Anglo-Saxon graves (Suzuki, 2000; Inker, 2006).

Brass alloy
Brass was a Roman alloy. It was used, for instance, in the production of sestertii coins in the earlier Roman empire, and its survival into the early medieval period points to continuing Roman metalworking traditions. It was employed in the manufacture of at least one hanging bowl (an early vessel from Field Dalling, Norfolk), which has openwork escutcheons that match those from the Tummel Bridge Hoard (Bruce-Mitford, 2005, 221).

Enamel work
After the fourth century, enamelling was predominantly red, since the range of colours current earlier in Roman (and pre-Roman) Britain had died out during the fourth century or earlier.

Enamelling was employed on many of the hanging bowls that are a prominent feature of the surviving metalwork of the fifth to seventh centuries (see below, pp 45–7). Apparent instances of yellow enamel on early hanging bowls have in most cases been shown by scientific analysis to be decayed red. Yellow seems to have been used on some bowls, most notably on two from Hitchin, Hertfordshire (Bruce-Mitford, 2005, 78). The use of colours other than red is also apparent on some bowls which date from the later seventh century onwards. Virtually all the analysis of the enamel on hanging bowls has concentrated on late (after *c.*600) examples. This shows that the composition of the enamel was different from that used in Roman Britain, as the red was derived from the re-use of metallurgical slag (Stapleton et al., 1999). Very little analysis has been carried out on the enamel used on penannular brooches and pins.

Despite the shared decorative devices and types of object, regional differences are apparent in England and Wales, Scotland and Ireland.

CELTIC ART IN ENGLAND AND WALES

Metalworking products found in England and Wales include dress accessories such as brooches and pins (which give insights into changes in fashion and status), hanging bowls and mounts from items that have not survived. Contacts between the Celts both within and outside the former Britannia, and the emergent Anglo-Saxon kingdoms (especially Northumbria), are clearly demonstrated through the surviving artworks.

Dress accessories
The development of new types of dress accessory reflected changes in fashion and lifestyle in the late Roman world. Around AD400, many artefact types appeared that were connected with status and new social values (Cool, 2000, 54).

The use of brooches and pins as insignia seems to have been acquired from the Late Antique world. Childeric (*c*.440–*c*.481, the Merovingian king of the Salian Franks), was buried with a brooch that copied a Roman crossbow brooch type, which Roman emperors pinned on officials at their investitures. The custom survived in Byzantium into the tenth century; Constantine Porphyrogenitos reported a ceremony in which the Byzantine emperor pinned a fibula on a new official's shoulder (James, 1977, 100).

Dress accessories from the later fourth century were larger than their antecedents. They were produced in silver (and in the case of crossbow brooches, also gold) as well as base metals. The material as well as the form was indicative of the status of the wearer. Crossbow brooches were used by the Roman army as marks of rank (Eagles, 1979, 66), which perhaps explains why the type did not survive the early fifth century. The Byzantine emperor Leo (AD457–474) passed legislation controlling who was permitted to wear what kind of brooch (Janes, 1996, 146). The most ornate was the *Kaiserfibel*, a gold brooch studded with gems worn by the emperor or on occasion an empress. The crossbow brooch was not permitted to include gems.

Brooches were major signifiers of rank in early medieval Ireland (and, it may be assumed, Britain too), a factor which stemmed from Roman traditions of social order and power (Nieke, 1993, 128; Whitfield, 2004). Youngs has suggested that brooches carried the same connotations of status as torcs (2007, 87–9). Within Celtic society, there was a belief that some were of great value, and their use in pledging is generally well-attested (Etchingham & Swift, 2004, 47; Whitfield, 2004). In the Goddodin poem, the warriors are frequently described as 'brooch-wearing in the front rank'.

It is likely that in the early medieval period males wore brooches on the shoulder, a custom directly derived from the Roman world, when soldiers and administrators pinned them on the right shoulder to keep the cloak back from the sword arm (Whitfield, 2004, 72). This method of wearing them can be seen represented on a sculpture from White Island, Co. Fermanagh (Ó Floinn, 1989, fig. 2). Females, however, wore them on the breast, a custom also found in the Mediterranean world, though there are relatively few depictions (Whitfield, 2004, 72). The custom of wearing a single disc brooch centrally was taken up in the Merovingian world, copying Mediterranean fashion. The centrally worn brooch is apparent in the representations of females wearing brooches in Pictland, such as on sculptures at Monifieth or Kirriemuir, Angus (Trench-Jellicoe, 1999a, 610).

There is some evidence from an eighth-century Irish law code that different types of brooches were associated with different groups of people, since it uses different words for Pictish and Anglo-Saxon brooches (Etchingham & Swift, 2004).

Brooch types Throughout the first to third centuries AD the majority of brooches in Britain were of the safety pin variety. There is a good series of prototypes in the brooches of La Tène Europe and Britain, but the safety pin brooch is also found from other cultures, including Classical Greece and the Roman Republic. In the Roman empire the safety pin brooch was very widespread, not only in areas which might have inherited it from La Tène sources. Concurrently with these, from the second century onwards, a diversity of plate brooches was produced. Some plate brooches were executed in openwork (for example with *trompetenmuster* ornament, or with lettering); some were of abstract shape (lozenges, crescents, peltas); some were circular (sometimes with projections), and some were shaped like animals, boats or equestrian figures (Hattatt 1982; 1985 for a series of these from Britain, but they are also found throughout the empire). Quite often they were enamelled. By the fourth century, however, the range of brooch-types had been greatly reduced, and the only safety pin type still current was the crossbow brooch. Plain disc brooches (often gilded or tinned, and sometimes enamelled or set with glass or stone), however, continued in fashion to the end of the Roman period. It has been suggested that these were an inspiration for the series of Anglo-Saxon disc brooches (Leeds, 1945, 52).

One type of brooch which had a different type of fastening mechanism from the safety pin and the plate brooch (both of which had either spring pins or hinged pins) was the penannular brooch. Found first in the pre-Roman Iron Age, the penannular brooch had a simple penannular hoop around which a pin swivelled, the hoop being rotated to complete the fastening. Penannular brooches are first encountered from the pre-Roman Iron Age, when they are found in both Britain and Spain, but in the Roman period they appear to be distinctively British and continued throughout the first four centuries AD and later (Fowler, 1960; Fowler, 1963; Laing, 1993a, 11–20; Laing, 2006, 153–60). The Iron Age penannular brooches have simple terminals – either rolled-over or knobbed (Fowler, 1960). The rolled-over terminal enjoyed a revival in the fourth century AD and later (Fowler, 1983). During the Roman period there evolved first brooches with turned over, thickened terminals and then more ornate solid terminals which have been seen as having zoomorphic features, that is, looking like an animal head with nostrils and ears (Fowler, 1963; Kilbride-Jones, 1980a; fig. 2.12).

Romano-British penannular brooches were relatively small, with fairly short pins, and a few survived into the post-Roman period. Around the end of the fourth century, however, penannular brooches became much larger, the pins became longer and instead of having simple looped heads, they acquired barrel-shaped heads that swivelled on the hoop. The zoomorphic type of terminal continued through the fifth and sixth centuries, with increasing amounts of decoration. At the same time other types appeared (including those with squared terminals), which were usually decorated with an incuse lozenge containing pellets. From the sixth century onwards, the brooch terminals were increasingly expanded, becoming flaring, sub-triangular plates.

There is no hard evidence that the crossbow brooch gave rise to post-Roman developments in the Celtic West, though there is what appears to be a native imitation of one in silver from a developed stone round-house of the Iron Age at Carn Liath, Sutherland, and one with a boar's head terminal from Sussex which may date to the fifth century (Johns, 1996, 169).

Ownership inscriptions survive in rare cases, such as on the backs of the Hunterston Brooch (Stevenson, 1974) and the Ballyspellan Brooch (Wallace & Ó Floinn, 2002, 226). Such inscriptions are not necessarily the

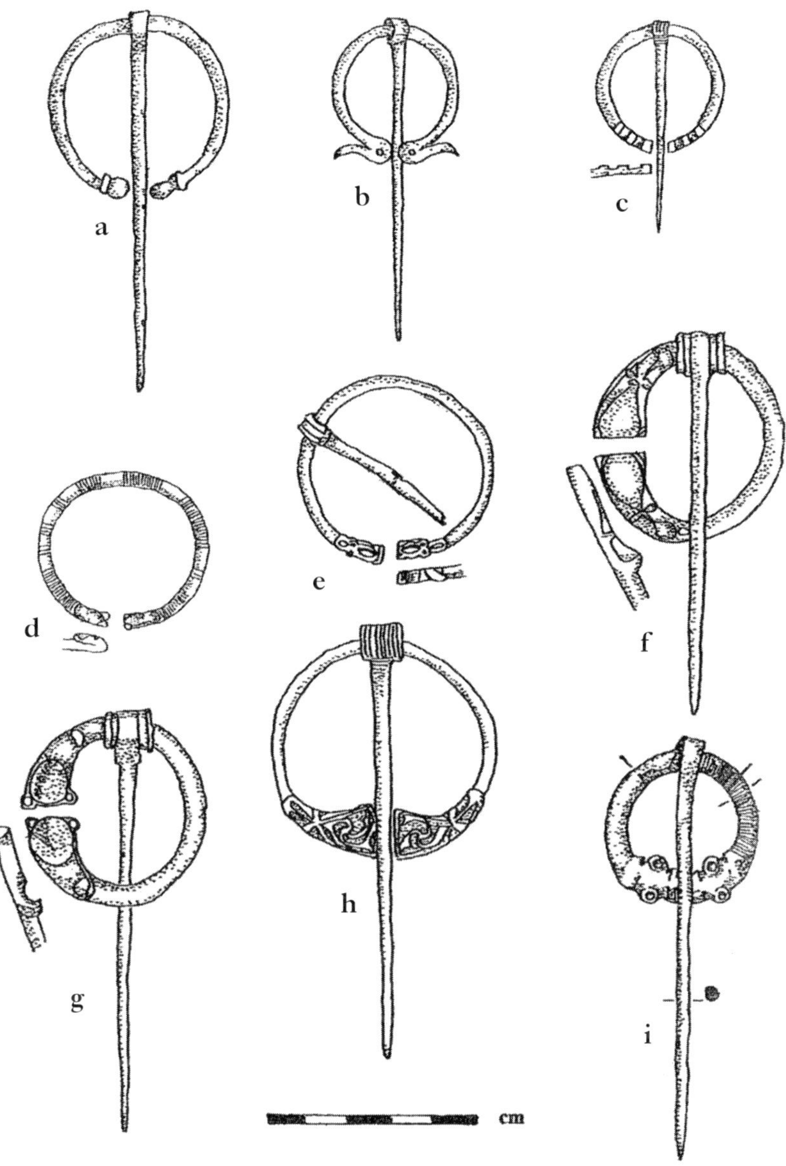

2.12 Penannular brooches. a: Lagore, Co. Meath; b: Ballyfallon, Co. Meath; c: Ballycatteen, Co. Cork; d: Lydney, Glos; e: Barnton, Edinburgh; f: Mullingar, Co. Westmeath; g: English, Co. Armagh; h: Belcoo, Enniskillen, Co. Fermanagh; i: Ireland, unprovenanced (not to scale).

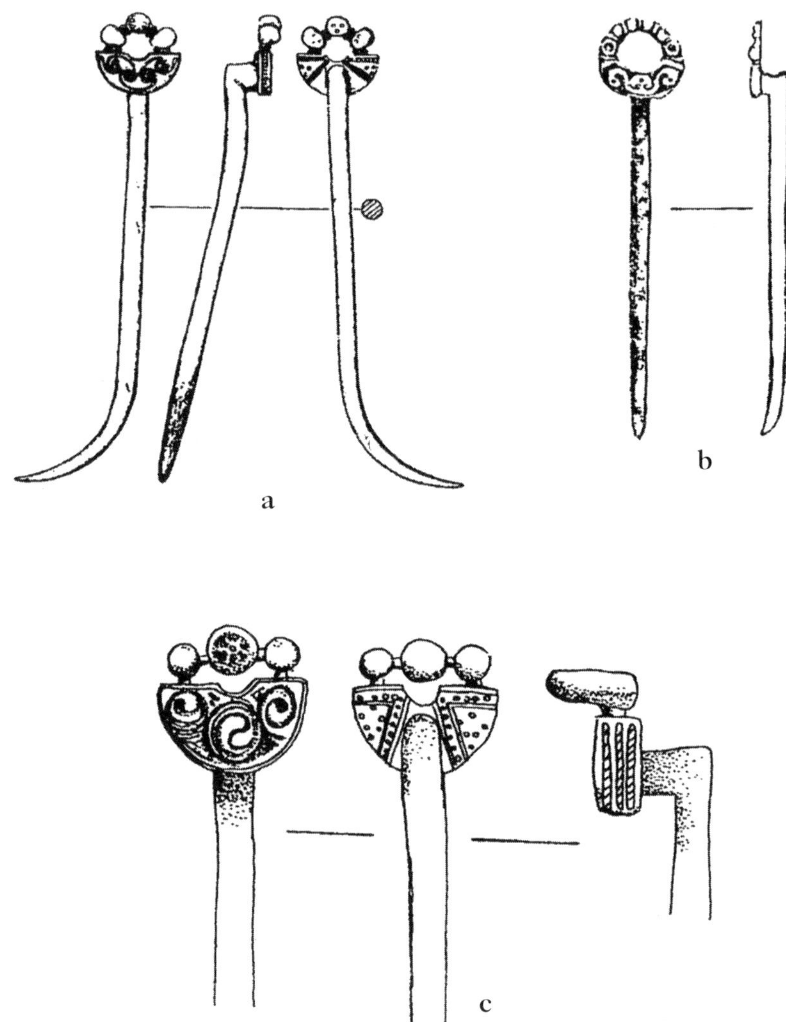

2.13 Roman proto-hand pins. a: Tripontium, Warks; b: Oldcroft, Glos; c: Long Sutton, Somt.

names of the original patrons – the Hunterston Brooch inscription relates to a Viking who acquired it much later than its date of production. The ogham inscription on the Ballyspellan Brooch indicated at least four Irish owners, possibly including the commissioner.

Stick pins In the first to third centuries, stick pins were furnished with a short shank and were used primarily as hairpins (Cool, 1990). In the fourth century, they acquired much longer shanks and were used additionally as a method of fastening clothing. The inspiration behind such dress-pins probably came from the Continent, where they are found in both silver and bronze and are often quite richly decorated. There are good examples from Xanten/Doderwaard and from Asselt (van Es, 1967). Closely related to the long dress pins found in Britain are the Fècamp pins, which have elaborate decoration and similarly served as dress fasteners (Böhme, 1974). In Britain, some of these pins have zoomorphic heads that copy the designs found on the terminals of penannular brooches, but there are also pins with plain round heads, sometimes enamelled, and what have been termed proto-hand pins. During the Roman period, these had comparatively short shanks and relatively simple heads. During the fifth to seventh centuries AD, the shanks became longer and the heads more elaborate, turning them into true hand pins (which have a crescentic plate with projecting 'fingers', giving the probably fortuitous appearance of a clenched fist (fig. 2.13).

Hanging bowls

Hanging bowls are metal vessels which were furnished with escutcheons and rings that show they were intended to be suspended. Probably due to the fact that no pagan burials survive from the Celtic areas from this period, hanging bowls are comparatively rare finds in south-west England, Wales, northern Scotland and Ireland. In the post-Roman period they were probably status symbols which represented the continuing values of Roman society. They were probably owned by the few. Some were very old when they were deposited. The majority (in some cases represented only by their mounts) have been found in Anglo-Saxon graves of the late sixth and earlier seventh centuries. Interestingly, however, it seems certain that most were made in Romano-Celtic workshops. This phenomenon may be the result of important seventh-century Anglo-Saxons favouring new styles of grave furniture, including different types of metal vessel (Geake, 1999). Some of these came from the east Mediterranean and the Rhineland, but British hanging bowls may have served as useful substitutes. They were sometimes copied, albeit badly, by Anglo-Saxon smiths (Laing, 2007).

A number of design elements in circulation in Roman Britain survived into the post-Roman period and were particularly widely employed in the decoration of hanging bowl mounts. Some, such as ring-and-dot, running scroll, c-scroll, swastika, laurel leaf wreath, herringbone, marigold, step-and key patterns, had a very long currency (Laing, 2005a, 161–5).

The most recent corpus of hanging bowls (Bruce-Mitford, 2005) lists 68 complete bowls and 106 further fragmentary bowls, though every year many more mounts come to light as the result of metal detecting. The total is likely to exceed 200. The bowls are very varied in size, the largest tending to be the latest in date. They are characterized by having three, sometimes four suspension hooks. They usually have a basal 'print' (another escutcheon or pair of escutcheons attached to the bottom of the bowl). Most are extremely well-made, usually having been finished on a lathe.

The function of hanging bowls has been debated, and they perhaps served different purposes at different times. They were probably intended for holding water, possibly for hand-washing (this certainly seems to have been one of their functions in post-Roman centuries), and some may have been suspended from tripods (Vierck, 1970; Fowler, 1968).

Some commentators have argued that hanging bowls cannot have been made before the sixth century, since they have not been found in securely dated contexts prior to this (see, for example, Brenan, 1991). However, current opinion favours a date for their production, following Roman antecedents, in the fifth and sixth centuries as well as later (Laing, 1993a, 22; Bruce-Mitford, 2005, 34–5).

Hanging bowls of various types were found in late Roman Britain, including silver examples from the Water Newton Hoard, Huntingdonshire (Painter, 2005) and from the Traprain Treasure, East Lothian (Bruce-Mitford, 2005, 443). A few, however, show direct design links with bowls of post-Roman date. Two bowls from Finningley, Yorkshire, contained what appeared to be smaller, made-to-measure bowls with embossed rims of a type well-known in the late Roman period (*basins à bord godronné*: Kennett, 1971). The Finningley bowls show two features found in all the presumed early bowls of the post-Roman period: the simple thickened rim form and the hooks and escutcheons cast as one. These are both features of Bruce Mitford's A Bowls (Bruce-Mitford 2005, 10).

The Finningley bowls were finished off by lathe-turning, a technique used on post-Roman hanging bowls (Bruce-Mitford, 2005, 308–11). The design of the Finningley bowls is closely related to a series of late Roman bowls (without provision for suspension) known as the Irchester type, which are exclusively from Roman Britain (Kennett, 1968).

Another hanging bowl of the same type as those from Finningley is known from Newnham Bog, Northumberland. It came from a hoard of vessels, which is a Roman, rather than post-Roman phenomenon. Its surviving lion-headed escutcheon hook is very similar to one from the Roman town of Silchester, Hampshire (Bruce-Mitford, 2005, 229).

It has been argued that the bowls with A-type rims all pre-date *c*.AD600, and that the B-type rims (which were more practically and technically

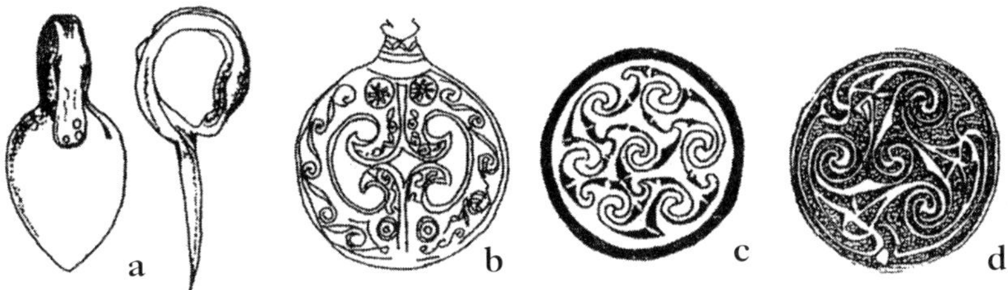

2.14 Hanging bowl designs. a: Sleaford, Lincs; b: Baginton, Warks; c: Winchester, Hants; d: 'near Oxford' (not to scale).

advanced, and were accompanied by composite escutcheons), succeeded them in the seventh century (Bruce-Mitford, 2005, 36).

The bowls with A-type rims include all those with plain escutcheons that are early in style, as well as a group with openwork escutcheons (the main design element of which seems to have been the pelta, as a pair or sometimes in an arrangement of four). In the same family are escutcheons which are themselves pelta-shaped. The openwork mounts from a bowl from Garton Station, Humberside, are more complex. The enamelled mounts have a triskele as the central element and an unenamelled basal print bearing a trumpet pattern triskele with terminal dodo-heads (Bruce-Mitford, 2005, corpus no. 30). One group of bowls and escutcheons bear decoration which was, in Bruce-Mitford's phrase, 'put together from the debris of late Romano-British art' (2005, 15).

Although Bruce-Mitford argued that the trumpet-spiral design found on Type B bowls was an innovation of the seventh century, the essence of many escutcheons with this type of ornament is in effect a trumpet pattern triskele, which was a feature of Romano-British art. The so-called Durrow spiral or yin-yang and the running scroll have also been seen as a feature of Romano-British art. The designs are in fact simply elaborations elements found earlier: the running scroll can be seen combined with dodo heads on the circular escutcheon in fine-line style from Faversham, Kent (Bruce-Mitford, 2005, corpus no. 39), which belongs with the Type A bowl series (fig. 2.14).

Miscellaneous post-Roman items of Romano-British origin
Other items which show continuing Romano-British metalworking traditions in the fifth and sixth centuries include various mounts, which were clearly not for hanging bowls, but could have decorated leatherwork, wooden objects or metal artefacts with flat surfaces such as caskets. They include a pelta-decorated enamelled mount from Liddington Castle, Wiltshire, which is probably late Roman. It can be compared to a mount

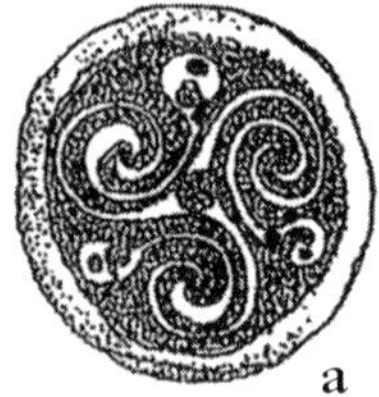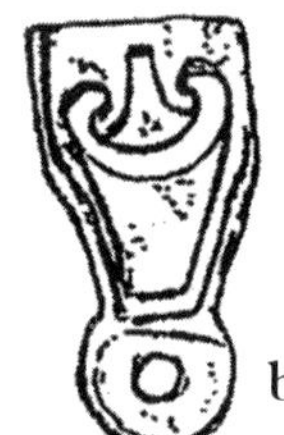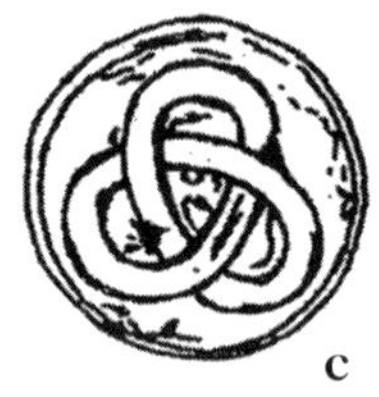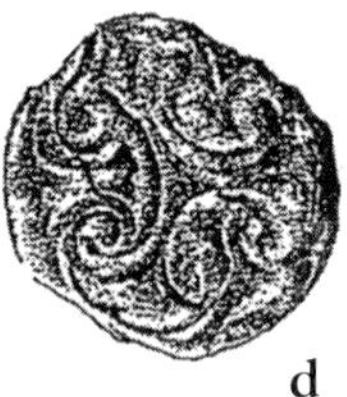

2.15 Mounts: a: near Coventry, Warks; b: Liddington, Wilts; c: Uffington, Berks; d: Clatchard Craig, Fife (not to scale).

from Dowkerbottom Cave, Yorkshire (Fowler, 1968, fig. 71.4; Laing 1993a, no. 181; for Dowkerbottom, Henry, 1936, 216, fig. 3); a triskele-shaped stud from Stanton St Bernard, Wiltshire (Laing, 1993a, no. 185; Bruce-Mitford, 2005, 434) and a millefiori and enamel sub-triangular mount from Bradwell-on-Sea, Essex (Laing, 1999; fig. 2.15).

It is also likely that the Romano-British tradition of making enamelled paterae continued through the fourth and probably into the fifth century. Such an item was found in a context post-dating 350 at Bradley Hill, Somerton, Somerset. It bears a laurel wreath scroll which is similar to one on a hanging bowl from Dover, Kent (Fowler, 1981), and to an example from Beadlam, North Yorkshire, which has running scroll ornament (Neal, 1996, illus. 7.2) (fig. 2.9/b). Some evidence for the survival of workshops producing this kind of enamelled vessel is provided by finds at New Market Hall, Gloucester, where excavations within the Roman town uncovered a bronze-worker's shop with a fragment of a bowl with geometric cloisons for enamel, a penannular brooch pin and other items including a sherd of imported Mediterranean amphora of the late fourth or fifth century (Hassall & Rhodes, 1974, 30).

CELTIC ART IN SCOTLAND

Roman influence in Scotland

In southern Scotland and Pictland there is evidence that towards the end of the fourth or early in the fifth century AD, élite groups assumed some of the status symbols of late Roman aristocratic and military society. This was probably due to respect for *Romanitas* and to absorb some of the authority it represented – there is growing evidence that Celtic communities north of Hadrian's Wall were considerably Romanized in the third and fourth centuries. In southern Scotland, good quality pottery and glass suggests that local leaders sought conspicuous display at the feast (Holmes & Hunter, 2001, 174). Some objects may have changed hands through subsidies and diplomatic gifts. This factor would explain a large hoard from Falkirk between the Forth and the Tay, which ends with a coin of AD230 (Todd, 1985). Such dealing would also explain some of the high-quality late Roman glass from Traprain Law, East Lothian. In the early Roman period, Traprain may have been a trading and manufacturing base, since there is abundant evidence for metalworking, with the type of finds implying direct connections with the nearby Roman military presence and its supply lines (Erdrich et al., 2000, 453).

A hoard of silverwork deposited at Traprain around the beginning of the fifth century (Curle, 1923), contained items showing specifically Christian subject matter, though there is some doubt as to whether this was significant to its owners; it could have been, for example, loot from further south. However, it might also have been the vestiges of a diplomatic gift from the Romans, or as has recently been suggested, the property of a Gothic army officer who had retired to Britain (Böhme, 1986, 488). None of these interpretations alter the fact that high-status Roman items were prized by the Britons of southern Scotland.

North of the Firth of Forth, the evidence for direct Roman impact is less strong, but growing. Of particular note is the native-style site at Birnie, Moray, which has produced two Roman coin hoards that were deposited in the early third century (Hunter, 2002). They are difficult to explain in terms of buy-offs or gifts, since they are heterogeneous collections of Roman coins with a wide chronological spread and include some with Greek inscriptions. They are probably the collection of a native leader with a respect for the Roman world. Similar evidence for the hoarding of Roman metalwork on a native metalworking site in use into the second or third century AD is provided from Culduthel, Inverness (Murray, 2007). Other finds of Roman status items include lathe-turned bronze bowls (related to the early hanging bowls) found as far north as Helmsdale, Sutherland (Spearman, 1990, 74–7: Curtis & Hunter, 2006).

A natural result of such contacts is that many motifs and techniques were assimilated into the Celtic artists' repertoire, which mostly survives in metalwork (especially for personal adornment and status), and monumental sculpture.

Metal artefacts for personal adornment in Scotland
It can be argued quite strongly that by the end of the Roman period, high-status Picts, in particular, adopted Roman-style insignia such as brooches and torcs.

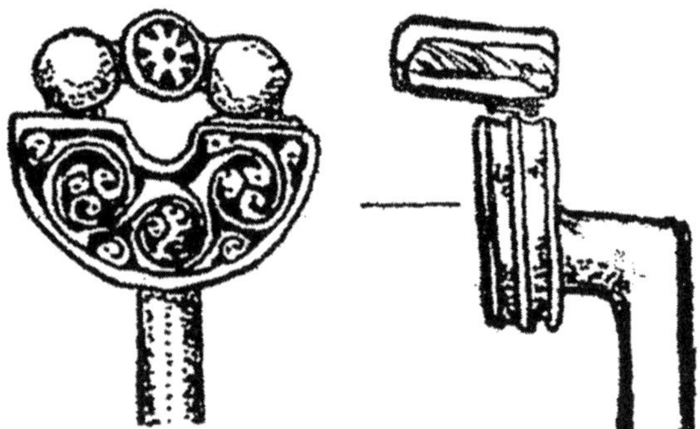

2.16 Scottish hand-pin, Gaulcross, Banff.

Brooches, pins and buckles Penannular zoomorphic brooches and their counterpart pins, seem to have spread into Pictland in the late fourth or early fifth centuries AD: there are, for example, three zoomorphic pins: from Skaill, Pool and Howe in Orkney. The pin from Skaill was furnished with a loop head, perhaps indicating its affinity to the linked pin sets also fashionable in late Roman Britain (Hunter, 1997). From Skaill and Howe have come penannular brooches of the late Roman Type E and fifth-century Type G, the latter a far-flung relative of a family found mainly in south-west England (for the Types, see Laing, 1993a, 11–20). The dodo-head, arguably a survivor of Romano-British art (see above, p. 32), decorates a silver hand-pin from Norrie's Law, Fife (Laing, 1990) and a similar pin from Gaulcross, Banff (Stevenson & Emery, 1963–4) (fig. 2.16). A buckle from Orkney with confronted animal heads on the bar may be a local imitation of the type of late Roman buckles that are associated with rank (Laing, 1972–4).

Torcs and chains Late Roman soldiers wore torcs on their chests as status and rank indicators. Such neck rings had originally been inspired by Celtic examples, but in the late Roman period were displayed trophy-fashion (as opposed to round the neck). A Pictish version may be represented in the Norrie's Law Hoard, which was deposited in Fife early in the post-Roman period, and was a composite treasure that included much Roman silverwork (Laing, 1994, 24–5). The terms 'torc-wearing' and 'gold torc resplendent' are used of kings in the poems of Aneurin (Williams, 1938, lines 21, 30, 39, 40, 46, 185), and also in the Gododdin poem (Jarman, 1988, lines 31, 40, 49, 50, 56, 195).

The Norrie's Law Hoard also contains three proto-hand pins. Two have strong affinities with examples from southern Britain (one has a Pictish symbol on the back), as well as with Pictish versions of Roman silver votive plaques of the type now well-known from the Water Newton Treasure.

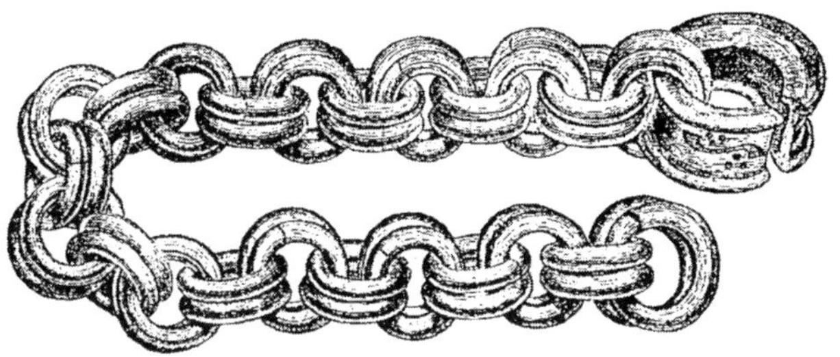

2.17 Pictish chain, Parkhill, Aberdeenshire (after Anderson, 1881).

A Roman ancestry can be postulated for a series of massive silver chains that are associated with the Picts since some display Pictish symbols (fig. 2.17). Inconveniently for this theory, most have been found in southern Scotland (Henderson & Henderson, 2004, 87) rather than Pictland. It is noteworthy, however, that one came from Haddington, East Lothian, which is less than seven miles from Traprain, and three more came from nearby Berwickshire. Probably made of re-used Roman silver (Stevenson 1954–6), they may well be Pictish versions of the massive gold chains current in the late Roman Empire. These items are represented in Britain by the body chain from Hoxne, Suffolk, which has been noted to be of a type worn by women of exceptionally high rank (Johns, 1996, 96). Of the silver chains found in Roman Britain, the Aesica (Greatchesters) chain from Hadrian's Wall has a system of links similar to those of the Pictish chains (Johns, 1996, 91). A prototype of the complex knitted wire chain represented in the Pictish Gaulcross Hoard can be found in the fourth-century Thetford Treasure, Norfolk (Johns, 1996, 94–5).

Sculpture – Pictish symbol stones
With a few exceptions, the Celts did not erect stone sculptures until the post-Roman period, which implies that the practice developed indirectly as a result of European contacts. For unknown reasons, it was initially developed in Pictland.

The tradition of incising symbols (abstract, as well as of real and imaginary animals) on undressed slabs of stone is a notable feature of northern Scotland in the early medieval period. Symbol stones have traditionally been dated to the sixth or seventh century, but there is growing evidence that they were used at least as early as the fourth century AD, since early forms of some of the designs were employed (Laing, 2006, 312–18). Although considerable debate has surrounded the interpretation of the Pictish symbols, it is likely that they were personal identifiers – the equivalent of names written in the Latin alphabet in the Roman world. The idea of creating symbol stones (in some cases as memorial stones to

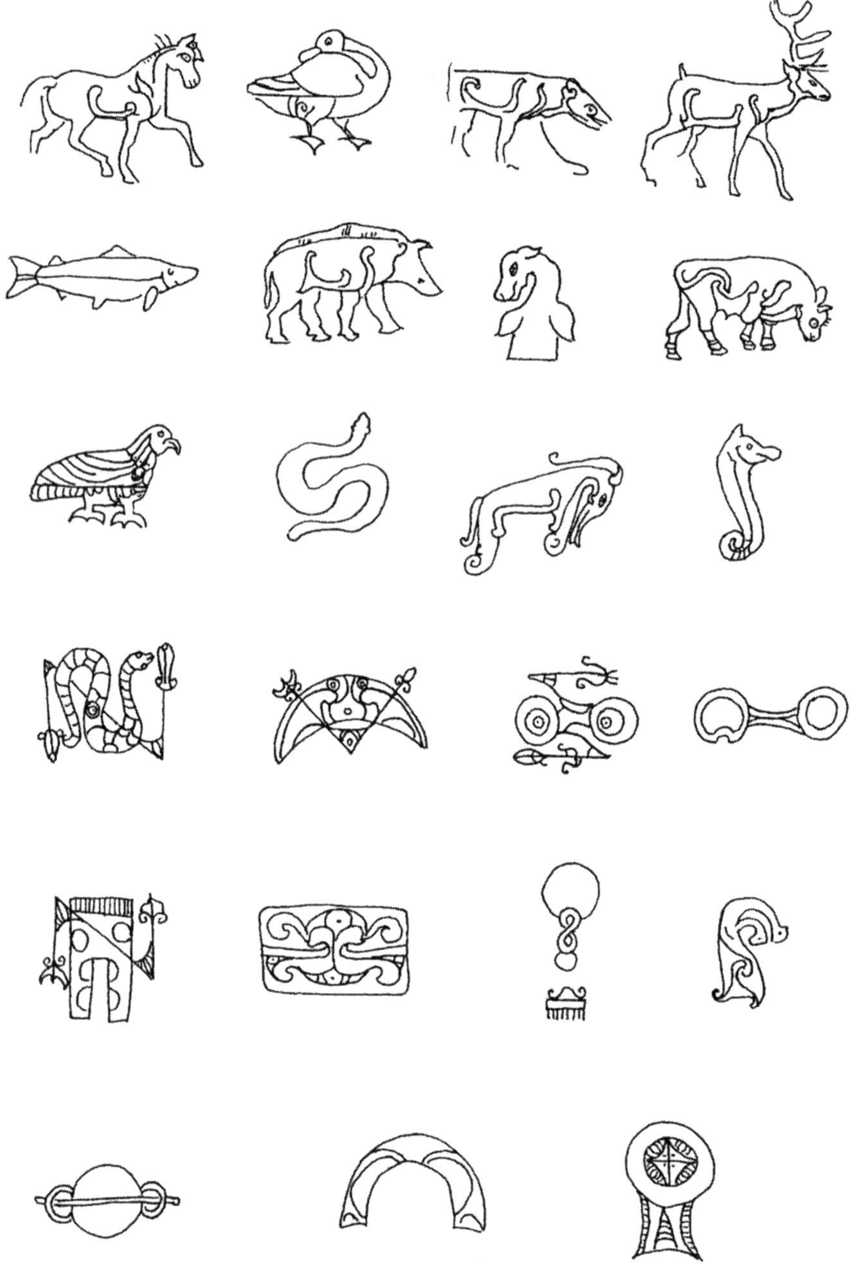

2.18 Pictish symbols.

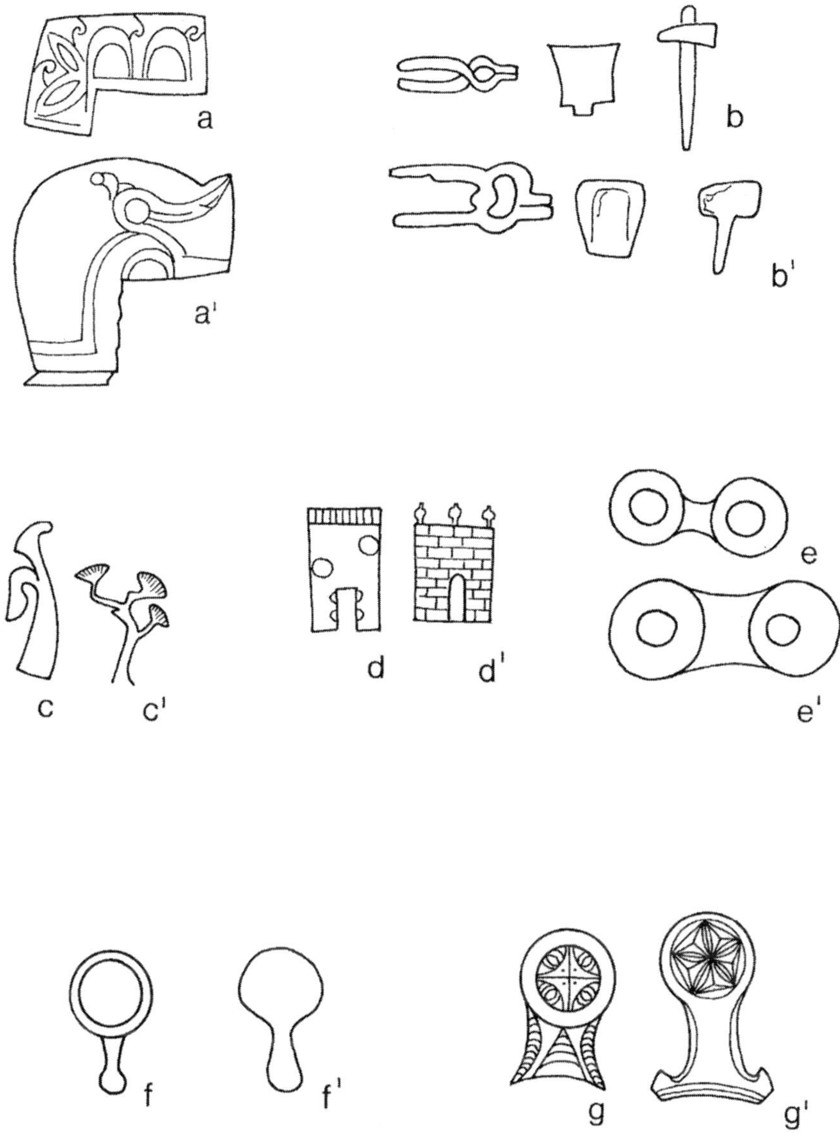

2.19 Roman inspiration for some Pictish symbols. a–g Pictish symbols. a1 Guisborough, Yorks, Roman helmet; b1: Colchester, Roman pot; c1: Corbridge, Northumberland, detail from silver lanx; d1: coin of House of Constantine, with Camp Gate reverse; e1: altar detail, Vindolanda, Northumberland; f1: Rudston, Roman mosaic mirror; g1: patera handle, Caernarvon.

the dead, in others perhaps as territorial markers), was probably inspired by a familiarity with Roman commemorative sculpture and inscriptions (fig. 2.18). Not only the form of the monuments copied Roman tradition – it is likely that the symbols themselves were first created during the period of Roman influence in Britain and were inspired by Romano-British art (fig. 2.19).

With one notable exception, the animals in Pictish art were found in the north of Scotland at the time the monuments were erected. The depictions imply that the artists had first-hand knowledge of the creatures, since, for example, they are shown as they would correctly appear in motion (Hicks, 1993a, 197). However, the animals are also found in Roman sculpture in north Britain – for example on altars, tombstones and distance slabs as well as in other media (Phillips, 1977; Keppie & Arnold, 1984; Coulson & Phillips, 1988).

The only Pictish creature found on the early incised stones that is not present in north British Roman art is the fish (Hicks, 1992, 200). However, it is found in Roman art further south. The remaining symbol which is known as the swimming elephant or Pictish beast, is not a real animal, but has much in common with the creature represented by dragonesque brooches (Laing & Laing, 1990, 196; Warner, 1987).

If the abstract symbols originated in Romano-British art, they must have developed at an early stage, before confronted trumpet patterns were common. The most common design element is the pelta, although a simple trumpet pattern, running scroll and ring-and-dot are also to be seen. Roman models for specific symbols can be suggested (Laing & Laing, 1984b).

CELTIC ART IN IRELAND

It is becoming increasingly clear that contact between Ireland and Britain in the Roman period was prolonged and far more extensive than was originally thought. There have even been suggestions that there may have been some attempt at invasion by Rome (Warner, 1994; 1995; Di Martino, 2003) and the Greek geographer Ptolemy (after AD83 to *c.*168), mapped Ireland, providing the names of tribes (Raftery, 1994, 206). Certainly, it is now accepted that Ireland had more contact with the Roman world than was traditionally thought, with the resultant new inspiration for Irish craftspeople and artists.

Influence from Roman Britain is apparent by the end of the first century AD in the use of broken-backed triskele designs and rosettes in the

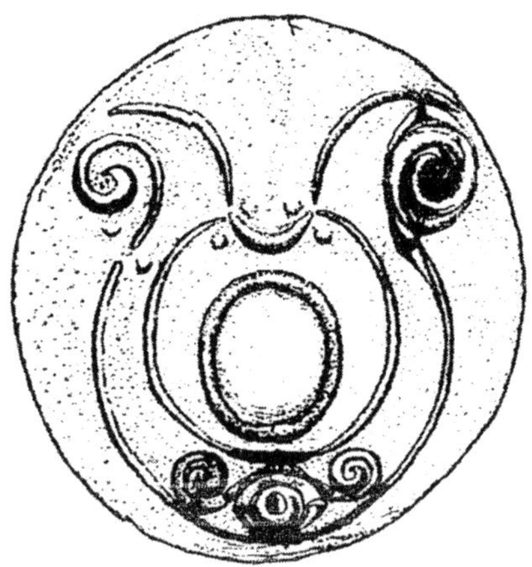

2.20 Monasterevin style disc, unprovenanced.

finds from Lambay Island, near Dublin, and on a bronze box from Navan, Co. Armagh (Raftery, 1984, 282). Slender-stemmed trumpet patterns and high relief modelling are apparent in the Irish repertoire. The Irish derivatives include a series of large discs known as the Monasterevin group, after one particular example (fig. 2.20). They were produced with repoussé hammering, and some have snail-shell coils with crests. The designs on some of these presumably religious objects (possibly votive plaques) are distant echoes of the lyre-scroll.

The Cork Horns (three horn-shaped objects, possibly joined by some perished material, and found in the River Lee in Cork city in 1909) and Petrie Crown (found in Co. Cork, and originally in the collection of George Petrie) are likely to be parts of head-pieces for ceremonial purposes, and display the same ornamental style (fig. 2.21). The discs on the Petrie Crown have designs which generally echo those on the Monasterevin discs and employ slender-stemmed confronted trumpets. Only one horn survives: it bears crested heads on its end coils, the heads being virtually identical to those that terminate the dragonesque brooches of Roman Britain. Bird head terminals to coils also appear on a disc from the River Bann, which has a triskele with yin-yang centre. The modelling on all three is in very shallow relief, and in the case of the Bann disc, was produced by cutting away the ground (O'Kelly, 1961). All these items could date to the late first- or second century.

Running scrolls, step patterns, peltas and triskeles are all employed on various pieces of metalwork connected with horsemanship, and are probably due to Romano-British influence (Laing & Laing, 1990, 191–3).

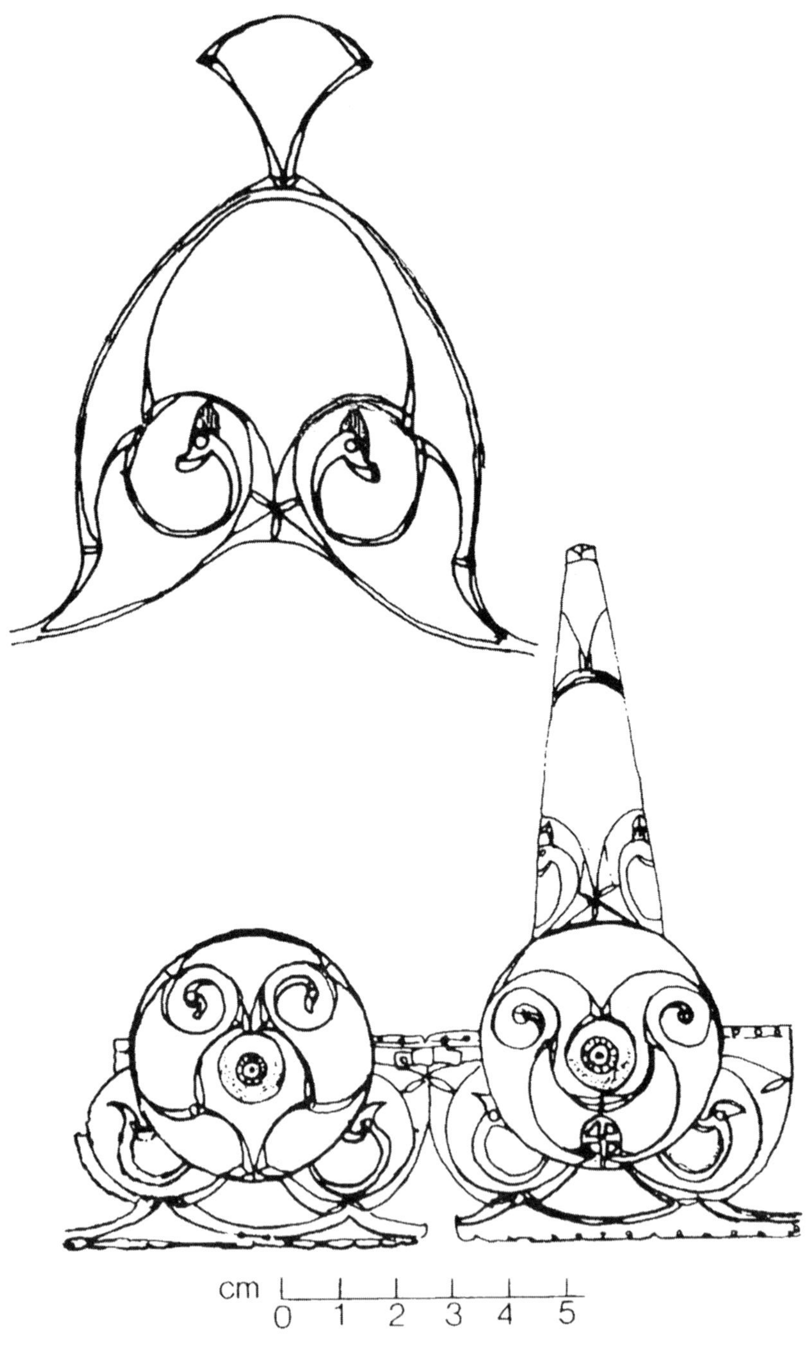

2.21 Petrie Crown.

Roman influence in fourth- and fifth-century Ireland
There is extensive evidence for the Romanization of material culture in Ireland in the fourth to fifth centuries, including the assimilation of Romano-British art (Laing, 2006, 273–6). Stray finds show, for example, a marked increase in fourth-century contact (Bateson, 1973; 1976). It seems likely that by the mid-fourth century the Irish Sea was under Celtic control (Charles-Edwards, 2000, 157), and Irish raids (and attempted Roman buy-offs) were avenues through which Roman material was introduced to Ireland. This is most easily demonstrated by the occurrence of Roman hoards of silverwork from Balline, Ballinrees and Coleraine, deposited in the late fourth to early fifth century (Ó Riordáin, 1947; Raftery, 1994, 214–16). Certainly in the fourth to fifth centuries there is evidence of Irish settlers as well as raiders in Britain. These include the Attacotti, the Déisi and the Uí Liatháin, who may have served as *foederati* (Roman federates – barbarian soldiers who were given lands in return for military service) in buffer areas (Rance, 2001).

Like its crested bird counterpart, the dodo-head appears in Ireland. A triskele with dodo-head figures on the end of a horse-bit from Attymon, Co. Galway (for which a date in the fourth or fifth century is acceptable) and the same device in variant form appears on a series of pins, mounts and penannular brooches from Ireland that probably spans the fifth and sixth centuries.

Irish dress-fasteners
Fourth-century types of Romano-British dress-fastener (penannular brooches and stick pins), and the ornament associated with them were used in Ireland. The earliest penannular brooches are concentrated near rivers, which suggests that they may have been votive offerings (Ó Floinn, 2001, 2).

Stick pins were also in use in Ireland. One series is clearly related to the Romano-British series; an example from Horn Head, Co. Donegal, is clearly closely related to the zoomorphic pins found in Britain (Newman, 1995, 19). This pin has its counterpart in the Irish series of penannular brooches, sharing a number of decorative features including a distinctive treatment of the 'eyes' on the animal (in this case a duck) head, which are also found on an Irish three-link horse bit (Raftery, 1984, fig. 11.1).

It has been argued that much of the stimulus for the development of ornamental metalwork in Ireland came from the Severn Estuary area and possibly south-west England (Laing & Laing, 1990, 208) since many of the Irish finds are enamelled – a technique that was popular in the area. Finds from Clogher, Co. Tyrone, imply that workshops were producing metalwork that was derivative of the Romano-British tradition – penannular brooches appear to have been made there in the late fifth to sixth centuries (dated by imported Mediterranean pottery (Warner, 1979). The Clogher brooches employ the basic range of scrolls, yin-yangs, peltas, spherical triangles and spirals that are part of mainstream late Romano-British art.

Fifth- and sixth-century contacts between Ireland and Britain

There is evidence of a two-way flow of objects (and probably also craftspeople) between Britain and Ireland in the fifth and sixth centuries. While there is no evidence that hanging bowls were produced in Ireland in this period, some may have been imported. It has been suggested that the openwork escutcheon from the River Bann is a local product (Bruce-Mitford, 2005, 329), but its close similarity to the escutcheons on a hanging bowl from Baginton, Warwickshire (Bruce-Mitford, 2005, no. 93) and fairly close affinity with that from Eastwell, Leicestershire (Bruce-Mitford, 2005, no. 45), argue more strongly in favour of a British provenance. It is pieces such as this, as well as proto-hand-pins that may have introduced the 'fine-line' style of decoration to Ireland. The proto-hand-pin from Castletown, Co. Meath (Kilbride-Jones, 1980b, fig. 68, no. 6), is closely similar to the proto-hand-pins from Britain, which suggests that it may be an import rather than a native Irish product. A similar conclusion may be drawn from the mount from Dundrum Castle, Co. Tipperary, which is decorated in a similar fine-line style (Waterman, 1951, 15–29). Bruce-Mitford linked this mount to a bowl from Jatten, Norway, and accordingly assigned it to the eighth century (2005, 438). However, this may be too late a date since (in addition to the fine-line style), it displays dodo-heads both in their simple, late Roman form, and in more evolved crested form, as found on hanging bowl 1 from the major treasure from Sutton Hoo, Suffolk, and on an escutcheon for a Type A bowl from Brill, Buckinghamshire (Bruce-Mitford, 2005, no. 174). Such imported models may have given rise to a series of more distinctively Irish products, such as the latchet from Dowris, Co. Offaly (though latchets, which are a distinctive type of dress fastener, may themselves be of Romano-British derivation: Laing, 1993a, 37).

Irish smiths in Britain

Irish smiths probably worked in Britain. A lead casting of a brooch, found at Dinas Powys, Glamorgan, may have been a model for making moulds. It is of a type well-known in Ireland but not otherwise represented in Britain (Alcock, 1963, 121; Graham-Campbell, 1991). Irish too is the penannular brooch from an Anglo-Saxon grave at High Down, Sussex

(Newman, 1995, 21). An Irish origin must surely be attributable to a large Class 1 penannular from Mull, with flaring terminals that show it to be on the cusp of development into the flaring terminal brooches of Fowler's Class H (Laing, 1993a, no. 1). The more evolved brooch from Pant-y-Saer, Anglesey (Laing, 1993a, no. 2) may also be Irish and should perhaps be seen as the starting point for the series of related Welsh brooches discussed by Youngs (2007).

ANGLO-SAXON INFLUENCE ON CELTIC ART

The influence of Anglo-Saxon art on that of the Celts may have begun in a secular context, through which they probably contributed a menagerie of animals as well as one of the most traditionally typical Celtic ornamental devices, interlace. The Anglo-Saxons are also likely to have introduced the Celts to filigree and granular work in gold, and chip-carved ornament.

Although it is clear that there was contact between Celtic British artisans and the Anglo-Saxons from the fifth century onwards, the main flow of ideas and technological innovation from the latter to the former probably came as a result of the growth of the Anglo-Saxon kingdom of Northumbria in the later sixth and early seventh centuries. This expansion resulted in the annexation of much of southern Scotland as far as the Firth of Forth. This undoubtedly explains why the Celts in the area adopted Anglo-Saxon technology and ornamental techniques. Fine Anglo-Saxon metalwork, including gold and garnet work, has been found in southern Scotland (Proudfoot & Aliaga-Kelly, 1996).

The transmission of Anglo-Saxon styles and techniques to Ireland was probably slightly later in the seventh century through the agency of Irish monastic activity and the strong connection with the monastery at Iona. Other links between Ireland and England from this period onward can be seen from burials of Anglo-Saxons that are now recognized to exist in Ireland (O'Brien, 1993; O'Brien, 1999, 179–86), where there is also substantial evidence for the presence of Anglo-Saxon monks (Charles-Edwards, 2003).

Beginning in the migration period with the Anglo-Saxon settlements in south-east England and continuing into the period of Northumbrian supremacy, several metalworking techniques were adopted and adapted by the Celts; filigree and granular work, chip carving, interlace and animal ornament being the most important.

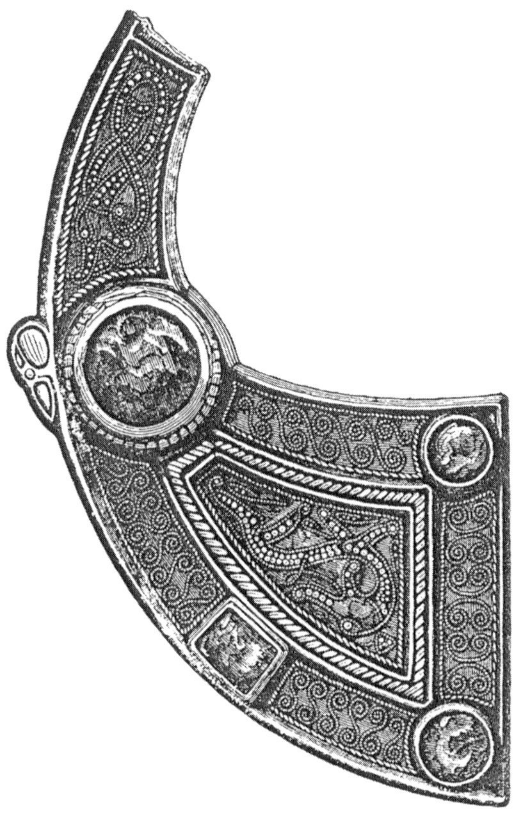

2.22 Dunbeath (Achavrole) Brooch (after Anderson, 1881).

Filigree and granular work

Filigree work involved the use of twisted gold wire, whereas in granular work beads of gold were employed, both attached to the metal base. Both techniques appear to have been developed in England during the late sixth and early seventh centuries as a result of Merovingian-Frankish influence. The ultimate origin of both lies in the east Mediterranean, but the techniques were probably acquired in Britain through the close ties between south-east England and the Merovingian world. During this period, gold was being imported into England from the Continent in the form of coins, which were apparently recycled as jewellery, the composition of which is closely similar to that of contemporaneous Merovingian coins (Hawkes, Merrick & Metcalf, 1966; Brown & Schweizer, 1973). By the early seventh century, filigree and granular work was being employed in the objects from the burial at Taplow, Buckinghamshire, and both types of decoration are found widely on disc brooches and buckles.

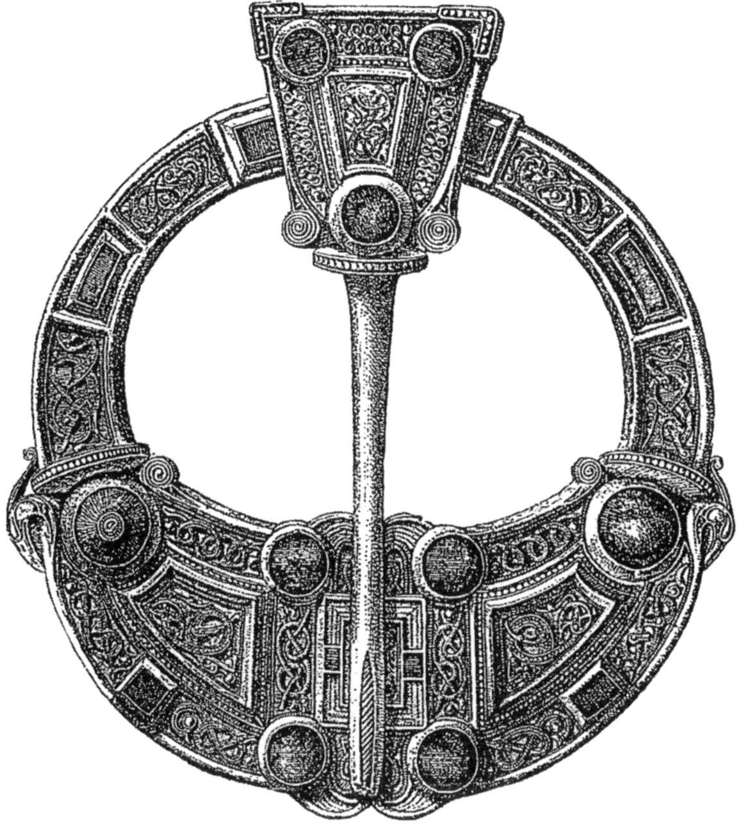

2.23 Hunterston Brooch (after Anderson, 1881).

In some cases, interlace was rendered in filigree (for example on the buckles from the Taplow burial).

It is likely that the package of Anglian ornamental metalworking arrived in the Celtic world through the late sixth- to early seventh-century Northumbrian expansion into southern Scotland. A detailed study of the filigree and granular work on Celtic metalwork has concluded that the techniques for the most part are directly modelled on those employed in Anglo-Saxon England, though many are also found on the Continent as well and direct continental models for their use cannot be totally ruled out (Whitfield 1987; 1993; 2001b; 2007). Two examples of filigree from Ireland (a gold bird from Garryduff, Co. Cork, and a mount from Lagore, Co. Meath), have been suggested from their associations as being from the late sixth to early seventh century AD, and to have been largely inspired by Anglo-Saxon techniques (Whitfield, 2001b). An ornate finger ring from

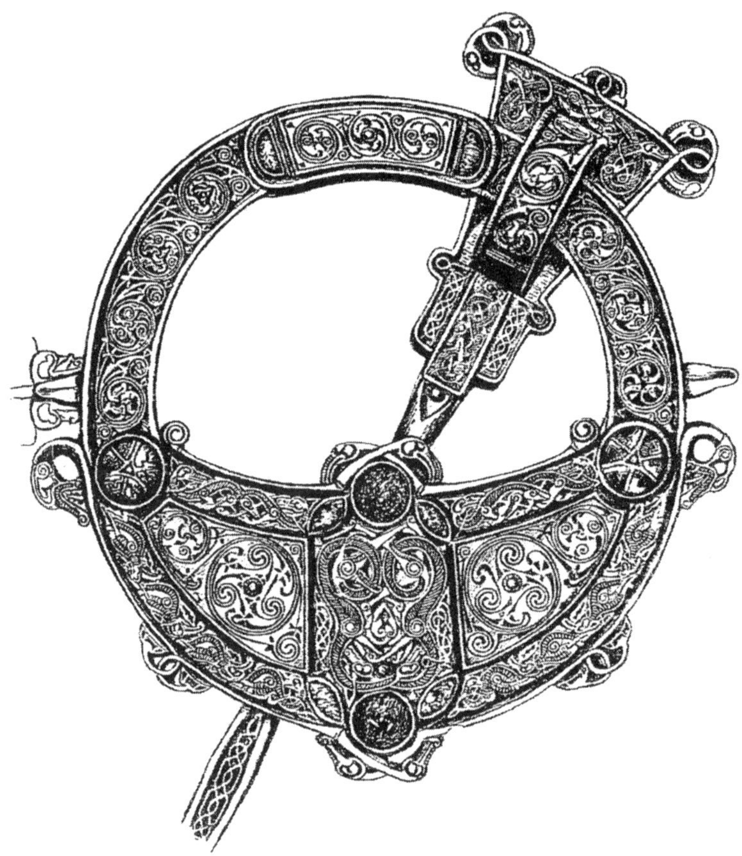

2.24 The 'Tara' Brooch (after Coffey, 1909).

Tipperary displays both filigree and cloisonné work. It may either be an import from the Merovingian world, or an attempt by an Irish artisan to imitate an ostentatious ring of late Roman date (Whitfield, 2001b, 151).

Two penannular brooches from Scotland (from Achavrole and Hunterston) display gold filigree and granular work, and seem to pre-date the earliest from Ireland stylistically. The Achavrole Brooch was found in the nineteenth century near the early monastic site of Ballachly, at Dunbeath, Caithness (fig. 2.22). The brooch is incomplete, but, despite a plausible suggestion that it was broken on discovery, the terminal has clearly been cut through, suggesting more strongly that it may have come from a hoard of scrap metal.

The Achavrole Brooch is made of silver with an inlaid tray ornamented with a filigree open-jawed dragon. A similar animal with open jaws adorns

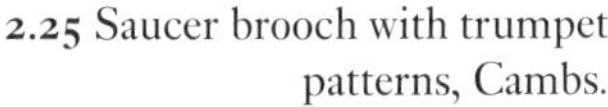

2.25 Saucer brooch with trumpet patterns, Cambs.

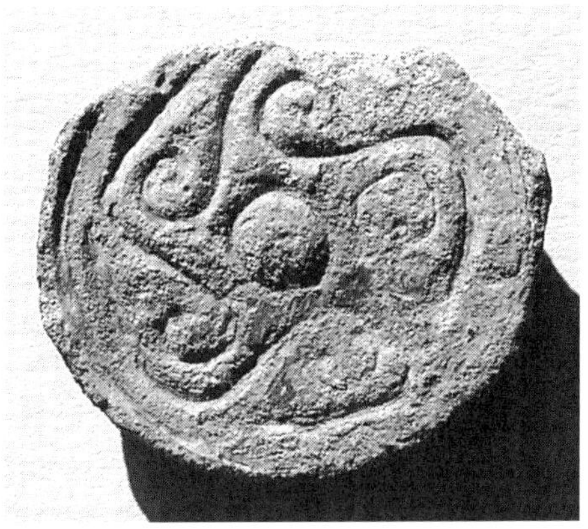

one of the panels on the hoop, and there are filigree running s-scrolls and c-scrolls inlaid in the remaining inlaid panels, which were separated by amber studs. The technique involved 'hollow platform' work, in which two back-plates were superimposed, the upper worked in relief with cut-out depressions.

The technique was employed more successfully on the Hunterston Brooch (fig. 2.23), but perhaps on the Achavrole it is an early attempt to imitate the technique which was widely employed on the Continent and in Anglo-Saxon gold work where it is seen for example, on a pair of buckles from Faversham, Kent (Whitfield, 1987, 78)

The Achavrole Brooch displays animal ornament very similar to that on the more sophisticated Hunterston Brooch (and the Irish Tara Brooch, which was named for romantic reasons and has no known connection with the royal cult site), and which has been seen as directly inspired by Anglo-Saxon filigree animals (fig. 2.24). However, the animal on the main Achavrole panel has a pronounced crest, which links it with the Pictish beast of Pictish symbol stones and the earlier crested bird heads of later Iron Age art. The crest on Hunterston is more pronounced, but on the Tara Brooch the crest is still there, but is much more attenuated, and the beaded granular infilling has been replaced by more sophisticated herringbone ornament.

Chip carving

This ornamental device seems to have originated as a woodcarving technique among the Germanic peoples. The ground is cut into by facets (often triangular) which reflect the light when polished or gilded. Some chip carving is apparent in late Roman metalwork used by Germanic people on the frontiers of the Roman Empire, and was widely employed in

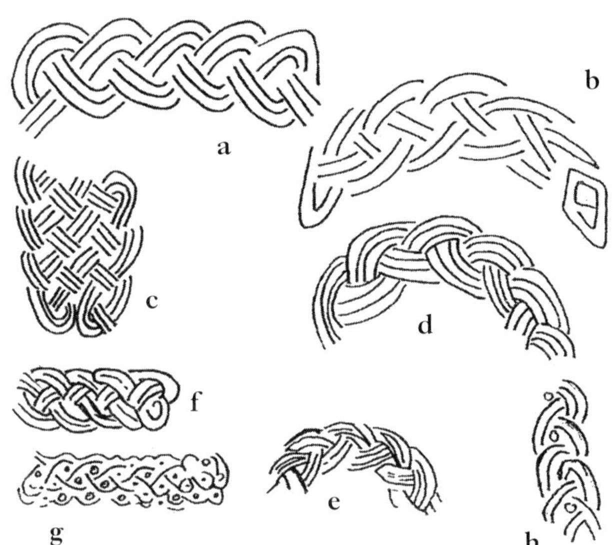

2.26 Interlace, Continental and Saxon. a: Freiweinheim, Germany, grave 10, from a brooch; b: Castel Trosino, Italy, radiate brooch; c: Szentendre, Hungary, brooch, grave 56; d: Hockwold, Suffolk, disc brooch; e: from a basal print of a hanging bowl, Ipswich, Suffolk; f: sword pommel, Coombe, Kent; g: Ruskington, Lincs, square-headed brooch detail; h: Thornborough, North Yorks, square-headed brooch detail.

northern Europe *c.*AD400. It was taken up by the Anglo-Saxons, being typical of saucer brooches in the later fifth and sixth centuries (fig. 2.25). Among the Celts it was used on some of the finest penannular brooches, such as the gold and silver Tara and Hunterston Brooches of the eighth and late-seventh century, and was used also on such masterpieces as the Ardagh Chalice, a richly-decorated liturgical vessel of the eighth century. Chip carving continued to be fashionable in the Celtic areas and in England, and was eventually employed in Viking period Ireland in the decoration of harness mounts.

Interlace

Interlace was unknown in the British Iron Age. Its earliest form (the only one found before the early medieval period) was plait work, in which strands were woven over and under one another and were never turned back on themselves. In this kind of work the ribbons are not changed into animals with the addition of heads and tails. Plait work/interlace was introduced to Britain during the Roman period, when it was used in the design of mosaic pavements and in metalwork. A fine example can be seen on a bracelet from Rhayader, South Wales, the design elements on which also include trumpet scrolls and small amounts of enamel, pointing to a native production in the second or third century AD (Cool, 1986; Henig, 1995, 91; Laing, 1997, 82). If a crude interlace design on the back of a penannular brooch from the Roman fort of Newstead is discounted

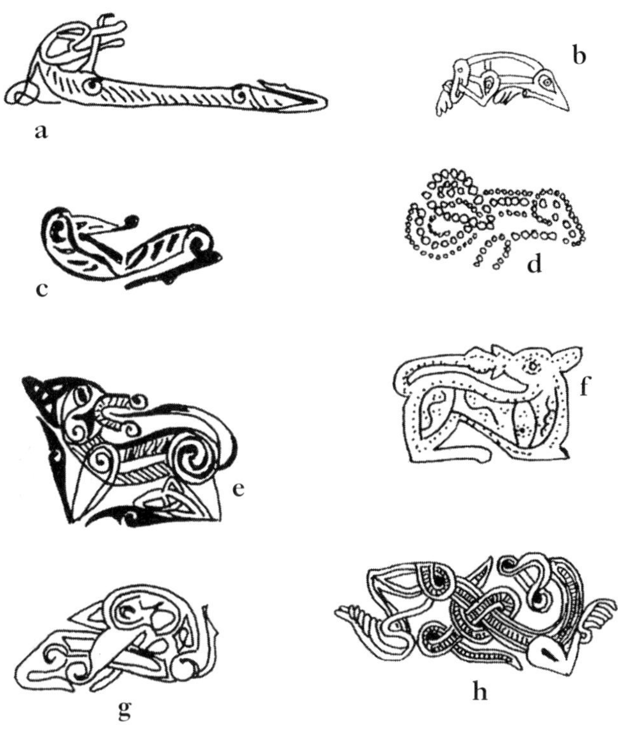

2.27 Animals of Whitfield's 4 types. a: brooch, Co. Cavan; b: Sutton Hoo, Suffolk, gold buckle; c: 'Londesborough' Brooch; d: shoulder clasp, Sutton Hoo; e: Killamery Brooch, Co. Kilkenny; f: Bidford-on-Avon, Warks, bucket; g: brooch said to be from Tara, Co. Meath; h: Sutton Hoo, Suffolk, shield animal (after Whitfield, 1995).

(Fowler, 1960, fig. 7), there are no Roman examples of plait work in metal from north Britain, and almost none from Wales or south-west England. It is therefore extremely unlikely that interlace was developed from an earlier native source, and must be seen as a contribution from outside the Celtic-speaking area (fig. 2.26).

Interlace in pagan Anglo-Saxon England is found in both abstract and zoomorphic form, in the latter case taking the guise of lacertines (a distinctive scrolling ornament of intertwining snakes). The sequence of ornament in Anglo-England (after the Quoit Brooch Style) comprises the two north European traditions termed Styles I and II by Bernhard Salin (1904). Style I seems to have evolved out of the strongly Roman-influenced Nydam Style (Haseloff, 1974; Chadwick, 1958, 50–7), and employed dismembered animal ornament and facing human masks. It was taken up in England around the end of the fifth century and was current thereafter through much of the sixth century. It had no obvious impact on the Celts. Style II seems to have evolved in the mid-sixth century, and predominantly employed lacertines, though in its earlier development it also made use of non-zoomorphic interlace. There has been active debate

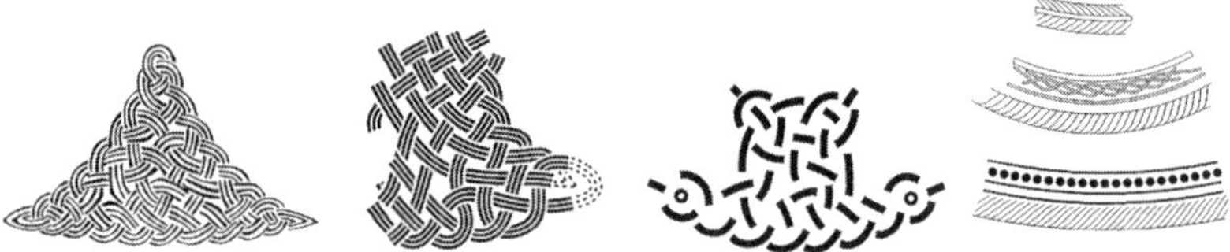

2.28 Mote of Mark, Kirkcudbright, types of interlace on moulds
(after Laing & Longley, 2006).

about the origins of Style II. In Scandinavia and in England it probably developed out of Style I, perhaps along parallel lines, but arguing against this is the fact that interlace is also found in different contexts in the later sixth century in areas of the Continent where Style I was absent (Speake, 1980; Davidson & Webster, 1967).

The earliest occurrence of non–zoomorphic interlace in England appears to be on a series of square-headed brooches dating from around the mid-sixth century, from Lincolnshire and North Yorkshire (Hines, 1992, 320–1). On these, in contrast to what is found in plait work, the cables bend back on themselves, as in Celtic interlace. The trend towards interlacing patterns is also apparent in a number of other media in sixth-century England, where plait work/interlace appears for example on some cremation urns from Spong Hill, Norfolk (Hills, 1981, fig. 76) and on a series of Style I pieces on which the animal bodies are extended into short pieces of interlace. The most notable examples of metalwork for which a date can be assigned are the mounts for a sword from Coombe, Kent, that were probably made between AD550 and 600. They employ zoomorphic and non-zoomorphic interlace as well as multi-strand ornament (Davidson & Webster, 1967).

Animal ornament

New types of animal ornament appeared in Celtic metalwork and manuscript art in the seventh century. Shown in profile, the animals are complete and anatomically structured, but do not represent specific species. They have no obvious antecedents in the Celtic world, but appear to be of Germanic ancestry (fig. 2.27). They were presumably borrowed directly from their Anglo-Saxon counterparts, though similar creatures can be found in Merovingian art. Four characteristic poses represented by the animals have been distinguished: (1) backward-looking animals with no forelegs; (2) backward-looking animals with raised forelegs; (3) backward-looking animals biting their forelegs; (4) backward-looking animals biting tails arched over their backs (Whitfield, 1995, 90–2). The first three poses

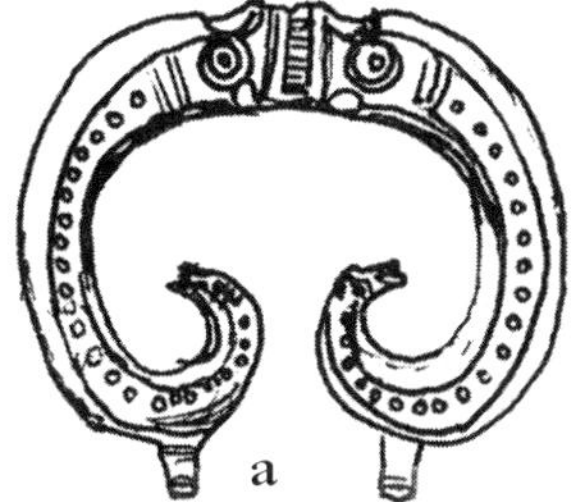
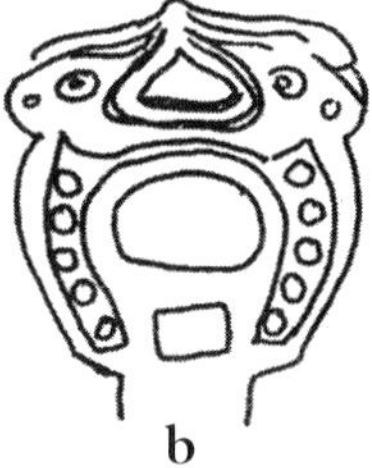

2.29 Buckles. a: Lakenheath, Suffolk; b: Mote of Mark, Kirkcudbright, mould.

can be seen in the metalwork from the Sutton Hoo Treasure, where pose 1 appears on the shoulder clasps; pose 2 on the shield and pose 3 on the great gold buckle (Whitfield, 1995, figs 1–4). Pose 4 is not found until the ninth century in Celtic art (it appears, for example, on the Killamery Brooch and in Pictish sculpture). Although found in the fifth century in England (on a bucket mount from Bidford-on-Avon, Warwickshire, for example) it did not gain popularity there until around the ninth century. These poses are not exclusive to Anglo-Saxon art, also being found in Continental Germanic art and occasionally in Antique art.

Compositions in Celtic art involving animals – in pairs or in processions – also have Germanic comparanda. Animals with a round object in the mouth (seen for example on the Hunterston Brooch) can be matched on the Sutton Hoo shoulder clasps and on earlier Germanic animals on the Continent (Whitfield, 1995, 93).

The ways in which the bodies are treated are matched in both Celtic and Anglo-Saxon art. These include the use of double contour lines, and speckled, hatched or herringbone infilling (Whitfield, 1995, 96–101).

THE MOTE OF MARK – A CASE STUDY IN CULTURAL
BORROWING

A workshop found at the Mote of Mark, Kirkcudbright, southern Scotland, displays the diversity of contributing elements in the art produced at the end of the sixth and in the early seventh century AD. The citadel lay in the British kingdom of Rheged, which subsequently became subject to Northumbria. Moulds discovered there were used for casting a diversity of objects, from penannular brooches and pins to items probably intended for horse harnesses. The ornament shows a mixture of elements from diverse sources, particularly Romano-British and Anglo-Saxon.

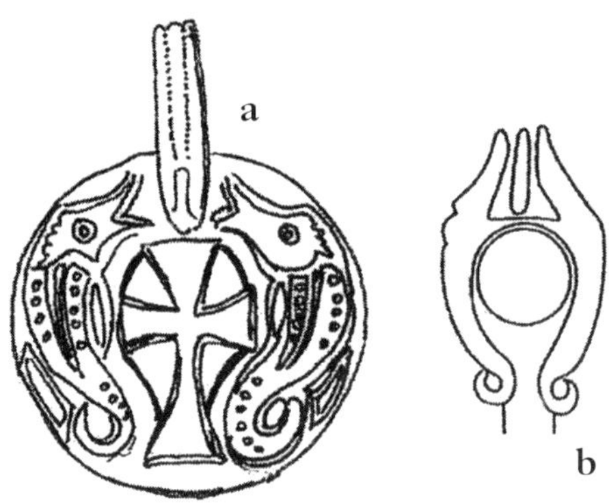

2.30 Confronted dolphins.
a: Faversham, Kent, hanging bowl
escutcheon; b: Mote of Mark,
Kirkcudbright, pin-head mould.

Roman influence at the Mote of Mark

The Mote of Mark moulds prove that Romano-British types of object and their associated ornament were being produced in southern Scotland in the post-Roman period, as they were in other parts of Britain. Moulds for plates display pelta patterns, running scrolls, yin-yangs and sunbursts (Laing & Longley, 2006, fig. 57).

Anglo-Saxon influence at the Mote of Mark

Anglo-Saxon influence is apparent at the Mote of Mark in the use of interlace, which seems to have been introduced as a result of contacts in the sixth century. Different types of interlace were employed. Most was double-strand, but both single-strand and triple-strand versions were also used. Only one of the designs might be seen as zoomorphic, since it shows what might be a vestigial 'eye' and a possible 'tail' (Laing & Longley, 2006, 151) (fig. 2.28).

Gold filigree and possibly granular work also appear at the Mote of Mark, presumably through introduction from Northumbria. Finds included crucibles, which proved that gold was cast into small objects. In addition, a strip of gold wire was found that was probably intended for use in wire work (Whitfield, 2006, 40). The interlace ornament on the moulds shows that filigree and granular work were being imitated in cast designs which were presumably gilded.

Stylistic fusion at the Mote of Mark

Just how intricately diverse decorative elements were fused together at the Mote of Mark can be seen in some moulds for buckles which have loops with pairs of confronted animal heads, in one case with bodies that show imitation filigree ornament.

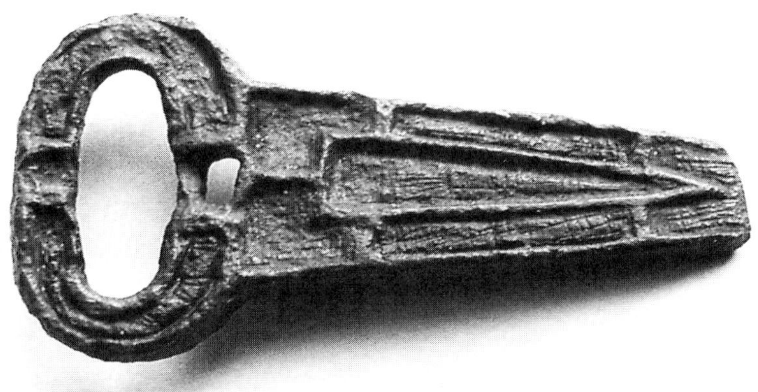

2.31 Buckle, with cells for enamel, North Yorks.

One decorative device encountered on moulds for buckles is reminiscent of decoration on late Roman provincial buckles that have often been assumed to have been signifiers of status. Found widely along the northern frontiers of the late Roman empire, the buckles have been found in Frankish burials such as those at Vermand and Haillot in northern France, as well as in Romano-British and Anglo-Saxon contexts. They vary in form, the most common having the loop decorated with a pair of confronted dolphins/hippocamps (sea horses) (Hawkes & Dunning, 1961). Once believed to be associated with federates, modern opinion now views them as being indicators of status in civilian society as well as military (fig. 2.29).

It is possible that the buckles were buried in Anglo-Saxon graves because of their associations with status, which may also account for their survival in a modified form at the Mote of Mark. There are no prototypes from Celtic areas, but the design of one from the Mote of Mark (Laing & Longley, 2006, fig. 57, 1212) seems to be a precursor of the penannulars with animal-headed terminals from Pictland. Similar confronted dolphins appear on a mould for a pin-head from the Mote of Mark, a motif that is very similar to that on the hanging bowl escutcheon from Faversham, Kent, where the dolphins face one another on each side of a cross (fig. 2.30).

The Mote of Mark buckles have a distinctive fastening mechanism, where the pin is fitted through a rectangular hole cut in the plate, which is cast in one piece with the loop. Found on late Roman buckles, the design continued in use in the Byzantine world, but is occasionally found in the Merovingian Empire. The fasteners are generally absent from purely

Anglo-Saxon assemblages in England (in which the buckle plate is usually hinged to the loop), but a few recent finds may imply surviving workshops. One Yorkshire example seems to be made to take inlays after the manner of seventh-century Anglo-Saxon gold and garnet buckles, but the cells appear keyed for enamel, which presumably would have been red in imitation of Saxon garnet (fig. 2.31).

Buckles of this type (decorated with enamel and millefiori), are known from Leicestershire, and from Rathtinaun, Lough Gara, Co. Sligo (Youngs, 1993). Such buckles may have been the models for the imitation buckle on the belt shrine from Moylough, Co. Sligo, which has a pair of long-beaked bird heads on the hoop and a square, flat plate behind. This is reminiscent of the Quoit Brooch belt buckle from Mucking, Essex (Evison, 1968).

CHAPTER 3

The impact of Christianity

Christianity was increasingly adopted in Celtic lands from the late-fifth century on. The organization of the church affected the patronage of art, the type of art objects and treasures that were produced and the ways in which religious beliefs were expressed in art. Iconography was taken straight from the Classical world through direct copying of Roman models and adaption into the media used by the Celts – especially metalwork, sculpture and manuscripts. As would be expected, the lay patrons were still from the higher levels of society, but their aims and therefore the artworks they commissioned were often more religious in appearance.

ORGANIZATION OF THE CELTIC CHURCH

Originally, the Church in the Celtic areas is likely to have been diocesan, and in the period immediately following the collapse of Britannia, ecclesiastical administration was probably based on urban bishoprics (a probable example is Caerwent, South Wales). Memorial stones of the fifth and sixth centuries in Britain (inscribed in debased Latin) make reference to bishops and priests. The term for bishop appears to have been *sacerdos*, below which was the *presbiter* (priest), and below that was the *diaconus* (deacon). The first two appear on memorial stones of the fifth to seventh centuries, but their appearance may have been a result of direct trans-plantation from the Continent (Thomas, 1998, 84–8). Bishops are mentioned in documentary sources. Gildas implies that the Church was diocesan in the sixth century, and SS Ninian and Patrick are both described by their biographers as bishops (Thomas, 1971, 13).

Towns declined in the former province of Britannia from the mid-fifth century. It is therefore likely that bishops became attached to courts and royal households rather than to permanent churches in towns (Thomas, 1998, 82–3). Similarly, in the Celtic areas, ecclesiastical sees (the areas under the jurisdiction of bishops) may have been focussed on major churches closely connected with royal strongholds.

Towns did not exist in Ireland: St Patrick set up churches adjacent to the royal centres of power. His centre was Armagh, less than two miles from Emain Macha, the royal capital (and cult centre) of Ulster. Two contemporaries of Patrick chose similar locations: Secundinus founded a church at Dunshaughlin (near the similarly important centre of Tara), and Auxilius founded his church at Killashee, near Dun Ailinne, also a traditional royal and ritual centre. From the outset, power was divided between secular and ecclesiastical authorities, which provided mutual support.

MONASTICISM

From the sixth century on, monasteries became the administrative centres of Celtic dioceses (although the Church was never totally monastic in its organization: Sharpe, 1984). This is of importance in the study of artworks, since monasteries not only preserved and guarded works of Christian art, but produced them in workshops and scriptoria. The needs of a formal Church, with considerable ritual involved in its dealings internally and with the outside world are the key to understanding some of the artworks produced.

St Patrick refers to men and women who became 'monks and virgins for Christ' (*Confession*, chs 41–2), which implies the existence of nuns from the outset. However, communities of women cannot easily be distinguished in either the documentary or the archaeological record in the early medieval period. St Brigit at Kildare, who presided over a double house for both monks and nuns, is the most prominent female ecclesiastical figure in the written sources.

Although some monasteries were founded in the fifth century, the majority of foundations were of the sixth century and later. Many seem to have been founded through the patronage of powerful landowners, who sometimes gave land for the purpose and on occasion established a family member as abbot or abbess. The proprietor of the monastic foundation at Iona was the Uí Néill family, who controlled Ulster, and a member of the family was normally the abbot. The fortunes of a monastery were therefore usually closely related to those of its patron, and the ecclesiastical communities could flourish or decline with the fortunes of their patrons.

Major monasteries were run by an abbot (though sometimes a bishop or even a secular landowner) ministering to daughter houses. In Wales, towards the end of the first millennium, a mother church emerged that was similar to an Anglo-Saxon Minster (*clas*). This was ruled by an abbot who presided over parishes that coincided with secular territories.

Monasteries in Celtic lands could comprise communities that ranged from a few monks or nuns to several hundred. There was some variation in the Rule followed by Celtic monasteries. The Rule of St Columbanus (a monk who was born in west Leinster, Ireland) is the earliest that survives. A similar programme seems to have been followed a century later, to judge by the *Antiphonary of Bangor* (an antiphonary is a liturgical book with the chants for mass), which gives the details of the offices (periods of prayer and the singing of specified psalms and hymns at 'hours'). The Rule of St Columbanus set out the arrangement for three night 'offices' and probably five day 'offices'. Times in between were filled with work and meals.

An important aspect of belief among Celtic ecclesiatics was *peregrinatio* (an expression of piety which included formal exile from a particular monastery to travel to another region and enter into the life of strangers). The biblical model for this was the quest for the Promised Land that had been pursued by the followers of Moses. However, the quest for the Promised Land was seen by Celtic ecclesiastics as an end in itself, since it was a method by which God might be sought. It was of vital significance in the spread of ideas as well as objects such as books and relics (body parts of saints or articles closely connected with them, that were seen to possess miraculous powers), between major centres in the Christian world.

Gildas alluded to the phenomenon in the early sixth century and Columba's journey from Ireland to Iona was in a sense in the spirit of *peregrinatio*. In the sixth century, *peregrinatio* brought Irish monks to Gaul: around 585, Columbanus set sail from Bangor, Co. Down, arriving in western Gaul with twelve followers. He subsequently established new monasteries in Gaul and Italy (Lapidge (ed.), 1997; O'Loughlin, 2001a). His first foundations included Luxeuil, on land given him by the Merovingian king Guntram, but he was subsequently exiled and went to Switzerland, where his name is linked with Zürich, Bregenz and Chur. He built a monastery in a former fort at Annegray, northern Burgundy, from which he was expelled in 610. He subsequently travelled to Italy, where he founded the monastery at Bobbio before he died there in 615. Columbanus and his fellow Irish clerics had a considerable influence on the Merovingian Church, altering its approach to private penance, for example. Their influence on the kings and nobles additionally changed the character of Merovingian monasticism, since it encouraged the foundation of rural monasteries.

Meanwhile, Irish clerics were active in Anglo-Saxon England, a factor which was certainly important in exposing Celtic art to outside influences. The monastery of Lindisfarne on Iona was founded by St Aidan on the invitation of King Oswald of Northumbria in 635. It became the mother church of Northumbria and the centre of the episcopal see until the Synod of Whitby in 664, when Northumbria agreed to follow the Roman version of the faith. Other monasteries were founded by Irish clerics in England, including Burgh Castle, Norfolk, a Roman fort which was taken over by St Fursa in the seventh century.

Many monks from Ireland were active in Germany, France, Switzerland, the Low Countries and Italy. The monastery founded by Columbanus at Bobbio for example, became a major centre of learning. Some of the earliest surviving manuscripts in Insular style may have been produced in Bobbio, and its library still holds three North African manuscripts of the fourth or fifth centuries, one allegedly carried by Columbanus in his book satchel (Lowe, 1935–72, iv, 465). Irish manuscripts, such as the *Antiphonary of Bangor*, were taken there (Hughes, 1966, 93). Luxeuil and Chur are also associated with major works of early medieval art, while the major monastery of St Gall in Switzerland was founded by one of Columbanus' followers.

Irish *peregrini* were not always welcome. They were unpopular in Carolingian circles because of their beliefs and monastic organization, though many, including Vergil of Salzburg, Dicuil, Sedulius Scotus, Marianus Scotus and John Eriugena were famous in Carolingian circles (Bitel, 1990, 227).

In addition to the *peregrini*, there were regular visits of pilgrims. Most of the early Irish saints seem to have made pilgrimages to Rome, and brought back 'earth for cemeteries, consecrated oil and wine, bones of Peter, Paul and Thomas, pieces of Christ's tomb and the Temple at Jerusalem, hair of the Virgin, garments of the apostles, croziers, books, gospels, vestments and bells' (Bitel, 1990, 231).

THE DEVELOPMENT OF NON-INSULAR CHRISTIAN ICONOGRAPHY

There is little evidence that external sources provided direct models for Christian artisans in the Celtic world before the end of the fifth century.

By that time a distinctive Christian artistic style had developed in the Roman and Byzantine worlds, particularly in wall paintings, murals and sculpture. Murals and mosaics were inappropriate in Celtic architecture, but individual symbols were adopted from mainstream Roman iconography in metalwork and used in manuscript art.

It is likely that some elements of early Christian art were introduced to the Celts directly from Roman Britain, though it is uncertain to what extent these had a direct survival into the later fifth century and beyond – many, possibly all, elements could have been re-introduced from the Continent at a later period.

The early Christians believed that image-making was pagan and it is not until the third century that images with clearly Christian iconography have been found. The earliest are in the Catacombs (underground passages and cemeteries) in Rome where, during periods of persecution, belief had to be covert. The figures in catacomb art were painted in a world unrelated to space or time, a feature that was pagan Classical in origin. Metaphors were drawn from Classical imagery and the form of presentation is sparse and rapidly executed since it was the symbolic content that mattered rather than the technical expertise. It has been termed 'signative' art and was carried forward into the fourth century when Christianity was tolerated, and could be used openly. Subsequently it was used in the Byzantine Empire and was taken up and adapted in the Celtic world (see below, pp 78–81).

The spread of ideas

The spread of Christian iconography from the eastern and western Roman worlds came about through a number of agencies and customs. The main foci of Christian art were the major monasteries such as Iona, Durrow and Clonmacnois, from which the monks travelled abroad, and to which visitors came from many parts of Europe. By the end of the fifth century or the beginning of the sixth, there is archaeological evidence for direct trading contacts between Celtic Britain, Ireland and the Mediterranean. The evidence primarily comprises pottery, imported mostly between *c*.475 and *c*.525, which came from sources in southern Greece, western Asia Minor and Carthage (Fulford & Peacock, 1984, 14–15; Campbell, 1988; Lane, 1994, Campbell, 1996). The greatest concentration of imports is in south-west England, but they are found widely distributed along the Irish Sea coast and in Wales, Ireland and Scotland as far north as the Firth of Clyde and Iona.

A scatter of Byzantine finds have been found in western Britain and Ireland. These include coins (Pearce, 2004, 2007; Harris, 2003, 154;

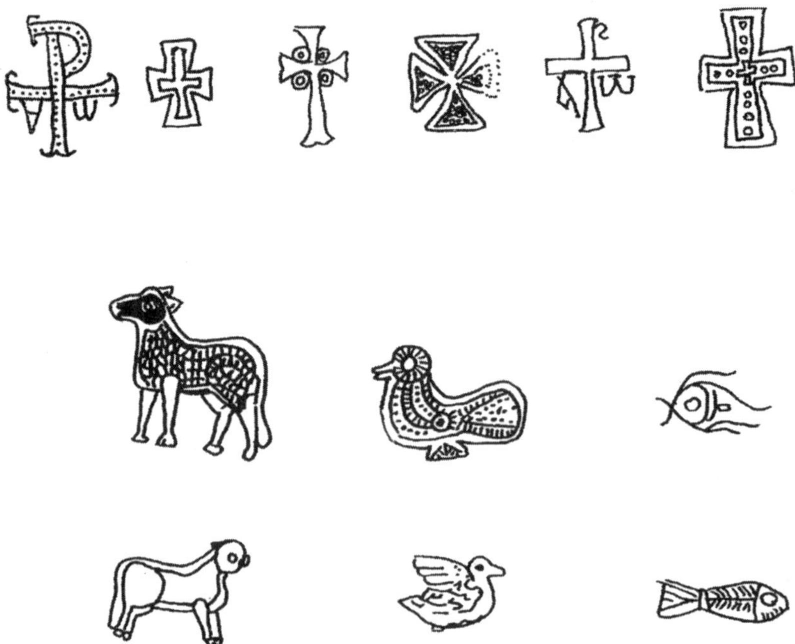

3.1 Motifs from imported North African pottery (after John Hayes, 1984).

Hillgarth, 1963, 177); a Byzantine coin weight from Entwhistle, Lancashire (Pearce, 2004, 237); pilgrim flasks from the shrine of St Menas, Alexandria, one of which was found at Meols, Cheshire (Bu'lock, 1972, 35) and a bronze censer produced in the Byzantine world which was found during construction work at Glastonbury, Somerset (Webster & Backhouse, 1991, 94, no. 68). Glass beads and glass objects that might have been tesserae used in Byzantine mosaics have been found at the Mote of Mark and Dunadd in Scotland. Some fragments of what were probably Egyptian glass vessels and an intaglio, have come from Anglesey (Denison, 2000).

The trade that brought the pottery (and arguably the other items) to Britain seems to have come directly from the sources of pottery production, and not through intermediaries, though some indirect trading from Gaul is possible (Wooding, 1996, 42; Fulford, 1989). The pottery trade is concentrated in the late fifth and early sixth centuries, which is compatible with the coin evidence, though there are later items, such as the censer from Glastonbury and a few coins which certainly indicate that connections continued into the seventh century.

Significantly, some of the imported pottery was decorated with stamped ornament, which in itself provides a direct source for some decorative devices in the Celtic world (fig. 3.1). Of these, the most significant are double-outline crosses, Chi-Rhos (the first two letters in Greek of the word Christ), peacocks, dolphins, fish and felines (Thomas, 1987). A Chi-Rho with alpha and omega also appears on an abraded sherd from Dinas Emrys, Gwynedd, North Wales (Savory, 1960).

There is strong evidence that the models for church plate used in the early Christian Celtic world were ultimately of Byzantine inspiration, even though there may have been intermediaries further west. St Patrick is reported to have come to Ireland accompanied by a bishop, Assicus, who was a bronze smith who fashioned altar plate. The source for this information is the seventh-century Tírechán, who claimed to have seen three patens made by Assicus that were at the churches at Armagh, Elphin and Saul (Bieler, 1979, 244). The importance lies not in the fact that St Patrick had liturgical plate produced, but that such a phenomenon was considered quite normal in the time of Tírechán.

The role of the Merovingian world in the dissemination of Christian ideas to the Celtic world has been recognized since the first studies of Irish connections abroad were made in the early twentieth century (Zimmer, 1902; 1909–10). Much detail in these studies has been rejected, but the overall conclusions that there were extensive networks of communication is now established. Fluctuating patterns of trade and the movement of individuals are increasingly being identified. The body of evidence relating to the trade networks that operated in the fifth to eighth centuries has been extensively studied in recent years (Wooding, 1996), and is complemented by studies of documentary sources (Mayr-Harting, 1972; James, 1982; Richter, 1999). The extent of Frankish/Merovingian influence in Ireland in the last quarter of the sixth and first quarter of the seventh century is apparent from the mounts for a saddle found at Hillquarter, Co. Westmeath. This indicates that saddles which were being made and used in Ireland were similar in design to, for example, one from Wesel-Bislich, Germany, which was made during a short period in the early Middle Ages, when saddles were fashionable in Europe. The likeliest source of inspiration is Gaul (Kelly, 2001).

The early Church in Celtic lands followed a similar theological and liturgical system to that of the Church in the Eastern Roman Empire, displaying a marked degree of conservatism (James, 2001, 164; Davies, 1992; Harris, 2003, 155). This probably extended to a view that possessions should be basic rather than sumptuary and that representational art was contrary to the teachings of the scriptures (Brown & Herren, 2001,

63). Brown and Herren have interpreted this as accounting for the lack of figurative Christian art before the late seventh and early eighth centuries (2001, 63).

CELTIC CHRISTIAN ART STYLES AND ICONOGRAPHY

Ambiguous Christian iconography

From the outset, early Christian art frequently used Classical symbols which could be interpreted in a Christian manner (Jensen, 2000, 32; Gough, 1961, 80–107). This feature was taken up by the Celts with such success that the hidden meanings behind much of the art have only recently been recognized as existing. One of the most prominent symbols in the Roman world was Orpheus surrounded by animals, which in a Christian context could be interpreted as the Good Shepherd without causing problems during periods of Christian persecution.

Another such motif represented in Britain and Ireland as well as elsewhere is the *orant* (a figure, usually female, standing with arms outstretched in attitude of prayer), which had both pagan and Christian connotations of prayer and piety (Jensen, 2000, 35). Orants appear for example at Llanhamllech, Brecknock (Allen, 1887, 29); on a cave wall in Arran (Laing, 1996), and quite frequently in the Book of Kells (Farr, 1997, 106) (fig. 3.2). Other motifs such as the vine (which was taken to represent Christ, its branches being the apostles and the Church) were used in early Christian Celtic art, along with some of the symbolic creatures found in early Christian iconography (peacocks, doves, deer, dolphins) and certain plants (such as palms, acanthus and laurel) that had symbolic connotations (Jensen, 2000, 59).

The use of the fish is the most common in a vast array of ambiguous symbols which might be read as Christian or non-Christian. The tendency to hide meanings was developed heavily in the Christian art of the Celts even though the original need to avoid social disapproval or even persecution, was obsolete. It had the effect of separating those who understood the iconography from those who did not. It possibly added to the mystique of the ecclesiastics, which in turn added to the authority of the Church.

Narrative art

Early Christian art developed the technique of narrative, which involved telling stories in a sequence of scenes, each of which encapsulated the essential significance of the moment (Kitzinger, 1977, ch. 2). The earliest

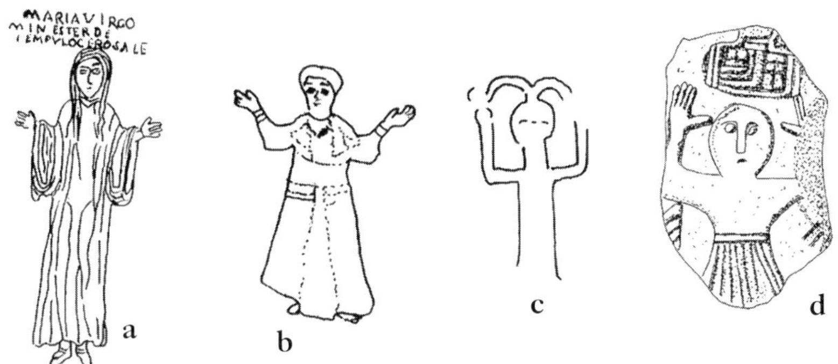

3.2 Orantes, Roman and later. a: Crypt of St Maximin, Provence, France; b: Lullingstone, Kent, Roman wall-painting; c: King's Cave, Arran; d: Seven Sisters, Glamorgan.

extant manifestation in a Christian context is a series of four sculptures now in Cleveland Museum, Ohio, which tell the biblical story of Jonah (Kitzinger, 1977, 21). Pagan Roman sarcophagi sometimes displayed a series of separate episodes which relate to a particular story (usually the life of the deceased). Christian artists took this further in the fourth century, using the multi-episode frieze on sarcophagi. Depictions of separate events were repeated without division, so that they appear as one narrative picture. The key figure appears repeatedly in the sequence. The only link between scenes is the ideology. Each episode speaks for itself, but significantly, the connection between each could only be understood by those who knew the context.

In addition, each scene was codified: details were incorporated to provide reference points so that the episode being depicted could be identified. This phenomenon developed during the fourth century, and as the century progressed the sequences became more complex, and two registers rather than one were used on sarcophagi (Kitzinger, 1977, 26).

The choice and arrangement of scenes in early Celtic Christian sculpture were determined by exactly these considerations but in different media. For example, on Irish High Crosses the panels are separated by frames, but are ordered in sequences. The connection between them can only be understood and appreciated with knowledge of the underlying ideology. Separate scenes linked only by ideology can also be found on panels. Thus, for example, on the Cross of Patrick and Columba at Kells, the biblical characters of Adam and Eve and of Cain and Abel are found in the same panel, connected by the fact that they were symbolic of the Fall from Grace (fig. 3.3).

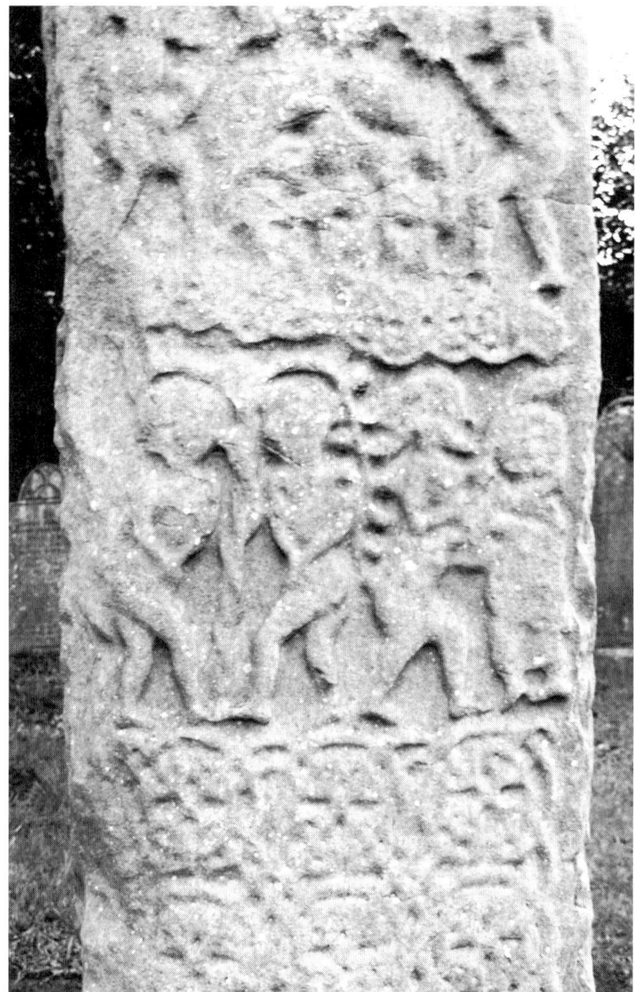

3.3 Adam and Cain, Cross of Patrick and Columba, Kells, Co. Meath.

Stylized figures

A characteristic feature of both pagan and Christian late Roman art is the stylization of figures. Roman representation of figures went through many stages of development, but in the fourth century figures had become stiff and uniform. This style can be seen on the Arch of Constantine (dedicated AD315) in a panel that shows the emperor addressing an assembly. The figures are flat and uniform, and depth is suggested by rows of heads one above the other. The influence behind this originated in the East, where

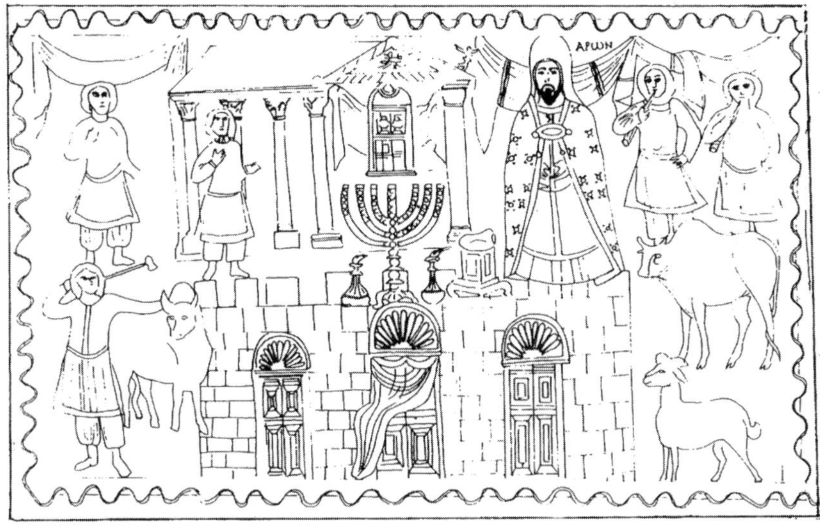

3.4 Dura-Europos, Syria, Synagogue painting, depicting Aaron and the Ark of the Covenant.

there were deep-rooted beliefs that art should express spiritual values rather than what the eye sees (Kitzinger, 1977, 8). It can be seen very clearly in the second-century-AD funerary sculptures from Palmyra, Syria, where the figures are stiff and hierarchical despite the figures in Roman dress and the lip-service paid to portraiture. The technique can also be seen clearly in the Synagogue at Dura-Europos on the Euphrates (fig. 3.4) where, in the scene of Aaron and the Ark of the Tabernacle, the architecture is without depth, the figures are frontal and staring, and the elements are in cavalier perspective, each representing a separate scene. Aaron is clearly the most important figure, since he is shown larger than the others and is dressed in an elaborate robe (Perkins, 1976; Laing & Laing, 1993, 208–9).

Such conventions were employed in Celtic figural work, initially in the rare representations of figures found in incised sculpture; later in the manuscripts and in relief sculptures of the eighth and ninth centuries (see below, chapter four).

Overtly Christian iconography

The least ambiguous Christian symbols are the Chi-Rho and the cross. The Chi-Rho was used on fourth-century coins (including as a sole reverse type of the Gallic usurper Magnentius (303–53), whose coins

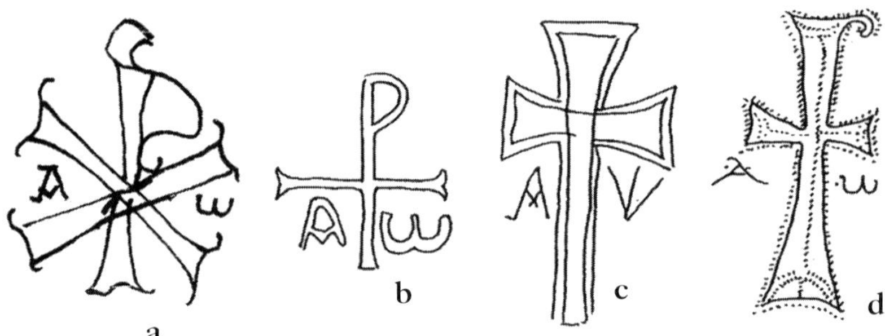

3.5 Chi-Rhos, with alpha and omega, Roman and later. a: Water Newton, Hunts, Roman
silver bowl; b: Vienne, France, memorial stone; c: Loher, Co. Kerry, pillar stone;
d: *Codex Usserianus Primus.*

circulated widely in Britain). It also appears in a wreath in the wall-
paintings of Lullingstone, Kent, which also displays orants (Thomas,
1981, 86–90, 94). The Chi-Rho occurs in various forms on a variety of
objects from all over Roman Britain (Thomas, 1981, 88–90). It is also
found in early Christian art in the Celtic areas, where the original models
were almost certainly inspired by the Antique world, but which were
passed on to the Celts from Gaul (see below, p. 84) (fig. 3.5).

Initially the cross is found mostly as a stone symbol of itself in the High
Crosses, though also incised on stone slabs and in metalwork.

CELTIC CHRISTIAN STONE-WORKING

There is an absence of obviously ecclesiastical metalwork before the mid-
seventh century and a total absence of surviving manuscripts, textiles or
wood carvings. The sole medium in which Christian art can be seen
displayed in the Celtic world is stone. Many outside influences are
discernible in stone sculptures of the early Christian period and by the
seventh century symbols appear on sculpture.

Inscriptions on stone

A series of inscribed stones are without ornamentation other than their
lettering. The earliest are the ogham stones in Ireland and the areas settled
by the Irish in Britain, which were similarly inspired by the Latin
alphabet. They probably began in the fourth century. Some have Latin
memorial inscriptions. Although there is a possibility that some of these
pre-date the period of direct Christian contact with the Continent, it is

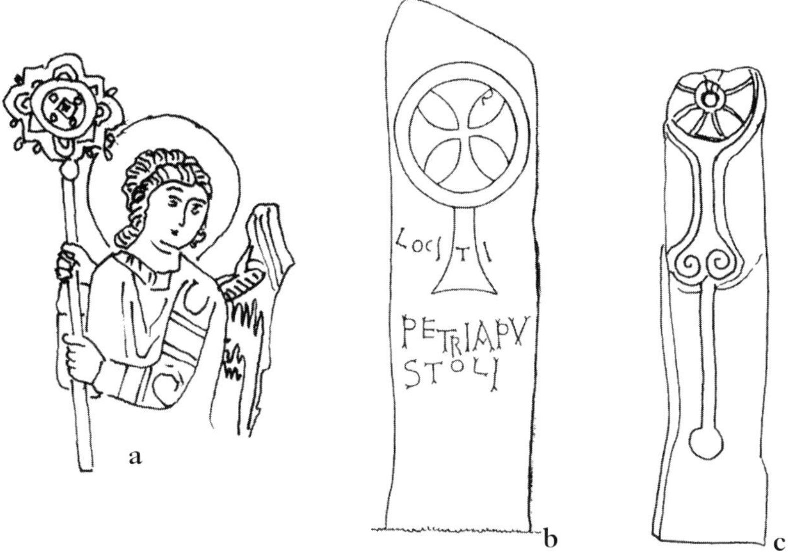

3.6 Flabella. a: Kiev, Cathedral of St Sophia, eleventh century; b: St Peter's Stone, Whithorn, Dumfries & Galloway; c: St Dogmaels 3, Pembroke.

clear that the main groups of memorial formulae are derivative of those found in Roman Gaul and in some cases north Africa. Links are very much apparent between the Insular inscriptions and those found in the vicinities of Lyon (central Gaul) and Camiac, Gaillardon and Protet (southern Gaul) (Knight, 1981; 1992; 1996). The Gallic inscriptions start in the fourth century (Knight, 1999, 106), and the HIC IACIT formula (a vulgar Latin form of HIC IACET – 'here he lies') appears in Gaul in the fifth century. A stone from Llanerfyl, Powys, uses the first formula in conjunction with IN PACE, a formula found in Gaul where it was used to end inscriptions. It probably dates from the fifth century, and shows the early date at which Gaulish influence was reaching Wales (Knight, 1999, 137). In Ireland, a number of stones inscribed in the ogham alphabet, sometimes found with additional incised crosses, can also be dated to the fifth century (Swift, 2001, 54–5).

Celtic Christian symbols on stone
The immediate models for the ornament on the early Christian incised slabs in Celtic areas seem also to be traceable to central and southern Gaul. The Gallic inscribed stones of the fifth century onwards also display various motifs, including symbols of the Eucharist (such as chalices, vine

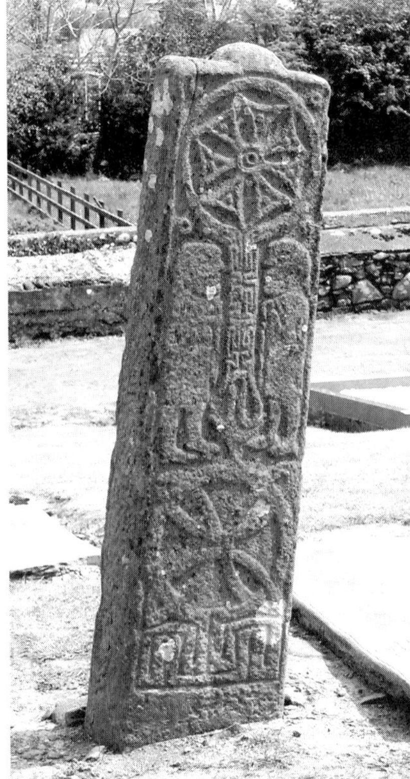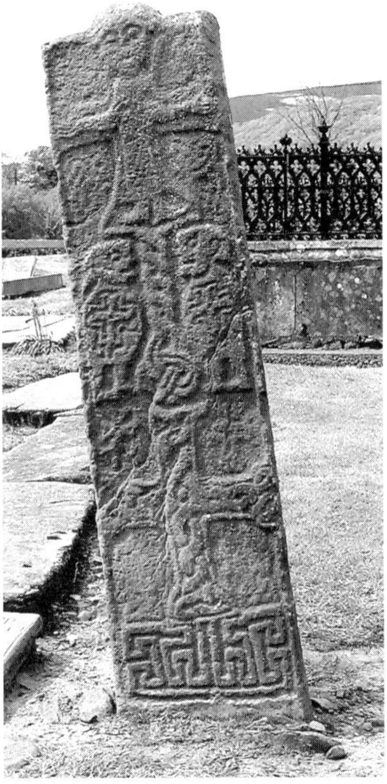

3.7 Marigold Stone, Carndonagh, Inishowen, Co. Donegal (photos: Eric Graff).

scrolls and birds), Chi-Rhos, monogram crosses (i.e., upright crosses with a loop on the upper arm forming a rho) and simple crosses, often within a ring (Knight, 1999, 177). The fish was also occasionally used in Gaul in conjunction with the cross and the *flabellum* (liturgical fan). Other Gaulish motifs include a design modelled on an altar cross; a marigold cross and a variety of crosses of arcs, double outline crosses and crosses with floriated ends. This list constitutes the major part of the repertoire of Celtic sculpture of the sixth and seventh centuries.

In the seventh century the inscribed monuments in both Gaul and Britain mostly gave way to slabs with various types of crosses.

The Chi-Rho in various forms is widely distributed along the Irish Sea coastal areas, as well as west and south-west Ireland, south Wales, the Isle of Man and Scotland, occurrences being documented as far north as Caithness. The earliest seem to date to the mid- or late sixth century, when

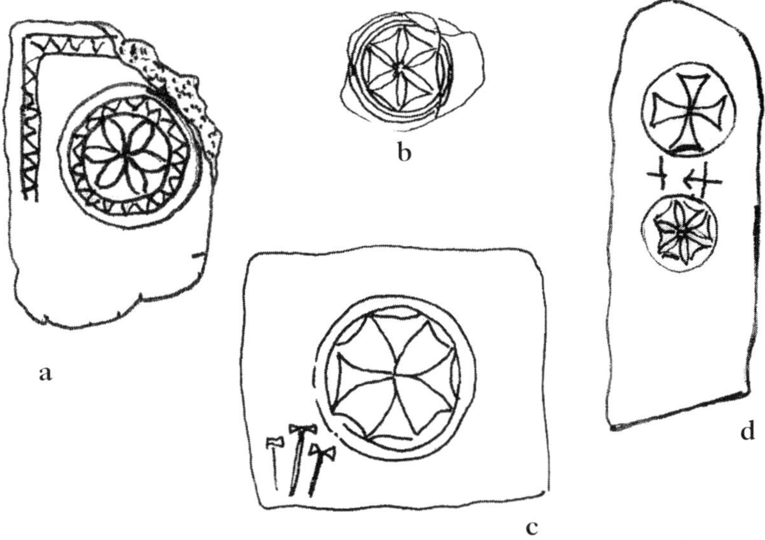

3.8 Marigold crosses. a: Pontoise, France; b: Gallon Priory, Co. Offaly; d: Maughold, Isle of Man; c: Ronaldsway, Isle of Man.

they also occur in France and Portugal. In Britain and Ireland they recur in different contexts through the seventh and eighth centuries (Hamlin, 1972; 1982; Edwards, 2007b, 190) (fig. 3.5).

The flabellum is an image which originates in the East, where a fan of peacock feathers, linen or vellum was used to keep flies off the bread and wine for the Eucharist. Eventually the fans were made of metal and had a symbolic function (Richardson, 1993, 27) (fig. 3.6). Western metal flabella survive, for example in Monza, but they went out of fashion by the fourteenth century. There is evidence for the use of flabella in Ireland in the seventh and eighth centuries, and the Irish had a specific word to describe them (Richardson, 1993, 30). St Columba possessed a famous example, and it would appear they were treasured as relics.

Flabella are first represented in Insular art on the seventh-century St Peter's stone, Whithorn, Galloway. The representations are also common in Gaul, and are widely distributed on stones in Wales, Scotland and Ireland in the sixth and seventh centuries, appearing as a stemmed cross, for example at Reask, Co. Kerry. The symbol also appears on the Marigold Stone at Carndonagh, Co. Donegal (which is named because of the marigold design on the head of the flabellum carved on it). It has been suggested that it is a representation of Columba's flabellum (Richardson,

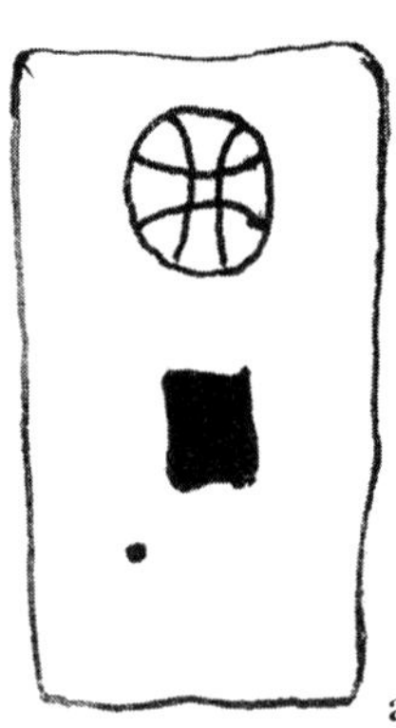

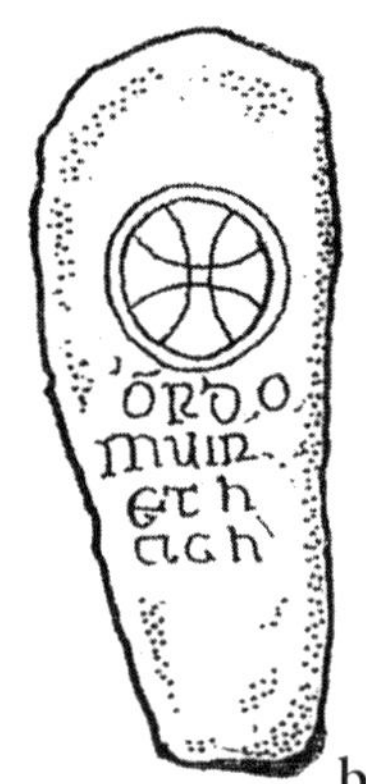

3.9 Crosses of arcs. a: Ablieges, France, grave 19; b: Clonmacnois, Co. Offaly.

1993) (fig. 3.7a). The flabellum motif also appears in angles on the Symbol page that precedes St Mark's Gospel (fo. 129v) in the Book of Kells (Richardson, 1993, 32–3).

It is also possible, however, that the symbol used in the Kells decoration and on the Marigold Stone is a representation of an *ostensorium*, a liturgical standard which had a circular head with a cross. Continental parallels for the depiction of these can be found, for example, on an altar front at Ferentillo, Italy (Newman & Walsh, 2007, 177). A similar depiction can be seen on an Irish slab, from Killedeas, Co. Fermanagh (Newman & Walsh, 2007, 178), and there is a series of round-headed crosses on stems in Merovingian sculpture.

In Scotland, the marigold motif appears on, for example, a stone from Cladh a'Bhile, Ellary (Fisher, 2001, 42), and on another from Great Cumbrae in the Firth of Clyde (Fisher, 2001, 71).

The marigold cross features in Celtic metalwork as well as sculpture, occurring on the terminals of zoomorphic penannular brooches including one that is datable to the late sixth century from Ballinderry 2 crannog, Co. Offaly (Hencken, 1942, fig. 11). It continued to be used in its more floriated form on Viking-Age metalwork, such as on a ringed pin from the Norse burial at Knock-y-Doonee on the Isle of Man (Laing, 1993a, no. 111). The marigold cross motif is found widely in late Roman art, and seems to have been adopted by Constantine the Great as the *labarum* (Christian standard). It survived in sixth-century Merovingian sculpture, on, for example, a frieze from the hypogeum at Poitiers (Salin, 1952, fig. 15). A version of it appears in conjunction with a depiction of a jewelled altar cross on the tombstone of a man called Boethius, who died in 603 (Salin, 1952, fig. 159) (fig. 3.8).

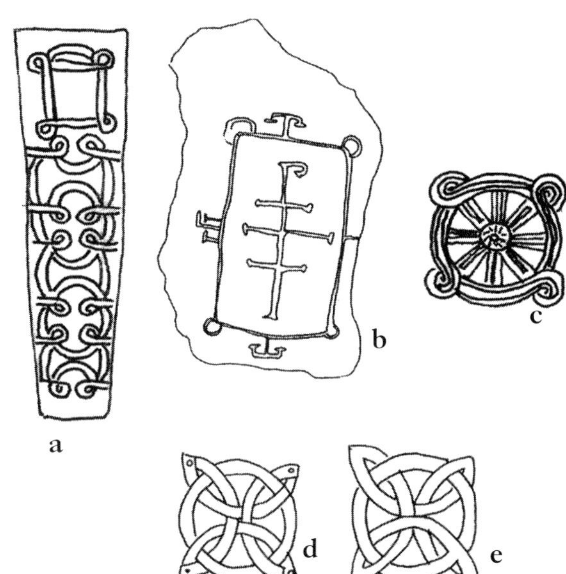

3.10 Ardmoneel Stone and Continental parallels for the looped corners. a: Sarcophagus cover, Vienne, France; b: Ardmoneel Stone, Co. Kerry; c: ornament on an ambo, Grado Cathedral, Italy; d: sarcophagus, Lunes, France; e: Carndonagh, Marigold Stone (after Sheehan, 1994 and Salin, 1952).

The cross of arcs is widespread in early Christian art, occurring on grave slabs from Gaul, such as one from Ableiges, Vexin (Sirat, 1966, 26). It also appears on sixth-century memorial stones in Iberia; for example on the tombstone of Simplicius at Mertola, Portugal, datable to 537 (Knight, 1999, fig. 39.3). It can be seen in Ireland at Caherlehillan, Co. Kerry (as the head of a flabellum); in Wales at Capel Colman and St Dogmaels (where on St Dogmaels 2 it appears to have a shaft, making it a flabellum or a processional cross), and in Scotland at A'Chill, the Isle of Muck, Inchmarnock, the Isle of Bute and Daltote Cottage, Argyll (Fisher, 2001, fig. 2).

Dating is indicated by a fragment of a cross of arcs from Whithorn, Galloway, that was found in a mid- to late seventh-century grave (Craig, 1997, 439). Crosses of arcs appear on some stones with ogham inscriptions, and on this evidence it would appear likely that they were current from the late sixth to the early eighth century (Swift, 2001, 58–9) (fig. 3.9).

A variant form appears on the Marigold Stone, where a cross of arcs can be seen beneath the flabellum (fig. 3.7b) and where the design is composed of rope-twist form (fig. 3.9). This form of cross is found widely in Lombard Italy, where many seem to have been carved in the time of Liutprand (712–44). One such example had a biographical epitaph to the

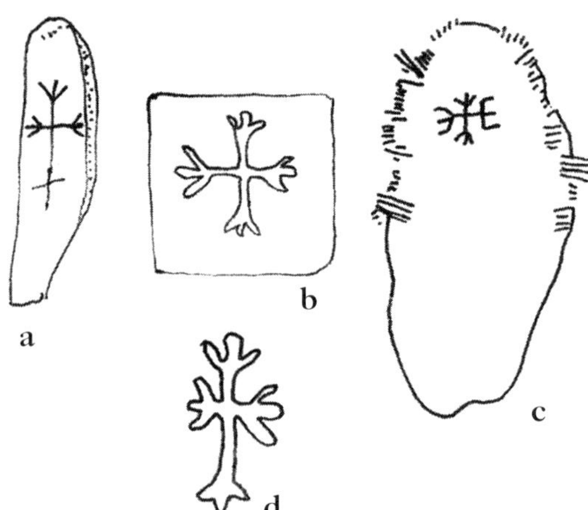

3.11 Crosses with trident-ended arms. a: Inchmarnock, Bute; b: Llansawel, Carmarthen; c: Ballintaggart, Co. Kerry; d: Llandeilo, Pembroke.

Irish monk Cummian of Bobbio on one side and a series of cable crosses and crosses with spiral terminals on the back (Newman & Walsh, 2007, 173). The exact parallel for the design on the Marigold Stone can, however, be found on a sarcophagus at Lunes in south-west Gaul (James, 1982, 385; Sheehan, 1994, 27).

Triple-armed crosses may be seen on a variety of monuments. On a stone from Ardmoneel, Co. Kerry, for example, a Chi-Rho crowns a triple-armed cross, the whole set within a frame with marginal elaboration (fig. 3.10).

The triple armed cross (the Cross of Lorraine) occurs often on sarcophagi in Aquitaine, especially Poitou. It was probably developed in the area, where it appears on buckles of the late sixth and seventh centuries (James, 1977, 73–5). Some buckles also employ a square with looped corners, which has led to the suggestion that this may have been the inspiration for the looped corners on the Ardmoneel Stone (Sheehan, 1994, 26). A similar looped-corner square appeared on a lost stone from Temple Brecan, Inishmore (Sheehan, 1994, 27), but is generally not well-represented in Ireland.

A trident motif, also found on Poitou monuments, is matched on a number of Irish stones, for example at Ballintaggart, Co. Kerry (fig. 3.11). This may date (on the evidence of associated ogham) to the late fifth century. A similar date is applicable for a similarly cross-inscribed stone with ogham inscription from Llandeilo, Pembrokeshire (Swift, 2001, 58). Inscriptional evidence suggests that the motif was current from the late fifth century (Swift, 2001, 59). The swastika and duplex knot also occur on Merovingian buckles as well as several stones in southern Ireland (Sheehan, 1994, 28).

3.12 Long-stemmed crosses. a: Sarcophagus, Lens (Gard), France; b–c: Isle Maree, Scotland; d: Glencolumbkille, Co. Donegal.

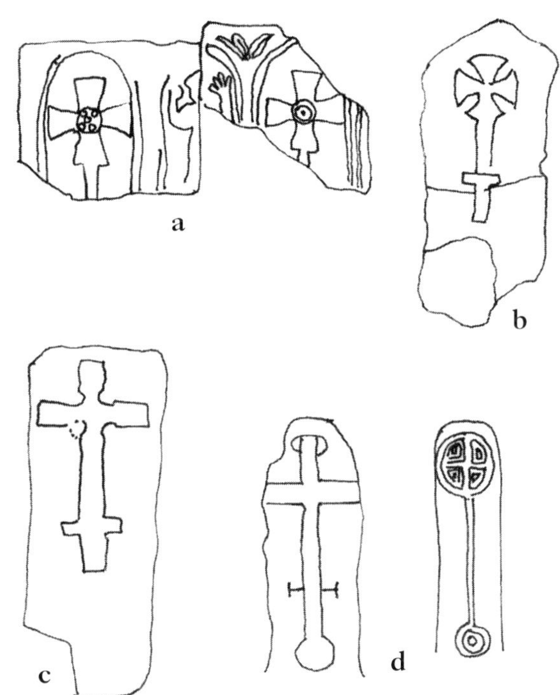

Long-stemmed crosses appear to have been representations of processional crosses and survive as, for example, the twelfth-century Cross of Cong from Co. Mayo. The motif also appears on the late eighth- to early ninth-century metal processional Tully Lough Cross. It appears first on Merovingian grave-slabs, for example on one of around 600 from Mandourel, Aude, where three long-stemmed crosses are depicted, the central one being surmounted by doves (Salin, 1952, fig. 44) (fig. 3.12). The same type of cross in simpler form is seen at Cheminot, Moselle (Salin, 1952, fig. 86) and Ableiges, Vexin (Sirat, 1966, no. 25).

The suspended cross is a more rare motif, appearing at Ballachly, Caithness and in Gaul on the gravestone of Bertislinde and Randoald at Mayence, which are datable to the sixth century (Salin, 1952, fig. 43) (fig. 3.13).

The anchor or anchor cross is rare. It was commonly used in Roman early Christian art in, for example, the catacombs in Rome and was probably disseminated by way of the Merovingian world (fig. 3.14).

The face cross is a relatively rare Celtic borrowing from the Merovingian world which probably originates as the Egyptian ankh symbol. The cross has a human head as its upper arm and is found for

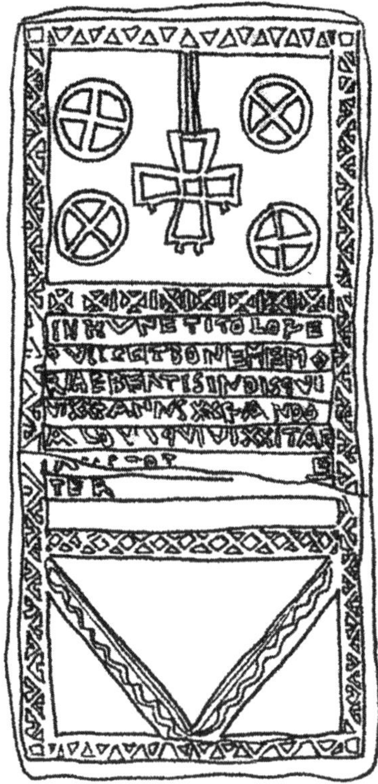

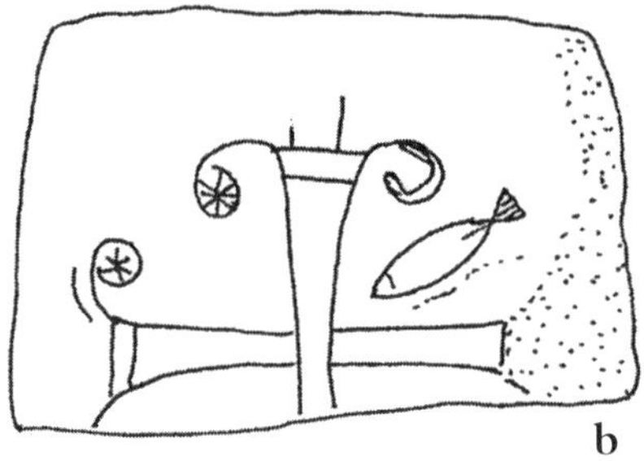

3.13 Suspended crosses, Gaul and Ireland.
a: memorial stone of Bertislinde and
Randoald, Mayence, France; b: Ballachly,
Dunbeath, Caithness.

example at Akhmim, Egypt, and later in Gaul and the Rhineland. In the
Celtic areas it can be seen at Skellig Michael off the coast of Co. Kerry,
and at Riskbuie on Colonsay (Thomas, 1971) (fig. 3.15).

The fish symbol in conjunction with a cross, is rare in Celtic areas. In
Ireland is can be seen on the stone of Oldscan, Fuerty (Allen, 1887, fig.
25) (fig. 3.16), and it appears in conjunction with the suspended cross at
Ballachly (fig. 3.17). Parallels for these can be seen on a fragmentary
sarcophagus from Cheminot (Moselle), dated to around the end of the
sixth century (Salin, 1952, 1, fig. 86). The fish and cross symbol seems,
however, to have been assimilated into manuscript art, appearing as an
initial ornament in the earliest surviving Insular manuscript, the Cathach
of St Columba (a Psalter – collection of psalms – believed to have
belonged to the saint).

The peacock is a symbol of resurrection that occurs quite frequently in
Gaul, and can be seen on each side of a pot containing a vine that appears
on a sarcophagus in the cathedral at Vienne (Salin, 1952, 1, fig. 83). It

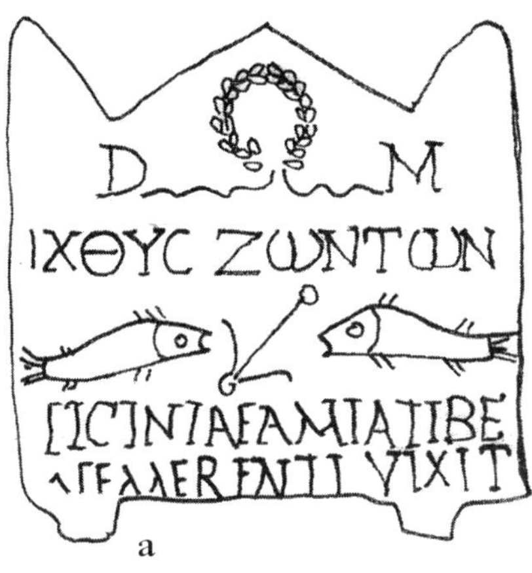

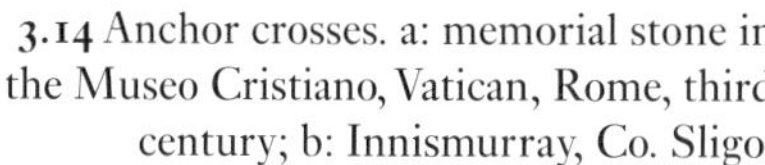

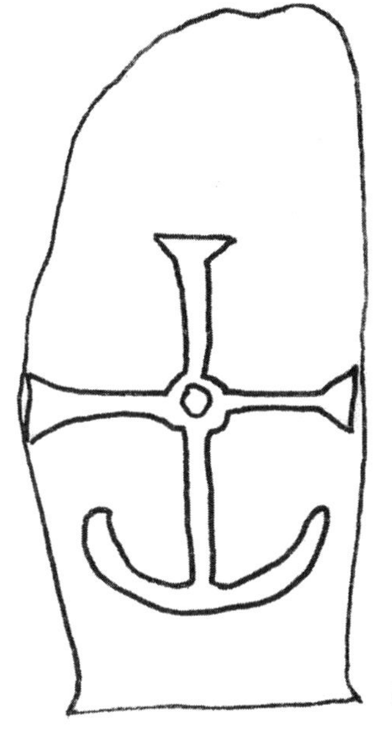

3.14 Anchor crosses. a: memorial stone in the Museo Cristiano, Vatican, Rome, third century; b: Innismurray, Co. Sligo.

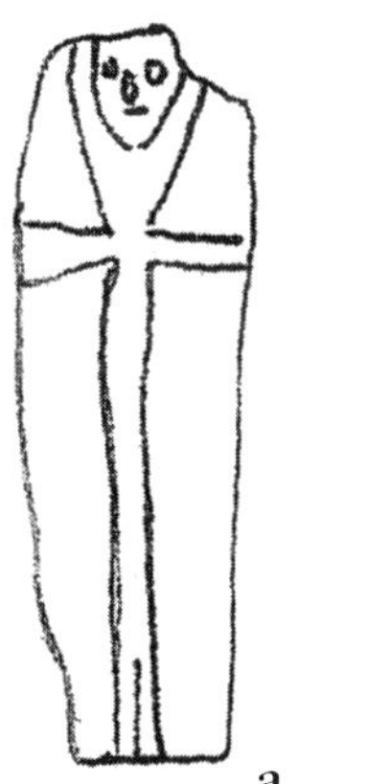

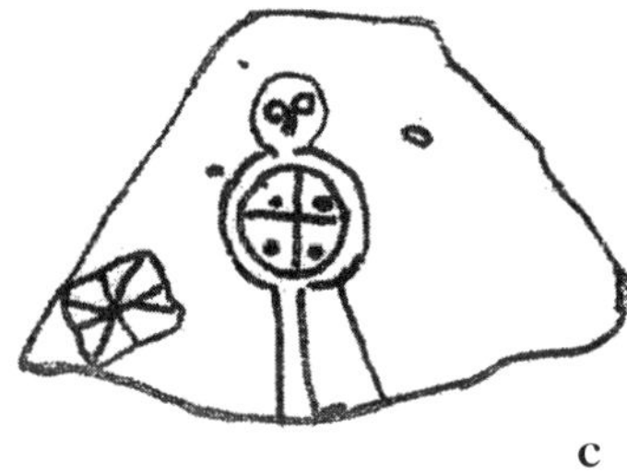

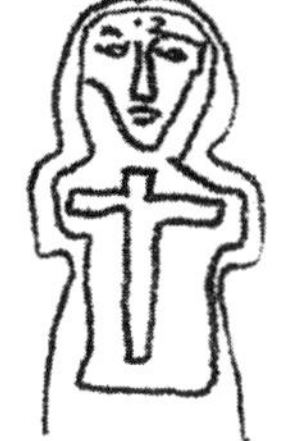

3.15 Face crosses. a: Faha, near Trier, Germany; b: Riskbuie, Colonsay; c: Knappaghmanagh, Co. Mayo; d: Kilbroney, Co. Down (after Charles Thomas, 1971).

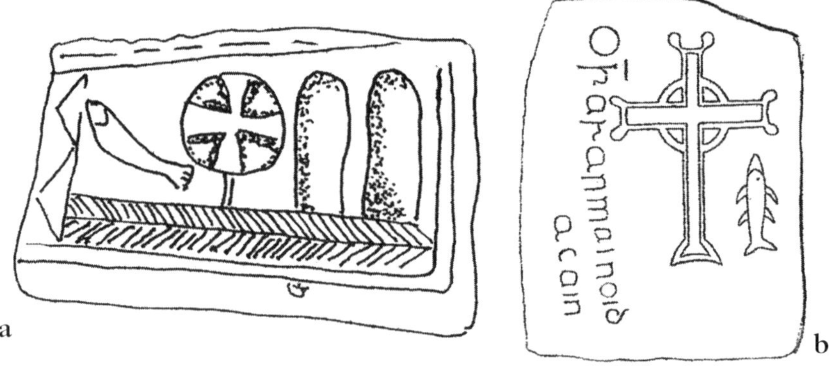

a

b

3.16 Fish symbols with crosses in Christian art. a: Cheminot, Moselle, France, sarcophagus fragment, *c*.700; b: Fuerty, Co. Roscommon, cross-slab.

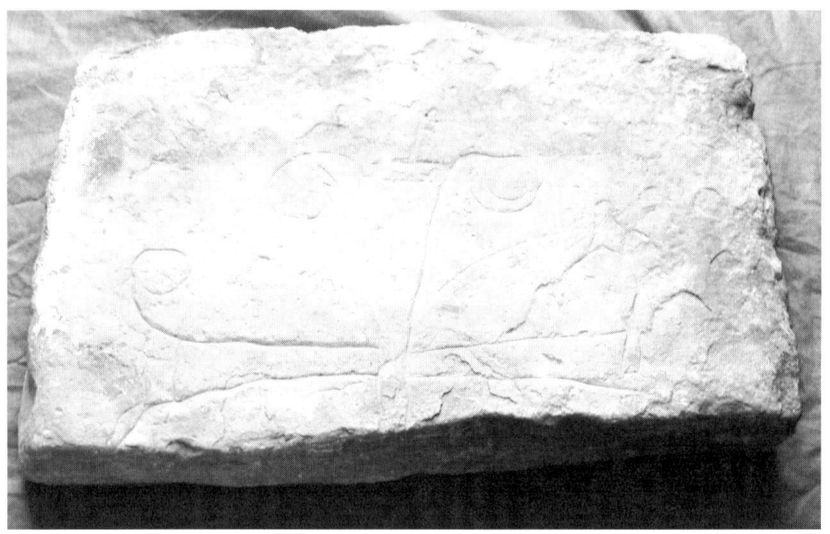

3.17 Ballachly, Dunbeath, Caithness, stone.

appears in Ireland at Reask and Caherlehillan, Co. Kerry, on cross slabs where it is associated with a flabellum (fig. 3.18).

CHRISTIAN METALWORK AND EMBELLISHED OBJECTS

Chalices and patens
The liturgical chalice (a drinking vessel used for the wine in the Christian communion service) is represented in Ireland by the ornate examples from

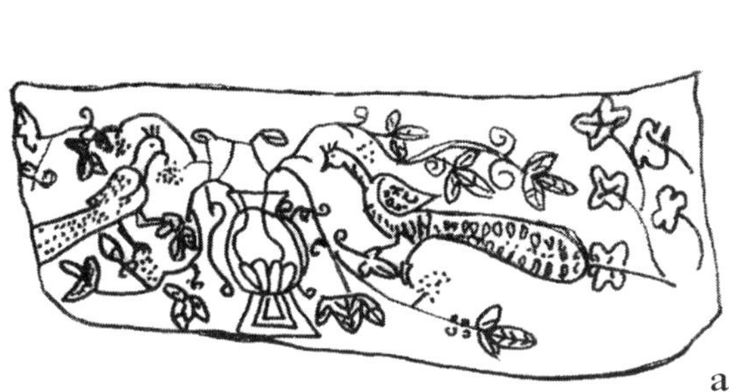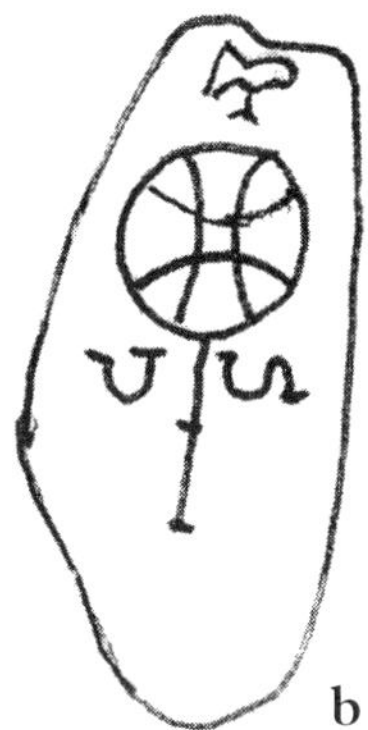

3.18 Peacocks. a: Vienne Cathedral, France, sarcophagus; b: Caherlehillan, Co. Kerry.

the hoards from Ardagh and Derrynaflan, and by plain examples without handles from Ardagh and Lough Kinale (Ryan, 1990a). The paten (a metal plate used in the Christian Communion service to carry the bread), is represented only at Derrynaflan. Both artefacts have models in the eastern Roman world (figs 3.19–20), but there are relatively few from early medieval western Europe – only thirty-seven examples of chalices have been listed, ranging in date from the fifth to the twelfth century (Elbern, 1963; 1965). Some, such as the examples from Trewhiddle, Cornwall, and from Hexham, Northumberland (both from Anglo-Saxon England), notably lack handles.

The two-handled chalice (originally a drinking vessel with no religious connotations) is found in the Roman world – an example was found associated with the fourth-century Water Newton Hoard of Christian silver. This is arguably the earliest example of a liturgical chalice in Europe. This chalice is plain.

Elaboration of chalice design was probably first undertaken in the Byzantine world and Byzantine influence on the design of the Irish chalices has frequently been argued (Gogan, 1932, 44; Ryan, 1984) (fig. 3.19). Syrian influence on the large size of the silver bowls has been considered (Ryan, 1990a).

The paten seems to have been inspired by late Roman vessels such as the dishes from the treasures found at Mildenhall, Suffolk, and Kaiseraugst, Germany, which had figures and animals as well as ornamental patterns around the rims. This type of vessel continued to be produced in the Byzantine world, and gave rise to comparable manifestations in Europe. The one Merovingian example that is known – the Exuperius plate – is lost. Another is recorded by Heiric in the ninth-century inventory of the treasuries of Auxerre (Ryan, 1987b, 72).

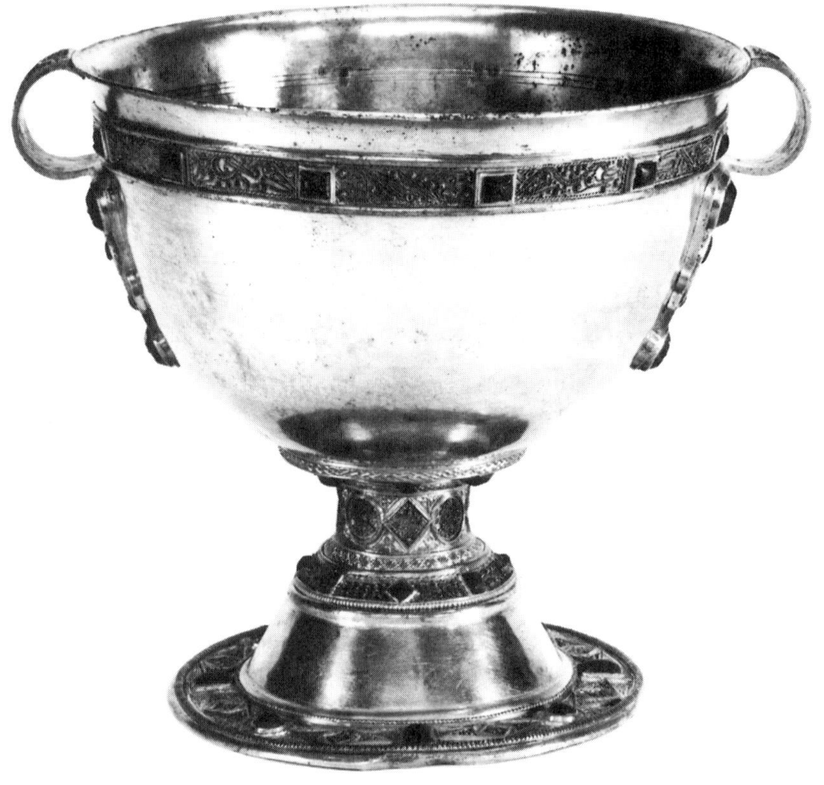

3.19 Derrynaflan Chalice (National Museum of Ireland, Dublin).

Jewelled crosses
The jewelled cross is sometimes depicted in the Celtic world. The prototypes are from the Byzantine world, although the idea probably reached Celtic lands indirectly, through intermediaries. The jewelled cross originated in Jerusalem, where a gemmed cross stood (and was seen by pilgrims) on Golgotha (the biblical name for the site of the Crucifixion) (Richardson, 1995). A jewelled cross appears in a Byzantine mosaic in Santa Pudenziana, Rome, datable to *c*.AD400, where it is shown on a small base behind the figure of Christ. It appears in the centre of the apse at Sant'Apollinare in Classe, Ravenna, which was put up in the time of Theodoric (the later fifth century).

Jewelled altar crosses, sometimes with a picture of alpha and omega suspended from chains, were widely adopted in the West (fig. 3.21). A good example is depicted on a stone from Drumhallagh, Co. Donegal

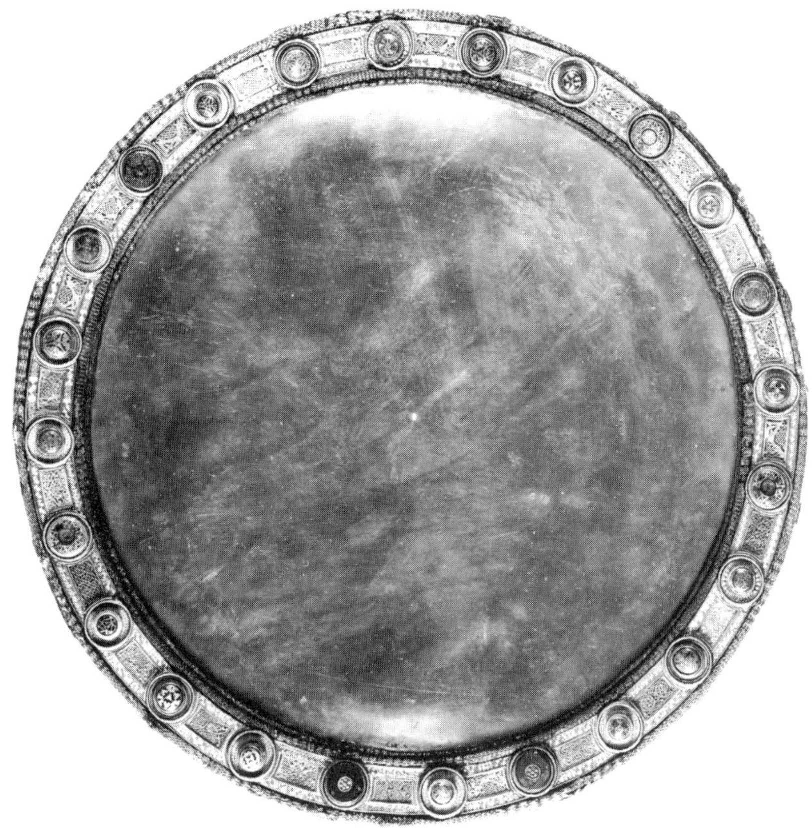

3.20 Derrynaflan Paten (National Museum of Ireland, Dublin).

(Newman & Walsh, 2007, 182). They appeared in Merovingian manuscripts, such as the seventh-century *Sacramentary of Gelasius* (Verzone, 1968, pl. facing p. 146), where one is shown under an arch with alpha and omega in the form of fish suspended on stylized chains. The same image appears in Merovingian sculpture, most notably on the sarcophagus of Boethius, where the alpha and omega are reversed (Salin, 1952, fig. 95). Without the alpha and omega, the jewelled altar cross is found widely throughout Europe down to the High Middle Ages (*c.*1000–1299). Surviving examples include the Cross of Angels, given in 808 by Alfonso II to Oviedo, Spain (Lasko, 1972, pl. 65), and the Altar Cross of Abbess Mathilde and Duke Otto made in 973/82 and now in Essen Minster Treasury (Lasko, 1972, pl. 93).

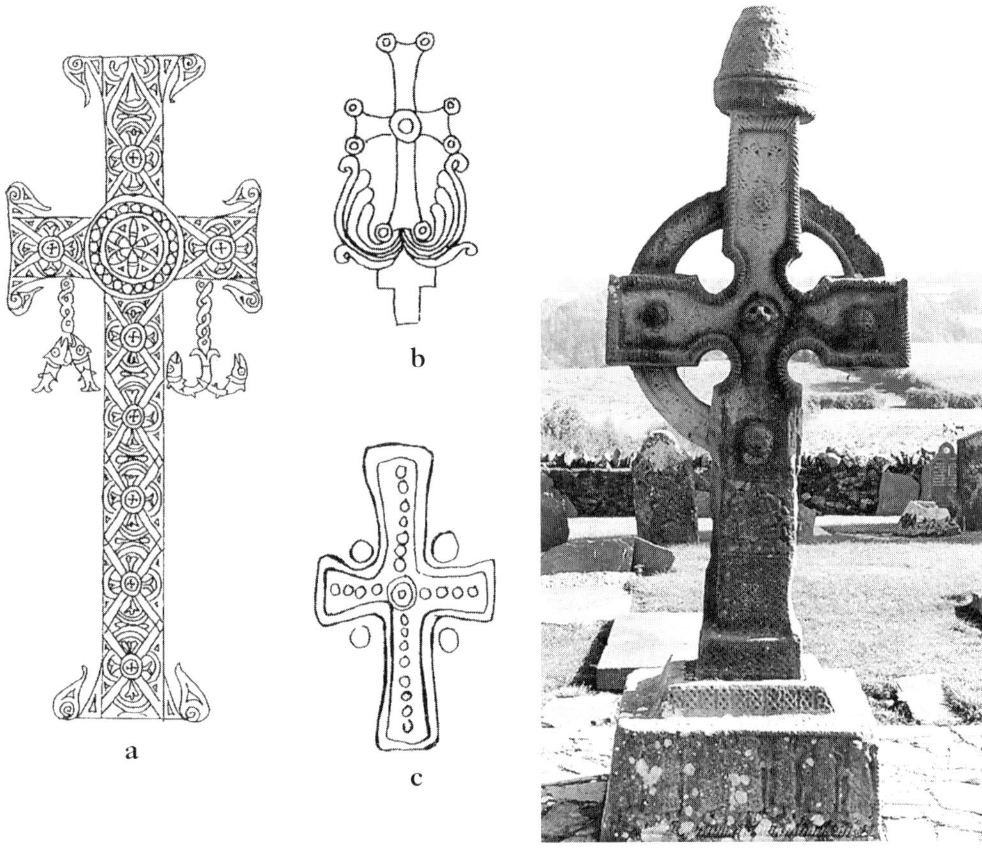

3.21 (*left*) Jewelled crosses from the East. a: Sacramentary of Gelasius; b: Armenian
Khatchkar, Etchmiadzin; c: Drumhallagh Stone.
3.22 (*right*) Ahenny, North Cross, Co. Tipperary (photo: Gavin Williams).

The jewelled cross has been seen as the inspiration for some of the early
High Crosses in Ireland, notably the ninth-century examples at Ahenny,
Co. Tipperary (Roe, 1965; Richardson, 1995), though there are other
possible models behind what are essentially early skeuomorphs of metal
crosses (see below, p. 205) (fig. 3.21).

CHAPTER 4

Mature Celtic art *c*.AD650–1200

By the middle of the seventh century, the Church was powerful and rich in Europe. Monasteries that had begun as small communities had grown to be centres of learning with wide contacts. They were becoming centres for industry and trade. They engaged in power-struggles which often centred on the possession of relics. Also of huge prestigious importance to monasteries was the possession and production of manuscripts of which the earliest that has survived from the Celtic areas, dates from the seventh century.

Many of the most important works in metal and manuscript form were produced in the eighth and ninth centuries, which has traditionally been known as the Golden Age of Celtic art. The art had developed into a maturity that produced some of the finest metalwork, which includes the Ardagh Chalice, the Derrynaflan Chalice and Paten, the Tara Brooch and the Monymusk and Moylough Reliquaries. The finest manuscripts have survived from the period, including the Book of Dimma, the Book of Kells and the Book of Armagh.

The wider European links continued and intensified during the eighth century and later. The Merovingian/Frankish world continued to look to the art of Classical Rome for models and inspiration, and respect for the Roman past was passed on to the Celts. With the growth of the Carolingian Empire respect for Roman culture on the Continent turned into a full-scale Classical revival. The impact on the Celts was particularly seen in the development of sculpture in the ninth and tenth centuries.

Anglo-Saxon animal art affected the Celts once again, as it had done in the fifth to seventh centuries (see above, p. 66). From the mid-ninth century onwards, Viking art styles were introduced to the Celtic world, primarily but not entirely from the Viking settlements in Dublin. The result was a newly invigorated flourishing of Celtic art before its fairly sudden decline around the end of the twelfth century.

IONA

The monastery on Iona (Ritchie, 1997a; Smyth, 1974), founded by St Columba in the sixth century, rapidly became a major centre of learning.

Its geographical situation, off the coast of Scotland and north of Ireland in the Atlantic Seaway, enabled it to be a particularly active receptor of ideas from a wide range of places. In turn, it spread ideas through its daughter-houses in Pictland and more particularly Ireland. The Book of Durrow, the earliest manuscript to display any significant ornament, was probably produced on Iona and although little relief sculpture was produced before the end of the eighth century, Iona was probably a major factor in the development and spread of the iconic monument of Celtic art, the Irish High Cross (see below, p. 205).

At Iona, Old Irish Law and Canon Law was set down. Books were collected in its library, some being sent out to the Anglo–Saxon monastery at Jarrow, Northumbria, where they were used by Bede. The Irish–born St Aidan was sent *c*.635, at the request of King Oswald to found the monastery at Lindisfarne in Northumbria, thus establishing an artistic interface between the Celtic and the Anglo–Saxon worlds. Monks from Iona too were responsible for initiating the conversion of the northern Picts. Links were established with Irish monasteries such as Bangor, Co. Down, and daughter houses of the Columban *familia* were established in Ireland (among them Durrow and later Kells), where they were in turn the focus of a flourishing art.

More is known about the resources of Iona than some of the other major monasteries such as Armagh because it is well-documented from the several Lives of St Columba, in particular that written by Adomnán. Much is known about the books available in Iona, largely through the writings of Adomnán.

Significantly, Adomnán also wrote *De Locis Sanctis*, a book about the holy places of the east Mediterranean. It may have been under Adomnán that the Book of Durrow was written and illuminated. He was prompted to write his book on the holy places through the visit of Arculf (or, more correctly probably Arnulf), a Gaulish bishop who was wrecked in the English Channel and who had brought relics and texts relating to miracles (Woods, 2002). According to Adomnán, Gaulish sailors regularly visited Iona (*Life of Columba*, I, 28).

The main Christian scriptural text used was the version of the Vulgate (an early version of the Bible in Latin) that had been compiled by St Jerome. Adomnán also alludes to a *sacramentary* (a liturgical book), and to the production of Psalters. He had a text of Athanasius' *Life of Anthony*, and one of Sulpicius Severus' *Life of St Martin*. He also had access to Augustine's *De civitate Dei and his De consensu evangeliorum*. The *Rule of St Benedict* was available to him, as was Cassiodorus' *Expositio psalmorum*, a sixth-century commentary originating in Italy. The known list of books available to Adomnán and his fellow clerics additionally includes: Constantius' *Life of St Germanus*; work by Dionysius Exiguus, who collected Canon Law in Latin; Eucherius' *Liber instructionum*; Pseudo-Eucherius; Gregory the Great's *Dialogi*; Hegesippus' *Historia* (a Latin version of Josephus); Isidore's *Etymologiae* and *De natura rerum*; six works of exegesis by Jerome; Juvencus' *Historia evangelica*; the sermons of Leo the Great; a corpus of the writings of Sulpicius Severus; and Virgil's *Aeneid* and *Georgics*. Inferences can also be made about other books that must have been available to the Ionan monks if they were to perform their duties (O'Loughlin, 2001a).

Although there is no universal agreement, is very likely that the Cathach of St Columba (which could have been written by his hand), the Book of Durrow and the Book of Kells were created at least in part in Iona (for the Cathach, Nordenfalk, 1947). The very earliest Insular-style manuscript, the *Codex Usserianus Primus*, may have been produced by Irish monks at Bobbio, but is more likely to have been the product of an Irish monastery (Brown, 1984, 312). The same may be said for a fragment of Isidore's *Etymologie* at St Gall (Brown, 1984, 313). The Iona scriptorium seems a likely contender as workshop for both.

Metalwork was also produced at Iona, where there is limited evidence for a workshop which includes moulds for glass studs (Graham-Campbell, 1981, 24; RCHAMS, 1982, 14–15). It is likely that the products included the surviving terminals of a substantial shrine which are now in St Germain-en-Laye, France. They display the type of snake-boss ornament that is characteristic of the Iona sculptured crosses and which may have originated in Pictland (Henderson, 1987a; MacLean, 1993 on snake bosses: St Germain reliquary terminals, Hunt, 1956). Another part of the same shrine with snake-boss ornament may survive as a panel from Gausel, Norway (Bakka, 1965, 39–40, Fisher, 2001, 15). Both the Hunterston Brooch and the Monymusk Reliquary may have been products of Iona workshops.

Iona was ideally placed to receive ideas from several nearby areas. Pictish influence is particularly seen in the Book of Kells (Henderson, 1982), and the archaeological evidence from Dunadd on the adjacent Scottish mainland shows that imports from the Anglo-Saxon world and further afield were reaching the monastery (Campbell & Lane, 1993; Lane & Campbell, 2000). Influences from both areas are apparent in the manuscripts and metalwork. Iona was also ideally positioned as the agent of transmission of new artistic impulses to and from Ireland and Pictland.

The High Crosses at Iona (see below, p. 205) are significant for seeing the processes of model-transmission in action. The sophistication of the iconography of St Martin's Cross on Iona provided models for individual pieces in Northumbria (for the Virgin and Child: Trench-Jellicoe, 1999, 621), Pictland and Ireland. The intellectual content of the overall design is concerned with Salvation (Hawkes, 2005).

EXTERNAL INFLUENCES IN MATURE CELTIC ART

The external stimuli that provided motifs, ideas and models in the preceding period continued to make a major contribution to the mature Celtic style, and new contributors were added. Mediterranean models for the liturgical vessels used in the Church had probably been introduced much earlier, but the surviving examples represented in the hoards from Ardagh and Derrynaflan belong to Celtic art's mature phase. Similarly, although the cult of relics made its impact on the Celts much earlier, it is only in this period that ornate shrines can be identified. Sculpture was originally only incised (see above, p. 83), which restricted its ornament to simple, drawn designs. In the mature phase relief work was added to the sculptor's repertoire, and opened up a range of new designs, inspired by Continental models.

Western Mediterranean models

The cult of relics and house-shaped shrines The cult of relics started in the Mediterranean even before the time of Constantine, with the veneration of the earliest Christian martyrs. It resulted in changes in architecture to accommodate relics or the tombs of saints and martyrs (Thomas, 1971, 132–66). Portable relics were enshrined in custom-made, usually richly decorated cases which sometimes saw further elaboration over a period of centuries. It is therefore not surprising that many of the most important surviving works of Celtic art from the mid-seventh century onwards are reliquaries.

A type of object frequently regarded as typical of the Celtic world is the house-shaped shrine/reliquary; a small box with roof-shaped top, usually furnished with hinges which originally took a strap to enable it to be carried round the neck. The ultimate prototypes lay in Late Antique sarcophagi such as the fourth-century 'City Gate' sarcophagus in Sant' Ambrogio, Milan, which has a gable adorned with a Chi-Rho in a wreath that is being pecked by doves. It has close parallels in a Roman wall-painting of similar date from Lullingstone, Kent (Gough, 1973, 110–11).

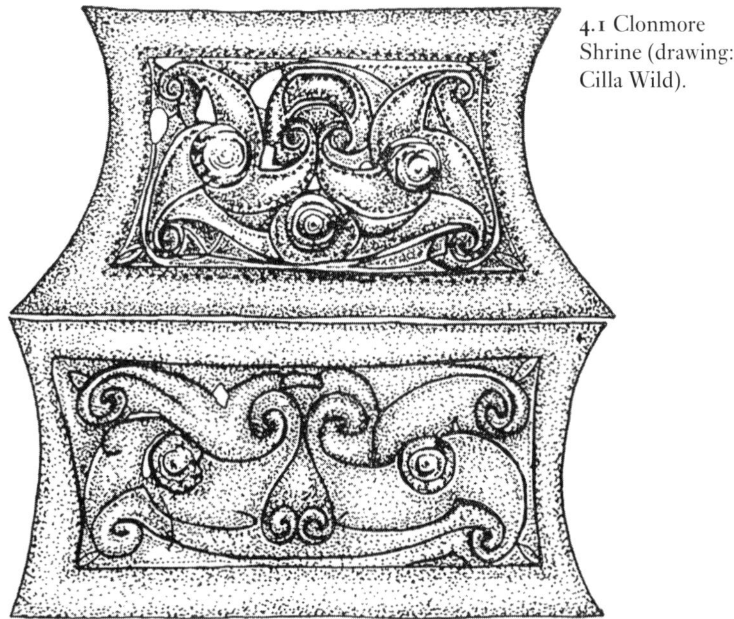

4.1 Clonmore Shrine (drawing: Cilla Wild).

The type is commonly represented in southern Gaul where, for example, Theodochilde's sarcophagus at Jouarre (Salin, 1952, fig. 77), dates from the end of the seventh century.

The design was followed in the portable reliquaries; one is shown being carried on a triumphal carriage on a sixth-century Byzantine ivory now at Trier (Van der Meer & Mohrmann, 1958, fig. 509). There are many shrines which come from all over Europe, the earliest dating from the seventh century (Braun, 1940, 163f, 19f). One of the earliest is the Clonmore Shrine from the River Blackwater, Co. Carlow, which, being a mere 8cm long, must have contained a very small relic (fig. 4.1). The ornament is entirely in the tradition of late Roman trumpet pattern decoration, and although the shape (with curving rather than straight sides) appears on panels from a shrine of Celtic design from Bobbio, Italy (Ryan, 1990b), it could be earlier seventh-century rather than later, as is usually assumed (for example, in Ó Floinn, 1994, 6).

Figural work Human figures first appeared in the Celtic Christian repertoire through the influence of the visual language of the Christian Mediterranean. Most Celtic art that survives from before the late eighth century is fairly unambitious in terms of iconography. It occurs mainly as metalwork produced for monasteries, which is lavish in its ornament but

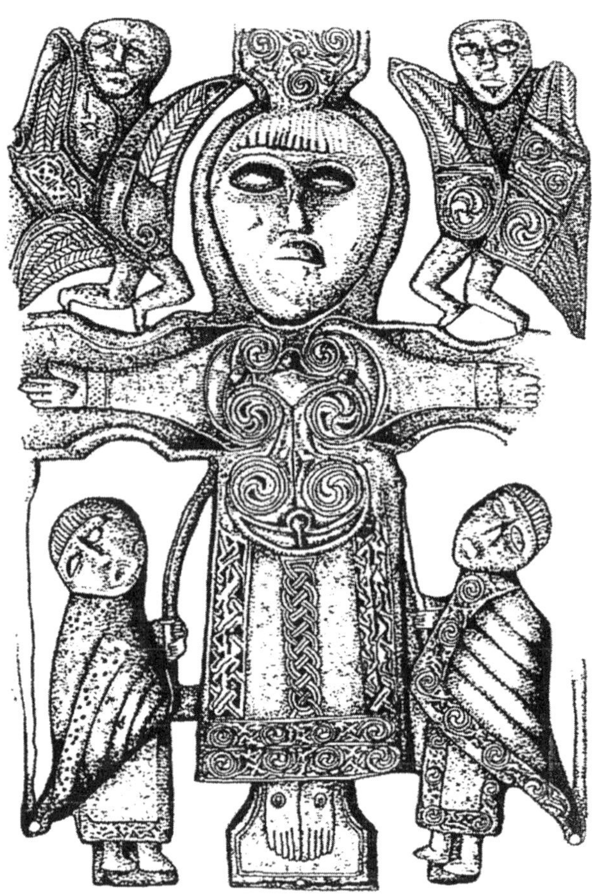

4.2 Rinnigan
(Athlone)
Crucifixion
Plaque
(drawing:
Cilla Wild).

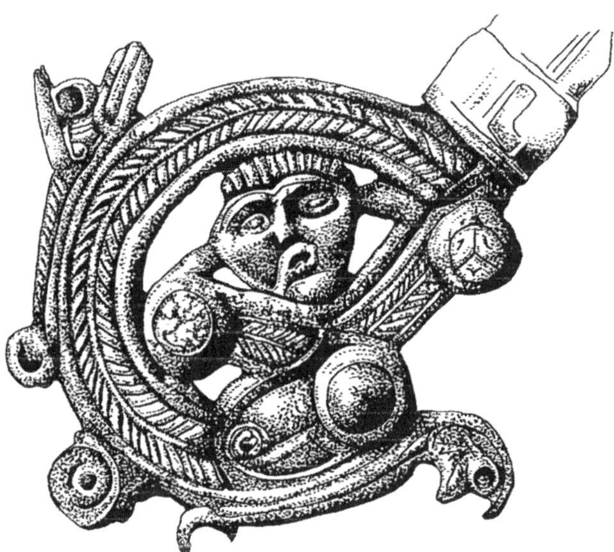

4.3 Ekerö
Crozier,
Sweden
(drawing:
Cilla Wild).

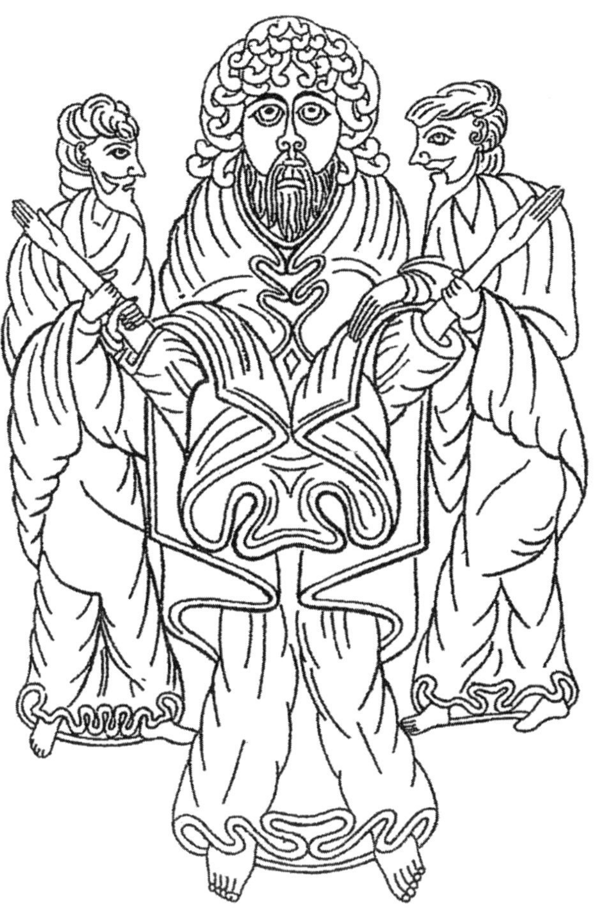

very limited iconographically. There are no human figures on, for example, the Hunterston, or Achavrole Brooches; the Ardagh Chalice, the Moylough Belt shrine or early reliquaries such as the Monymusk. The sole concessions to humanity in the entirety of the St Ninian's Isle Treasure are the tiny masks on the escutcheon attached to the base of one of the bowls (Laing, 1993a, no. 227). The only ornamental metalwork with more extensive figural iconography is the Rinnigan (Athlone) book mount, which depicts the Crucifixion with cherubim above and the Roman soldiers, Stephaton and Longinus, below (fig. 4.2). The date, however, has been debated, some scholars preferring to place it in the ninth century rather than earlier (Harbison, 1984). A symbolic depiction of Jonah and the Whale may appear on the Ekerö Crozier (pastoral staff), which was found in a grave in Sweden (fig. 4.3).

Similarly, the seventh- and eighth-century Irish cross-slabs are noteworthy for their lack of scriptural iconography, though a few do bear simple human figures. In Pictland, there is little relief sculpture before the end of the eighth or beginning of the ninth century. The area is notably devoid of the kind of scriptural scenes found in the ninth- and tenth-century Irish High Crosses and a few of the later Pictish cross-slabs. In Wales, Scotland and south-west England, human figures are generally absent; when they do appear, they remain in isolation, not as part of iconographic schemes.

Except for evangelists and their symbols, figural work is also absent from manuscripts. The first appearance of figures is in the Book of Kells, and shows Roman models. Thus, in folio 114 (usually called the 'Arrest of Christ'), the figure of Christ stands facing, eyes staring, arms out, in a long robe, very similar in treatment to the figure in the Dura-Europos Synagogue (fig. 4.4). The rows of heads on the Temple page in the Book of Kells (fo. 202v) are similarly comparable to the close ranks of figures from the Arch of Constantine some half a millennium earlier.

There seems to have been a massive increase in the use of figural (particularly scriptural), iconography in the ninth century, particularly in Irish sculpture (it may have existed before this, but not in surviving media). Cogitosus described the seventh-century basilica of St Brigit at Kildare, making reference to paintings and commenting that the church 'was adorned with painted pictures'. He describes a partition wall which was 'painted with pictures and covered with wall hangings'. This has been noted as having the appearance of a later Byzantine iconostasis (a screen used by the Eastern Church on which to mount images) (Stalley 1990, 148).

Many Irish clerics visited Italy (Tommasini, 1937); one group from Armagh went to Rome in 631 to celebrate Easter and returned with relics (Doherty, 1984, 193). Cogitosus states that one member of the group, Bishop Conleth of Kildare, had 'vestments from overseas'. Models, in the form of manuscripts, panel paintings and even textiles, could have been taken to Ireland by monks returning from the Continent, where they would also have been exposed to other depictions of Christian subjects. A surviving textile from Llan-gors crannog, Glamorgan, appears to have been a native product ornamented with lions, vine scroll and birds, which were directly modelled on Byzantine or Eastern textiles (Granger-Taylor & Pritchard, 2001). It has been suggested that pilgrimage was the source of much of the iconography of the Irish High Crosses, and that there was a deliberate attempt to create Rome on Irish soil through the use of imported Roman iconography (Verkerk, 2001, 23).

Roman sarcophagi Much of the imagery of Celtic figural sculpture is clearly ultimately derived from the eastern and western Roman empires where conventions were formulated for depicting particular events in the Old and New Testaments. They were employed in surviving media such as sculpture, manuscripts and mosaic. It is particularly likely that Roman sarcophagi were the sources of much iconography in Celtic art. It has been noted that the Arrest of Christ on Muiredach's Cross, Monasterboice, is very similar to the Arrest of Peter on, for example, the Passion Sarcophagus in the Vatican Museum (Verkerk, 2001, 15). It has been suggested that the animal under Christ's feet on Muiredach's Cross was a misunderstanding of the figure of Coelus on the sarcophagus of Junius Bassus (Henry 1967, 185). Muiredach's Cross and the sarcophagus of Junius Bassus have six scenes in common (Stalley, 1990). It has also been suggested that the Irish *traditio clavium* scene is modelled on the *traditio legis* iconography of Roman sarcophagi, a subject which is also found in wall paintings and apse mosaics.

The West Cross at Monasterboice has, on each side of the Crucifixion, scenes of the milking and shearing of sheep, which may have been connected with early Christian imagery of Christ the Good Shepherd (Roe, 1981, 46). A shepherd milking sheep occurs on a sarcophagus from the Catacomb of Praetextatus, Rome, for example, as well as in murals. It has been suggested that the original meaning may have been lost, and that the parallel is being drawn between Christ sacrificing himself for his Flock, and Patrick as shepherd tending his flock (Verkerk, 2001, 17). It has also been suggested that the hunting and herding scenes that appear on the bases of monuments such as the Cross of the Scriptures at Clonmacnois are modelled on similar scenes on sarcophagi, though the meaning has probably changed on the Irish monuments to a prayer for deliverance (Verkerk, 2001, 18). The Tall Cross at Monasterboice and the Market Cross at Kells both depict St Peter walking on water, a subject found on some sarcophagi (Henry, 1967, 187).

Roman in origin are depictions of the 'raised Christ'; the 'washing of the Christ child' and scenes from the early life of the Virgin, the latter two rarely found outside Rome. One series of scenes was illustrated on the walls of St Paulo fuore le Muro, Rome (known from copies made in the seventeenth and eighteenth centuries, since the originals were destroyed in a fire in 1823). They provide models for scenes such as Joseph in the Pit and Moses changing the Waters of Egypt into Blood, which appear on High Crosses. A date of around AD700 has been suggested for this fresco cycle, but is not certain (Harbison, 1992, 314).

Roman models probably lie behind a number of non-biblical scenes on High Crosses, such as the Romulus and Remus figures on the cross at Donaghmore, Co. Tyrone. They may have been the source for the scenes on the base of the cross at Ahenny and the Market Cross at Kells (Harbison, 1992, 317). Roman models have also been seen to lie behind some of the animal iconography on both Irish and Scottish sculptures (for the Irish, Harbison, 2007).

It is very possible that Roman silverwork provided inspiration for Celtic artists. It has been suggested that the filigree figural work on the rim of the Derrynaflan Paten was inspired by figures that are arranged round the rims of Roman plates, such as some in the Mildenhall Treasure. There is some literary evidence for the availability of late Roman plate in Continental treasuries (Ryan, 1987b). There is also the possibility that the silver pronged implement from the St Ninian's Isle Treasure (Wilson, 1973, 58, no. 10) is a direct copy of a Roman implement of similar shape.

Eastern Mediterranean models
There has been vigorous debate about the extent of the east Mediterranean contribution to Celtic art. The influence of models originating in the east Mediterranean have been particularly debated in the case of manuscripts.

The *Diatessaron* The *Diatessaron* by Tatian (*c*.150–160), is the most prominent attempt to merge the Gospels of Matthew, Mark, Luke and John into one narrative. Carl Nordenfalk suggested that the Evangelist figures in prominent Celtic works were modelled on those in a Persian copy of the *Diatessaron*. This argument was based on the only surviving copy (of the sixteenth century) that is now in the Laurentian library, Florence. It was pointed out that the poses of the evangelist symbols were the same, which suggested that a manuscript version of the *Diatessaron* with a similar frontispiece must have been available to monks in the Celtic and Northumbrian scriptoria (Nordenfalk, 1968; 1973; 1987) (fig. 4.5). Nordenfalk was of the view that the first carpet page in Durrow was directly inspired by a similar carpet page in the *Diatessaron*, which implies that the inspiration for carpet pages originated in the East. This model for Durrow has been endorsed by Werner, who has further considered the first carpet page and argued that its design is modelled on the double cross of St Helen (Werner, 1990b) (fig. 4.6). More recently, it has been suggested that the depiction of the symbol of St Matthew is not modelled on millefiori and metalwork, but is a rendering of the sumptuous garments worn by ecclesiastics in the eastern Church. Depictions of these can be seen, for example, on saints flanking the Madonna and Child on an icon

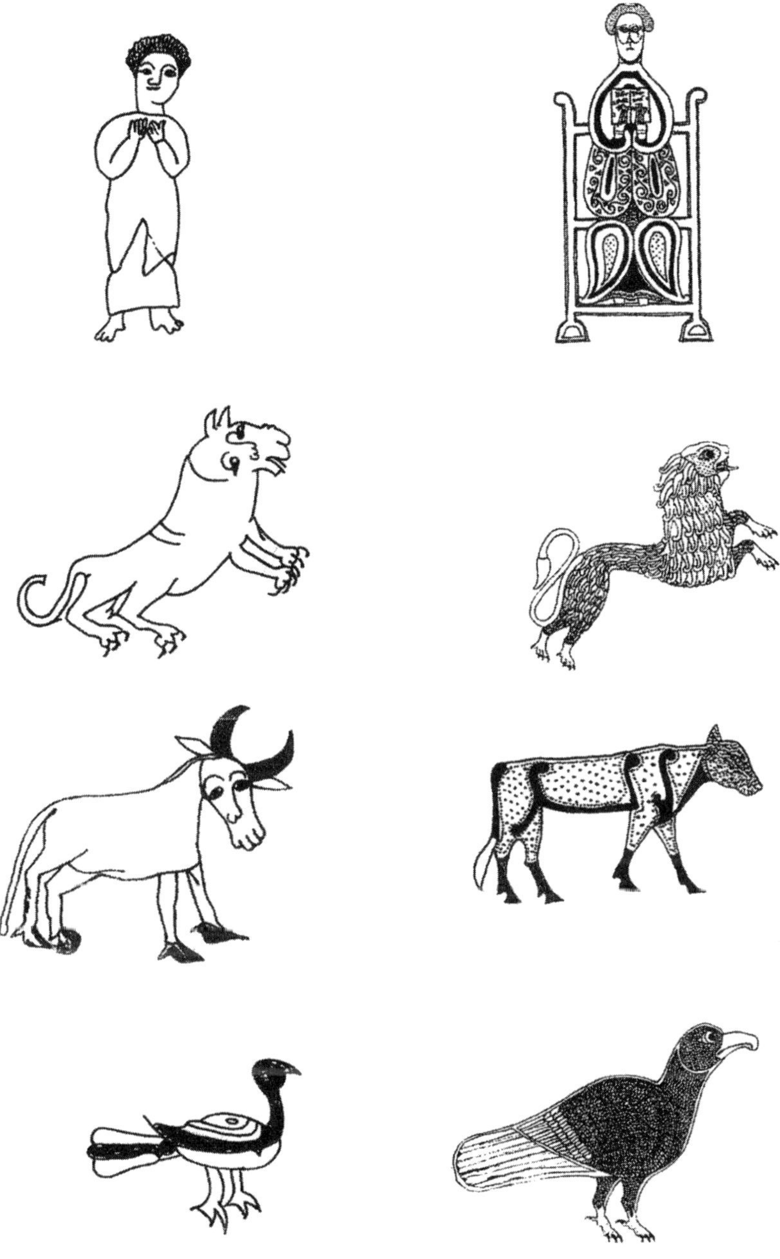

4.5 Diatessaron (left) and Echternach (right) evangelist symbols compared (drawing: Dayanna Knight, after Nordenfalk).

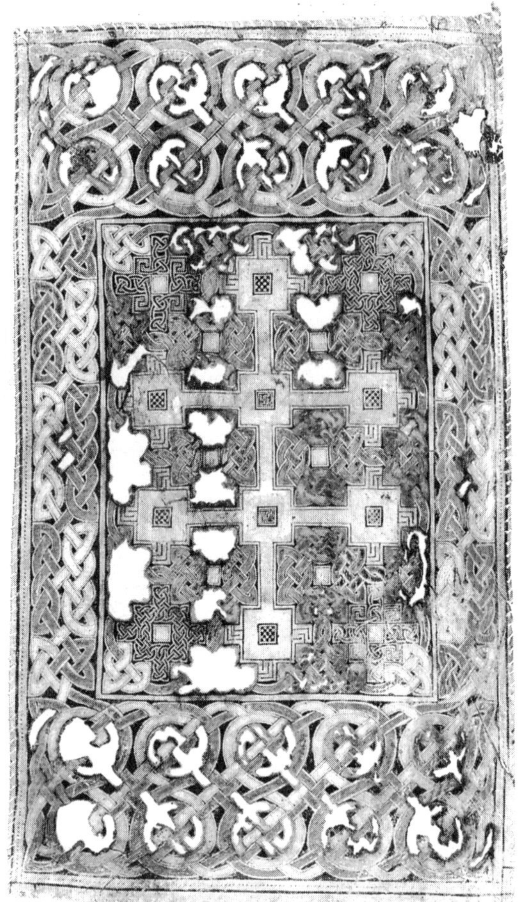

a

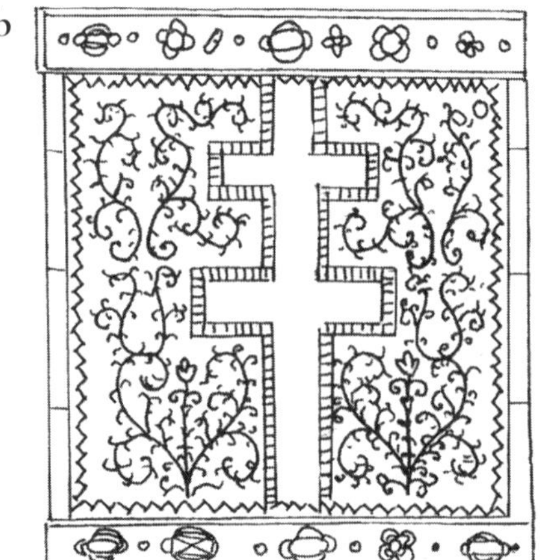

b

4.6 a: Carpet page, Book of Durrow, fo. 1v (The Board of Trinity College, Dublin); and b: central section of Reliquary of St Croix, Poitiers, sent by Justin II to St Radegunde, allegedly in 569, but the reliquary is probably later.

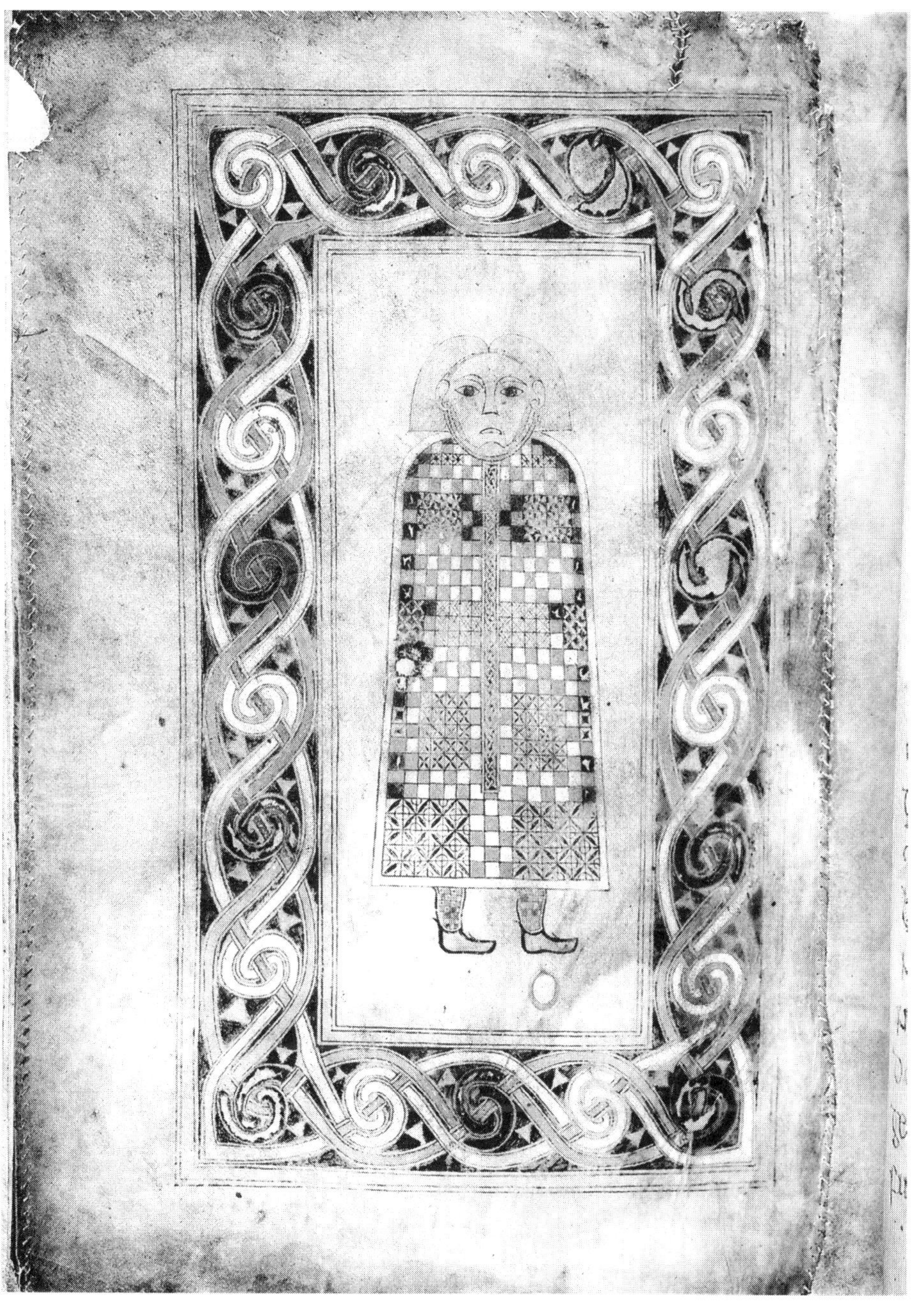

4.7 Symbol of St Matthew, Book of Durrow, fo. 21v
(The Board of Trinity College, Dublin).

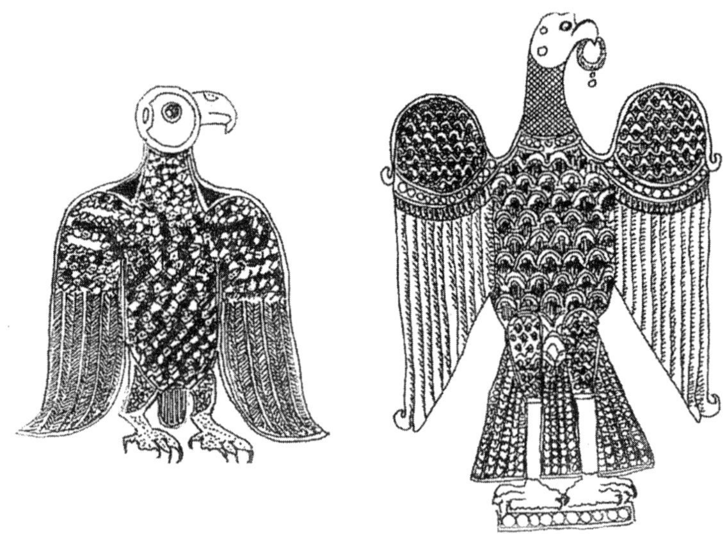

4.8 Eagle symbols, Book of Durrow and Byzantine textile, grave cloth of St Germain, St Eusebius, Auxerre, France, tenth century AD.

from Mount Sinai, or are worn by St Demetrius in a mosaic at Salonika (Newman, 2006, 223). Whether this is a reflection of an east Mediterranean model for the book, or a reflection of the extent to which Eastern ideas about vestments were adopted in the Church in Celtic lands, remains in some measure open to debate (fig. 4.7). A similar observation could be made about the eagle symbol in the Book of Durrow, which though also having fairly close relatives in areas nearer to the Celts, is most closely matched in the Byzantine world (fig. 4.8).

The *Diatessaron* may have been the inspiration for the design of the Pictish cross-slab at Rosemarkie, Ross, which employs a stepped cross design very similar to that in the Cross-Carpet page in Durrow (Henderson, 1978, 50).

The Virgin and Child Eastern Mediterranean models may have lain behind other manuscript decoration. This may have been the case with the full-page illustrations in the Book of Kells, though a single model probably does not lie behind any one of them. The Virgin and Child page (fo. 7v) most probably has an ultimately Eastern antecedent, since the image of the Virgin with Child on her knee recurs frequently in early Christian and Byzantine iconography. There, the convention is also followed of representing the Virgin on a jewelled throne flanked by angels. Where the

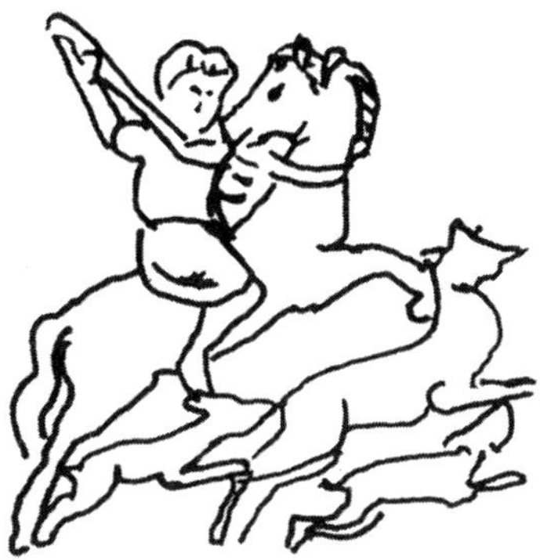

4.9 Roman horseman. Hippolytus, from a sarcophagus, Arles, France.

precise model originated is debatable – it has been suggested that the lozenge-shaped 'brooch' on the Virgin's cloak is derived from a cross, sometimes represented as a lozenge of pellet in Late Antique art. An example of this can be seen in a seventh-century fresco at Santa Maria Antiqua, Rome, and in an eighth-century mosaic formerly in the mortuary chapel of Pope John VII in Old St Peter's, Rome (Whitfield, 1996). A distinctive feature of the Virgin and Child is that the Child is represented in profile, which is also the case with depictions of the Adoration of the Magi on Roman sarcophagi. However, the direct inspiration is more probably Eastern, as Kitzinger pointed out when comparing the Kells Madonna with the similar subject on the coffin of St Cuthbert in Durham Cathedral (Kitzinger, 1956).

In Celtic early Christian art, the Virgin and Child is a comparatively rare subject, though it seems to have been favoured on Iona, appearing on the Iona crosses and on High Crosses erected at Iona's daughter houses in Ireland. The normal depiction shows the Virgin seated facing, with a facing Christ on her knee, which is the usual iconographic convention in the Mediterranean and is that used on Eastern icons. The model used for the Virgin and Child on the Iona crosses, where the two are surmounted by angels raising their wings to form a canopy, seems to be of ultimately Eastern origin, possibly Armenia or Coptic Egypt (Werner, 1972, 8–9).

Other possible eastern Mediterranean models The East has also been seen as a source for some of the iconography in the Pictish sculptures, as first suggested by Cecil Mowbray (later Curle) in connection with the St Andrews Sarcophagus and the cross-slab at Nigg (1936). Curle compared the hunt scene on the sarcophagus with Sassanian silverwork (1936, pl. IV) and argued that the image of David slaying the

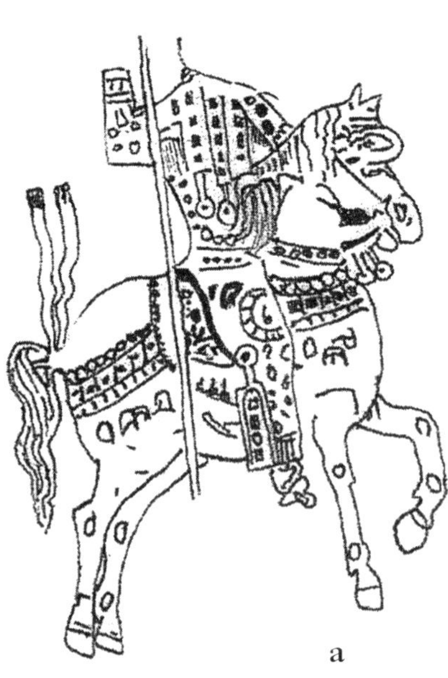

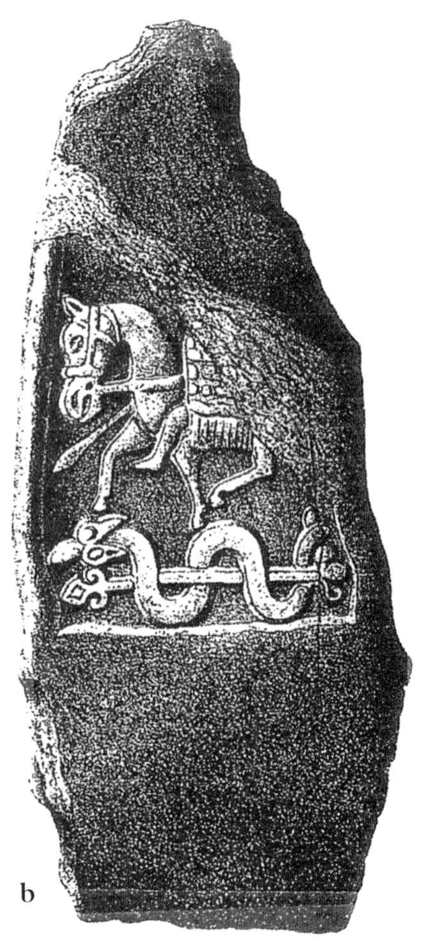

4.10 a: Detail from Byzantine textile,
Lyon, France; b: Pictish sculpture,
Logierait, Perths (after Allen, in Allen &
Anderson, 1903).

lion that appears on this work has an ancestry going back to depictions of
Gilgamesh employed in Assyria, but transmitted via Antique sources
(fig. 4.9). It was to the East, too, that Curle attributed the vegetation and
figure of a monkey on the St Andrews Sarcophagus, seeing links in its
iconography with the Nigg cross-slab. Later commentators have followed
these suggestions, but have argued for additional, Late Antique influence
and have seen the medium of transmission as being the textiles that were
reaching the West from the seventh century on (Henderson, 1998).

   The David and the Lion motif has been seen as of Eastern inspiration,
but, along with another similar relief of the subject from Drainie, Moray,
may have been modelled on an Italo-Byzantine ivory (Henderson, 1998,
130). The tree, hinds, wolf and cubs that appear on the St Andrews

Sarcophagus have also been seen as inspired by Eastern (though different) models (Henderson, 1998, 144). A few other elements point east in the sculpture of Pictland, for example, a figure depicted on one of the sculptures from Logierait is very close in style to a warrior depicted in a tapestry from Mozac, in the Tapestry Museum at Lyon, which is datable to the ninth century. The similarity includes the bejewelled Byzantine imperial dress, though as has been noted, the ultimate model for the textile probably lay in Sassanian Persia (Talbot Rice, 1963, 71) (fig. 4.10). A figure that may be the Persian god Ahuramazda can also be seen on one of the stones from Meigle, Perthshire.

Influence from the Frankish world
Frankish influence continued to make itself felt in the eighth century and later. Sixth-century and later Frankish and Burgundian buckles seem to have had some impact on Celtic art as late as the eighth century. Their influence on the design of the Moylough Belt-Shrine has been suggested (Werner, 1978), and the Daniel in the Lions' Den iconography that they often employ has been seen to have influenced the design of the shrine crest formerly at Killua Castle, Co. Westmeath (Ryan, 1991).

The model for the brooch from Ardakillen, Co. Tipperary, has been much debated. It has usually been seen as copying a type of ansate (handle-shaped) brooch that was current in the Carolingian world (Henry, 1965). However, the type in simple form is first seen in Denmark in the sixth century, and was taken up in England particularly in the eighth century, appearing in many different forms. An Anglo-Saxon model is therefore equally likely for this object.

One of the most active debates on the sources for Celtic iconography has centred on the extent to which the models were drawn from the Carolingian world, or from a common pool originating in the Late Antique world. While the Late Antique sources for much of the iconography are not disputed, it has been argued that the inspiration for the iconography came indirectly through the Frankish world, where there was a marked revival of Classical iconography as part of the wider process of revival. This view was shared by Henry and later Harbison (Harbison, 1987; 1992; Henry, 1967). For Henry, the main agency of transmission was Carolingian ivories, but as several commentators have noted, no ivories, Carolingian or otherwise, have been found in Ireland. Furthermore, most of those that were produced on the Continent were (due to the scarcity of ivory) confined to limited circles and did not travel (Harbison, 1992, 310; Stalley, 1990, 146). Harbison suggested that stucco might have been a medium of transmission (1987), however, no stuccoes are known from Ireland either and they would not have travelled easily (Stalley, 1990, 146).

There may well have been many avenues of transmission of the iconography. For instance, some images and ideas may have may have arrived in Ireland and Britain as a result of peregrinations, pilgrimages and the deliberate acquisition of works of art from the seventh or even sixth century onwards. This would have been reinforced by new sources of imagery from the Carolingian world in the ninth century.

The Book of Kells has been a central element in this debate, since it was first suggested that its Canon Tables were directly inspired by a Carolingian model, specifically a Gospel Book produced in the Palace School of Charlemagne, *c*.800 (Friend, 1939). A Carolingian source has also been suggested for the full-page illustrations in the book (Harbison, 1985). Although there is a considerable measure of agreement about the link between the Carolingian court school manuscripts and the Canon Tables, it has also been suggested that there was an earlier, now lost, series of tables available in Ireland, and the borrowing went the other way (Netzer, 1994).

A similar chicken-and-egg debate has attended discussions of the source of the biblical iconography on the Irish High Crosses. There is wide agreement that many of the compositions originated in Late Antique art, but less certainty as to whether they came directly from the Antique world or indirectly from the Carolingian. Some ninety scenes have been identified on the Irish High Crosses, a very high proportion of which employ the same iconographic conventions as are found in the Carolingian world of Louis the Pious (778–840). Biblical narrative is relatively rare from the court of Charlemagne, although it appears on an ivory datable to c.800, now in Oxford (Harbison, 1987, 106). Pope Pascal I (817–24) prepared the way for a revival of Antique biblical iconography in Rome, and at a Council held in Paris in 825 it was decreed that religious pictures could be used for instruction and meditation (Harbison, 1987, 106). Louis the Pious decorated his palace at Ingelheim with now lost 'Biblical Cycles'. Several other such cycles are documented, though they too are lost. A surviving fresco cycle at the monastery of Müstair, Switzerland, provides striking parallels (despite modern 'restoration') for the iconography found on the Irish High Crosses. Most of the scenes illustrated on the Irish Crosses are represented in the cycle or are described in contemporary accounts of lost Carolingian frescoes (Harbison, 1987, 107).

Parallels between Irish and Carolingian art can be found in other media besides High Crosses, but the chronology is problematic, since several of the items are conventionally dated prior to the Carolingian age.

Carolingian influence has been seen in the use of a beardless Christ on the Rinnigan (Athlone) Crucifixion Plaque, which is usually dated to the eighth century (Harbison, 1984) (fig. 4.2). However, at this time in Western art Christ was usually shown with a beard (as opposed to the beardless Christ of Late Antique art), and certainly the later series of openwork Crucifixion plaques from Ireland show him as bearded (Bourke, 1995). It has also been suggested that the Moylough Belt-Shrine displays Carolingian influence (Harbison, 1981).

Late Saxon influence in the eighth and ninth centuries
The influence of Anglo-Saxon England in the development of Celtic art in the eighth and ninth centuries is demonstrated in particular, by new techniques of metalworking and fresh types of plant and animal ornament that were employed in the Anglo-Saxon world before being added to the Celtic repertoire.

Animal ornament Among the earliest examples of animal ornament of Anglo-Saxon derivation are in the Book of Durrow, where both lacertines (in the tradition of Style II in England), and anatomically proportioned profile animals of the general type already discussed (see above, p. 65) are found (figs 4.11 and 4.12). Of these, the processions of biting 'horses' on fo. 192v are of particular interest. They display 'ankle bracelets' which are found on the lacertines on the same page and on the creatures on the Sutton Hoo maple wood bottles as well as on the interlinked horses on a sword pommel from Crundale Down. This feature has been traced to an element in Swedish Vendel (Merovingian period) animal depictions (Speake, 1980, 43).

The Durrow 'horses' display other features that clearly are derived from Anglo-Saxon art. For example, attenuated jaws which cross one another can be seen prominently displayed on an openwork buckle from Kingston Down, Kent (Speake, 1980, fig. 6l and pl. 9h). Details of the design (biting the body of the beast in front; legs folded under them; frond-ended feet; double outline and oval hips and shoulders) can be matched on a series of creatures for which the sword pommel from Crundale Down again provides the closest comparison (Speake, 1980, fig. 3h). For the lacertines on Durrow fo. 192v there are many possible models in Anglo-Saxon art, including one on the die from Icklingham, Suffolk (Speake, 1980, fig. 14f).

There need be no great time-lag between the use of such animal ornament in Anglo-Saxon England and its adoption by the Celts, for the

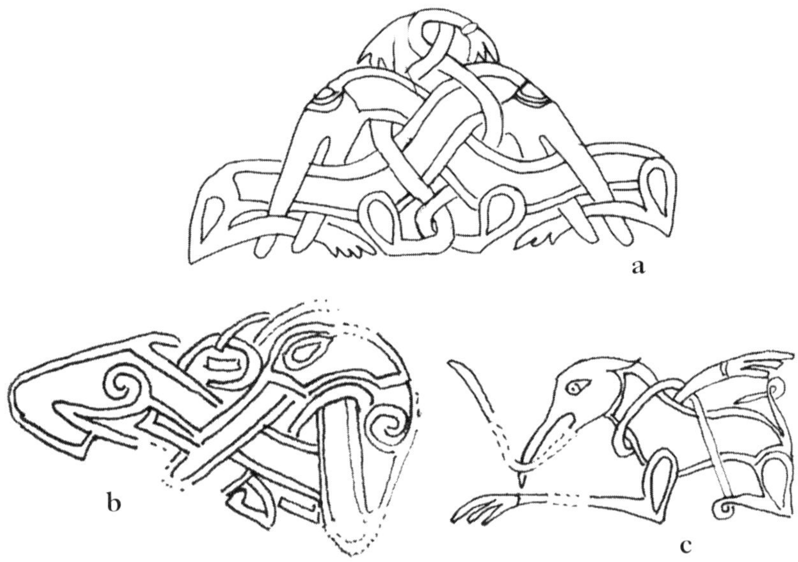

4.11 Durrow animals, with examples from a: Crundale Down, Kent, sword pommel
b: Dunadd, Argyll; c: Book of Durrow.

Crundale Pommel does not need to be much earlier than the mid-seventh century, simply because it came from a pagan Saxon burial. It is possible to trace the transmission of such animals into Celtic art, since examples in the same tradition are apparent on the gold mount from Bamburgh, Northumberland (Bailey, 1996b) and on the die-stamped imported plate from Dunadd, Argyll (Lane & Campbell, 2000). This type of animal passed into sculpture as well as manuscript art: just such a creature is displayed in a relief from Wamphray, Dumfriesshire (Bailey, 1996b).

Another type of animal image apparent in the Book of Durrow is also found in other Gospel books such as the Northumbrian-produced Echternach Gospels. These animals appear as the evangelist symbols of calf (ox), eagle and lion. The calf displays a double outline and dotted infilling, features that are notably found in animals on Anglo-Saxon metalwork. It also has hip- and shoulder spirals (quite different from the muscle-lines that appear on Pictish symbol animals, although they are often compared) combined with confronted trumpets. The head is segmented off from the body. The same kind of treatment of the hips and shoulders can be seen on the stags that decorate the hanging bowl from Lullingstone, Kent, which may in fact have been produced by an Anglo-

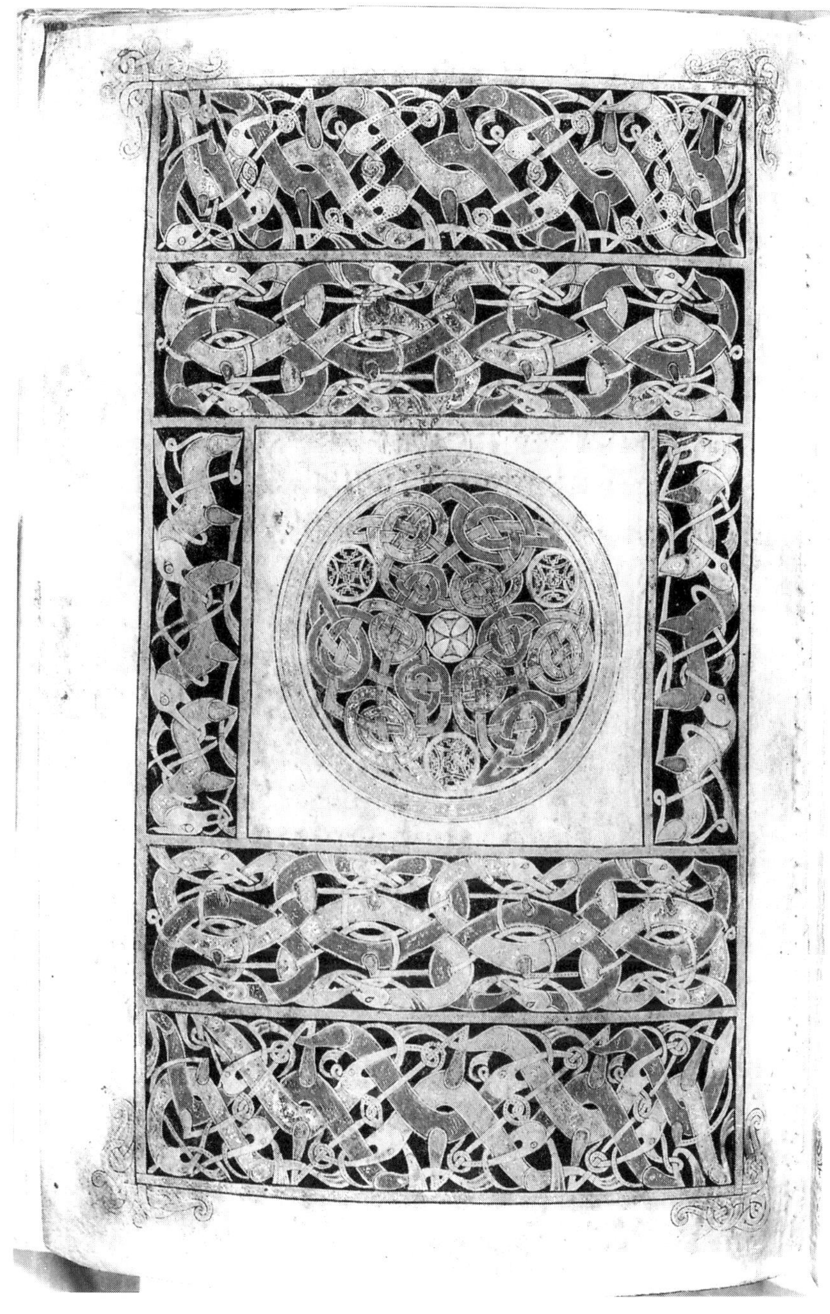

4.12 Book of Durrow, fo. 192v (The Board of Trinity College, Dublin).

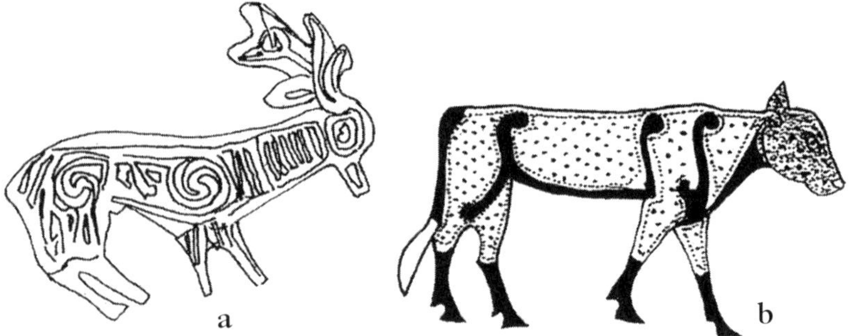

4.13 Lullingstone stag, from a hanging bowl and Echternach calf symbol.

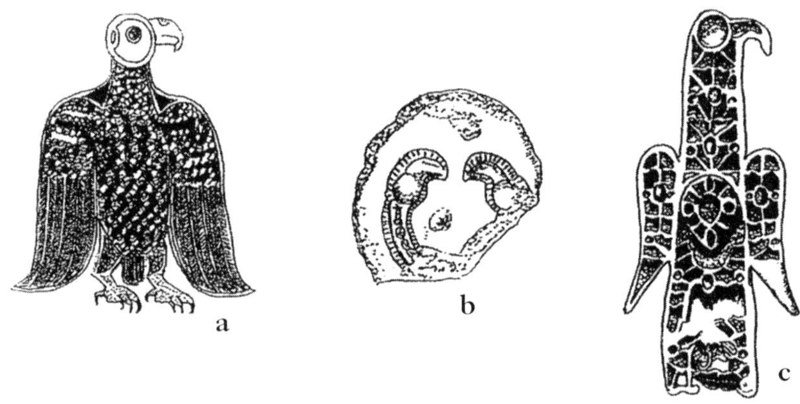

4.14 Eagles. a: Durrow evangelist symbol; b: Dunadd, Argyll, brooch mould;
c: Merovingian gold and garnet brooch.

Saxon artisan (fig. 4.13). The segmented head probably originates in Anglo-Saxon Style I ornament, but continues in Style II, where it can be seen, for example, in the way the heads are separated on the great gold buckle from Sutton Hoo.

The eagle symbol has frequently been noted as having features which are Germanic in origin, and has been compared with images on Visigothic cloisonné brooches. The eagle however, has a series of close relations in Anglo-Saxon metalwork, where the eye can also be seen to occupy the entirety of the head, for example on a shield mount from Hacklington, Kent (Speake, 1980, fig. 17c) and a mount from Asthall, Oxfordshire (Speake, 1980, fig. 17j).

The treatment of the eagle's head in the Book of Durrow is matched by the eagle heads on the Hunterston Brooch (Stevenson, 1974), and the same design appears on moulds for penannular brooches from Dunadd, Argyll, in Scottic Dál Riata (fig. 4.14). The Durrow lion displays a double outline and dotted infilling, as well as feathered feet. Its tail is curled back over its back. The poses of the evangelist figures may have a different model (see below, p. 106).

Bird heads (specifically, raptors with hooked beaks) occur with some frequency as extensions to the ornate penannular brooches. They occur for example on the Tara, Dunbeath and Hunterston Brooches. Raptors were common in Anglo-Saxon art, occurring in both Style I and Style II. They are represented, for example, at Sutton Hoo and on a pair of gold buckles from Faversham, Kent (Speake, 1980, pl. 3h). They also especially feature in a category of Anglian ring brooches, found particularly in the north of England, which have two pairs of confronted raptor heads at opposite points on the hoop.

A feature of the birds on the Hunterston Brooch is that they have crests, as do the Pictish beast of symbol stones and the stylized birds of the Petrie Crown and Bann disc (a feature not shared by the bird heads on the Tara Brooch). This might suggest that the Hunterston Brooch was produced in Dál Riata, where Pictish influence in other aspects of art is apparent.

The type of creature represented in the Anglo-Saxon Lindisfarne Gospels is also found in metalwork produced in the Irish Midlands, particularly the Donore Hoard from Co. Meath (Ryan, 1987d; 1991).

The Tara Brooch also displays an animal head viewed from above with flaring nostrils and ribbed snout. It is seen in a slightly variant form on the animal head that grips the ring on the door handle from the Donore Hoard (Ryan, 1987d; 1991), for which the closest counterparts are the (later) handles of the Palace Chapel at Aachen. This type of head is also found in Anglo-Saxon sculpture and metalwork, from which it probably derives (fig. 4.15). It appears initially on the crest of the Sutton Hoo helmet, then somewhat later on the Coppergate helmet from York (Tweddle, 1984). In sculpture, it appears as a corbel in the church at Deerhurst, Gloucestershire (Webster & Backhouse, 1991, fig. 27).

In Anglo-Saxon England, a new type of prancing, yapping animal appeared in the eighth century, probably in Mercia initially. It found its way on to metalwork and manuscripts. Classic examples can be seen on the linked pins from Witham, Lincolnshire, and the brooch from Flixborough, south Humberside (Webster & Backhouse, 1991, nos 184 and 69c). These evolved into a type of animal that is distinctive of the Trewhiddle Style (named after a hoard in Cornwall: Wilson & Blunt,

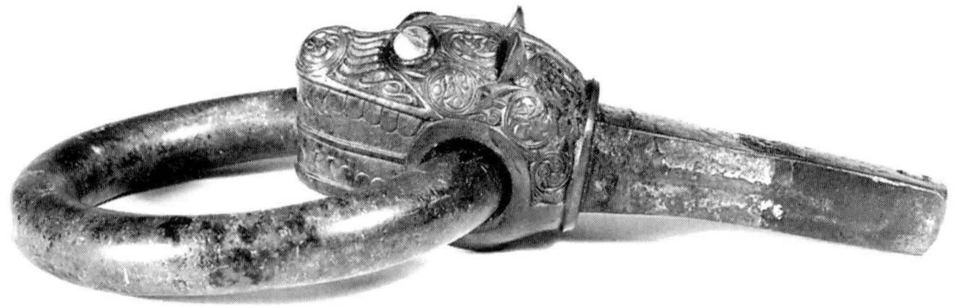

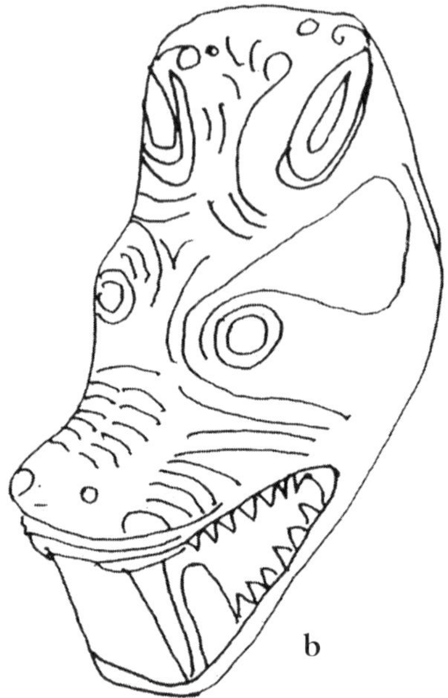

4.15 a: Animal head, Donore, Co. Meath, door handle (National Museum, Dublin); b: stone corbel, Deerhurst, Glos.

1961). A transitional stage in their evolution is represented by animals on the Tassilo Chalice, which was made for Duke Tassilo at Kresmunster, Austria, in the late eighth century by an artist who had been trained in the Anglo-Saxon world (Haseloff, 1950) (fig. 4.16).

Trewhiddle animals are ubiquitous in ninth-century Anglo-Saxon art, appearing in particular on strap-ends with animal-head terminals, of which over 1500 are now known, though not all have animal ornament (Thomas, 2001). Typical of these creatures are speckled bodies, yapping mouths and contorted limbs, which are often twisted to fit irregularly shaped panels. They proliferated all over England and crossed into Celtic-speaking areas, where they lingered on to become a key element in the decoration of the crozier of Cú Dúilig (the Kells Crozier). This is datable

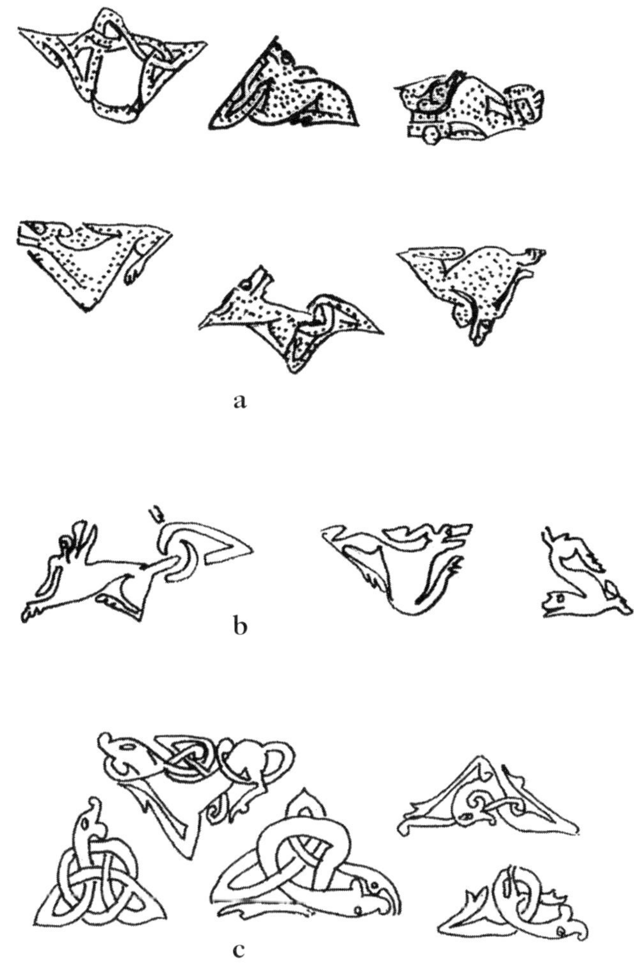

4.16 Anglo-Saxon animal ornament and Irish versions. a: Trewhiddle Hoard, Cornwall; b: Tassilo Chalice, Kresmünster; c: Crozier of Cú Dúilig.

to the early eleventh century (MacDermott, 1955; Michelli, 1996), though the creatures had acquired forward-pointing eyes, which have been taken to be a Viking feature.

Trewhiddle-Style animals are also found on motif pieces from Christ Church Place, Dublin, in a Norse context of the tenth to eleventh centuries (O'Meahdra, 1987b, 161). If Celtic metalwork examples of Trewhiddle animals point to a continuing tradition in the tenth century and beyond in Ireland, their relatives were already present in ninth-century metalwork, notably on the Bologna Shrine (Blindheim, 1984) and in Pictish sculpture, notably on the Roadside Cross at Aberlemno, Angus, and at Dunfallandy, Perthshire (Laing, 2001a, fig. 22.6).

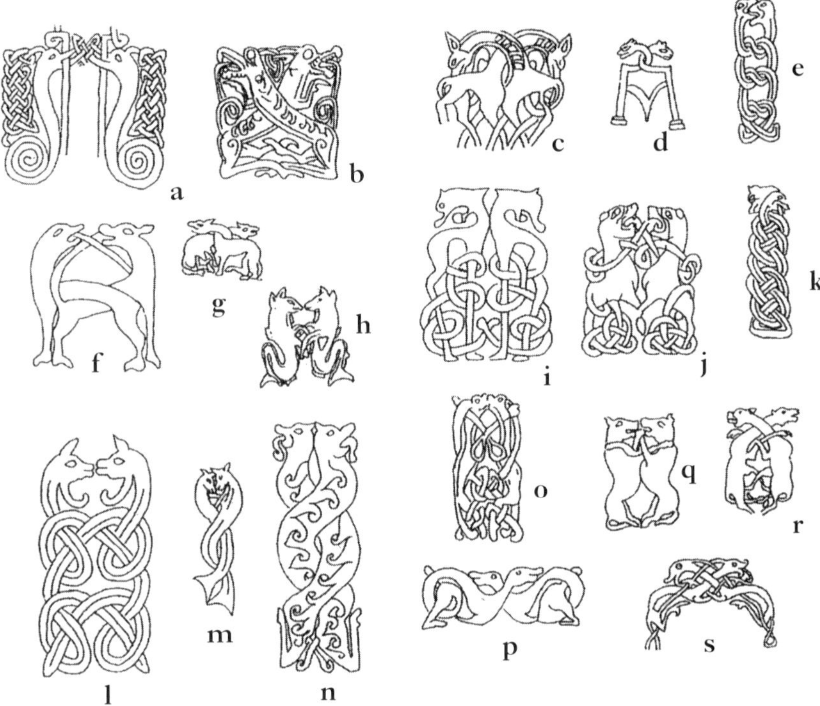

4.17 Confronted beasts in art. a: Skinnet; b: Invergowrie; c: Crofton; d: Durham Ritual; e: Dogtown; f: Kettins; g: Meigle, no. 23; h: Murthly; i: Thornhill; j: Gloucester; k: Kirriemuir; l: Romsemarkie; m: Largo; n: Benvie; o: Collingham 2; p: Kilkieran; q: Dupplin; r: Tower Cross, Kells; s: Crozier of Cú Dúilig.

In sculpture, other animals, oriental in origin, first appeared in late-eighth-century Anglo-Saxon carvings. Initially, they were fairly naturalistic, representing lions or griffins (part-lion and part-eagle), with a plant-scroll background. These evolved into confronted pairs of canines, long-necked creatures and bipeds with lizard features. In the following stage of development they were not confined to England, being also seen in Scotland, having trails which extended from their tongues and were wrapped around their legs (Cramp, 1978, 13). Classic English examples have been found at Masham, Yorkshire, and Newent, Gloucestershire. This stage was reached in the early ninth century, after which the animals became more flattened, and had double-outlined hip joints and back-thrown heads. These versions belong to the early tenth century, and show Viking influence (Cramp, 1978, 14). The paired creatures facing or crossing one another can be seen in Pictish sculpture on the stones known

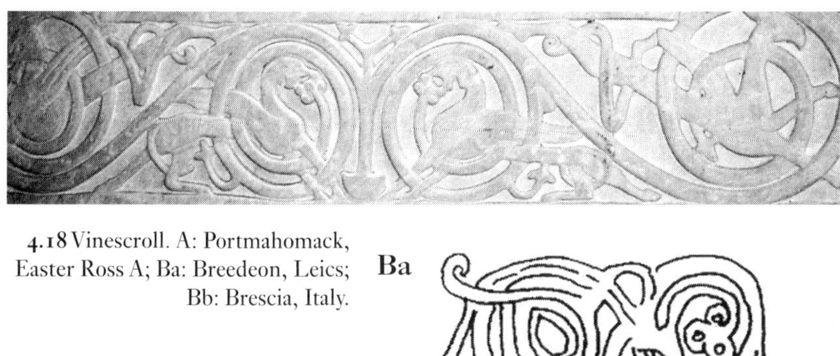

4.18 Vinescroll. A: Portmahomack, Easter Ross A; Ba: Breedeon, Leics; Bb: Brescia, Italy.

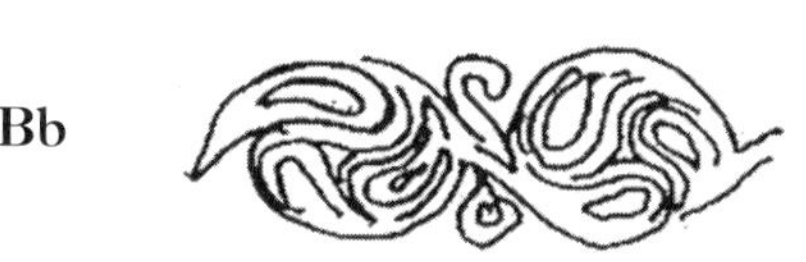

as Meigle 2, Dogtown, Kettins, Meigle 23, Murthly, Kirriemuir 3, Rosemarkie 1, Largo, Aberlemno Churchyard Cross (on which they are sea-horses), Benvie, Kilkieran and the Dupplin Cross. Outside Pictland, they appear on the stone from Thornhill, Dumfriesshire (Laing, 2000a, 106–7) (fig. 4.17). In Ireland, they are much rarer, but a good example can be seen on the North Cross at Clonmacnois.

Plant ornament Vine-scroll ornament (fig. 4.18) is characteristic of Anglo-Saxon sculpture in the eighth century. Its ultimate origins lie in the Mediterranean, where the vine symbolizes Christ and the birds and animals eating the fruit represent the Faithful. It apparently originated in the Byzantine east, where the Dome of the Rock shrine in Jerusalem provides prototypes, but it probably reached England more directly from Rome (Bailey, 1996a, 52–5). It arrived in the Celtic world comparatively late – in the ninth century – and seems to have been derived from the Anglo-Saxon repertoire. It is represented on fifteen sculptures from Pictland, of which the most notable are the cross-slab at Hilton of Cadboll, Easter Ross, and the St Andrews Sarcophagus (Crawford, 1937; Henderson, 1983). The closest sculptural models for the Hilton of Cadboll slab are to be found in Northumbria at York and Croft, Yorkshire (Crawford, 1937, 470), though it has been suggested that there are closer parallels for the animals in manuscripts such as the Rome Gospels (Henderson, 1983, 252). Vine-scroll with human inhabitants is found on

Sueno's stone, Moray, where it has been suggested that an English model is likely (Henderson, 1983, 260).

In Ireland, vine-scroll occurs on the crosses known as Clonmacnois South, Kells South, Monasterboice South, Clonmacnois West and Durrow. It is also found in metalwork. It has been argued that the animals in plant-scroll ornament were the inspiration for the quadrupeds that appear on the Romfojellen mount found in Norway (where it had been taken from Ireland); the Vatne mount and possibly the Steeple Bumpstead mount, a close comparison for which has been seen in the vine-scroll – derivative ornament on the Anglo-Saxon – made Brunswick (Gandersheim) casket (Ryan, 1991). Vine-scroll appears more obviously on a panel on the Corp Naomh, which is probably of tenth-century date (Edwards, 1986, 32). In Pictish sculpture, it is most prominent on the Hilton of Cadboll stone, for which the closest parallels are to be found on a cross at Croft, Yorkshire (Henderson, 1983).

A different type of vine – the bush vine – is occasionally apparent in Irish and Pictish sculpture. It appears in Ireland on the cross known as Duleek North (Edwards, 1986, 32). Metalwork models have been compared. In Pictland it occurs on a sculptural fragment from Rosemarkie (Henderson, 1983, 260–2) (fig. 4.19). In Wales, plant ornament derived from vine-scroll is found on Penally 1, Glamorgan, while on Penally 2 the influence of Carolingian acanthus ornament is apparent (Edwards, 2007a, 81). In Ireland, a derivative of the vine-scroll appears on a unique stone from Clonmore, Co. Carlow, for which the only parallel is to be found at Barnack, Northamptonshire, where a similarly designed slab is built into the tower of the Anglo-Saxon church (Harbison, 1988).

Decorative techniques and design Apart from the procedures involving filigree, granular work and inlays, other techniques used by the Celtic smith seem to have been derived from the Germanic world, most notably die-stamping and the use of niello as an inlay.

Die-stamping Pressblech (die-stamping) involved using dies to impress designs on thin sheets of metal, or (more often) pressing the metal into an underlying die. Die-stamping was employed in the Roman period in the production of casket ornament work and later in creating some composite disc brooches, but does not seem to have continued into the late Roman period. Die-stamped work is apparent on some early (fifth-century) composite disc brooches from Anglo-Saxon England, and subsequently was routinely employed in the creation of bracteate pendants and similarly impressed scutiform pendants. It seems to have been still in use in the

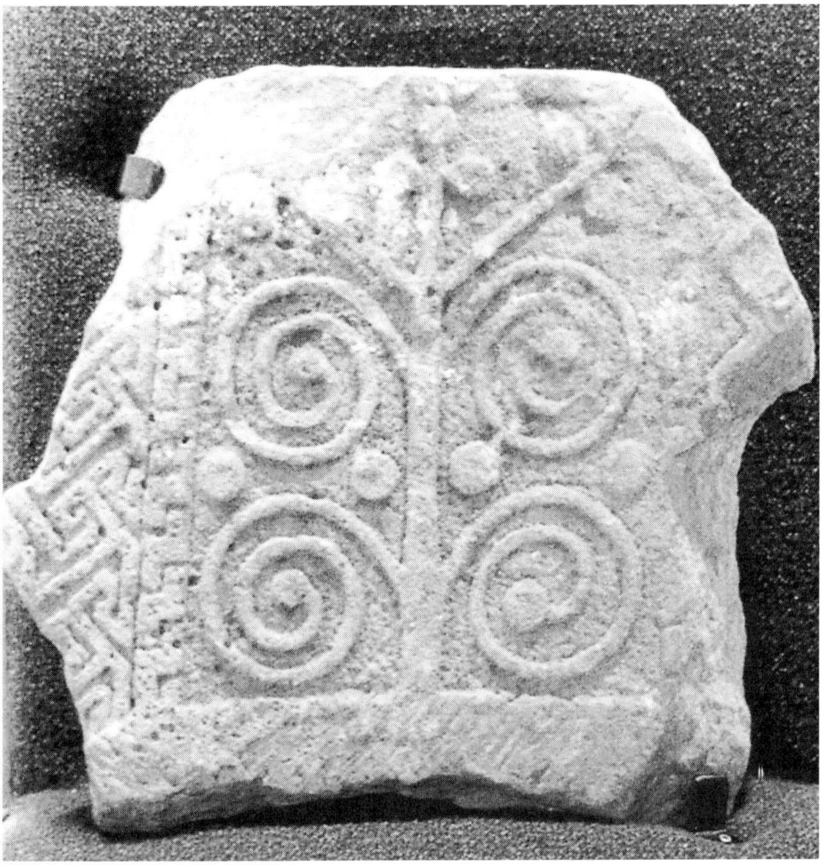

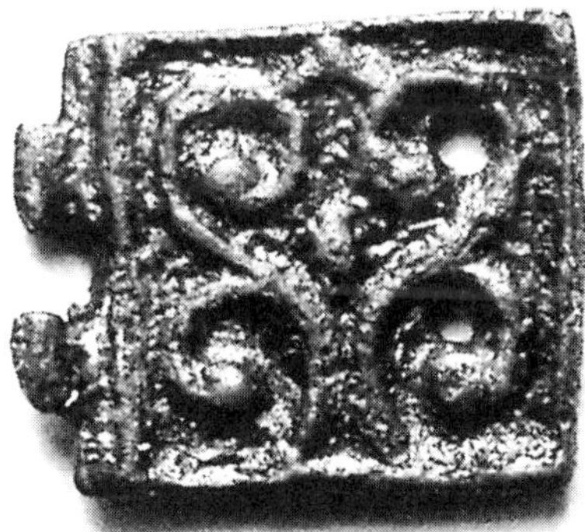

4.19 Bush vine.
a: Rosemarkie, Ross;
b: Anglo–Saxon bronze
buckle plate, Yorks.

seventh century, when the mounts were made for the bag from
Swallowcliffe Down, Wiltshire, but later it is comparatively rare from
Anglo-Saxon England. A die for making foils decorated with pelta and

other Romano-Celtic ornament was found at Louth, Lincolnshire, suggesting that the tradition continued there (Youngs (ed.), 1989, 192–3, no. 184). It was taken up by Celtic artisans, however, and was used to great effect on such items as the Moylough Belt-Shrine and the stand for the Derrynaflan Paten.

Niello Niello was probably adopted from the Anglo-Saxon world in the ninth century and was used extensively in Trewhiddle Style metalwork. It is a silver- or copper sulphide based material, which produces a black paste that can be inlaid into silver to produce a striking black-and-white effect (La Neice, 1983; La Neice & Stapleton, 1993). It became popular in the Roman Empire, and continued in use for a time on post-Roman British and pagan Anglo-Saxon metalwork. There is no firm evidence for its use in Ireland before the ninth century, and it was not until the twelfth that it was used extensively on, for example, the decoration of such works as the Crozier of the Abbots of Clonmacnois and the Shrine of St Lachtin's Arm.

Sculpture Anglo-Saxon sculpture probably influenced design in Pictland. It has been suggested that Northumbrian cross-incised grave-slabs of the late seventh century may have been the models for Pictish cross-slabs. In particular, the Herebericht Stone, Monkwearmouth, has been seen as a model for cross-slabs such as that in Aberlemno Churchyard, Angus (Henderson, 1983, but Henderson & Henderson, 2004, 176 sound a note of caution). The Northumbrian slabs, however, are appreciably earlier in date than most of the Pictish cross-slabs, and it is probable that the form was inspired by the cross-incised stones of Merovingian Gaul, which in turn gave rise to the various cross-incised stones in Ireland and Scotland (see above, p. 83). It is likely that the form of the cross on Pictish cross-slabs (effectively a cross head surmounting a pillar) is derived from Anglo-Saxon free-standing crosses, since they are different in design from the Irish High Cross series. It is also notable that the Northumbrian cross-on-a-pillar form was universally employed in Wales (Kelly, 1993, 223).

The development of high-relief carving in Pictland and Ireland in the ninth century was probably due to the influence of a similar trend in Anglo-Saxon sculpture at the same time.

The Norse contribution to Celtic art

The Norse raided and subsequently settled along the Atlantic coastline of Britain and Ireland. The first recorded Viking raid in Scotland was that on Iona in 795, but for the previous year the Irish Annals of Ulster recorded that 'all the isles of Britain' were devastated by the 'gentiles' (pagans) (Crawford, 1987, 40). Subsequently, raids on Iona in 795, 802 and 806, and attacks on the Hebrides were documented from 798 to the 830s (Graham-Campbell & Batey, 1998, 24). Settlement followed in the ninth century, in the Northern Isles, north Scottish Mainland and Hebrides (Crawford, 1987, ch. 5).

Similar raids affected other parts of the west, notably Ireland, where fortified longphorts were established in the 840s, at Dublin and Annagassan (Ó Cróinín, 1995, ch. 9; Doherty, 1998; Larsen, 2001). In Ireland, marriage and military alliances were made between Irish and Norse. Following the foundation of Dublin, other towns grew up at Waterford, Limerick, Wexford and Cork, but subsequently the Viking towns and their territories came under the control of Irish kings.

In the Isle of Man, settlement began around 900 (Cubbon, 1983, 13). Place-name evidence suggests that the settlers were predominantly from Norway and are likely to have been colonists from Scotland (Fellows-Jensen, 1983, 45).

Viking attacks on Wales began with a raid on Anglesey in 852, but there was a succession of raids up to 919. A 'second Viking Age' followed the death of Hwyel Dda (949/50) and was marked by targetted attacks from the Norse colonies elsewhere in Celtic Britain or Ireland. A further phase followed in the eleventh century, with an increased Norse presence in the Severn Estuary (Redknap, 2000).

The artistic contribution of the Norse was felt through the Scandinavian settlements in the Celtic areas. In Celtic Britain, the settlements seem to have given rise to the development of a hybrid Celtic-Scandinavian sculptural tradition, which can be compared to the Anglo-Scandinavian tradition in the north of England, with which there was some cross-fertilization of ideas. In Ireland, the impact of Scandinavian styles on sculpture was fairly minimal, but the Norse influence is very much more apparent in metalwork and manuscript art, and in the bone and woodwork that has been recovered in Dublin.

In Scandinavia, the seventh-century Style II was succeeded by a style represented in the Viking ship-burial from Oseberg, Norway. This was current in Scandinavia before the time of the Viking settlements in Celtic areas. However, the styles that developed from these have counterparts in Britain and Ireland: Borre (*c*.850–1000); Jellinge (*c*.875–975); Mammen (*c*.950–1025); Ringerike (*c*.975–1050) and Urnes (*c*.1025–1150) (fig. 4.20). To some extent, these overlapped with one another. Of these, the last two made a particular impact on art in Ireland.

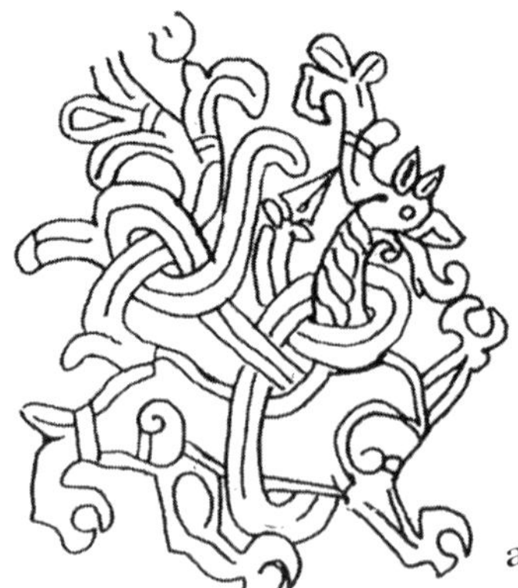

4.20 Viking styles of animal. a: Mammen style, Harald Gormsson's monument, Jelling, Denmark; b: Ringerike, weather vane for ship, Heggen, Norway; c: Urnes, runestone, Ytterselö, Sweden.

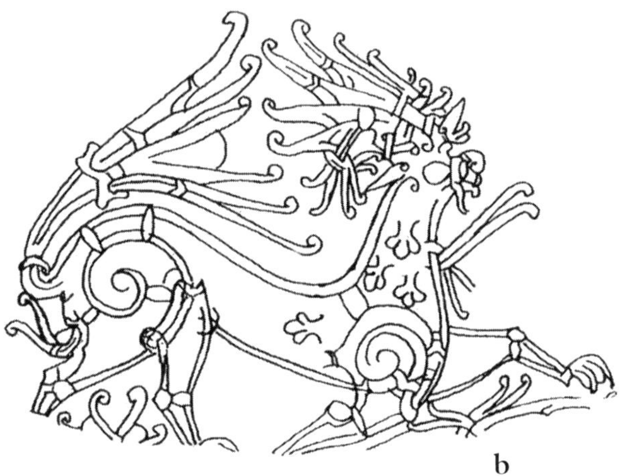

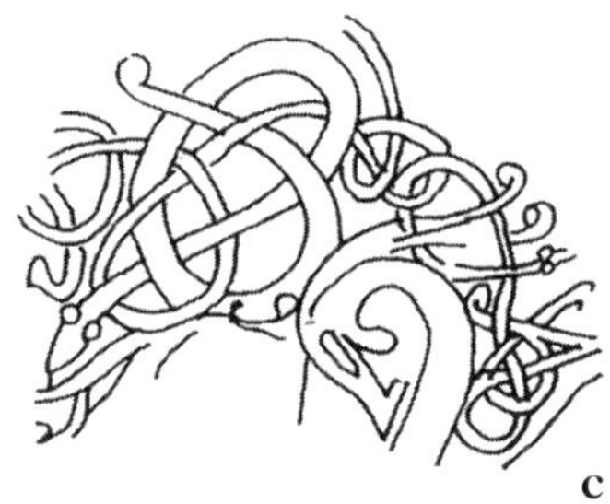

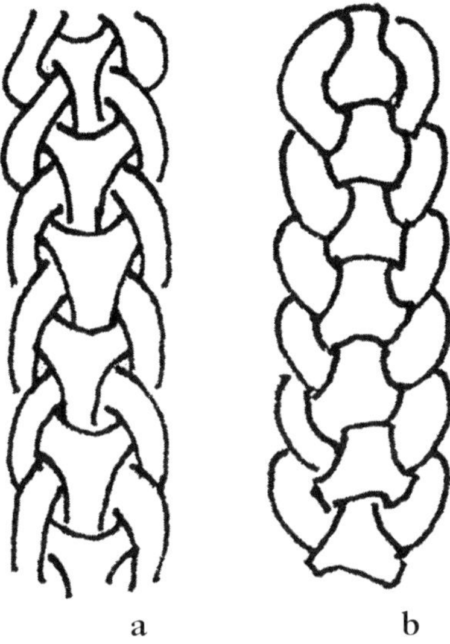

4.21 Borre ring-chain. a: Manx; b: Gosforth, Cumbria.

The Borre style The earliest Scandinavian style to make an impact on Celtic art was the Borre (named after the finds from the ship-burial at Borre, Vestfold, Norway: Wilson & Klindt-Jensen, 1966, 87). The most distinctive feature of Borre is a ribbon-plait. This is notable for having a symmetrical interlace with a circle containing a concave-sided lozenge at the point that the strands intersect (fig. 4.21). Also known as 'ring-chain', this is often found with an animal-head terminal. Quadrupeds with ribbon bodies and mask-like heads are often associated with Borre (Wilson & Klindt-Jensen, 1966, 88).

Borre, and in particular ring-chain, enjoyed some popularity in Insular art. It is found in Scandinavian areas of settlement in England, and in the areas of Norse colonization in Ireland and the Isle of Man. It is very sparse in the areas of Scandinavian settlement in Atlantic Scotland, despite the claim that it 'flourished all round the Irish Sea' (Wilson, 1983, 183): there are only a few stray strap-ends from North Uist decorated in this style (Graham-Campbell, 1973). A considerable corpus of Borre-influenced sculpture on the Isle of Man includes a cross-slab from Kirk Michael, which carries a runic inscription noting that 'Gautr carved this and all in Man'. Although ring-chain is very apparent on Gautr's slab, other elements of Borre (notably the animals), are absent, and it may be that the Borre style found here is derivative of the fashion for its use in the Anglo-Saxon world (Wilson, 1983, 180). It is also possible that ring-chain was developed in the Isle of Man and taken to Norway rather than vice-versa (Lang, 1984, 127). The Borre style is most apparent in the finds from

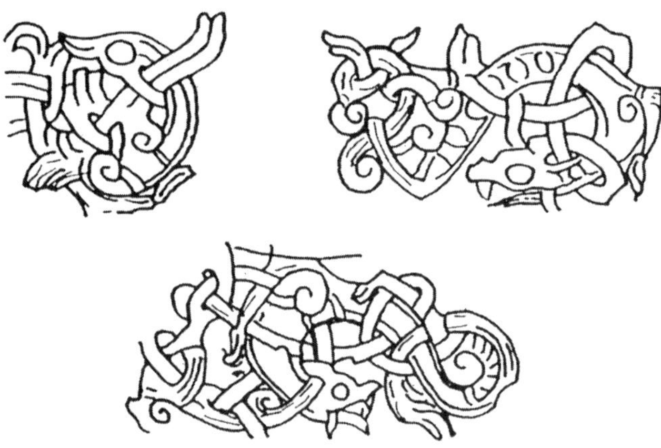

4.22 Motifs from brooch at Skaill, Orkney.

excavations in Dublin, where pure Borre is not found – the style seems to be a regional response in which ring-chain is found on strap-ends, woodwork and a couple of motif pieces (Graham-Campbell, 1987, 150; O'Meadhra, 1987a, 161). Ring-chain is also found as a border on a gaming board from Ballinderry 1 crannog (Hencken, 1936), probably made in Dublin. This crannog is now seen as Norse (Johnson, 1999).

Jellinge/Mammen style The Jellinge style, named after a silver cup found in the tenth-century royal cemetery at Jellinge, Denmark, typically displays an animal with double outline, lip lappet and pigtail. The closely related Mammen style is named after a Danish find which included an iron axe inlaid in silver, which bears a biped. Its head is small in relation to its body, and it displays a lip lappet, double contoured body and spiral hip from which extend ribbon tendrils. The same kind of animal appears on the large stone monument set up at Jellinge some time after 983 (Wilson & Klindt-Jensen, 1966, 96). The Jellinge/Mammen style appears in the Isle of Man on a series of crosses at Braddan, and on thistle brooches from Skaill, Orkney (fig. 4.22).

In Ireland, a wood carving shaped like an animal head that was originally part of a chair, was found at Fishamble Street, Dublin, and is in the Jellinge/Mammen style (Lang, 1987) (fig. 4.23). This displays one of the earliest manifestations of Viking idiosyncrasy – the forward-pointing profile eye, a feature which is particularly associated with Ringerike and Urnes (see below, p. 136).

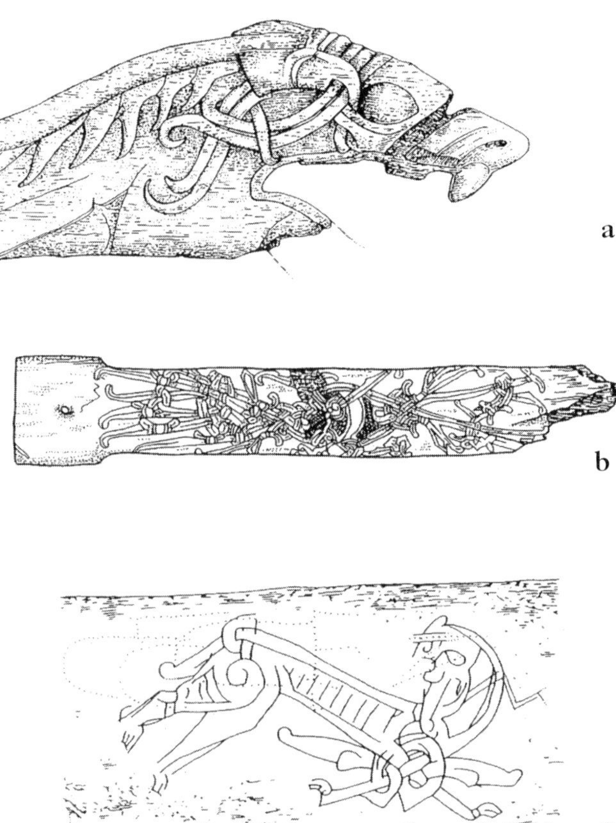

4.23 Norse ornament on items from Dublin. a: chair pommel, Fishamble St; b: box lid, Fishamble St; c: spatula, Christ Church Place (Cilla Wild, after James Lang, 1987).

In Scotland, the Jellinge style had some impact in Pictland, where it inspired the design of a cross-slab in Elgin, Moray, on which four quadrupeds with lateral tendrils, are biting each other's bodies. They lack the lip-lappet and pigtail of the true Jellinge animal, but the use of pellets to infill their bodies is a feature of Norse-period stones on the Isle of Man. A closer parallel to the creatures on the Jellinge cup can be seen on a stone at Dunblane 2, Perth & Kinross, which also has its counterparts in the Isle of Man (Laing, 2000a, 100). In the west of Scotland, direct Viking influence is apparent on two stones from Iona (Fisher, 2001, 16) and on a few other monuments such as a cross-slab from Doid Mháiri on Islay which displays Jellinge influence (Fisher, 2001, no. 136) (fig. 4.24).

Ringerike style The Ringerike style is named after a district near Oslo, and the animals characteristic of this style display the elements of the

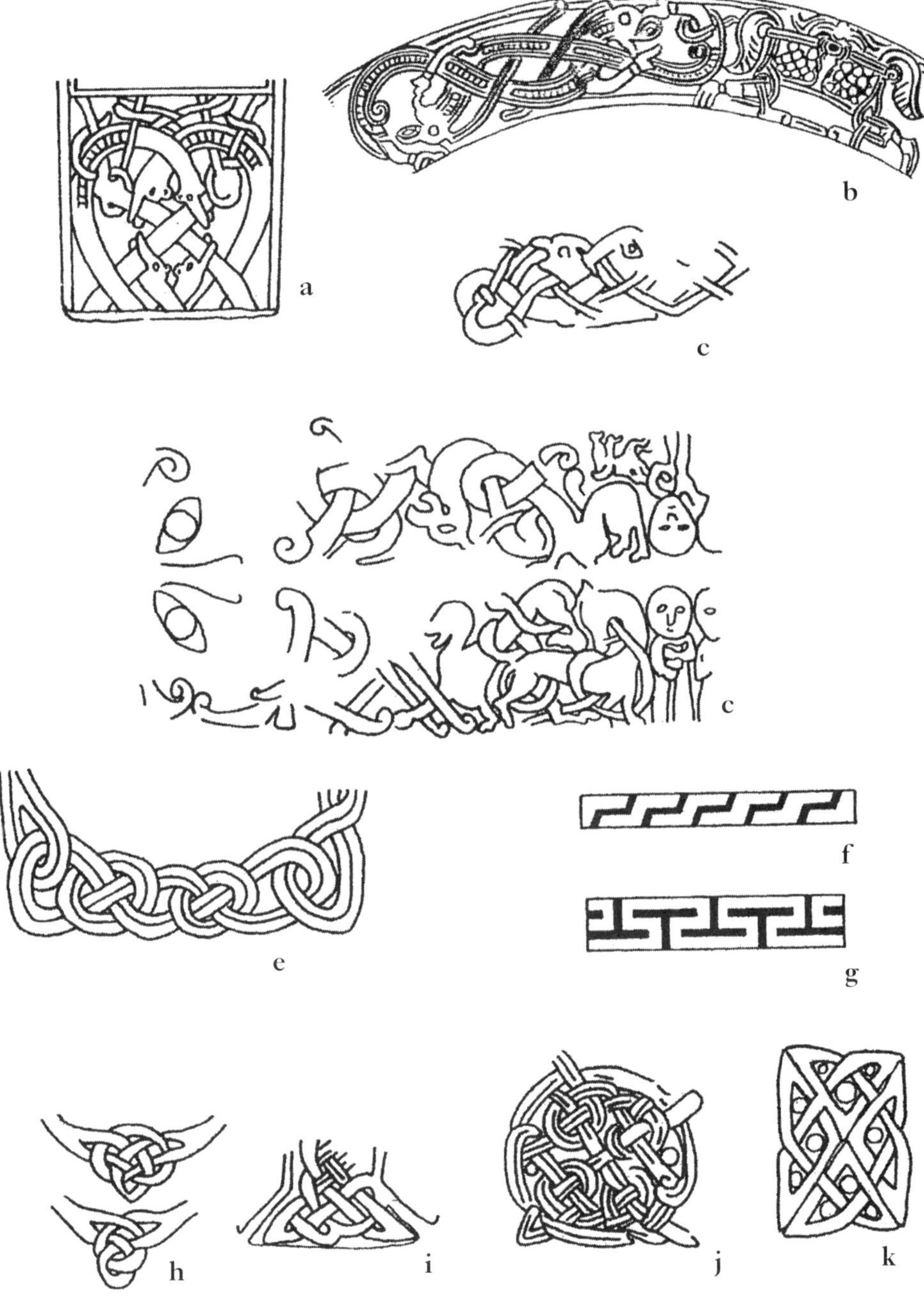

4.24 Norse ornament on sculptures from Scotland, with Danish Jellinge for comparison
a: Elgin; b: animal on Jellinge cup; c: Dunblane 2; d: Brechin, hogback; e: Bressay; f: Fortingall;
g: Menmuir 2 (restored); h: Rosemarkie 1; i: Menmuir 1; j: Collieburn; k: Forteviot 3.

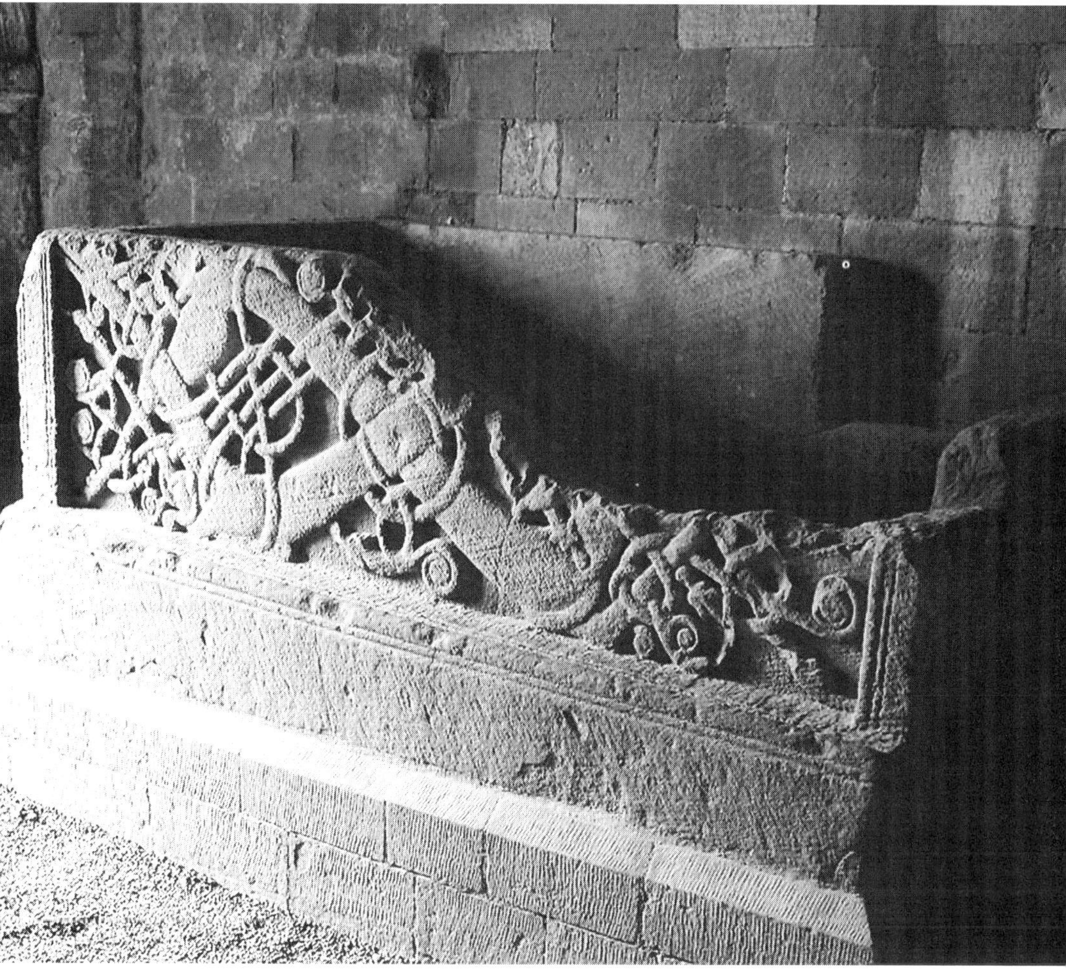

4.25 Cashel, Co. Tipperary, sarcophagus with Urnes ornament (photo: PD photo.org).

Mammen beasts. The Ringerike animal (sometimes called the 'Great Beast') is essentially a lion with extended, fleshy tendrils. In its homeland, it is sometimes combined with a snake. Another element of Ringerike is an elongated scroll which is ultimately derived from Mammen acanthus ornament, sometimes with an angular thickening half-way down its length, ending in a curled tendril (Wilson & Klindt-Jensen, 1966, 136–8).

Ringerike was first applied in sculpture, but is also used in jewellery. It is found in England in its native form (for example on the stone from St Paul's Churchyard, London, which may have been carved by a Swedish artisan). In the Celtic west it is apparent in a more modified guise: in

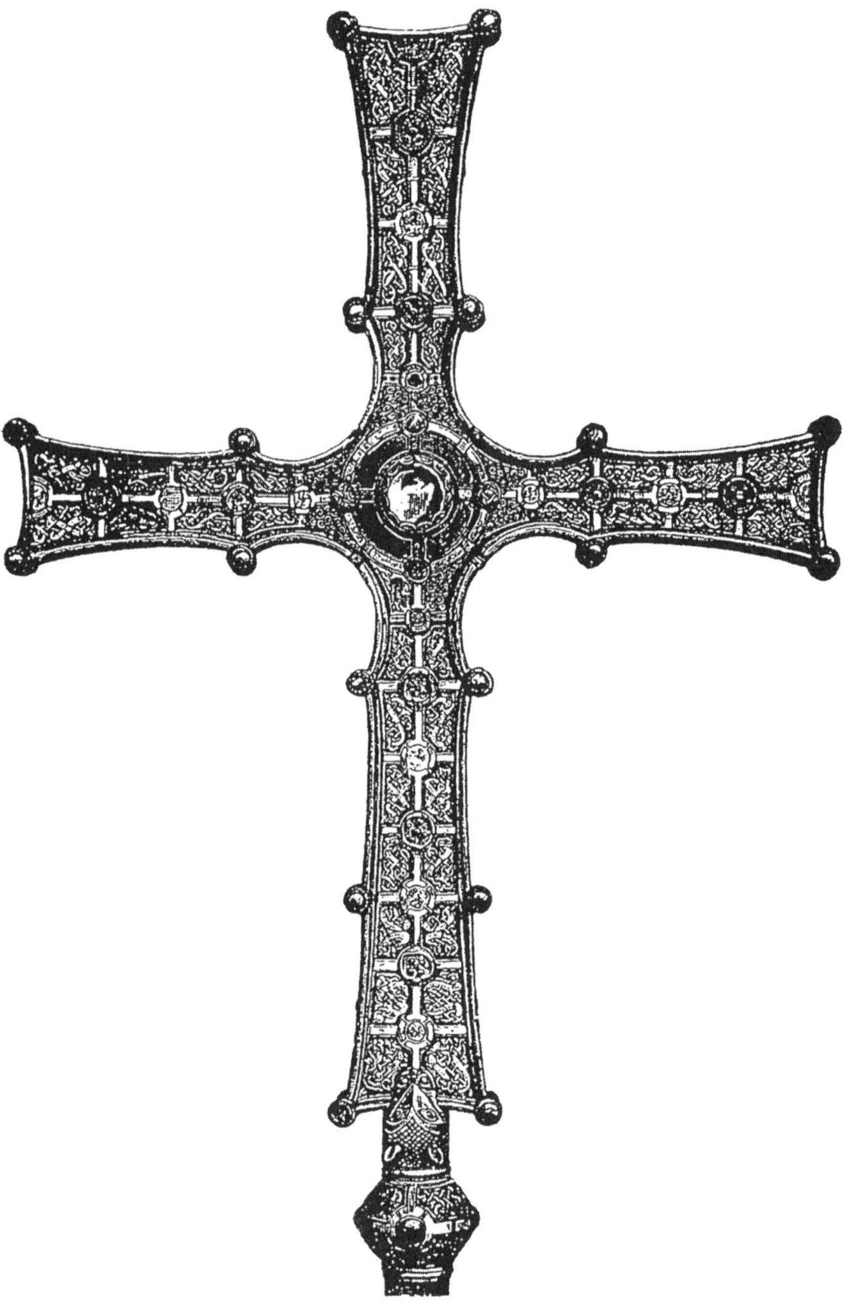

4.26 Cross of Cong (after Margaret Stokes, 1894).

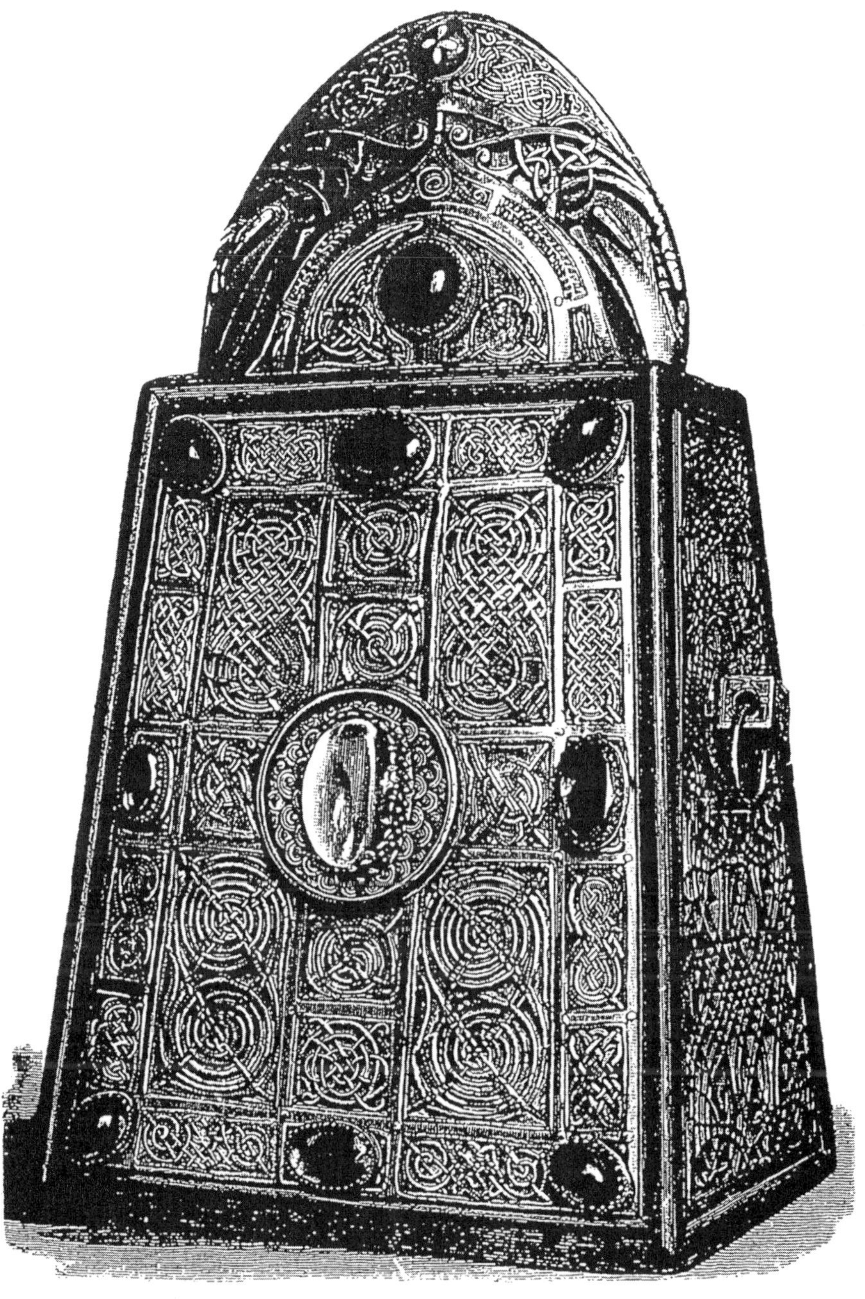

4.27 Shrine of Patrick's Bell (after Margaret Stokes, 1894).

Ireland, a Ringerike animal head, dated to the second quarter of the eleventh century, adorns an awl from Fishamble Street, Dublin. It has a forward-pointing eye, tendrils and volutes, though is clearly a native adaptation of the style (Lang, 1987, 175) (fig. 4.23).

The same type of creature appears on a hogback from Brechin, Angus (Lang, 1972–4, pl. 13). In Irish manuscript art, the impact of Ringerike was largely confined to the introduction of foliage elements that are appended to animal ornament. This is apparent in the animals that appear in the *Chronicle* of Marianus of Mainz (Vatican Library Pal. Ms Lat. 830), which, though written in Germany, was the work of an Irish scribe and datable to 1072–3. The animals have foliate ends to their tails, and seem to be trapped in plant tendrils (Henry, 1970, 54–6). A similar liking for Ringerike-derived foliage is apparent in the animals in the late-eleventh-century *Liber Hymnorum*, of which two copies survive (Henry, 1970, 56–66). The traditional ornament on the British Library Harley Ms 1802 (a gospel book written at Armagh in 1138), is also embellished with interlacing foliate strands (Edwards, 1990, 160).

Urnes style The final Scandinavian style to impact upon Celtic art was Urnes, which is named after the decoration carved on a wooden (stave) church at Urnes, Norway. Of all the Scandinavian styles, Urnes had the greatest impact on the Celts. It is characterized by interlacing ribbons that are associated with a standing quadruped and a snake–like animal with two legs. The animals in Urnes interlace bite one another, and the ribbons intertwine as interlace (Wilson & Klindt-Jensen, 1960, 147).

In sculptural form it can be seen at its finest on the sarcophagus from Cashel, Co. Tipperary, which is decorated with two elongated, crossed beasts (Kendrick, 1949, 114; Henry, 1970, 146) (fig. 4.25). Elsewhere on Irish sculpture, its influence was confined to interwoven tendrils such as appear on the crosses at Dysert O'Dea, Roscrea and Tuam. In metalwork, Urnes had a major impact in the design of some of the important pieces that survive from the twelfth century: the Shrine of St Patrick's Bell, the Lismore Crozier and the Shrine of St Lachtin's Arm (Henry, 1970, 201–2) (fig. 4.26–27). It also influenced the Lemanaghan Shrine (Shrine of St Manchan) at Boho, Co. Fermanagh.

In manuscript art, pure Urnes ornament is not discernible, but its influence is very clear in the tendrils that intertwine from the bodies of animals in, for example, the British Library version of the *Liber Hymnorum* (Rawlinson, Ms B502) and the Corpus Missal (Oxford, Corpus Christi Ms 282). This employs an Irish version of beast–and–snake Urnes-style

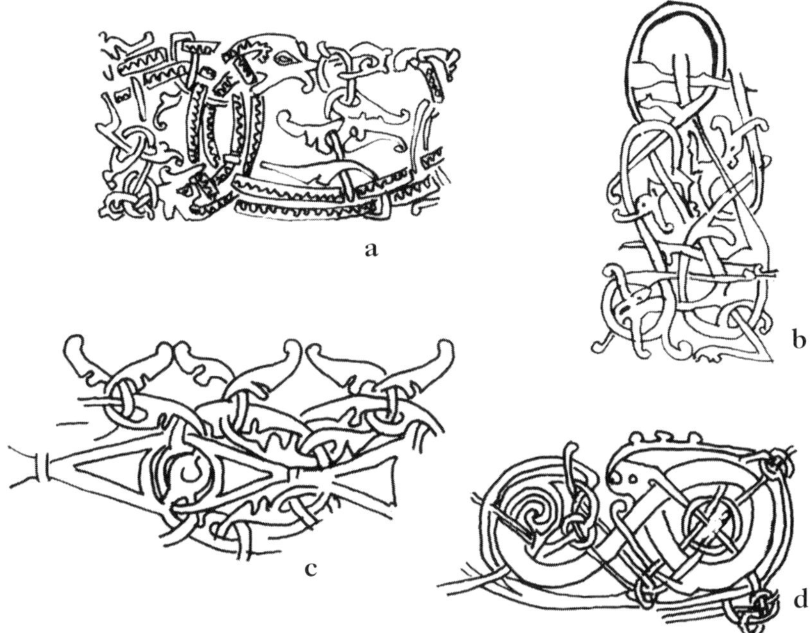

4.28 Viking-influenced ornament in Ireland. a: Cumdach of the Cathach of St Columba, side ornament; b: Shrine of St Lachtin's Arm; c: upper knop of Crozier of Cú Dúilig; d: Inisfallen Crozier, from crook (after Françoise Henry, 1970).

initials, which is very comparable to metalwork ornament on the Cross of Cong (Henry & Marsh-Micheli, 1932), and in Cormac's Psalter (British Library Additional Ms 36.929) (Henry, 1970, 72) (fig. 4.28).

The Celto-Scandinavian style in sculpture In the areas of Britain settled by the Norse, a distinctive sculptural tradition emerged in the tenth and eleventh centuries. Prior to their colonization, the Norse had no native tradition of sculpture, and were therefore directly influenced by the existing sculpture in Celtic areas when developing their own sculptural art. This art can be seen most definitively in the Isle of Man, but is also discernible in Galloway, Strathclyde, Dál Riata and the Northern Isles and north Scottish mainland.

The Isle of Man Norse tradition of sculpture In the Isle of Man, some sculpture was produced around the time of the Viking raids and settlement (the ninth to tenth centuries). One group, apparently centred on the monastery at Maughold (Trench-Jellicoe, 1999), seems to have been influenced by Pictish art. Manx sculptures of the Viking period characteristically comprise larger cross-slabs (perhaps modelled on the Pictish-influenced predecessors) which are executed in false relief. In some cases, they carry Norse runic inscriptions and employ iconography of pagan Norse origin as well as earlier Celtic motifs and a repertoire of distinctive abstract designs. They were probably produced for secular patrons (Trench-Jellicoe, 1999b, 198).

The detailed Norse iconography on these stones has been subject to some debate, especially since much occurs on very fragmentary stones. The subjects that have been identified include themes from the story of Sigurd. Most of the key elements in the story as given in literature are depicted in later art that appears on the Manx stones. Odin, Thor, Gerdr and Heimdallr are also featured (Margeson, 1983). Of the abstract ornament, ring chain (ultimately derived from Borre), with the tongue of the chain pointing downwards, is a feature also found in the comparable Viking-Age sculpture in the north of England, although there the tongue normally points upwards rather than downwards (Bailey, 1980, 217) (fig. 4.29).

Also found on the Isle of Man is a type of plait with a curling tendril offshoot (of which rare examples are known in Yorkshire), that must ultimately be of Scandinavian origin (Bailey, 1980, 218–19). The Manx cross-slabs additionally display a type of interlace which runs diagonally across the arms of the cross head, as opposed to from one arm to the adjacent one. This is universal on the Manx stones, but very rare outside Man, though it is sometimes found in Yorkshire (Bailey, 1980, 221). A type of lobed motif also occurs in Man, and has been found in Cumbria, pointing to the fact that these design elements are widespread in Insular Scandinavian sculpture (Bailey, 1980, 222).

The Govan school of Strathclyde The so-called Govan School of Scandinavian-inspired sculpture flourished in the Strathclyde area, though the term is misleading since there were probably more centres than solely Govan, Glasgow (Ritchie (ed.), 1994; Driscoll, O'Grady & Forsyth, 2005). Best known from the sculptures at Govan, there are related monuments from a wide area, extending to sites such as Kingarth on Bute, and Barochan, near Paisley. Characteristic of these monuments, which typically comprise recumbent cross-slabs, is the use of relatively simple interlace patterns, particularly 'stopped plait' and free-ring knot work (Driscoll, O'Grady & Forsyth, 145). A median line incised on the strands and bifurcating interlace are also features.

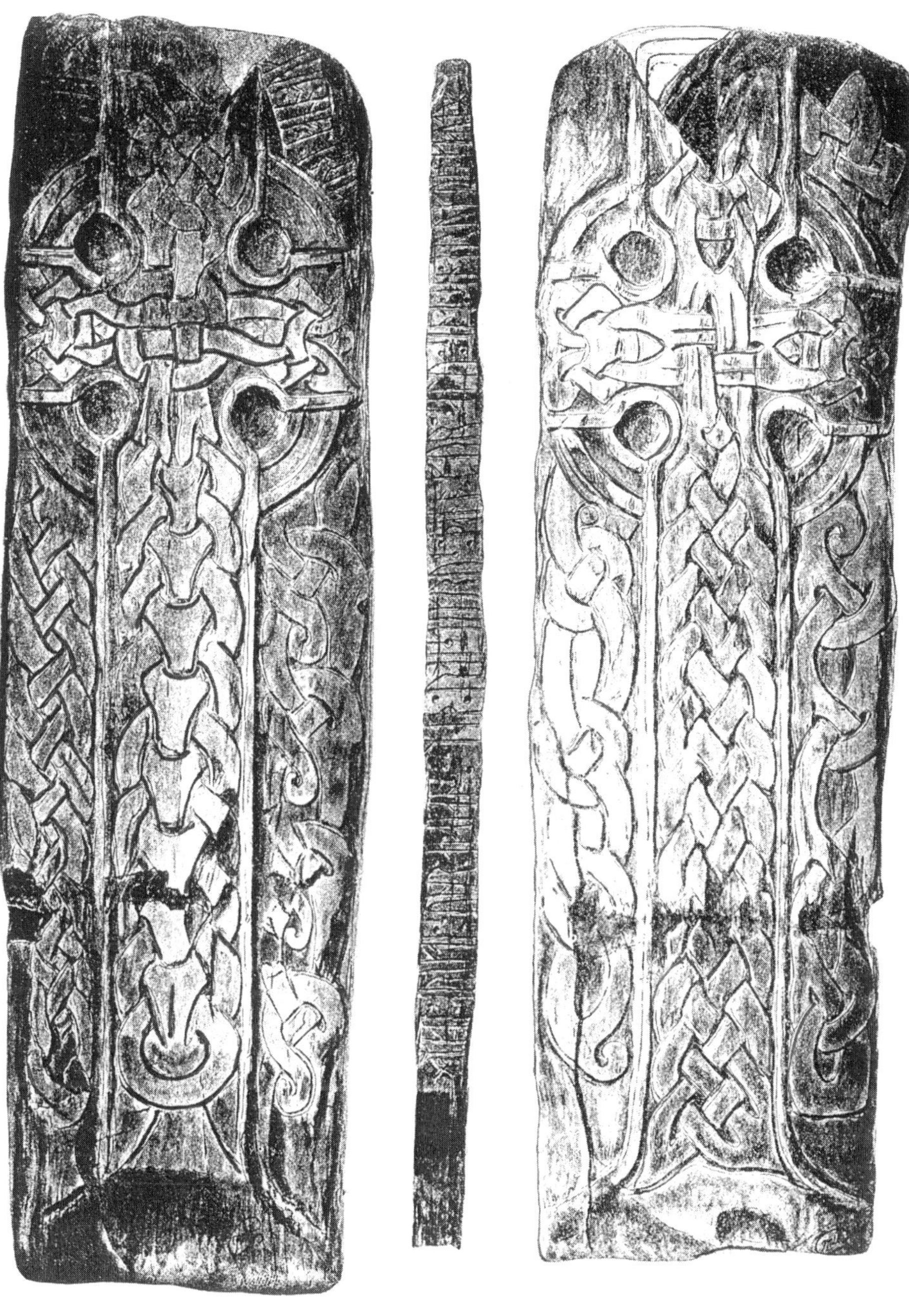

4.29 Gaut's Cross-Slab, Maughold, Isle of Man (after P.M.C. Kermode, 1907).

These types of interlace, though not originating in Scandinavia, seem to have been a Scandinavian contribution to the ornamental repertoire. Concurrent with the interlace are types of fret pattern that were previously employed in manuscript art but first appear in sculpture in the Viking Age. These distinctive types of decoration are found not only in the areas settled by the Norse, but in Pictland (Laing, 2000a) and Wales (Nash-Williams, 1950; Redknap, 1991). Some of the abstract patterns generally associated with Norse colonial sculpture appear in the west of Scotland on a few stones, notably key pattern at Kilmartin 11, Kilmichael Glassary, Eilean Mhor, Kilfinan, Kilmory Knap and Iona.

Other features of Norse-influenced sculpture include mounted warriors, usually poorly executed (such as are found on Man), and the relative flatness of the carving. Such features are shared by a further so-called School centred on Whithorn, Galloway (Craig, 1991). One side of a stone from Begerin, Co. Wexford, in the National Museum of Ireland, Dublin, has a cross with bifurcating interlace in low relief that is closely related to work done in the Isle of Man (O'Connor, 1983). Another stone from the same site has a mounted warrior, though the cross on this stone has closest links with Cornwall (Harbison, 1988).

In Wales, Scandinavian influence is apparent in the sculpture, particularly in south-east Anglesey and Clwyd, where the Viking impact was most strongly felt. Viking decorative elements are found, for example, on the stones known as Carew 1, Nevern 4 and Llantwit Major 4 in south-west Wales (Edwards, 2007a, 118). In south-east Wales, the Viking-period styles of interlace and fretwork are very much apparent.

CHAPTER 5

Workshops and artisans

Understanding how Celtic artisans worked in the period between *c*.350 and *c*.1200 – how they organized their work and what techniques they had at their disposal – furthers an understanding of the art they produced. It is clear that the makers of important works of art held high status, almost certainly because of the importance that such items held for the commissioning patrons. Information comes from law codes, as well as incidental references, all of which tend to reflect a rigid organization. However, it is clear from anecdotal material that society sometimes deviated from the legal requirements.

While the art objects themselves rarely have archaeological association, there is a substantial body of archaeological information relating to Celtic workshops and to craft practice. The material relates especially to metalworking, manuscript production and sculpting – and is particularly abundant in comparison with what is known about the craft workshops elsewhere in Europe. In general, it is quite clear that Celtic craftspeople functioned in the same way as those in neighbouring regions and mostly used the same techniques.

THE STATUS OF THE ARTISAN

Ireland provides a ready source of information about the status of the artisan in Celtic society, based on data from contemporary law codes. It is clear that craftspeople belonged to the *áes dána*, a social division that comprised the 'men of art'. They enjoyed free status, owned and inherited property, entered into contracts, made oaths and attended assemblies as part of the group known as *nemed* – those who had religious status and privilege (Kelly, 1988, 10, 62–3; Gillies, 1981, 76–7). Within the *nemed* class, those who possessed a *dán* (a craft or art) were recognized as a distinct group. Some of this status came from the fact that they were the possessors of arcane knowledge. They were also perceived to possess curative powers, and had the power to impose curses.

The *áes dána* were able to travel, and thus link 'mutually suspicious communities'. They were seen as 'the law, the personification of tradition, and had personal command of some of its superhuman and extra-social force' (Court, 1985, 10–11).

An eighth-century charm for travellers, significantly seeks help against 'the spells of women and smiths and druids' (Greene & O'Connor, 1967, 29). The *Life of St Abban* (who allegedly lived in the fifth century) refers to a certain Gobanus as a 'most illustrious craftsman, the most skilled in every woodcraft and stone craft in Ireland'. Gobanus was made blind, but had his sight restored by the saint so that he could build a church (Gillies, 1981, 73–4). It may be of significance that in a pagan context Gobniu was a smith god – the name appears in variant forms.

Nemed status was reserved for the *prim-goba* (the master smith) and distinguished him from the *fear imearta* who worked under his supervision (Gillies, 1981, 76).

Eighth- and ninth-century law tracts show highly formalized organization, and emphasize ranking in artisanship. The laws may not represent the reality so much as the ideal, but nevertheless they probably reflect how ranks were perceived. Some of the informative glosses in the surviving texts, however, were not added until the fourteenth century, so the material must be viewed with caution.

The skills of the master smith were valued more highly than the honour price accorded to the rank in the Irish law code known as the *Crith Gabhlach* (Kelly, 1988, 62–3). In particular, the text known as the *Uraicecht becc* relates specifically to those who worked with their hands (MacLean, 1995b). The law code makes it clear that the master artisans were 'dependent professionals', who enjoyed the privilege of 'noble dignitaries'. Although they were dependent on their patrons, they had the same honour price as the nobility.

The *gobae* was the blacksmith. Coppersmiths are referred to as *umaige* and goldsmiths and silversmiths (*cerd*) were considered to be of comparable status to judges and physicians (MacLean, 1995b, 131).

The *sáer* was the artisan who worked in wood; who could put up buildings and make boats and mills. From the late eighth to early ninth centuries onwards, the *sáer* was also a stone-worker. A master stone-wright could attain a rank higher than not only a master metalworker, but higher also than some grades of jurist. A later gloss lists the things that a wright might produce. They ranged from cashels (stone-walled forts or farmsteads) to mills, chariots and crosses (stone monumental crosses) (MacLean, 1995b, 134). The chief master wright was paid one-sixth of the two cows paid for making wicker houses, bridges, shields, chariots and crosses (Maclean, 1995b, 135). The *sáer* could rise in status as more skills were acquired.

The earliest reference to the existence of workshops is provided by Cogitosus in his *Life of St Brigit of Kildare*, written in the mid-seventh century. The account described those concerned with the production of millstones, but it is clear that the same artisans worked in both wood and stone (Connolly & Picard, 1987, 24–6).

According to the *Uraicecht becc* law code, workshops were organized into a hierarchy in which the apprentices were clients of the master artisan, just as he was a client of his patron. Within the workshop there was a master, assistants with independent legal standing, and dependent apprentices (MacLean, 1995b, 137). Training, food and clothing were given by the master to his apprentices, but all the earnings of the apprentice went to the master. When the apprenticeship ended, the first earnings of the newly qualified artisan went to the master, who was also entitled to support in his old age (MacLean, 1995b, 130). It is notable that a distinction was made between the artisan who designed a cross and the person who carved it. The designer was of aristocratic status; the relief carver simply a workman (MacLean 1995b, 136).

The high status of the smith was not unique to the Celtic areas. Documentary evidence indicates that in Anglo-Saxon England skilled smiths had a similar status to that of their counterparts in Celtic lands (Hinton, 1998, 11). It is evident from an early-seventh-century Frankish burial (in Grave 4), Wallerststadten, Germany, that the deceased was a goldsmith who had warrior status (Moller, 1987, 65). Another high-status burial of a smith was found at Vendel, Sweden (Arrhenius, 1979). At Hérouvillette, Normandy, a warrior burial contained both the ferrous and non-ferrous equipment of a smith (DeCaens, 1971, 83–90). The Laws of Aethelberht of Kent (552–616) indicate that a smith had the same value as a freeman, even though he was not formally free (Hinton, 1998, 9).

It is rare for the death of an artisan to be mentioned in documents before the eleventh century, when the death in 1029 of Mael Brígde ua Brolcháin is recorded in the *Annals of Ulster* (Ní Brolcháin, 1986, 44–5). Mael Brígde ua Brolcháin is described as *primsaer Erenn*, i.e., chief wright of Ireland.

The manuscript artist was often the same person as the scribe and is sometimes named. In some instances, both scribe and illuminator are named. The earlier manuscripts do not bear the name of a scribe, though the eighth-century *Book of Dimma* was allegedly written at Roscrea by a scribe called Dimma, who had been given a day to complete a copy of the gospels. This may be a later myth since the book is clearly by several hands (Alexander, 1978, 69).

Attributions in the ninth century occasionally occur. The *Book of Mac Regol* is attributed to Mac Regol of Birr, who died in 822 (Hemphill, 1911–12), and the *Book of MacDurnan* is attributed to an abbot of Armagh who died in 927 (Henry, 1967, 102–5). The Welsh *Psalter of Rhygyfach* was written *c.*1079 at Llanbadarn Fawr, by a scribe called Ithael. It was illuminated by Ieuan to whom an illuminated text of Augustine's *De Trinitate* (Corpus Christi Ms 199), is also attributed (Edwards, 1995). The twelfth century was a period when manuscripts such as *Cormac's Psalter* were most frequently attributed to specific scribes.

Sculptors are sometimes named in inscriptions on Irish stone crosses, though it is not always clear whether the person who is described as having made the monument was the sculptor or the patron. In Ireland, the Kinitty Cross asks for a prayer to be said for its maker, Colman, who fashioned it for the king of Ireland (Harbison, 1992, 356). The Cross of the Scriptures at Clonmacnois requests a prayer for Ronan who made it in memory of Flann (Harbison, 1992, 357). A cross at Delgany names two people for whom prayers should be said, the second being Odran the *saer* (who probably cut the inscription) (Harbison, 1992, 358). At Iniscealtra a cross requests a prayer for Tornoc 'who made the cross' (Harbison, 1992, 361), while the Broken Cross at Kells may originally have had an inscription seeking a prayer for Artgal who made it (Harbison, 1992, 362). A fragmentary cross in Tuam calls for the prayer for 'the artisan, for Gillachrist, descendant of Tuathal' (Harbison, 1992, 366), indicating that it continued to be common to name the artisans on crosses down to the twelfth century.

ITINERANT ARTISANS

The extent to which artisans travelled had great impact on the distribution of artefacts, the availability of source materials, the dissemination of ideas and the development of local styles or 'Schools' in some artistic enterprises.

Obtaining raw materials for stone carving did not generally necessitate extensive travel, but ornamental metalworking and manuscript illumination required a considerable range of materials that were unlikely to have been found locally. Artisans are not likely to have travelled to the source of the materials they required in all instances, and must have mostly relied on networks of trade. In some cases, however, they may have travelled personally in search of suitable sources.

Members of the *aes dána* were permitted to travel beyond the limits of their *tuath*, and were given protection outside their territory (Binchy (ed.), 1978, 2333, 23–29). However, the extent and nature of individual itinerancy is difficult to assess, since there is little documentation, most of which relates to the travels of churchmen. There is a difference between itinerant artisans (such as tinkers who constantly move around with no fixed base) and travelling artisans (who travel to execute particular commissions for patrons but who then return to base). The movement of objects themselves can be traced in some cases. Sometimes ecclesiastical or diplomatic gifts could change hands many times, not simply with close neighbours, but across hundreds of miles. Commissions could also be ordered from considerable distance from the workshop.

In the *Life of Colmán mac Lúacháin* (datable to *c.*1122) an artisan called Anniraid residing in the Abbot's lodging at Lann, is reported to have saved a criminal from the hangman by exchanging him for a bridle of gold and silver. Significantly, Anniraid had made the bridle himself and had been intending to deliver to the king of Offaly (Kenney, 1929, 454–5).

Relics were sometimes sent away to other centres to be enshrined (placed in specially made containers) (Hughes, 1972, 255). A good example of this is the Cumdach (Shrine) of the Cathach of St Columba. This may have been one of the relics known to have been sent in 1090 from Donegal to Kells for enshrinement (Henry, 1970, 89–91). The inscription on it names its metal-smith maker as Sitric Mac Meic Aeda. Since Sitric was a name used by both Norse and Irish, it is possible that the smith originally came from Dublin. This theory is partially supported by the similarity between a motif used on the Cumdach of the Cathach of St Columba and one employed on a motif piece found in Dublin (O'Meadhra, 1987b, 164).

CENTRES OF PRODUCTION

Despite the necessity for artisans to travel occasionally, it is likely that most had a base from which to work. It is probable that the craftspeople who carved monuments did so once the stone had been transported to its final resting place, whereas metal smiths would have needed complex workshops and manuscript illuminators would have required suitable scriptoria. It is likely that even stone masons returned to a base from which commissions were ordered, plans and designs were drawn up, and where suitable stone and helpers were available.

Certainly, corroborative of this view is the fact that regional characteristics can be distinguished in the surviving artworks. The existence of 'Schools' (or perhaps, more accurately, centres of production) of Irish metalworking has been suggested because some groups of surviving objects have close similarities in their decoration and their provenance (where known). Most of the process of grouping works is applicable to the eleventh and twelfth centuries. In this period, five main groups have been distinguished. The first group is thought to be centred on Kells, Co. Meath, and includes the Cumdach of the Cathach of St Columba, the Misach (a shrine for an uncertain type of relic), part of the Crozier of Cú Dúilig, and two bell shrines. The second group, thought to be associated with Clonmacnois, is characterized by various croziers and crozier fragments, including the Clonmacnois Crozier. The third group is more debatable since it is not associated with a specific site. It includes the Shrine of St Lachtin's arm. The fourth group is characterized by the Lismore crozier, and the fifth group, by the Cross of Cong (Ó Floinn, 1987).

PATTERN BOOKS AND MODELS

Evidence points to the use of models and pattern books. Models could include descriptions. One account, from a collection of Irish texts set down between 663 and 800, explains how to paint the tonsures (distinctive ecclesiastical hairstyles in which the crown of the head is shaved) of the Apostles in Roman style. The description notes that 'Matthew has grey hair and a beard. / Peter is grey and has a round tonsure. / Andrew has a grey beard and the sign of the cross in his hair' (Davis-Weyer, 1971, 78–9).

The idea of tabulae (design sketches) was probably inherited from the Antique world, where pattern books for mosaics in particular, are known to have existed. Wax tablets, parchment pages and motif pieces in stone, bone, wood and probably leather, are likely to have been used, although none survive in organic materials. Later medieval model-books are known – they include designs for abstract patterns such as those found in a thirteenth-century manuscript in the National Library in Vienna (Cod. 507, fo. 13) (Scheller, 1963).

Artisans had limited creative licence. In the eighth century, the Nicene Council stipulated that 'the composition of the figures is not the invention of the painters, but the law of tradition in the Catholic Church' (cited in Cust, 1902, 94).

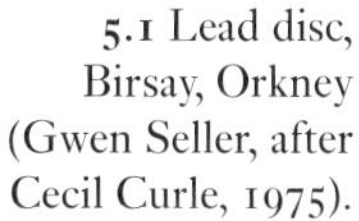

5.1 Lead disc,
Birsay, Orkney
(Gwen Seller, after
Cecil Curle, 1975).

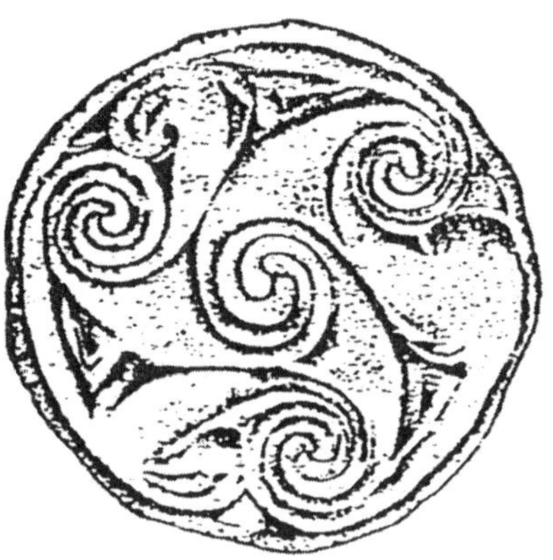

The best-known designs on parchment (a creamy yellow material derived from sheepskin or goatskin) are the late Anglo-Saxon sketches on two pages of a copy of the poems of Caedmon (a seventh-century Anglo-Saxon monk). The book is known as the *Junius 11*, and is preserved in the Bodleian Library, Oxford. One sketch is usually assumed to be the design for a book binding (though it could be for a box). The other two sketches, on the second page, are arguably for clasps. Both were made by the same person, who was clearly designing for two media – bookbinding and metalwork (Fuglesang, 1980, no. 110).

An unfinished designer's sketch for a developed trumpet pattern appears on a lead disc from Birsay, Orkney, which has been suggested as a master model (Curle, 1975) (fig. 5.1). It has also been more persuasively interpreted as a design template, of which only one section has been completed, the others being repetitions of the first (O'Meadhra, 1987b, 115). The back of an unprovenanced Irish enamelled mount (National Museum of Ireland, 1906.38) bears a sketch of interlace and a fish, which O'Meadhtra has suggested may be a designer's model (1987b, 116).

There is a substantial series of around 350, of motif pieces, in wood, bone and stone (O'Meahdra, 1987; 1987b; 1993). Although most are from Ireland, they are also found in Scotland and more rarely in Wales (fig. 5.2). They date mainly from the Viking Age, but there are examples from the eighth century or earlier. In essence, most appear to be trial designs for ornament that was destined to be used in metalwork or other media. Some work perhaps originated with apprentices undergoing training. Since many come from archaeological contexts, the pieces can often be dated fairly closely, and are invaluable for studying the chronology of motifs on surviving objects. A few show the guidelines employed in setting out the designs, and at least two have designs for penannular brooches.

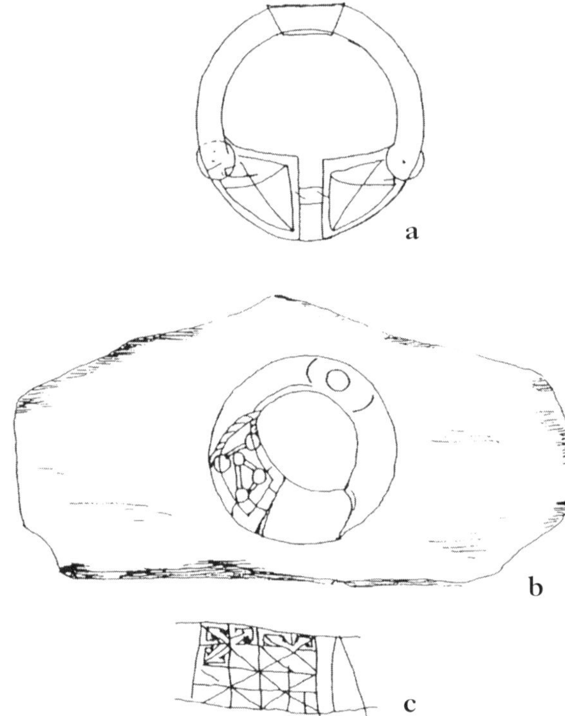

5.2 Motif piece designs. a: penannular brooch, Nendrum Co. Down; b: penannular brooch, Dunadd, Argyll; c: Ballinderry, Co. Offaly (after Uaininn O'Meadhra, 1987).

METALWORKING

Metalworking was carried out on both secular and ecclesiastical sites and much of the workshop evidence relates to non-ferrous metalworking. Most evidence comes from Ireland, where over forty sites have produced evidence for non-ferrous metalworking, though most of them also produced lesser evidence for working in iron as well (Comber, 2004, 46).

Secular workshops
Key secular workshop sites in Ireland include Garranes and Garryduff, Co. Cork (O'Riordain, 1942; O'Kelly, 1963); Lagore (Hencken, 1950, re-appraised in Comber, 2004); and Moynagh Lough, Co. Meath (Bradley, 1993). A study of Irish settlements has suggested that non-ferrous metalworking was carried out only on sites of medium-to-large size, whereas iron was worked on at sites of all sizes (Comber, 2004, 45). It is clear that ornamental metalworking is a feature of sites known from other sources to have been the residences of kings or chiefs.

The evidence from Britain is less abundant, but several sites, most notably the Mote of Mark, Kirkcudbright (Laing & Longley, 2006), Dunadd, Argyll (Lane and Campbell, 2000), and Birsay, Orkney (Curle, 1982), have produced fairly extensive evidence of both the techniques used and the items produced. Of secular sites in Britain, the Mote of Mark had a three-sided stone structure of uncertain function, perhaps a bench, associated with metalworking (Laing & Longley, 2006, 19). For the most part, the evidence from secular sites and from some ecclesiastical suggests that most of the metalworking was carried on out of doors.

Most sites in both Britain and Ireland can be classified as high status, though in a sense this has tended to be a chicken-and-egg argument, since the presence of ornamental non-ferrous metalworking on a site is often taken to imply a high status for its occupants.

Monastic workshops

Although most sites producing evidence of workshops are secular, a number of monastic sites have produced important evidence of industry. These include Clonmacnois, Co. Offaly (King, 1992); Reask, Co. Kerry (Fanning, 1981); Cathedral Hill, Armagh (Gaskell Brown & Harper, 1984); Tullylish, Co. Down (Ivens, 1987); Kilpatrick (Swan, 1995); Kiltiernan (Waddell & Clyne, 1995); Nendrum (Lawlor, 1925) and Movilla Abbey, Co. Down (Ivens, 1984). In Britain, there is evidence of industry from Iona (Barber, 1981), Portmahomack, Easter Ross (Carver, 2008), Whithorn (Hill, 1997) and Kingarth, Bute (Laing, Laing & Longley, 1998). In general, the evidence from monastic sites spans a longer period than the secular.

Monasteries in the Celtic areas were major land-owning centres, with lay clients who included high-ranking secular nobles. The population of lay dependants could be large and the layout of the buildings reflected the complexity of the organization.

Production workshops were arranged along streets, and markets were held. Monasteries with this organization were in effect the closest to towns that the Celts reached in the pre-Viking Age (Doherty, 1980; 1985; Ryan, 1989; Laing, 2006, 215). The model for such foundations can be found in Merovingian and Carolingian Gaul, where monasteries such as Centula-St Riquier had quarters occupied by artisans and dependent merchants (McKitterick, 1979).

A ninth-century plan survives of the layout of the monastery at St Gall in Switzerland. A route led to the artisans' areas to the south and west of the cloister where shoemakers, shield-makers, saddlers, sword-makers, wood-turners and tanners were all represented. At the end of the route lay the workshops of the goldsmiths, blacksmiths and fullers (Schwind, 1984). The arrangement at St Gall was modelled on Corbie in north-east France, for which there is documentary evidence of carpenters, masons, founders and parchment-makers. The swords and shields may seem incongruous products for a monastery, but they served as gifts for important laymen (Schwind, 1984, 115). A documentary reference indirectly suggests that there was a street or terrace at Kildare, with a comb-maker's shop in the tenth century (Doherty, 1985, 67).

On both secular and monastic sites the workshops tended to be away from the domestic occupation areas (presumably because of fire and pollution risk). In the case of the larger monasteries such as Clonmacnois and Portmahomack, metalworking areas were grouped with other industrial activities. At Clonmacnois, large areas on each side of a metalled road were given over to specialist workshops for iron, bone, lignite, glass, bronze and gold.

At Portmahomack there was a parchment makers' hall with yard, and a timber smith's hall, which was substantially built (then later rebuilt), set within an enclosure wall. Associated with this building were whetstones, mould fragments, crucibles and slag. The crucibles had been used for silver, copper, tin, zinc and lead. There were also fragments of a glass rod, glass droplets, lumps of raw glass and a vessel with a coating of yellow glass.

Among the items produced at Portmahomack were examples of church plate and studs inlaid with metal wire and coloured glass, similar to those on the Ardagh Chalice (Carver, 2008, 134). Similar components of liturgical vessels or shrines were produced at Clonmacnois.

On a few ecclesiastical sites there is evidence that (as at Portmahomack) particular buildings were designated for artisans. Thus at Reask, iron and non-ferrous metalworking was carried out in the same stone-built round hut. A stone hut seems to have been used at Nendrum in the same way. Post-holes of a timber structure were associated with metalworking at Armagh, and some sort of enclosure may have defined the metalworking at Kilpatrick (Swan, 1994–5).

Metalworking tools and equipment
There is evidence for most of the techniques and processes involved in the production of metalwork. Most of the tools that would have been needed have been found in excavations (Comber, 2004, 39–43). They include the tools necessary for creating the objects and for designing the ornament.

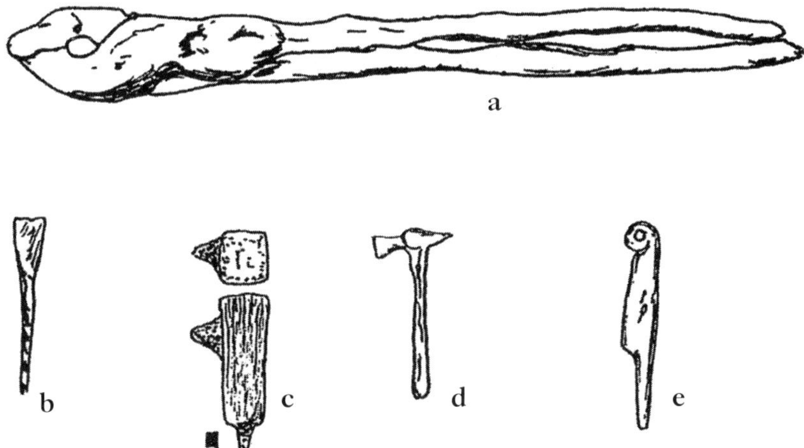

5.3 Metalworking tools. a: Tongs, Garranes, Co. Cork; b: stylus, Carraig Aille, Co. Limerick; c: anvil, Garryduff, Co. Cork; d: fine hammer, Lagore, Co. Meath; e: dividers, Garryduff (not to scale).

These include the (possible) dividers from Garryduff (O'Kelly, 1963) and the compass needles from Kilpatrick (Swan, 1994–5) (fig. 5.3). The most abundant finds are two-piece clay moulds (that were broken and discarded after being used once); the small, usually triangular, crucibles for melting the metal, and moulds for small ingots. Some lead models or dies for making moulds have also been found. The evidence for gold-working includes residue in crucibles, touchstones (for assaying the metal) and shallow trays for separating gold and silver. Other finds relate to glass and enamel working.

The only items of equipment that have not been found are a lathe and a tool for making trichinopoly work (a kind of circular knitting using wire). The techniques and tools of the smith have been discussed (Laing, 2006, chs 4–5; Comber, 2004).

The raw materials for metalworking
Gold is found as a raw material in fifteen of the thirty-two counties of Ireland, and Gerald of Wales called Ireland 'the golden island'. It is probable that the ore was obtained from relatively local sources (Whitfield, 1993, 127). Silver may initially have been derived from Roman scrap material – it may be significant that the Irish word for silver (*airgid*), is derived from the Roman word argenteus (Ryan, 2002, 5). This source

must have been in short supply by the seventh century, however. Although there are some places where argentiferous lead is found in Ireland, from which silver can be extracted, the later source was probably coins introduced by the Vikings. Copper mines were worked in Ireland, most notably those at Ross Island, Co. Kerry, which were being exploited around the eighth century AD (O'Brien, 2004). Tin would probably have come from Cornwall. More exotic materials such as amber (for which there is no known local source in the Celtic areas) and some of the pigments used in creating manuscripts, must have been imported.

There is very little evidence that the original smelting of the ores was carried out on the sites where the metalwork was produced – the raw materials seem to have been brought from outside the areas. Smelting furnaces of the early Christian period were associated with the copper mines on Ross Island (O'Brien, 2004), and there is the possibility that smelting was carried out at Moynagh Lough (Bradley, 1991).

SCULPTURE AND STONE MASONRY

A considerable amount of sculpture survives from the Celtic areas, though true relief sculpture was not developed until the eighth century. The earliest monuments (from the fifth century on) comprised either slabs with incised motifs (sometimes accompanying inscriptions), or work in false relief in which the ground was removed to leave the design in relief. It seems that this technique was developed from the later seventh century onwards, after which it was employed intermittently (as was incised work). The majority of relief sculpture in Ireland and Scotland belongs to the ninth and tenth centuries, and includes the series of High Crosses and Pictish cross-slabs (see below, p. 205).

Raw material for sculpture
There is good evidence to suggest that sculptures were generally made from locally quarried stone. This is hardly surprising, since with the exception of smaller grave-slabs, most of the sculptures are substantial enough to have required a team of men to move them from the quarry to the ox cart, wagon or boat in which they were to be transported to the place where they were to be erected. A similar team would have been needed to lift them off the transport and erect them on site. It is therefore probable that preliminary shaping and dressing would have been carried out at the quarry, with the more careful carving done on site.

Geological analysis of the large collection of Pictish monuments at St Vigeans, Angus, suggests that all the stone was obtained locally but outside a radius of 1km. The stones used at Aberlemno, Angus, and for the cross at Dupplin, Perthshire, were also interpreted as of local derivation (Miller & Ruckley, 2005).

The stone used for the sculptures at Portmahomack seems to have come from four sources, one of which was probably the adjacent beach. Several of the stones came from the same source as that of other major sculptures found in the Tarbat peninsula (on which Portmahomack is located). The stone for one grave-slab, however, seems to have been imported from further south in the peninsula (Carver, 2008, 103).

Few studies have been carried out in Wales and Ireland, but the evidence supports the use of local rock (Redknap & Lewis, 2007, 125). An analysis of the lithology of sculptures in south Wales suggested that with very rare exceptions the stone had been quarried within 5km of the site where they were erected. Only two or three had been brought from outside the immediate area. These include a cross from Glamorgan that was made from a stone not native to Wales, but which could have come from the area round Bath, Somerset (Redknap & Lewis, 2007).

In Ireland, all the crosses at Clonmacnois appear to have been carved from local material. A common source of very pure quartz sandstone was employed in making the Cross of Muiredach, Monasterboice; the crosses at Kells and the cross at Castlekieran, Co. Meath. The quarry may have been at Carrickleck, which is eighteen kilometres from Kells and twenty-two from Monasterboice (Stalley, 2007, 161). The nature of the locally available stone at Moone, Co. Kildare (granite) meant that there were serious limitations on the results that could be achieved (Henry, 1967).

Carving techniques

It is probable that once transported to the site, the initial marking out and carving would have been done with the stone lying flat or propped up on a bank of earth. The investigators of Conbelin's Cross, Margam, Glamorgan, concluded that the sculptor moved round the cross head to carve it (Redknap & Lewis, 2007, 125).

Cross-slabs were usually carved out of one piece of stone, but High Crosses were composite monuments. The techniques used in making and assembling High Crosses suggests very strongly that carpentry techniques were adapted to the stone medium. It is significant that free-standing crosses were preceded by timber ones, and *saers* worked in both wood and stone.

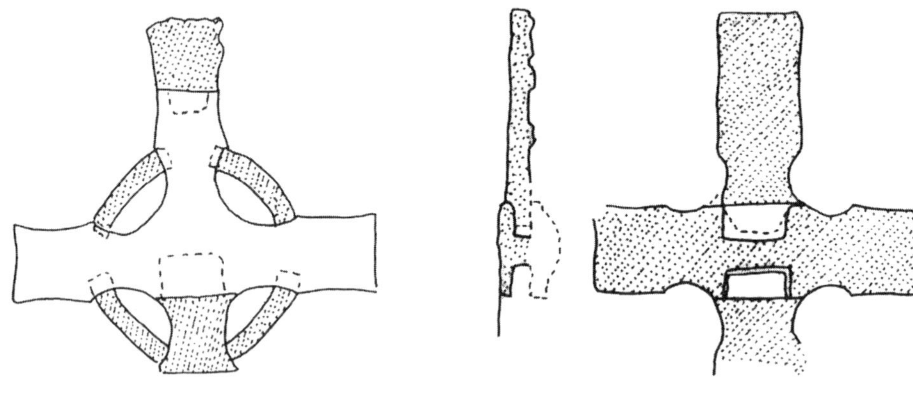

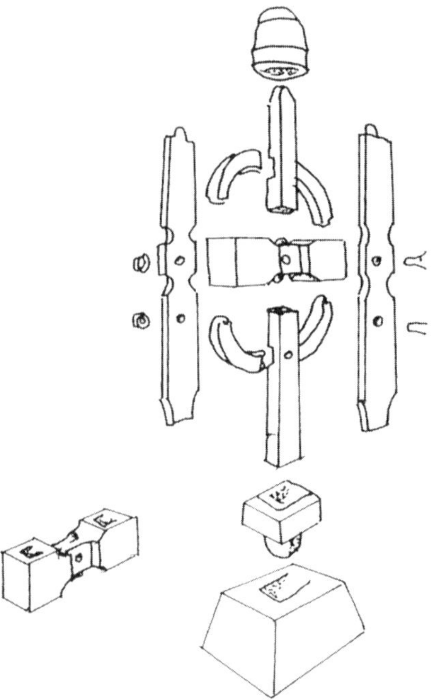

5.4 Constructional carpentry. Iona crosses and Ahenny cross (after Dorothy Kelly, 1991 and Douglas MacLean, 1995).

Techniques for assembly were varied. On St Oran's Cross on Iona (the earliest of the Iona crosses), the assembly involved three sections, the upper arm being tenoned down and the shaft tenoned up into the transom. The same method was employed on St John's Cross (Kelly, 1993, 223; MacLean, 1995a, 171). Tenoning from below was also used on the cross-head from Edzell, Angus (MacLean, 1995a, 171). Three other groups of carpentry-inspired crosses are distinguishable in the Celtic world – they copy different timber constructions. The most complex is that represented by the Ahenny crosses, Co. Tipperary which have a considerable number of pieces tenoned and pegged together (Kelly, 1991) (fig. 5.4).

The carving was laid out according to mathematical principals, using grids and circles (see below, p. 165). There is some evidence that the guide points were first drilled to mark the intersections of the grids or the centres of the circles. This is apparent even on the Pictish incised symbol stones (notably on a slab from Westfield, Fife). On this, the centres of the concentric circles on the symbols appear not merely as an element in the design (as they appear on some clearly free-hand circles on other stones) but as the centre points for compasses – a further arc of a circle for some unfinished element of the decoration appears below (Ritchie & Ritchie, 1984 for illustration of the stone).

In relief work the laying-out can be seen on, for example, the Pictish slab from Invergowrie, Angus, which depicts a drinking, mounted Pict angled as though riding uphill (fig. 5.5). The hocks of the horse are deeply drilled and the natural grain of the stone has been used as a base-line. Diagonals can be established running at forty-five degree angles, but a governing diagonal is also in place running at fifty-five degrees, which is the angle apparent on other monuments, including the Viking-period cross slab at Kirk Andreas in the Isle of Man (Lang, 1986, 158).

Blocking-out was employed, as shown by sections of unfinished interlace at Llandyfaelog Fach and Llangyfelach, south Wales, where median lines were cut on the interlace after the broad outlines had been blocked out (Redknap & Lewis, 2007, 126).

Unfinished sculptures

Some information about the carving of monuments is provided by unfinished examples, such as that from Errigal Keerogue, Co. Tyrone, and the more prominent Unfinished Cross at Kells (fig. 5.6). In both instances, the head was designed using compass circles. At Kells, the laying and blocking-out of the panels on the Unfinished Cross was done next and in

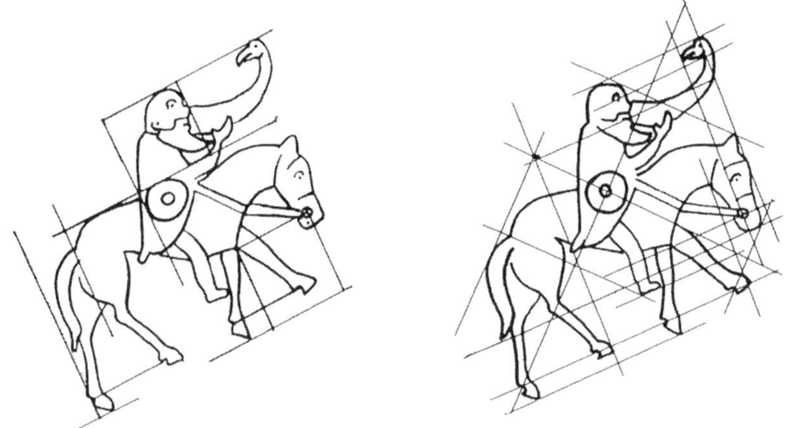

5.5 Diagram of constructional lines used at Invergowrie, Angus
(after James Lang, 1986).

point of fact was all that was done on the east face. In doing this, the depth
of the proposed relief was evidently considered, higher relief requiring
stone to be retained higher than the level of the moulding. The blocking-
out employed standard units of measurement – the panels seem to have
been divided into halves, thirds or quarters (Gelly, 1995, 165). The laying
out of the design used fixed points, which sometimes involved drill work
and in the crosses of the ninth and tenth centuries, probably high-quality
iron tools (Gelly, 1995, 158). Then, somewhat surprisingly, the interlace
on the ring seems to have been done along with the Crucifixion on the
face. Three figures were simply roughly incised on the north arm, but may
have been meant to be the three Marys being met by the angel on Easter
Sunday (Harbison, 1994a, 75). The south arm is simply marked by some
incisions where figures were intended to be placed.

It is very possible that templates, perhaps of leather, were used
to reproduce fixed elements in the decorative scheme. This has been
clearly demonstrated for early medieval sculpture in England (Bailey,
1980, ch. 10). Few comparable studies have been carried out on Celtic
sculpture, but there is good reason to assume the use of templates. In
Monmouthshire, the angels on each side of the St Arvans 1 cross seem to
have been produced using a template which was simply reversed to carve
each one (Redknap & Lewis, 2007, 126). Gelly has suggested that
templates as such were not necessarily employed on Irish High Crosses,
but that figures were created using a standard plan and a grid. Standing
profile men appear not only to have been similarly posed, but to follow the

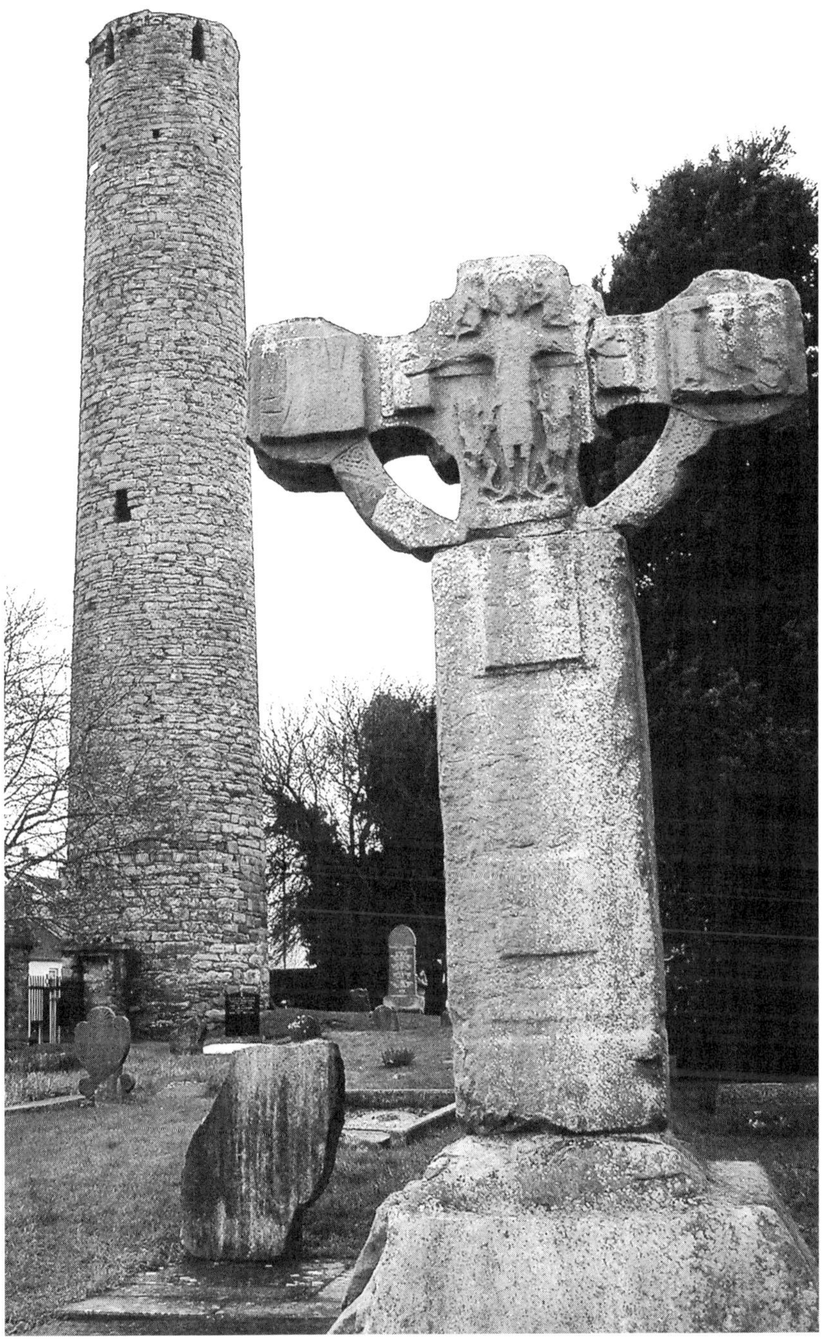

5.6 Unfinished Cross, Kells, Co. Meath (photo: C. Loveluck).

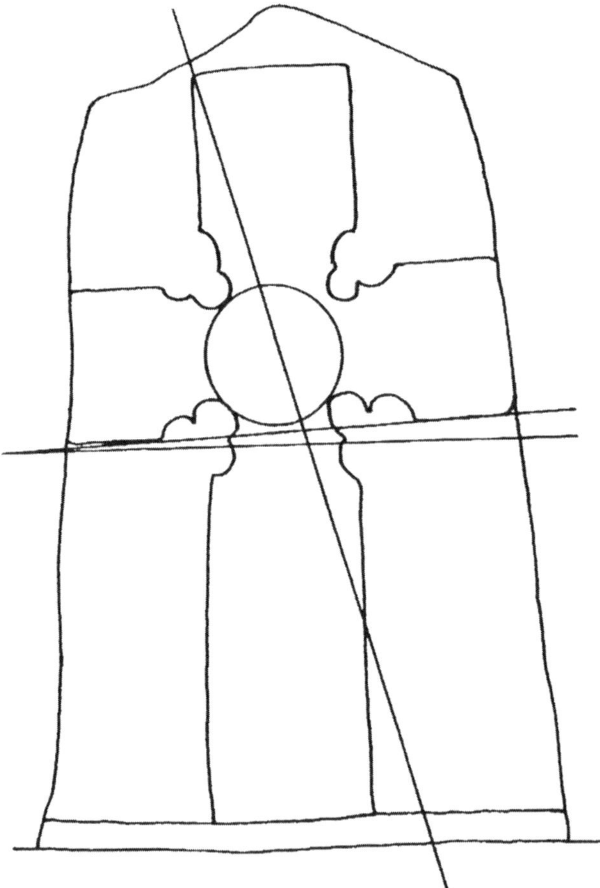

5.7 Glamis Manse stone, Angus, errors in layout.

same measurements. At Durrow, on the Cross of the Scriptures at Clonmacnois and on the Market Cross at Kells, the figures have 4-inch heads, 6-inch torsos and 3.5- to 4-inch lower legs (Gelly, 1995, 161). It is likely that a design was drawn out before carving, possibly directly on the stone, but possibly also using a cloth which could be punched through to provide the guide points (Gelly, 1995, 165).

Sometimes sculptors seem to have made mistakes in their layouts. This was the case with the slab known as Glamis Manse, Angus. Here, the right arm of the cross is higher than the left, and the area on the left arm, which contains interlace, is smaller than that on the right. There is a difference in the width of the upper lobe of the armpit on the left and right; the interlace on each arm differs, and the axis is skewed. These features all suggest that the design was laid out freehand (Laing, 2001b, 226) (fig. 5.7).

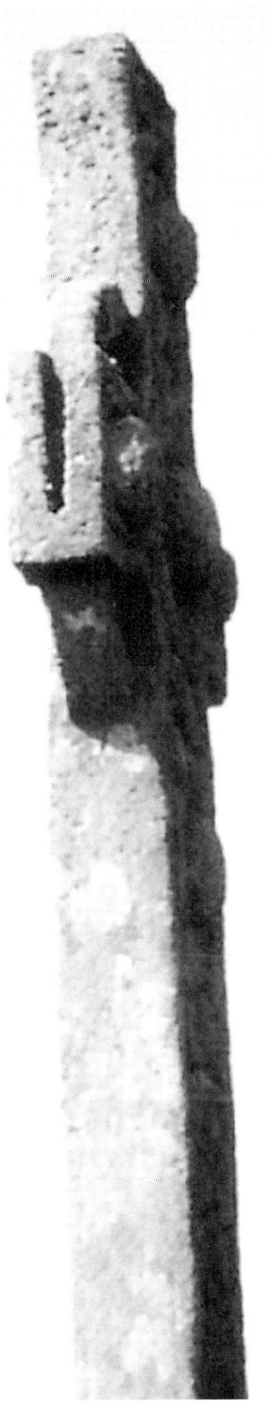

5.8 Slot in arm of St Martin's Cross, Iona.

Stone-carving tools

Stone-carving tools were probably similar to those employed by modern sculptors – wooden mallets, various iron chisels, punches and hammer picks. The techniques for cutting letters in Welsh inscriptions appear to have been fairly varied; some letters being chased, others picked or stabbed (Redknap & Lewis, 2007, 122–3). Relief sculpture seems to have been cut using pick hammers ('jadds') and points (point chisels). It is also possible that drilled holes were used, the spaces between them being picked. This is apparent at Llangynwyd, Glamorgan, and on Margam 2 (Redknap & Lewis, 2007, 125).

Excavations on the site of Sueno's Stone have revealed the post-holes of the temporary supporting structure used to lift the stone into position (James, 2005, 102). Several Pictish stones have projecting bosses on the sides, which may have been to aid the ropes or lifting gear used to hoist the sculptures upright.

Additions to sculptures in other materials

Features to be noted on a few crosses are the sockets that appear to have been intended for additions. Thus the St Martin's Cross on Iona has slots on the arms which may have been to take metal or wooden extensions, or ornamental panels (Fisher, 2001, 133) (fig. 5.8). Holes have similarly been drilled in the arms of the cross from Dysert O'Dea, Co. Clare, which dates from the twelfth century, and there are mortise sockets in the sides of the shaft of the cross at Drumcliff, Co. Sligo. The phenomenon of metal attachments to sculptures is well-attested in Anglo-Saxon work (Bailey, 1996a, 6–10). In Wales, Margam 2, Glamorgan, may have had metal fittings on the side bosses (Redknap & Lewis, 2007, 129).

Painted sculptures

The final stage in the production of sculpture involved painting. Traces of what may be white gesso under-painting survive in some of the incisions on the cross slabs from Meigle, Angus. However, whether this belongs to the period when the stones were rebuilt into the church walls or from the original use could only be ascertained by the analysis of the pigment. In Wales, the only evidence for painting is from Llantwit Major 2, on which traces of black were detected (Redknap & Lewis, 2007, 128).

It is extremely likely that the blank panels on some of the monuments were originally intended for painted ornament, probably inscriptions.

Workshops and groups of sculptures

As with metalworking, characteristic types of ornament and design that occur within a restricted area, point to the existence of 'Schools' of sculpture.

In Ireland, a Clonmacnois school of sculpture has been defined, which includes monuments at Clonmacnois, Bealin, and a shaft from Banagher (Hicks, 1980). It has also been suggested that the crosses at Ahenny, Kilkieran and related cross bases at Lorrha are products of a local workshop tradition which had connections with Clonmacnois (Edwards, 1983). Various groups of crosses have been defined in Ireland: a Midlands and North Leinster Group; an Ulster Group; a South Leinster Group; a Bealin-Banagher Group; a Tipperary-Kilkenny Group; and a West Munster Group (Harbison, 1992, ch. 9). Henry distinguished seven groups which cannot be meaningfully defined as Schools (1964, 21–34), though Henry employed the term 'Monasterboice School' (1967, 156). There has been wide acceptance that the crosses at Kells represent a workshop tradition. A recent study (Stalley, 2007) has suggested that it is possible to distinguish a 'Monasterboice Master' who worked on the Midland Scripture Crosses, notably those at Monasterboice, Durrow and Clonmacnois. Stalley has also suggested that the Market Cross and Tower Cross at Kells may have been by the same master's hand.

In Scotland, a number of distinct groups of sculptures can be distinguished, which appear to be the products of particular workshop traditions. These include the tenth- to eleventh-century sculptures at St Andrews (Hay Fleming, 1931); the Whithorn 'School' (Craig, 1991); the Govan or Strathclyde 'School' of roughly contemporaneous date (Ritchie (ed.), 1990; Driscoll, O'Grady & Forsyth, 2001); the earlier Pictish workshop traditions associated with Abernethy (Proudfoot, 1997; Harden, 1995; Meyer, 2005); Rosemarkie; Meigle (Ritchie, 1995, 1997b); St Vigeans, Kirriemuir (Alcock, 1998) and Aberlemno (Trench-Jellicoe, 1999a, 616; Laing, 2000a; Laing, 2001a). In the east of Scotland, an Iona tradition is recognizable, with outlying products such as the Kildalton Cross on Islay.

In Wales, workshop traditions are associated with St Davids (Edwards, 2007, 84–87); St Dogmaels (Edwards, 2007, 87); Penally (Edwards, 2007, 88); Carew and Nevern (Edwards, 2007, 89–90); Margam and Llantwit Major (Edwards, 2007). These seem to belong to a series of related workshop traditions (Redknap & Lewis, 2007, 115). Another workshop tradition seems to link the 'panelled cartwheel crosses' that are concentrated in the Vale of Glamorgan (Redknap & Lewis, 2007, 117). Four of the Monmouthshire cross-slabs (Caerleon 1, St Arvans 1, Christchurch 1 and Llan-wern 1) may have been the work of the same sculptor, operating in the tenth century (Redknap & Lewis, 2007, 117).

MANUSCRIPTS

The evidence for the production of manuscripts is very limited. Wax tablets were used for writing, as shown by those from Springmount, Ireland (Armstrong & Macallister, 1920). Most written material was in book form – codices or volumes of pages which had generally replaced rolls in the later Roman period. Although papyrus was known in the ancient world and was used in the east Mediterranean, the material used for books was vellum (untanned animal skin, ideally from a calf), which after preparation was folded in a traditional manner into bundles (quires) which were then bound.

A workshop believed to have been used in the production of vellum for manuscripts has been found at Portmahomack, where a large timber building and associated yard was shown by excavation to have been in use from the late seventh to late eighth century. Lime was obtained from sea shells burnt in a reducing atmosphere, and used to preserve hide. The hides were thinned and scraped with iron knives, two of which were found, associated with whetstones. This part of the operation was carried out inside the building. The skins were further tawed (tanned white) and taken out to the yards for stretching and finishing on a wooden frame. To avoid ripping the skins by perforating them before attaching them to the stretcher, each corner was wrapped round a pebble (forty-two were found) and then tied with a leather thong attached to a peg. On this site a cattle metapodial was used for the peg. The taut skin was rubbed with stones (three pumice rubbers and ten burnishing stones were found) and then finished with a skiving knife (lunellarium), which had a curved blade to allow the skin to be depressed without being cut. One of these came from the site (Carver & Spall, 2004; Carver, 2008, 122–5).

There is reason to believe that monasteries did not necessarily possess their own vellum production facilities. It has been pointed out that the vellum used in the Book of Durrow was inferior, which might be because it had to be bought in (Neuman de Vegvar, 1984, 84).

Scriptoria
There is little direct evidence for the scriptoria in which the manuscripts were written – none is known from Portmahomack for example. Oyster shells found at Glastonbury, Somerset, appear to have been used to hold pigments, and presumably must have been associated with a scriptorium.

Pigments for manuscripts
Recent work on the Book of Kells has identified some materials used by the artists. It is likely that all the pigments available to Insular illuminators were used, since the range is closely comparable to that on the Lindisfarne Gospels, the Stockholm Codex Aureus and the Barberini Gospels (Fuchs & Oltrogger, 1994, 149).

The most significant colour is yellow, mainly derived from orpiment. Red is derived from inorganic red lead. These are the most commonly used pigments in medieval manuscripts, and are also known from Antique and medieval pigment recipe texts. Other shades were derived from yellow and red ochre. The green appears to have been derived from a copper pigment, probably malachite. Other pigments included vergaut (a mixture of orpiment and indigo) and sap green (from the sap of leeks, cabbage and lilies). The origins of the purple and pink colours are less certain – the most likely source for the purple being a purple-coloured dye. Pink was probably achieved by mixing purple dye with chalk. The most likely purple dye was folium. Black came from iron gall, white from chalk. Brown was produced from brown ochre, iron gall ink, or a mixture of vergaut and iron gall ink. Several agents were used to produce blue. The main one was indigo, but a blue was also achieved by mixing lapis lazuli, indigo and chalk. The binding agent was probably egg yolk in the case of the red and pink (Fuchs & Oltrogger, 1994).

Analysis has also been carried out on the pigments employed in the Book of Durrow, the Book of Armagh, the Book of Dimma and the Book of Mulling. These, and books such as the Lindisfarne Gospels from Insular sources other than Ireland, show a similar range of pigments. The same range, particularly red lead and orpiment, is found in a wide range of manuscripts from European contexts from the fifth century onwards (Fuchs & Oltrogger, 1994, 146). Methods of preparing red lead were discussed by Pliny the Elder (*c*.AD23–79), and recipes for artificial green copper pigments were provided by Theophrastus (371–287BC), Pliny and Vitruvius (the first-century-AD Roman architect and author of *De Architectura*, 25BC).

Glazes in manuscripts

A feature of the Book of Kells is an apparently unique method of applying glazes. This usually involved the over-painting of a colour with a translucent dye, but on the Christ miniature in the Book of Kells (fo. 32v), a more complex method was used. As was standard practice, the outlines were drawn in black ink (iron gall) after which one colour was normally added in the appropriate areas, before the final drawing was done on top. On the Christ miniature page, however, the border for the capitals was drawn with orpiment, then filled in with red lead, which was in turn covered with pink. More complex still was the painting of the peacocks. The left peacock was painted with a blue body, ink lines and red dots; the right-hand side peacock was painted green. Over-painting was employed firstly to make the two peacocks match one another, and secondly to give a sense of perspective – each bird had one leg over-glazed with purple and the other over-glazed with opaque pink, applied unevenly (Fuchs & Oltrogger, 1994, 151).

DESIGN CONSTRAINTS ON CELTIC ARTISTS/ARTISANS

Probably as a result of the way art was organized, all Celtic Christian art, whatever the medium, was designed according to mathematical principles and used standard units of measurement. The scheme began with objects and was extended to architecture from the eighth century on, when the Celts began building churches in stone. Cocke and Kidson, writing about medieval architecture, noted that 'The essential principal was that all major dimensions should form themselves into a mathematical system in the sense of being related to one another by means of ratios. To get things started, a fundamental dimension, nearly always a width, was chosen first ...' (1993, 62).

It has been argued that poetry and artistic design followed geometric principles. This has been demonstrated in the case of the design of Insular manuscript pages and the composition of Anglo-Saxon poetry. In early medieval Europe, using mathematical principles in constructional plans was seen to replicate spiritual truths and thus fit into Christian metaphysical doctrine and theological beliefs (Stevick, 1994a, 13). Ratios employing integers smaller than ten are arithmetical proportions; those expressing irrational numbers (such as $\sqrt{2}$, $\sqrt{5}$ or φ) are geometrical (Stevick, 1994, 211).

On the simplest level, in creating frames, the formula of the height in relation to the width is the equivalent of the diagonal in relation to one of the sides, that is: $\sqrt{2}{:}1$. This is the first of the 'two true measures of geometry'. It can be created simply using an underlying square which is quartered. This can then be used to create the necessary form by one of several methods, with or without the use of compasses (Stevick, 1994a, 17). The method is used in the Book of Kells, the Macdurnan Gospels and the Book of Mulling.

The second 'true measure of geometry' is the 'Golden Section' or 'Golden Ratio', which is the 'division of a line so that one segment is to the other as that is to the whole' (*Chambers Dictionary*). In arithmetical terms this is expressed as 3:2 (0.618). Its opposite counterpart, the 'Golden Number', was defined in the thirteenth century on the basis of the rate at which rabbits left to themselves would multiply, each number in the sequence representing the sum of the two previous numbers. It was calculated that even with an infinite number of rabbits, they would only multiply by 1.618 times what they numbered originally. The resulting number is 1.618 (or φ). It is a governing factor at which in nature all things multiply – in shells each spiral is 1.618 times the radius of the one before (Carver, 2008, 130). In manuscripts it is used in determining the page sizes and the area occupied by the text. It can be seen, for example, in the Macdurnan Gospels, where the portrait pages were constructed using a square as a base, from which Golden Section rectangles were constructed, using the long side. The frame's dimensions are established by doubling the measure by which the square was extended (Stevick, 1994a).

The mathematical principles of design are very well exemplified by the Book of Durrow, where asymmetry is apparent on the Cross page (fo. iv).

Detailed study of the Book of Kells has shown a similar geometry employed on the full-page illuminations, which used a commodular construction employing a circle and a cross (Stevick, 1994b).

In metalwork, too, similar mathematical principles were employed. It has been suggested that a unit of measurement of 9mm was employed in the design of the ninth-century Westness Brooch (Stevenson, 1989, 242), and a similar measurement was employed on some late-tenth-century bossed brooches in Ireland. Such a unit seems to have been used in designing the Hunterston Brooch, which followed the geometry of circle and square employed in the Book of Kells (Whitfield, 1999). The Irish Laws indicate that various items made of precious metal were of regular dimensions (Kelly, 1988, 583), which would support the idea of fixed units. Whitfield has suggested that 9mm represents a third of an 'inch' of 27mm – effectively a twelfth of a Roman foot (1999, 311). It is to be noted that the guide-points for laying out the designs on penannular brooches are apparent from motif pieces from Dunadd and Nendrum, and are also apparent on a brooch from Loch Glashan crannog, Argyll. A similar geometry, employing compasses and straight edge, is apparent in the Tara Brooch. It may be that the design was created in parallel with some Anglo-Saxon disc brooches, which display the same kind of design characteristics (Whitfield, 2001a). A book shrine, the Soiscél Molaise, uses the same kind of commodular construction as the pages in the Book of Kells (Stevick, 1994b, 243).

The design methods used in constructing Irish High Crosses have been extensively studied. Stevick has argued that they were designed using constructive geometry proceeding from a given measure (1999; 2001, 227). There have been suggestions that the unit used in calculations was the inch or half-inch of imperial measurement (Lang, 1986; Gelly, 1995, 160) but more recent study has suggested that, as was proposed for metalwork, the unit of reckoning was in fact based on the Roman foot (Gelly, 1996, 138). The diagonal of a square based on the foot seems to have been particularly favoured as an ideal. This was used to follow design based on the well-known principles laid down by Vitruvius, including both rational and irrational ratios. Of these $1:\sqrt{2}$ was most commonly employed, and is used on crosses in both Ireland and Scotland.

Fifths also seem too have been employed in architecture, sculpture, and metalwork. The discs from Donore, Co. Meath, seem to have been designed by dividing the circular area on the disc into six, using three diameters, after which each was divided into fifths, and five circles were marked out, each with a radius one-fifth of the circular area. The roundels on the circles were surrounded by voluted trumpet spirals, made from circles half the size of each roundel (Ryan, 1995, 27, fig. 3).

The same principle was employed in architecture. The original structure of a building used as a smith's hall in the monastery at Portmahomack, for example, was laid out according to the same mathematical principles that can be seen in the design of gospel pages or sculptures. Here, the perimeter wall and the timber structure within were laid out as a combination of a semi-circle and a trapezium, in accordance with the Golden Section (Carver, 2008, 128–35).

CHAPTER 6

Patrons

Closely connected with the role and status of the artist or artisan in society were the patrons. To appreciate the art fully, it is important to know who commissioned the works, why they were commissioned and how the ideas and aspirations of the patrons influenced the form of the art itself. The opportunities and needs for expensive art objects as status symbols and gifts were numerous. Patronage is distinct from market forces, which operate at even the lowest and most impoverished level of society (whether with a monetary or a bartering system), and are often more concerned with need or perceived need rather than ideals, status or ostentatious display.

In the fifth and sixth centuries, art patrons were chiefly concerned with commissioning items that reflected their secular rank and status and that could be gifts to their followers. With the growing role and wealth of the Church in society, ecclesiastics became leading patrons, and the works they commissioned entirely reflected ecclesiastical concerns. Similarly, from the late eighth century, secular patrons were increasingly involved in commissioning works for the Church, and increasingly, subject matter was chosen for its relevance to both an ecclesiastical audience and secular authority.

THE SOCIAL CONTEXT OF CELTIC PATRONAGE

Society in all the Celtic areas centred on the kings and high kings who ruled over a nobility within a tribal structure. The majority of people were probably farmers, with slaves at the bottom rank. In the middle was a rank of professionals (*áes dána*) that included poets, legal scholars and experts in genealogy and history, as well as druids – and skilled smiths.

The Irish law codes of the seventh and more particularly eighth century provide a valuable insight into the functioning of Irish society. Later Welsh laws suggest a similar social organization in Wales. The evidence for the different areas reflects broadly similar societies – for example, generally similar kinship systems are described in both Ireland and Wales (Charles-Edwards, 1993, 477). However, such deductions should be treated with caution.

The Irish law codes show the importance of the clan (*cenél*, or extended family) and the lineage or kin-group (*fine*): all the males who had a great-grandfather in common, up to and including second cousins. Within the fine each member might be in part responsible for another members actions – if a man killed someone and could not pay the 'honour price' the *fine* was liable for it. The clan maintained its own warrior aristocracy, which took part in battles and cattle-raids.

Clientship was important – the 'lord' handed over a 'gift' (generally cattle, produce or labour) in return for defined dues (Patterson, 1991; 1995). Over-kings (notably the kings of provinces), demanded tribute from those of lesser status (Gibson, 1995). However, by the Viking Age, high kings (*ard-rí*) appear to have outranked them. Their legal position is unclear. In Ireland, kings ruled over the *túath* (tribal territory), which could include members of more than one clan (Byrne, 1973, ch. 2). Geographically, the *túath* typically extended to an area about 16km across, and was comparable to baronies in the later middle ages (Patterson, 1991, 88–93).

In the sixth to eighth centuries, evidence suggests that there were between 100 and 150 kings in Ireland (Byrne, 1973, 7). The king led his nobles and freemen into battle but had no powers of legislation. He protected his *túath*, and presided over the *oenach* (the assembly of those with political power). In return, the nobility were obliged to provide him with hostages, tribute and hospitality as he travelled about his lands.

With the adoption of Christianity, bishops had the same honour-price as kings. It is clear from this structure that patronage of the arts – producing fine objects as gifts and as status symbols would have been of prime importance in Celtic society.

Patronage of skilled crafts: fifth to eighth century
In the fifth and sixth centuries the patrons of art in the Celtic areas were from the upper levels of society and the driving forces behind patronage were shared by many societies in migration-period Europe. By having in their employment particularly skilled 'men of art', the patrons would also have increased their own stature in the eyes of their peers (Helms, 1993, 68–9).

The overlords used skilled craftsmanship to reinforce their status by re-affirming traditions. It was therefore important to employ an art which looked back to the past (Helms, 1993, 17–18). The first requirements would have been for the insignia of rank (such as items of regalia including brooches and pins), for particularly fine weaponry, horse-trappings, or the mounts for drinking vessels to display in the feasting hall. Next in importance came the adornment of women, which also had to signal their rank in the social order. Thirdly, objects had to be created that could be used as gifts. These could range from swords and other weaponry to items of adornment.

The cost of artworks

The Celts did not use coinage until the time of the Vikings (and then only to a limited extent, in Ireland). The economy functioned on barter and accepted values were accorded to, for example, cattle, with major values being expressed in terms of numbers of cattle.

While the works of art had to reinforce traditional values, the rarity of the materials from which they were made and the sumptuousness of overall effect was vitally important. The barbarians of migration-period Europe were very much concerned with this, and the financial value of the materials used was in itself important (Dodwell, 1982, 25). Importance would have been placed on the exotic: materials obtained from outside the area under the control of the ruler were certainly prized (Helms, 1993; Laing, J., 2000, 103). Significantly, status could have been increased by seeking the services of artisans from outside their immediate area.

Artisans gained prestige through travelling widely; the journeying to external regions being as important as the materials and ideas that were brought back (Helms, 1993, 32–3). It is noteworthy that amber (probably from Scandinavia) was the most common stone used in inlays in ornate penannular brooches.

The equivalent material in Anglo-Saxon England was garnet, which was also not found naturally in Britain (except in small pieces unsuited for cutting into inlays), but obtained from the East by way of Byzantium and the Merovingian and Carolingian worlds. Occasionally, pieces of garnet arrived in Scotland, presumably on Anglo-Saxon artefacts such as the sword pyramid from Western Craigie, West Lothian (Proudfoot & Aliaga-Kelly, 1996, 5) and the gold and garnet stud from Dunadd, Argyll (Lane & Campbell, 2000). Such a source must account for eleven garnets on the terminal of a silver penannular brooch from the hoard at Croy, Inverness, which had clearly been recycled (Laing, 1993a, no. 22).

An insight into the range of prized sumptuary art in the Celtic world can be seen from the list of equipment in the ninth-century Irish saga of *Táin Bó Fraích* which was provided by his mother for Fraech and his retinue: 'Fifty blue mantles … with four dark grey corners on each mantle; and a red gold (animal) brooch with each mantle, and brilliant-white tunics with twisting animals in gold all around them; and fifty silver shields with golden rims round them, and a palace-candle [i.e., spear] in the hand of each person, with fifty rivets of white-gold on each one. Fifty coils of refined gold around each one of them. Their butts of carbuncle, and their tips of precious stones; they blazed at night as though they were rays of sunlight. And fifty golden-hilted swords with them; and a light grey horse under each man, with golden bridle bits. A silver peytrel with golden bells under the throat of each horse. Fifty purple saddlecloths with silver threads trailing from them, with gold and silver pins with animal patterns on their heads. Fifty white-gold wands with a golden crook on the end of each one. And seven greyhounds on silver chains with a golden apple between each greyhound. Bronze greaves on them; there was no colour which was not represented on them' (trans. Meid, 1967, 1–2).

Allowing for this to contain some poetic exaggeration, all these creations were within the capabilities of Celtic artisans – indeed, there is some evidence for silver-covered shields from the Pictish hoard at Norrie's Law, Fife (Laing, 1994, 36).

Association of rank with artwork types
Irish law codes, though slightly more prosaic in their descriptions, are quite clear about the association of certain types of item with particular ranks in society. An account of the laws concerning fosterage, includes a commentary on the text, which notes that if the fosterling were the son of a king, he should have swords with silver on their scabbards, and hurling sticks bound with bronze. Those of lesser rank should have tin instead of silver on their scabbards, and an inferior grade of bronze on their hurling sticks. The laws also set out that the brooch of a king's son should be of gold with crystal inset, while lesser ranks should have silver (Gillies, 1981, 79). The commentary is a later addition to the original law codes, but was presumably still valid.

In early seventh-century England, the extent of royal and noble patronage of artisans can be seen in the assemblage of artefacts from Sutton Hoo, Suffolk (Evans, 1994); Prittlewell, Essex, and that from Taplow, Bucks (Bruce-Mitford, 1974). Similar collections have been found in continental Europe in the burials of Childeric at Tournai (Brulet, 1966) and Arnegunde at St Denis (if the burial was actually of the queen and not a noblewoman in her circle (Werner, 1964). It is this type of patronage that led to the creation of early Anglo-Saxon gold-work (Coatsworth & Pinder, 2002). There are, however, no pagan burials of the fifth to seventh centuries in the Celtic areas which can be compared, only isolated artefacts, so there is no hard evidence that this pattern was followed in the Celtic areas.

Gift exchange of artworks

Some documentary sources relate to the prizing and distribution of works of high craftsmanship in Celtic society. The distribution of wealth by the leader to his followers could either be as a reward for services already given, or as a kind of advance payment for services expected to be rendered in the future (Evans, 1997, 109). Such distribution of largesse (matched in the distribution of booty) served several functions. The more magnificent the gifts, the more readily the leader could recruit to his service. The *Gododdin*, a very early poem attributed to Aneurin and probably dating in origin to the period between AD550 and 570 (Evans, 1997, 148), describes the leader Mynyddog as *mymynfawr* ('wealthy') and extols the range of his largesse (Evans, 1997, 110). The same poem refers to Llif, who 'gave a bright array [of objects], shining, to the brave' (line 257). Another warrior listed in the *Gododdin* was Gwefryfawr, who was noted for 'wearing a brooch, leading in battle, a wolf in fury, the sharing torqued warrior gained amber beads' (lines 49–50).

The *Gododdin* refers to a goldsmith, and repeatedly refers to torcs as marks of status. The poems of Taliesin (apparently first composed in the mid-sixth century), reflect a similar situation, in which the giving of wealth was as important as its personal display. Taliesin says of Owain, one of the key figures in his poems, that 'although he hoarded wealth … for his soul's sake he gave it' (Pt X, 21–2). The acquisition and distribution of booty was a major element in the operation of early medieval war bands – the Laws of Hwel Dda seem to suggest that the lord kept one third of the spoils of war and distributed two thirds to his followers (Richards, 1954, 112). The process of capturing and distributing booty was no doubt a factor in the dissemination of design elements in the repertoire of early medieval smiths.

Memorial stones

The earliest inscribed stones of Wales (which rarely have ornament beyond their inscription) mostly appear to be either the memorial stones of a secular élite, or used to demarcate the limits of their lands. In some cases they appear to be located with a sense of continuity from prehistoric and Roman remains (Edwards, 2001, 38–9). The same can be said for the memorial stones of southern Scotland, the earliest of which commemorate a similar secular nobility (with women, however, named more often than in Wales). The stones were clearly generated in a framework of Roman memorial tradition (Forsyth, 2006, 130), a situation repeated in south-west England (Okasha, 1993). It may have been the driving force behind the creation of the earliest Pictish symbol stones, which could have been both funerary and on occasion demarcatory of territory (Driscoll, 1988, 176–88). The ogham stones in Ireland proclaim a similar patronage (Charles-Edwards, 2000, 173). While not strictly speaking art, these monuments were all the work of artisans who are unlikely to have been employed solely in carving inscriptions.

ECCLESIASTICAL PATRONAGE

In the sixth and seventh centuries, when patronage was sometimes turned towards the creation of specifically Christian artefacts, the products were essentially pagan status symbols given a Christian meaning. Ecclesiastical metalwork reflects the styles and techniques of lay craftsmanship: the Ardagh Chalice displays the range of techniques and ornament seen in the Tara Brooch, which has been assumed (though not necessarily correctly) to have been produced for a lay patron. The best documented example of metalwork that was produced for both lay and ecclesiastical patrons, is contained in Dado's *Life of St Eligius*. The saint is said to have made vessels of silver and gold as well as jewels for the king. He is recorded as producing these in what appears to have been a sunken floor building (Roth, 1986, 676). St Eligius worked for several royal patrons in the seventh century, producing gold-work and coins (James, 1988, 196–7). Some of his metalwork for lay and ecclesiastical patrons seems to have survived until the French Revolution, but the only extant record of his work (apart from a few coins) are pictures of the chalice he made for the abbey of Chelles (Lasko, 1971, fig. 89). Clearly, his skills extended to the production of cloisonné work as well as more simply wrought gold and silver.

In the eighth and probably the seventh century, the Church was the main patron of ecclesiastical art. Alongside the secular memorial stones of southern Scotland were other monuments which displayed more art and which were clearly ecclesiastical in origin. They commemorate ecclesiastics (notably at Kirkmadrine, Galloway and Curghie) but even though they are associated with church sites, they are not all funerary memorials (notably the St Peter stone at Whithorn, Galloway: Thomas, 1992). In Wales, uninscribed cross-decorated stones began to be set up in the seventh century, and are associated with churchyards. Most are probably grave-markers for Christian, probably ecclesiastical, dead but some were probably used to demarcate church land in the way that earlier monuments had demarcated secular holdings (Edwards, 2000, 39). A similar explanation may account for the simple cross-marked stones in northern Scotland (Henderson, 1987b), which are not obviously associated with monastic foundations.

CHANGING PATTERNS OF PATRONAGE

Lay patronage for the production of objects used in status-building in secular society undoubtedly continued through the eighth century and beyond. Lay patrons must have continued to commission items of personal adornment that declared their status, most notably the ornate penannular brooches and dress pins that have survived from the eighth to the tenth centuries.

From the seventh century, kings and other laity only indirectly patronized the ecclesiastical arts, their patronage being felt through their general support of the Church and in particular monastic foundations. Kings and monasteries co-operated to support one another's authority (Byrne, 1973, 40), and hagiography is full of accounts of successful partnerships between kings and saints. In many cases the tales not only reflect the situation in the seventh century, but were also symbolic of the political relationships that operated from the ninth to twelfth centuries (Bitel, 1990, 157). The major monasteries were frequently closely associated with powerful lay families. At Iona for example, the patrons were members of the royal dynasty of Cenel nGabráin (Fraser, 2004), and at Clonmacnois patronage came from the dynasty of the Connacht kings. Armagh, the dominant monastery in Ireland, claimed to have enjoyed the patronage of the dominant royal dynasty, the Uí Néill (Bitel, 1990, 157).

As far as is known, the laity in the seventh or eighth century did not often directly commission specific sculptures or manuscripts. The major artworks of the eighth century were products of monastic workshops and scriptoria, some of which were run by laymen in the service of the monastery. Individual abbots were probably the specific patrons insofar as they ordered particular commissions. For the most part, the patrons remain anonymous, since it would have been against their beliefs to seek status for themselves by declaring their hand in commissions.

The Bealin Cross, Co. Westmeath, appears to name an abbot of Clonmacnois, Tuathgall, who lived *c*.800 and may have been its patron

(Harbison, 1992, 355; 1994a, 24). Apart from this, the only works which carry the names of individuals in the eighth century are funerary monuments naming clerics. The monastery at Clonmacnois is known to have enjoyed the patronage of the kings of Connacht in the eighth century. The long series of cross-incised slabs begin around the mid-eighth century, and it is possible that the earliest datable example was set up in memory of Ailill Medraige (who died in 764), presumably on the order of the abbot (Fanning & Ó hÉaildhe, 1980, 7; Ó Floinn, 1995, 252; but not all accept this identification). Other kings were allegedly buried at Clonmacnois, but the evidence is late, literary, and suspect (Swift, 2003). Swift has pointed out that of over 700 slabs surviving at Clonmacnois, only one certainly commemorated a king (of the mid-tenth century). Where a named person is identifiable on the other stones, most are churchmen (Swift, 2000, 119). Swift also pointed out that where similar cross-slabs are found on local church sites, for example in Islay or in the middle Shannon basin, they were on ecclesiastical estates belonging to major monasteries. They were the monuments of both clerics and non-clerics who could draw on the services of artisans from the mother monastery. In essence, they were the markers of the graves of dedicated Christians and the funding was undoubtedly provided by the taxes imposed by the mother houses (Swift, 2003, 120).

In seventh-century Wales, king Cadfan was buried at Llangadwaladr, Anglesey, *c*.625 with a plain memorial stone which bears a grandiloquent formula reminiscent of those that might have been used in Byzantium – 'Catamanus wisest and most renowned of kings' (Nash-Williams, 1950, 57, no. 13). This monument remains an isolated example.

It has been suggested that since sculpture represents considerable economic outlay, the larger and more elaborately decorated the work, the more it meant in economic terms and the more important it was as a symbol of wealth and power (Gondek, 2006, 108–12). The increasing investment in sculpture, it has been argued, reflects the increasing power of local kings, and, in some cases, monasteries, as well as the changes in power bases which vary from region to region and period to period (Gondek, 2006, 137). While this is probably true, the creation of sculpture was probably a secondary outcome of the growth of individual royal power.

In other media for this period, direct evidence of inscriptions is for the most part lacking. The custom of naming patrons and artisans on metalwork did not become established until the tenth and eleventh centuries. A possible exception is the sword chape from the St Ninian's Isle Treasure, which is probably datable to the late eighth century. There has been some debate about how it should be read, but the most widely accepted current interpretation is 'In the name of God, of the Son and the Holy Spirit, Resad' (Graham-Campbell, 2003, 31–2). Although the object is one which most certainly represents the 'Church militant', Resad could have been an ecclesiastical rather than a secular patron.

There is occasional written reference to those who produced manuscripts, and why they did so, but it is not always known upon whose orders they were created. No surviving manuscripts pre-date the mid-seventh century. However, a tenth-century colophon added to the seventh-century Lindisfarne Gospels, provides the names of the writer and illuminator, Eadfrith, bishop of Lindisfarne; of the binder, Ethelwald (also a bishop of Lindisfarne); and the man who decorated the cover with metal and gem embellishments, Billfrith, the anchorite (Backhouse, 1981, 12–16). It is probable that the commissioner in this instance was Eadfrith himself. Similarly, the Book of Armagh appears to have been written by Ferdomnach, a scribe working under the direction of Torbach, abbot of Armagh in 807–8 (Henry, 1967, 101). The Book of Mac Durnan takes its name from Maelbrigte Mac Durnan, Abbot of Armagh (AD888–927), who is likely to have been the commissioner rather than the scribe. A royal connection with this book is apparent from the fact that it was acquired by the Anglo-Saxon king Aethelstan who gave it to Canterbury Cathedral (Henry, 1967, 103).

The concerns of the ecclesiastical patrons were firmly focussed on ecclesiastical matters, and the subject matter chosen was essentially scriptural. It was used to teach the major themes of the faith visually, though occasionally with a layered content so that some inner meanings could only be understood by the most highly educated monks themselves, since they contained allusions to texts by the fathers of the Church (see ch. 7).

The influence of lay patronage from the Carolingian world
The accession of Charlemagne and the subsequent formation of the Carolingian Empire in the 770s and 780s, brought about a considerable change in attitudes to art and learning and to the role of royal and noble lay patronage of the arts (McKitterick, 2005; Dodwell, 1993, 52). This impacted on other neighbouring societies. In England, from the ninth century on, it is clear that different levels of patronage were affecting the art in monasteries and subsequently in manorial and local churches. As a result, much ecclesiastical art was not purely ecclesiastical in origin (Gameson, 1995, 241–60).

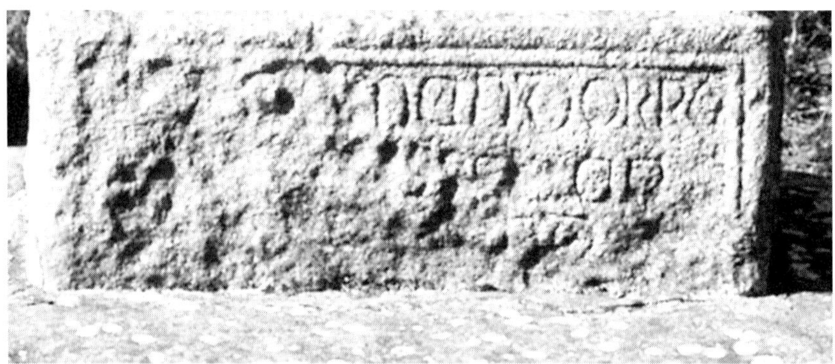

6.1 Inscriptions. a (*above*): Cross of the Scriptures, Clonmacnois (from the replica); b (*below*): Carew.

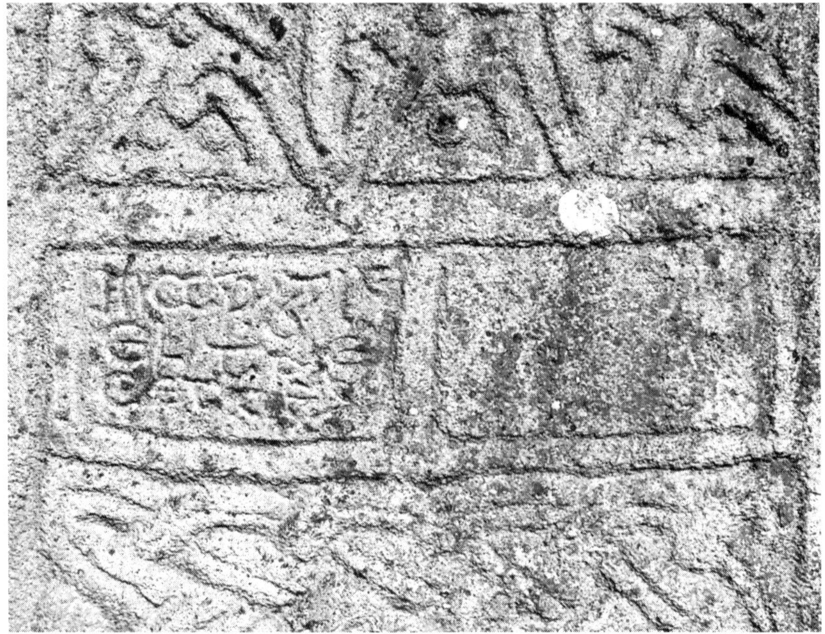

The extent to which Pictland and the united kingdom of Picts and Scots (Alba) that succeeded it, followed the Carolingian ideal has been debated, but there is growing reason to believe that the kings of Alba saw themselves as ruling from a court in the Carolingian model (Wormald, 1996). The same model was followed elsewhere in the Celtic world in the reigns of Brian Bóruma in Ireland (Byrne, 1973, 11), and Rhodri Mawr and Hwyel Dda in Wales (Davies, 1982, 105–7).

PATRONAGE IN INSCRIPTIONS

In the mid-ninth century, for the first time royal patrons were named on sculptures erected in ecclesiastical contexts (fig. 6.1). They occur in Ireland and Scotland, and slightly later in Wales and the Isle of Man. The earliest are in Ireland during the reign of Maelsechnaill (846–62), when the erection of crosses seems to have been not merely to endow a church but to further the name of the sponsoring king (Harbison, 1994a, 14). Inscriptions naming Maelsechnaill and also his son, Flann, have been deciphered in Co. Offaly at Kinitty, Durrow and Clonmacnois. An inscription on the High Cross at Killamery has also been read as naming Maelsechnaill (Harbison, 1992, 363). The tradition can be seen to continue by the inscriptions on the crosses at Tuam, Co. Galway, which name Turlough Ó Conor (1119–1156) (Harbison, 1994b, 78–80). Other inscriptions on Irish High Crosses seem to relate to abbots: one at Galloon, for example, may name abbots of Clones who died in the late ninth and tenth centuries (Harbison, 1992, 361), or to name the artisan.

Inscriptions in Wales
In Wales, virtually no relief sculpture pre-dates the Viking Age, but although some sculpture is associated with monasteries (Llantwit Major, Margam, Penmon and St Davids, for example), many examples seem to have been erected in local churches. Patronage of sculpture can be seen for the first time, reflected in inscriptions (Nash-Williams, 1950, 43). There are twenty-one inscribed crosses or fragments of crosses, most of which appear to be carrying memorial texts. Nine employ a formula referring to the patron (Higgitt, 1986b, 139–40). In most cases the people named on the Welsh stones do not appear to have been royal, but a few definitely were. The most notable example is on the round shaft known as the Pillar of Eliseg, Llangollen, which has a very long inscription apparently stating that it was set up in commemoration of king Eliseg by his great-grandson, Concenn. A date in the second quarter of the ninth century is likely for this monument (Edwards, 2001, 33). A cross from Llantwit Major names Hywel ap Rhys, a late-ninth-century king, and at Margam there are several stones with inscriptions, including a free-standing cross of the late-ninth century that bears an inscription declaring it was set up by Conbelin in memory of Ric.

A similar situation is reflected in the Isle of Man, where the small amount of pre-Viking sculpture appears to be associated chiefly with the monastery at Maughold. However, Viking-Age sculpture is found in both monastic contexts and in local churchyards (Trench-Jellicoe, 1999b, 198). On Man, royal, or at least noble patronage is implied by the inscription on the 'Crux Guriat' stone at Maughold (Kermode, 1907, 121–3). Guriat is often identified with the Welsh prince Gwriad who was apparently in Man *c*.825, though some scholars would prefer to see it dated in the tenth or eleventh century.

Inscriptions in Pictland

In Pictland, there is one inscription dating from around the mid-ninth century on the Drosten Stone, St Vigeans, Angus, which has been read as naming Uurad son of Bargoit, a Pictish king (r.839–42), and two other Picts, Drosten and Forcus (Clancy, 1993). It has been suggested that the royal patronage of both St Vigeans and Meigle lay behind the wealth of sculpture on these sites (Clancy, 1993, 350; Ritchie, 1995, 4). An inscription on the Dupplin Cross, Perthshire, seems to name King Constantine mac Fergusa, who died *c*.825 (Forsyth, 1995). These inscriptions, like the main body of the stones, were probably painted. There were traces of black paint on the inscription on the Welsh cross known as Llantwit Major 4 (Nash-Williams, 1950, no. 222; Redknap & Lewis, 2007, 387; Higgitt, 1986b, 138). It has been suggested the formula on the Pillar of Eliseg 'Conmarch pinxit hoc chirografium' might imply that it was painted, though other interpretations are possible (Higgitt, 1986b, 139).

The blank panels on some monuments may originally have carried inscriptions. This is presumably the case with the blank panel on the base of St Andrews 14; and only slightly less certainly the panel at the base of the cross at Crieff (Allen & Anderson, 1903, fig. 328); the bottom section of St Vigeans, 10 (Allen & Anderson, 1903, 281); and the blank panel on the base of the Aldbar cross-slab (Allen & Anderson, 1903, fig. 259). This is probably also the case with some of the Irish High Crosses. A panel on the base of the South Cross, Castledermot, displays what has been seen as the Kiss of Judas (but it could be two kings greeting). Next to it is a blank panel, with another outlined blank panel beneath. A similar blank panel can be seen at the bottom of the cross shaft at Donaghmore, Co. Down.

A regional type of monument in Wales, of the tenth to eleventh century, known as a cartwheel cross has, in some cases, panels with carved inscriptions. In a few instances the outlined panel is present, but it is blank. On Welsh stones, this is apparent on, for example, a panelled cartwheel cross at Tythegeston, Glamorgan (Nash-Williams, 1950, no. 270a; Redknap & Lewis, 2007, G120), and on an almost identical cross from Kenfig. An outline panel appears on the base of a cross from St

Ishmaels. This can also explain the blank panels on many other stones. A monument from Margam, Glamorgan (Nash-Williams, 1950, no. 237; Redknap & Lewis, 2007, G85), has an inscription in a panel on the front, but no inscription on the back where there is an identical panel.

Inscriptions on metal shrines
Particular insights into the operation of patronage in the eleventh and early twelfth centuries (before the arrival of the Normans in Ireland) are provided by the inscriptions that appear on a series of eleven metal shrines from Ireland, ranging in date from the crozier of St Dympna (*c*.1000) to the Cross of Cong (*c*.1123–34), with a further (lost) example which was the Cumdach (shrine) of the Book of Durrow. The texts are organized in either two or three parts, relating to the commissioners, the interested parties and the artisans. The commissioners appear at the beginning and end of the inscription. Where they occur, the interested parties are in the middle (Michelli, 1996, 11). The recording of the first and the last names emphasizes that the shrine was a significant work of art, socially, and provides a date for its creation. Some insight into how such commissions were perceived is provided by the Martyrology of Oengus, a calendar of feast days set down in the early ninth century. An eleventh-century preface explained that there were four requisites for a work of art: a Place, a Time, an Author and a Cause of Invention (Stokes (ed.), 1905, preface 3–9). This was clearly a widely held view in the period, since it is alluded to in another manuscript, which, though relating to the creation of texts, makes it clear that this principle covered all works of art (Michelli, 1996, 4).

It is clear that the commissioners were members of a family who had connections with the relic for which the reliquary was made, and that within these families only those of highest rank could commission. The interested parties had political connections with the commissioners, and could sometimes outrank them (Michelli, 1996, 11). The commissioners recorded in five inscriptions consist of three kings, one *rigdamna* (heir-apparent of a king) and one abbot.

SCULPTURAL ICONOGRAPHY OF SECULAR PATRONS

Secular patrons seem to have favoured somewhat different subject matter from that of the clergy, even though the main topics still reflected a Christian message, as was appropriate for a monument erected in a sacred space.

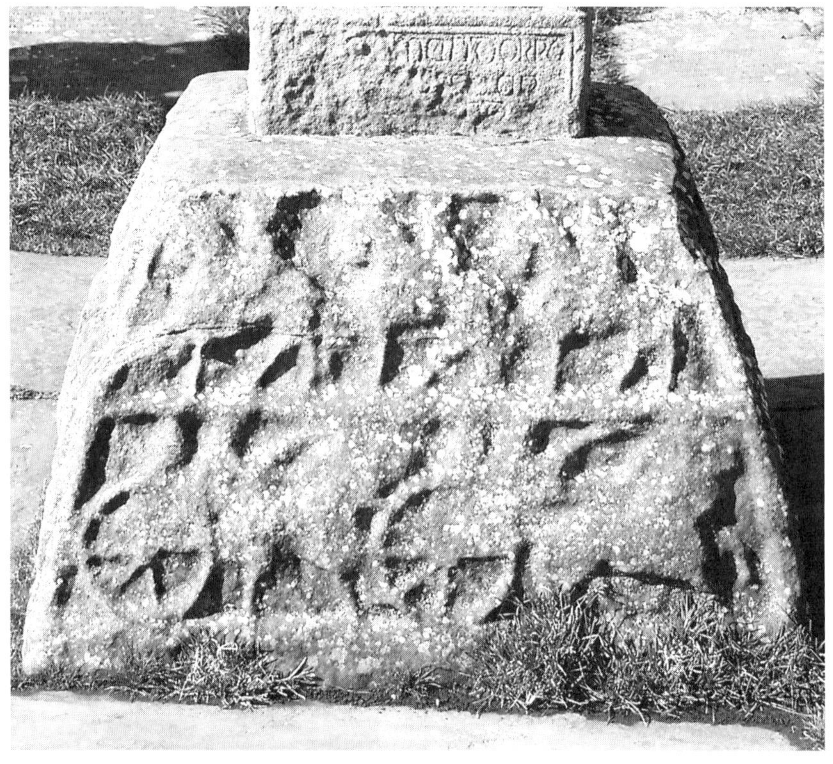

6.2 Chariots on base of Cross of Scriptures, Clonmacnois.

6.3 Combat scene, Market Cross, Kells.

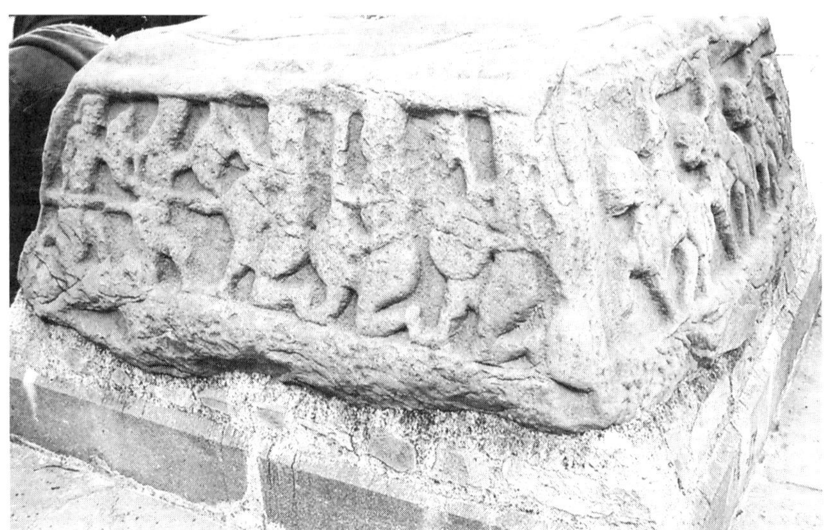

Secular patronage in Ireland

By and large in Ireland the taste of the secular patrons was kept very much subordinate to the biblical narrative displayed on the stones (Harbison, 1992, 330), although secular subject matter was clearly seen as acceptable for the base of Irish High Crosses. Hunting scenes were sometimes employed, reflecting the new taste for the activity that, although Classical in inspiration, was part of the accoutrements of Carolingian kingship. Oddly, although it was a major subject in Carolingian literature, it did not figure prominently in Carolingian art.

The base of the South Cross, Castledermot, displays two spear-wielding huntsmen in pursuit of a variety of animals. The base of the Cross of the Scriptures at Clonmacnois displays two registers, the lower depicting two chariots, the upper three horsemen riding in the opposite direction (fig. 6.2). One face of the base of the Market Cross at Kells displays four horsemen with shields and the other has soldiers with spears fighting one another (fig. 6.3). The Cross of Patrick and Columba at Kells has a chariot procession reminiscent of that at Clonmacnois, while the Cross of Muiredach at Monasterboice displays a chariot procession on the base.

Secular patronage in Pictland

In Pictland, it is noteworthy that the corpus of Pictish sculpture is generally lacking in biblical iconography, though some apparently secular scenes may be of biblical inspiration. In contrast with the contemporaneous Irish High Crosses, which display a very wide array of biblical scenes (Harbison, 1992, 330), Pictish sculpture is characterized more by abstract ornament, by animals (Henderson, 1997; Hicks, 1993a), and by what appear to be secular figures. Allen and Anderson noted only Old Testament iconography at twelve locations in Pictland (1903, pt 3, 405), and, if angels are excluded, a similar number of locations were noted for New Testament subjects (1903, pt 3, 405–6). In point of fact, the only Old Testament scenes documented by Allen and Anderson were scenes relating to David, Jonah and the Whale, and Daniel in the Lions' Den (both concerned with Salvation), and the only New Testament scenes, apart from depictions of Christ, are the Flight into Egypt and the Raising of Lazarus (1903, pt 3, 406).

Certain categories of apparently secular iconography recur throughout Pictland, notably solitary horsemen, hunt scenes and scenes of combat that cannot be explained from solely biblical tradition.

Horsemen appear either in the context of the hunt, or carrying shields and weaponry (fig. 6.4). They occur on stones throughout Pictland, from Shandwick and Hilton of Cadboll in the north, to Largo in Fife, after

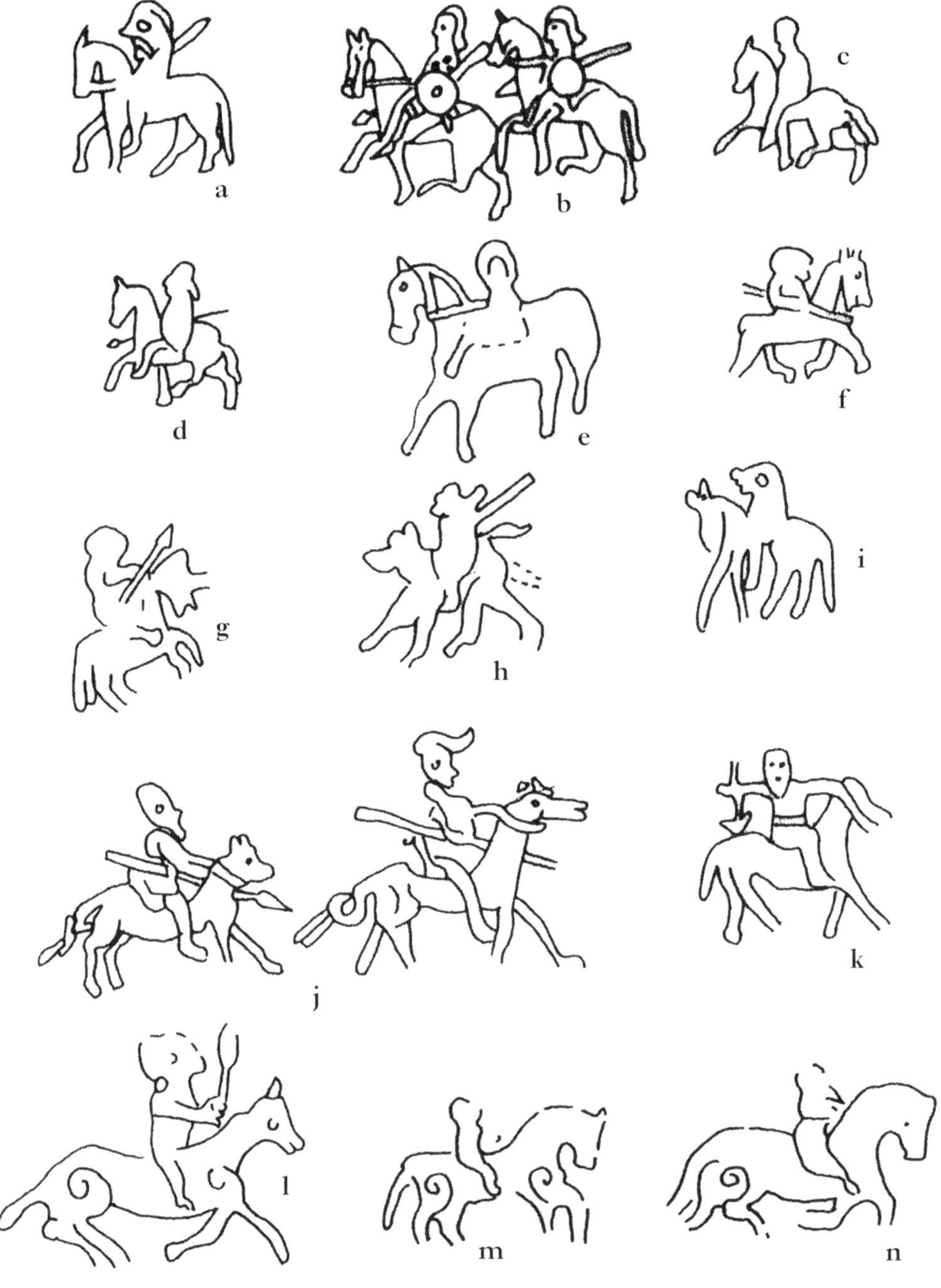

6.4 Horsemen from various sculptures. a: Dupplin, Perths; b: Edderton, Ross; c: Balluderon, Angus; d: Fordoun, Kikcardine; e: Llandough, South Glamorgan; f: Barochan, Renfrews; g: St Andrews, Fife; h, i: Govan, Lanarks; j: Sockburn, Co. Durham; k: Gosforth, Cumbria; l, m, n: Michael, Isle of Man.

which come hunting scenes and finally scenes which seem to depict military engagements. In addition, there are a few depictions of animals being dragged down by hounds, which were presumably part of more extensive hunt scenes, now lost. These horsemen cannot readily be explained in terms of normal early Christian iconography.

Warriors

There are sufficient references to battles in the Old Testament to provide the inspiration for warriors on Christian cross-slabs and, although not numerous, models can be found from many areas of early medieval Europe. The warriors that appear on the Franks Casket (a small carved whalebone chest, of Anglo-Saxon make, named after its nineteenth-century owner, not the people) are exceptional, and almost certainly inspired by a Late Antique manuscript in a monastic milieu (Webster, 1982). Horsemen adorn the Merovingian Pliezhausen disc brooch and some, possibly Lombard, pendants from the Merovingian world, which may represent Christ militant (Lasko, 1971, 81). There is a relief of clearly Antique inspiration at Civita Castellana in Italy (Harbison, 1992, fig. 978), and a remarkable example in sculpture in the Merovingian world at Hornhausen, Thuringia (a work for long believed to be a seventh-century grave-slab, but now re-appraised as part of a screen) (Roth, 1986, pl. 79). There is a further depiction of a Frankish warrior at Niederdollendorf (Lasko, 1982, 89).

In Britain, the earliest sculptural example of a mounted warrior is on a slab from Repton, ascribed to the reign of Aethelbald of Mercia (r.716 to 757) (Biddle & Biddle, 1985; Hawkes, 2006, 107), but which is just as likely to be of the ninth or tenth century.

Battle scenes

The most notable battle scenes are found in Pictland, on the Churchyard Stone at Aberlemno, Angus, and on the exceptionally tall monument known as Sueno's Stone (fig. 6.5). The back of the Aberlemno slab has two confronted armies, represented in vertical perspective. Suggestions have been made that this represents the battle of Nechtansmere, fought between the Picts and the invading Anglo-Saxons, probably at Dunnichen (see for example, Cruikshank, 1999). While this is an attractive suggestion, the slab dates from the ninth century, making it difficult to explain why it should be commemorating a battle fought over a century previously (Laing, 2001a). The back of Sueno's Stone shows more complex iconography, which certainly seem to represent events surrounding a battle. Named in the eighteenth century because of unsubstantiated romantic

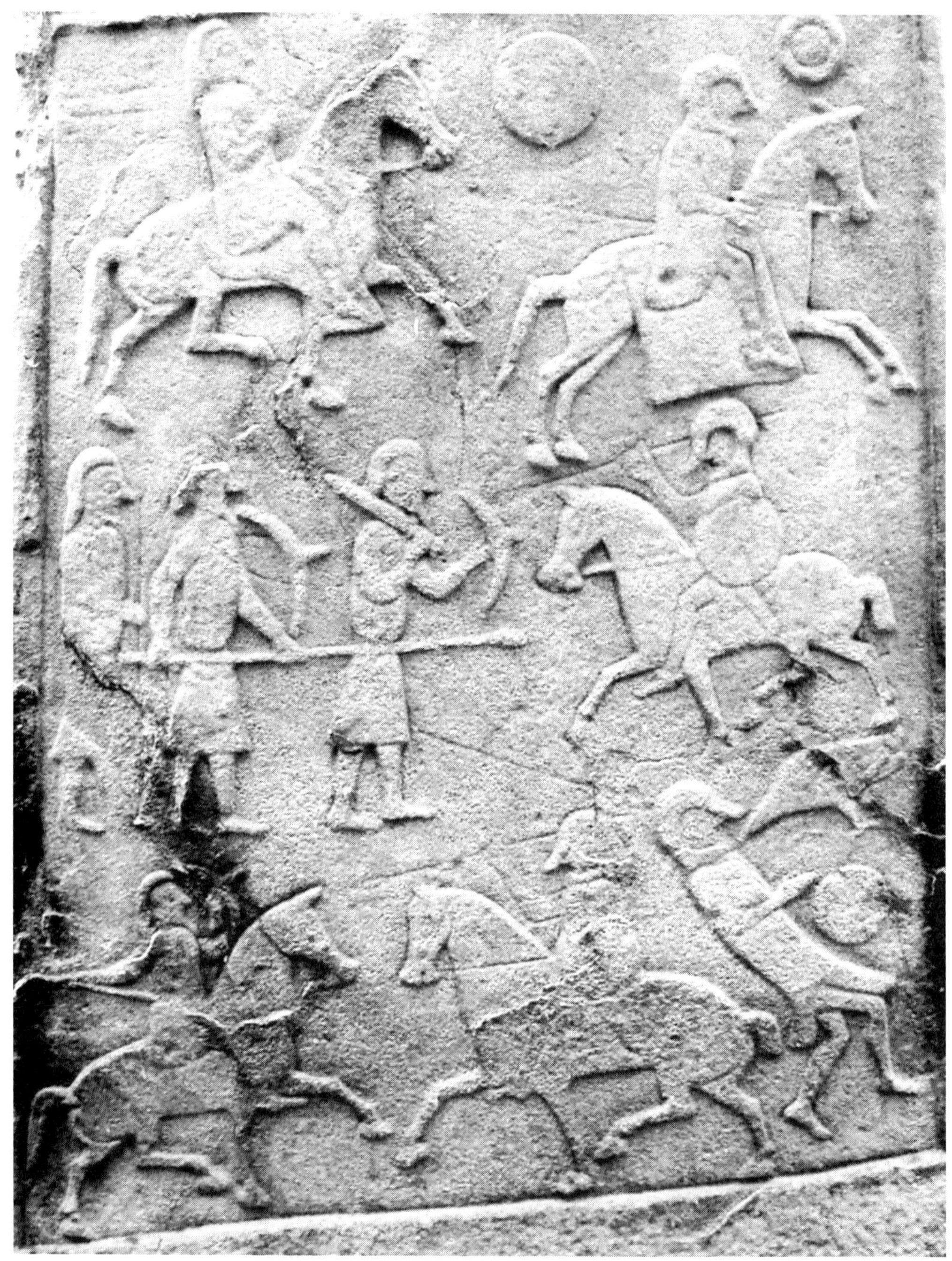

6.5 Aberlemno Churchyard, Angus, back showing battle scene.

ideas that it commemorated a victory over the Norse, it is nonetheless probable that it is datable to the tenth century. One suggestion is that it commemorates a victory by the men of Forres over the Scottish king Dubh in 966, when he was replaced by his cousin (Ritchie, 1989). The scenes depict cavalry, foot soldiers and executed prisoners. Details include what appears to be a bridge and a broch (a Scottish Iron Age round tower).

REVIVAL OF ANTIQUE MODELS AND ITS IMPACT ON CELTIC SCULPTURE

The Carolingian renaissance led to a conscious revival of Antique models in art, as well as of Classical learning and Late Antique ideas of kingship (Christie, 2005, 167–82). In the north of England this is very apparent in the Classical models that inspired such works as the Masham Pillar and the Otley Shaft in Yorkshire, which seem to be taken directly from Classical Rome rather than through a Carolingian intermediary (Lang, 2000).

Warriors and horsemen

The ultimate models for horsemen and hunt scenes can be found in Late Antique art. Sassanian Persian models are apparent in fifth-century silver dishes as, for example, one that allegedly comes from Qazvin (Kent & Painter, 1977, no. 308).

Warriors, horsemen and hunt scenes also occur widely in sculpture of the Viking Age. In Wales, where the relief sculpture is mostly tenth- or eleventh-century, there are few human figures, but a horseman can be seen on the base of a pillar cross at Llandough, South Glamorgan (Nash-Williams, 1950, 206). It is dated to the late tenth or eleventh century and bears an inscription saying that it commemorated Irbic (fig. 6.6). Horsemen occur on stones from Penmon (Nash-Williams, 1950, no. 38) and Whitford, Clwyd (Nash-Williams, 1950, 190), both of Scando-Insular tradition. In the Isle of Man, the horseman and warrior duo occurs in a number of contexts. On Irish High Crosses, purely secular scenes appear to be confined to the bases, as for example, on the ninth-century Market Cross at Kells, Co. Meath (Harbison, 1992, 126 & fig. 974), which has a battle scene (fig. 6.3).

From Northumbria, there are full-face warriors on the stones named Middleton 2, Levisham 1 and Kirbymoorside 2 (Yorkshire), which are dated to the tenth century. A school producing similar figures was centred on Otley in the East Riding of Yorkshire. Hunt scenes appeared on Middleton 1 and Stonegrave 7 (Lang, 1991, III, 37), and very Pictish-

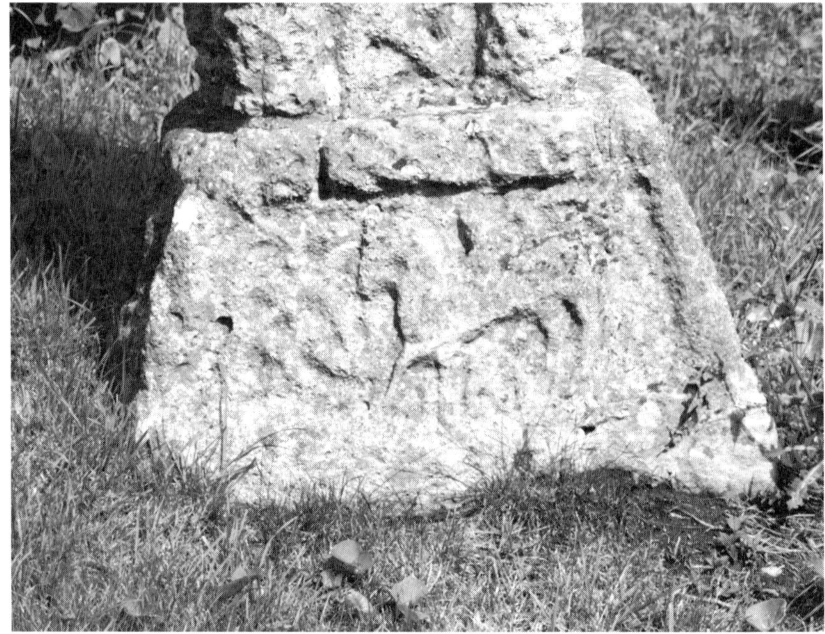

6.6 Horseman at base of Llandough Cross, Glamorgan.

looking horsemen appear at Sockburn, Co. Durham (Bailey, 1980, fig. 69). Lang pointed out that in northern Yorkshire, secular figures became popular from *c*.920 onwards, with the Viking shift in patronage from ecclesiastical to secular, and noted the wide occurrence of warriors. A School at Allertonshire produced profile warriors. The Rydedale School in eastern Yorkshire and Wharfedale in the West Riding produced warrior portraits (Lang, 2001, 36). In north-west England, figures are less apparent, but a fine horseman appears on the Gosforth Cross, Cumbria (Bailey & Cramp, 1988).

In Strathclyde, the warrior as a motif features in the strongly-Scandinavian Govan 'School' (Ritchie (ed.), 1994), at Govan itself, where it is well exemplified by the sarcophagus of St Constantine (Spearman, 1994), and in the related Strathclyde sculptures, most notably those from St Blane's, Kingarth; Rothesay 2, Bute; Mountblow, Glasgow (Allen & Anderson, 1903, fig. 471), and on the Barochan Cross in Renfrewshire (Allen & Anderson, 1903, fig. 475).

The royal hunt, popular in the Carolingian world, is also reflected in art of the period in Scotland. Hunt scenes involving falconry and their Carolingian background have been reviewed by Carrington (1996). Falconers appear on stones at St Andrews, Elgin and Fowlis Wester, as well

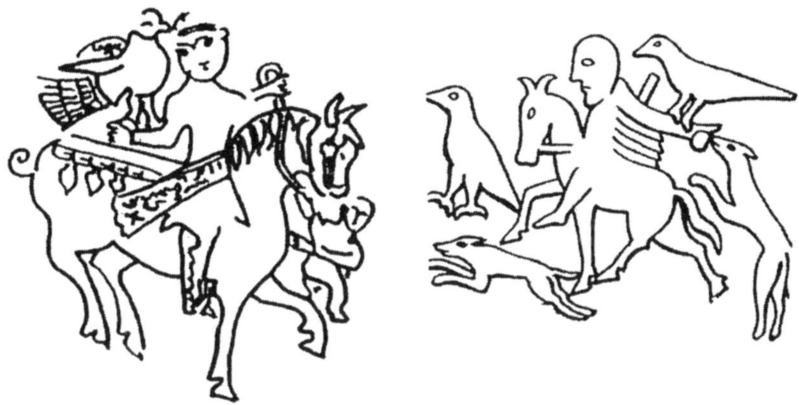

6.7 Falconers. a: Sassanian dish, Vyatsky, south Russia; b: Elgin, Nairn.

as probably at Kingarth, Bute (Laing, 1998, 21 and fig. 7) (fig. 6.7). The models for hunt scenes and for mounted warriors were ultimately Classical, but all need not have been.

David iconography

A theme which became widely popular in ninth-century Pictland, but also found a place in Irish sculpture, was the story of David (fig. 6.8). The popularity of David iconography is almost certainly a reflection of royal patronage, since David was first and foremost a king. He was also given particular prominence as one of the Old Testament forerunners of Christ.

Late Antique models include those on silver plates from the Cyprus Treasure, which show David iconography (Kent & Painter, 1977, nos 179 and 184); images of mounted emperors on coins and medallions of the fourth century, for example the Beaurains (Arras) Treasure (Abdy, 2006, 52–7); the fifth-century Ambrosian Illiad, and the mosaics of Santa Maria Maggiore in Rome. Earlier models can be sought in the Roman Battle Sarcophagi. In Ireland, David battling with Goliath figures on the base of the North Cross at Ahenny, and he also appears on two panels on the cross at Arboe. David can also be seen on the crosses at Armagh, Castledermot, Clonmacnois (The Cross of the Scriptures, which had a royal patron, see above, p. 177), Donaghmore, Drumcliff, Durrow, Kells (both the Market Cross and the Cross of Patrick and Columba) and at Monasterboice on both the Cross of Muiredach and the Tall Cross. In Wales and the Isle of Man, David does not appear, but he is prominent in Pictish sculpture, and is the main subject of the St Andrews Sarcophagus.

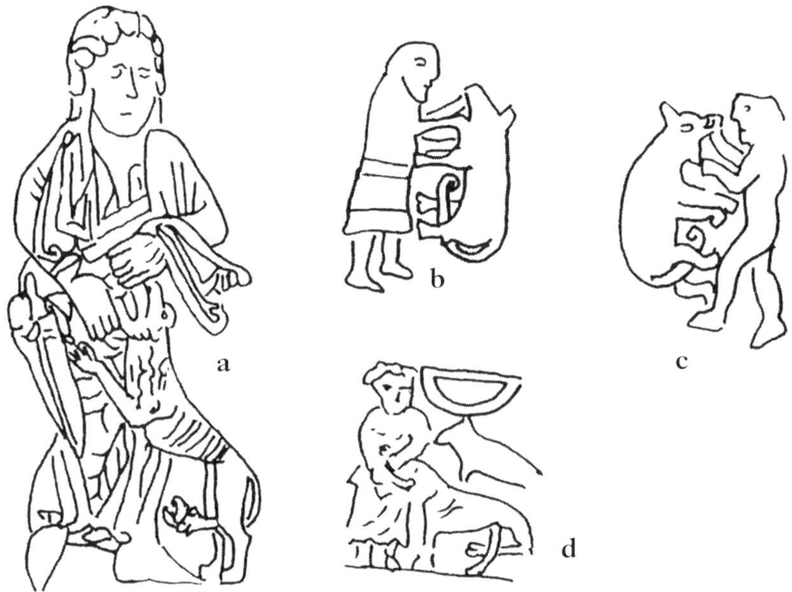

6.8 David iconography. a: St Andrews Sarcophagus; b: Aldbar, Angus; c: Dupplin, Perths; d: Aberlemno 3, Angus.

David iconography is first seen in the eighth century, when it was used, not surprisingly, in the ornament of Psalters in Anglo-Saxon England (for the iconography as a whole, Curle, 1940; Roe, 1945; Henderson, 1967; Henderson, 1986; Henderson, 1997). In sculpture, there is little evidence for its use before the ninth century, the earliest instances in Scotland appearing on St Oran's Cross and St Martin's Cross on Iona and on the Kildalton Cross on Islay. These have usually been dated to the end of the eighth century (Fisher, 2001, 15). David iconography is very rare in Anglo-Saxon sculpture, appearing on a worn column of the ninth century at Masham, Yorkshire (Lawson, 1981), and on a fragmentary cross-shaft at Sockburn, Co. Durham (Bailey, 1980, fig. 36). Its origins lie in Eastern models (Mowbray, 1936), as is apparent both in Anglo-Saxon Mercian sculpture and in Pictland, where its finest manifestation is on the St Andrews Sarcophagus. It is extremely unlikely that this implies that Eastern works were present in Pictland or Ireland; the designs probably travelled by way of Byzantium and Anglo-Saxon England (Henderson, 1986, 102). There are distinctive features to the Pictish David iconography, which differ in some instances from both the Anglo-Saxon and the Irish models (Henderson, 1986, 105–6).

CHAPTER 7

Symbol and image

The art of the early Christian Celts reflected the way early medieval ecclesiastics thought about the Christian god and his works. It was the Church's method of 'thinking out loud on the "problem of Christ"' (Mathews, 1993, 141). Like the rest of the clerical world in early medieval Europe, Celtic ecclesiastics were profoundly influenced by the writings of Roman and later theologians in Europe and North Africa. They were engaged in the quest for the hidden truths in the scriptures, and their art was intended to further that quest. By contemplating the images, the observer could come to a greater understanding of God and the order of his universe.

The early Christians were fascinated by numbers and the ways in which they could be used. Number and geometry were therefore fundamental to ecclesiastical thinking and to symbolism. This importance extended from the numbers chosen for figures and motifs, to the layout of pages in manuscripts and the design of architecture. All God's creatures had their own 'natures', which could be used to teach lessons about proper behaviour in humankind. The Divine existed in an eternal present, and events that had happened centuries before in the records of the Old Testament were considered relevant to events in the New, so that links had to be sought in order to further illuminate God's purpose. Much of the basic 'language' of ecclesiastical art was imported from outside the Celtic areas, but the Celts (especially in Ireland) excelled in its implementation, which reached its most complex in the Book of Kells and the ornament on the High Crosses of the ninth and tenth centuries.

CELTIC SCHOLARSHIP

Much early Christian Celtic thinking was based on the writings of Christian theologians (the Church Fathers) in the period up to the fifth century. Some scholars were writing before the Council of Nicea in AD325 (the first general synod of the Church, which established the Nicene Creed, setting out the basic beliefs of the faith, most of which are still accepted Christian doctrine). The early theologians contemplated the concepts of the Trinity and of Salvation, and were responsible for the organization of the Church. They also fought heresy, which was a particular problem at the time of Constantine, but which had also been discussed by Irenaeus of Lyon as early as the second century. Among the earliest Church Fathers were Origen of Alexandria (*c*.185–204); Tertullian (*c*.160–225) of Carthage; Athanasius (*c*.296–373), bishop of Alexandria; Jerome (*c*.342–420) from Italy and Augustine of Hippo in North Africa (354–430).

The Celtic clerics, in common with their contemporaries, studied the patristic (that is of the Church Fathers) writings and particularly the exegesis (commentaries on the Bible intended to further an understanding of it from the information contained in the scriptures). The Celts contributed their own commentaries, and in Ireland studied the language and literature not only of their own language but also Classical, sometimes pagan, writers. They were concerned with philosophical speculation on astronomy and geography: in the late eighth century, Dicuil, an Irish monk from Iona, wrote a book on astronomy and a treatise on the extent of the earth, which included an account of a journey to Iceland.

CELTIC ART AND THE QUEST FOR HIDDEN TRUTHS

Celtic art contained hidden clues for the seeker of truth. This phenomenon was first mentioned by Gerald of Wales, who recorded the mysterious 'shrines' (arcana) of what is now known as Celtic ornament (Pirotte, 2001, 203). The interpretation becomes complex because there can be layers of meaning within images, that were intended to lead the viewer to consider different aspects of the theme being explored. Sometimes these are fairly clearly conveyed, but as some of them stem from biblical exegesis and patristic writings, it requires a fairly thorough understanding of the intellectual climate of the time to disentangle the message.

The art that contains this complex symbolism was primarily created within and for the monastic community. The daily contemplation (*ruminatio*) of the gospel was part of the *lectio divina* – a thought-process that involved making links between texts. These were so subtle that they might lie only in their common use of a word or some liturgical function (O'Reilly, 1993, 110). Much of this originated in the intention of demonstrating that the ability to perceive the true nature of Christ was what distinguished the Saved from the Damned, and that the five senses were essential in this perception. A church ceremony (the *apertio aurium*) was part of the preparation of the catechumen for baptism. It was the 'opening of the ears' and had to be accompanied by the rinsing of the eyes, since blindness was a metaphor for sin. It was important that the message was not obvious; it had to be sought out, just as under the literal reading of the scriptures a more profound spiritual meaning had to be sought.

In approaching the meaning, the viewer must first recognize the importance of number, then appreciate the medieval principle of 'four-fold interpretation' – literal or historical, allegorical, tropological (moral) and anagogical (a mystical interpretation of scriptural exegesis), which may contain interlocking layers of meaning (Neuman de Vegvar, 2007, 243).

Iconography was not always directly copied from a previous model, but altered to isolate specific hidden meanings. The early medieval Church did not have concepts of linear sequential time; it existed in timelessness, so events that were chronologically separate could be seen as existing in the same dimension (Veelenturf, 2001).

The liturgy was also important in the way images were arranged in both manuscripts and sculpture. Gospel manuscripts were used in the liturgy – passages (*pericopes*) were selected daily, preceded by readings from the Epistles or from the Acts of the Apostles. In the earliest liturgies, there were also readings from the Old Testament. The sermon which followed the readings was usually chosen by the abbot and based on the writings of one of the Church Fathers. The physical presence of large and ornate gospel books, such as the Book of Kells, as objects of veneration was important. However, it has been suggested that these were not directly read out during the liturgy, but were placed open on the altar. On balance, however, it is likely that they were used for both reading aloud and for private contemplation (Farr, 1997, 41–3). Certainly, the larger illustrations in works such as the Book of Kells must have been intended to be seen by the congregation (Ó Carragáin, 1994). An illustration in the Echternach Gospels shows St Matthew displaying his gospel book open to the viewer (Meehan, 1994, 29).

Some manuscripts seem to have been designed for use by the individual reader, for whom the marginal drawings could have served as a commentary on the text. This was particularly a feature of Byzantine manuscripts of the ninth century and later, but the use of marginal 'illustration' goes back to Late Antique traditions (Nees, 2007). The Book of Armagh (*c*.AD807), for example, has a plan of the New Jerusalem, which was intended as a commentary on the text (O'Loughlin, 2000). Such additions to the text can sometimes be 'visual exegesis', in which the images draw upon patristic and contemporaneous commentary on the scriptures, as well as from the liturgy (Pulliam, 2006; 2007, 257).

The canon tables in manuscripts were not simply frames or arcades, but were metaphorical architectural entrances that provided a ceremonial way into the texts (Nordenfalk, 1963). Architectural forms were seen by the clerics as carrying meaning, and could signal key points for approaching the broader context (Neuman de Vegvar, 2007, 256).

Symbolism is visible even on comparatively simple monuments. In the sixth- and seventh-century art of the Mediterranean and Gaul, the chalice was popular as a symbol of Eucharist (Mass or Communion) and of baptism. Combined with the cross it united the death of the individual with the Crucifixion, through the wine of the Eucharist. This is most commonly seen on memorial stones. On some, such as one from Gallen Priory, Co. Offaly, the arms of the cross take the form of chalices (Karkov, 1993).

Hidden messages are apparent in all media, but are most complex when juxtaposed with text in manuscript illumination. They are somewhat less difficult to read in the case of sculpture, and are seldom very complex in metalwork (except in the case of a few composite shrines, where there is figural work as well as the symbolic content of the ornament and the animal art).

Extensive time-damage means, however, that many images in Celtic sculpture are difficult to identify with any degree of certainty, as has been well demonstrated from the Shandwick, Ross-shire, cross-slab (Meyer, 2005).

NUMEROLOGY

The roots of the Celtic ecclesiastical fascination with numerology lie in particular in the neo-Platonist school of philosophy centred on Alexandria in the third century AD, which recognized a scheme of celestial arithmetic. It was built on by St Augustine (AD354–430), and set out very clearly by Isidore of Seville (*c.*AD560–636), in his *Liber Numerorum*. The work of Isidore was familiar in Ireland, and might explain the ready adoption of number symbolism in the art there. Numbers could be used to convey the final truth, and both numbers and geometry governed the rules of architecture and the layout of art (Hopper, 1969).

There is some evidence that the use of key numbers, acrostics and number patterns was familiar in Roman Britain (Thomas, 1998, 54), and numbers seem to have been employed in inscriptions in the Celtic West in the fifth and sixth centuries, where they may represent a survival or possibly a re-introduction from Gaul (Thomas, 1998). It has been suggested (though not universally accepted) that in some cases, the numbers in the texts could have been used to create visual images. Examples of this may be the plan of the Temple of Solomon in Jerusalem (on the Latinus stone at Whithorn: Thomas, 1998, 110) and possibly an outline of the deceased's body on the Carausius stone from Penmachno, Gwynedd (Thomas, 1998, 143–9).

By the ninth century, a guidebook for number symbolism was provided by John Scotus Eriugena (*c.*815–77), who lived in the Carolingian Empire but was of Irish origin (O'Meara, 1969). Eriugena based his definitions on the work of Pseudo-Dionysius the Areopagite, Maximus the Confessor and Boethius (*c.*480 to *c.*525), the philosopher, poet and politician. In addition, Eriugena's reasoning was coloured by that of St Augustine, who followed neo-Pythagorean ideas (Richardson, 1984a).

In his *Division of Nature*, Eriugena defined six as the perfect number, because the elements of which it was composed – 3, 2 and 1 – when added together, produced the same number again. Six is contained in twelve, the number of the disciples; three is the number of the Trinity (the 'triad of the Creator' in Eriugena's words) and eight is the symbol of the Resurrection (Christ rose on the eighth day). Eight was doubly symbolic since it included the number five and the number three, which also carried symbolic meanings. It was also symbolic of Easter, Sunday, baptism and immortality.

Four was the number of the evangelists, but was also the symbol of the material world (Earth, Air, Fire and Water, the points of the compass and the four seasons) and the Rivers of Paradise. It is also the number of the Cross (Child & Colles, 1971, 229). Five, the 'pentad of the Creator' in Eriugena, also represented the wounds of Christ. Other important numbers in Christian iconography include nine (the nine orders of angels) and forty, which represents trial or testing (Child & Colles, 1971, 230).

These numbers constantly recur in the composition of works of art. In metalwork, eight is used on the Ardagh Chalice, which has eight glass studs serving as feet. The central stud on the base is surrounded by five dark blue studs, each containing three filigree c-shapes. On each side of each stud there is a gilt bronze triskele (important for the number three). The inner band of filigree has six animals (Berger, 1979; Richardson, 1984a, 31). The Derrynaflan Chalice likewise uses eight zones of decoration. The eight configuration also occurs on the die-stamped plates on the Moylough Belt-Shrine. Number symbolism is apparent on the Derrynaflan Paten, which had twelve studs round the rim. The assembly marks on this and on the Ardagh Chalice point to number symbolism in their construction (Brown, 1993, 163).

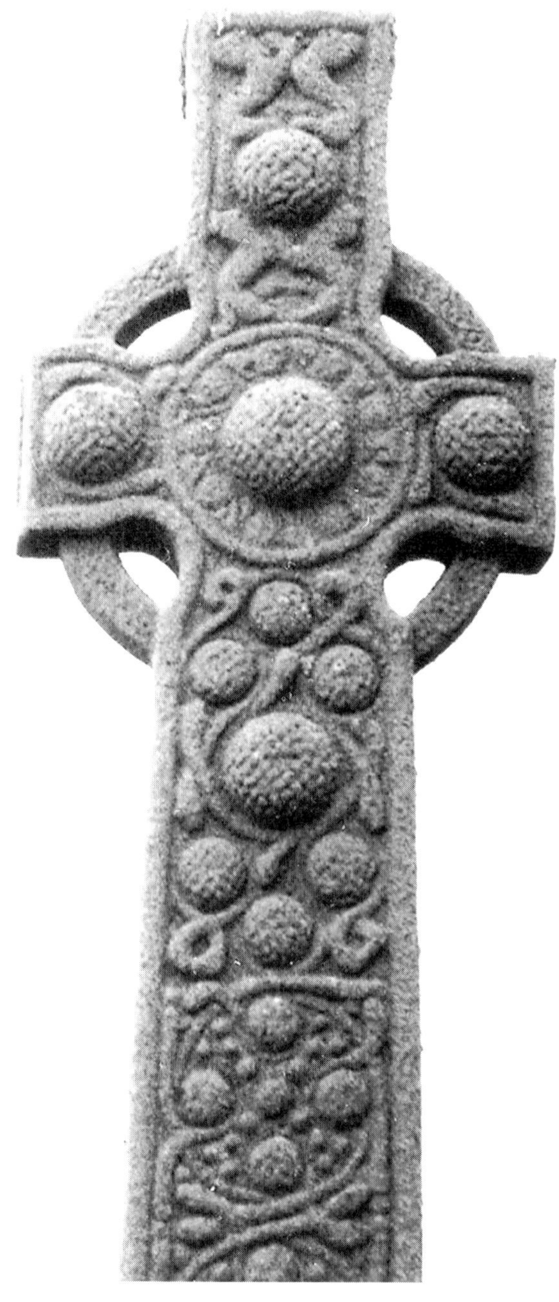

7.1 Bosses on crosses, St Martin's, Iona.

Similar symbolism can be seen in other media (fig. 7.1). The arrangement of the bosses on crosses and cross-slabs in Ireland and Scotland in the ninth century follow numerical symbolism. The eight bosses on the back of the South Cross at Clonmacnois, for example, are the counterparts of the Crucifixion on the other face. On the cross at Lisnakea, Co. Fermanagh, there are thirty-two bosses (Richardson, 1990, 44), while at Tihilly, Co. Offaly, there is a circle for seven bosses (Richardson, 1990, 49). St Martin's Cross on Iona has a central boss on the head and one on each of the arms, representing the Five Wounds of Christ. The bottom of these large bosses is set within a further setting of six bosses, three on each side, while below there are twelve still smaller bosses, surrounded by even smaller bosses.

Equally complex is the arrangement of the bosses on the cross head of the Pictish Meigle 2 in Perthshire, where in the centre of the cross are eight bosses around a central one, with eight bosses in the ring (two are now missing) and four bosses on each of the arms, making a configuration of eight for the uprights and the cross. The recurrent pattern of eight may therefore designate the cross as symbolic of the Resurrection.

In manuscripts, number symbolism is apparent in folio 192v of the Book of Durrow (fig. 4.12), where the innermost circle may represent a chalice around which are zones of ten animals – the number of unity in St Augustine's scheme – which also contained the symbolic numbers seven and three (Hicks, 1993a, 89). The central cross is surrounded by three small roundels (symbolic of the Trinity), which is set within a circle (the symbol of Eternity). In turn, the whole design lies within a double square, which is also significant since a square has four sides and a double square has eight. Eight appears on the Eight Circle Page in the Book of Kells, in which number symbolism is important.

Interlace contains the elements of number symbolism, subsumed into the geometry of the construction (O'Meadhra, 1987b, 158–9), but it also has other symbolic connotations (Budny, 2001). The triquetra, duplex, trefoil, quartrefoil, quadrilobate knot and quadriloop are particularly significant. The 'closed' nature of these makes them representative of Eternity (O'Meadhra, 1987b, 158).

Knots were considered to be a method of trapping Satan, and the serpent was of particular symbolic importance. Zoomorphic interlace assumed a particular importance, since adding a head to a strand brought it to life and strengthened its power (Kitzinger, 1993). It has also been suggested that the intricacy of the interlace was intended as an aid to focusing on the multiple layers of meaning in the text it embellished (Werkmeister, 1967).

Interlace was also used to create reserved negative crosses (concealed crosses within crosses). The device is apparent in the sophisticated interlace of the Book of Durrow. Red, yellow and green were used 'disruptively' (as R.B.K. Stevenson put it) on individual strands to hide their continuity or to emphasize complex knots (1981–2, 12). In folio 125v, the carpet page displays coloured interlace against a black background to project three main crosses, two half crosses and small crosses in the upper and lower borders (Stevenson, 1981–2, 16).

ANIMAL SYMBOLISM

Animals play an important part in early Christian symbolism, and the acquisition of their symbolic meanings seems to have been cumulative. The use of the peacock, dove, fish, dolphin and stag were very early symbols in the Church, some appearing in Britannia. The fish as a symbol of Christ appears on, for example, a pewter dish from Appleshaw; a tag from Beadlam, Yorkshire, and a silver spoon from Dorchester (Thomas, 1981, fig. 6). The Greek name for fish, ιχθυς, is an acronym for Ιησούς Χριστος Θεου Υιος Σωτήρ (Jesus Christ, Son of God and Saviour'). The use of this acrostic was cited by Eusebius in the fourth century, and alluded to by St Augustine of Hippo (Allen, 1887, 121).

Other symbols found in Roman Britain include doves, which represented the peace of Christ (at, for example, Lullingtone and Fifeshead Neville). Peacocks were symbols of rebirth and appear on a buckle plate from Tripontium, Warwickshire; on a bowl from the Isle of Ely and on a tag from Orton Longueville (Thomas, 1981, fig. 8).

The peacock appears on one of the terminals of a penannular brooch from Bath. It has a background of red enamel, the opposite terminal being adorned with an eagle and fish. This can be assumed to be an example of surviving Christian symbolism from the Romano-British past, since the eagle and fish motif in a Christian context symbolizes Christ carrying the Soul. Like a number of other early Christian symbols, the peacock is deeply rooted in pagan Mediterranean tradition – it appears as a Greek coin-type, for example. It decorates a Roman bronze plate from Wroxeter, Shropshire, and is possibly what is intended to be symbolized by the decoration on the Lullingstone hanging bowl, which has not only eagle and fish, but also deer. These symbols appear in later early Christian art in the Celtic world but their models were almost certainly re-introductions.

An extended repertoire of symbolic animals was contained in the *Physiologus*, an early Christian (probably Alexandrian) Natural History,

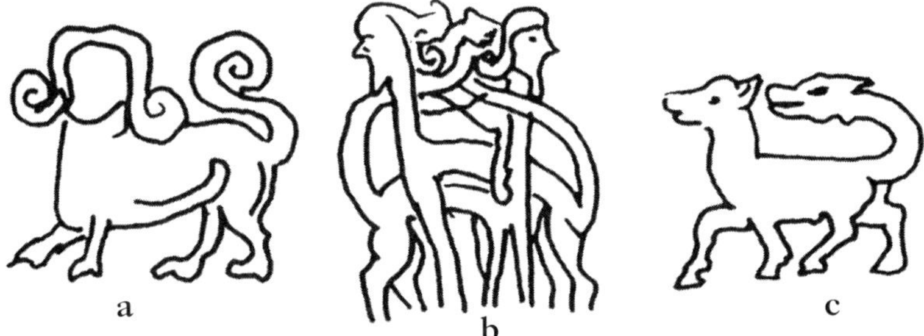

7.2 Mythical beasts on Pictish stones (all Perths). a: Gask; b: Rossie; c: Gask.

which borrowed from earlier Eastern tradition. Sections from Isidore of Seville were incorporated into versions of the *Physiologus*, though these survive only in later manuscripts. The purpose of the *Physiologus* was to define Christian behaviour, and the 'natures' of animals were used as allegories for the nature of Christ and Christian doctrine. There were short lessons about these natures, with biblical quotations, used to explain the nature of Christ; Salvation; proper Christian behaviour; heresies and the consequences of sin (Henderson, 1996, 3). As well as real animals, such as the pelican, the *Physiologus* included mythical creatures, such as the phoenix, the mermaid, the basilisk, the unicorn, the griffin, and the manticore (a beast which ate men). With the notable exceptions of the griffin, the manticore and the mermaid, most of the fantastic beasts do not figure in Celtic Christian art.

Complex animal symbolism can be seen clearly in, for example, the filigree panels on the Derrynaflan Paten, on which forty-seven panels bear filigree animals, either alone or in various combinations. Thus, a stag representing Christ confronts a serpent which represents evil (Ryan, 1983; Ryan, 1987, 72). The same motif appears on a slab from Gallen Priory, Co. Offaly (Henry, 1965, 123 and pl. 64).

It is difficult to be certain how far the animals that appear in Celtic sculpture are directly rather than indirectly inspired by the *Physiologus*. In Ireland, however, a good range of the bestiary from this source appears on a cross at Tybroughney (also known as Tibberaghny), Co. Kilkenny; notably a manticore, hyaena, and an axe-wielding centaur (Roe, 1958, 31) (fig. 7.2).

The serpent had many symbolic meanings, depending on context. It is most famous as a symbol of evil – the tempter of Eve. The snake could also be used as a symbol of eternity, since it casts off its skin and emerges alive. This may be its correct interpretation in sculpture (where 'snake bosses' are employed, for example on the Iona crosses), or in metalwork (such as on the Romfojellen mount), and in manuscript art (as in the Book of Kells (Henry, 1974, 208; Henderson, 1987, 64)).

The lion symbol is ubiquitous, representing power over death and perpetual vigilance. It was therefore an allegory of Christ (still used in the twentieth century in the form of Aslan in C.S. Lewis' fiction). It was also one of its 'natures' to conceal its tracks by swishing its tail and brushing them out, just as Christ concealed his divinity through incarnation in the womb of the Virgin. Association with Mary may have resulted in the conjunction of lions with the Virgin and Child on St Martin's Cross on Iona (Henderson, 1996, 8). The extensive animal symbolism on the Kildalton Cross, Islay (the probable work of Iona sculptors), includes crouching lions on the arms, posed in the ever-vigilant position that is illustrated in one of the earliest surviving texts of the *Physiologus*; and a lion tangled in serpents. The cross also displays a pair of peacocks pecking at grapes (RCHAMS, 1984, 208). In Irish sculpture, the lion is equally apparent as, for example, on the pillars from Banagher and Clonmacnois, Co. Offaly, and on a cross at Bealin in Co. Westmeath (Harbison, 2007, 215–16).

Other exotic creatures that may have come from the *Physiologus* include a possible hyaena and panther on a Pictish frieze from Meigle (Hicks, 1993, 149), and a monkey (a symbol of evil incarnate) on the St Andrews Sarcophagus (Henderson, 1996, 11). A monkey also figures with other animals apparently from the *Physiologus*, on the cross at Moone, Co. Kildare.

The clearest animal symbolism can be found in the evangelist symbols that appear in manuscript illumination, starting with the Book of Durrow. The origin of the symbols lies with the Revelation of St John (4:7), where the four creatures surrounding the throne of God are a lion, a calf (or ox), an eagle and a man (all with wings). The origin of this imagery is rooted in the Book of Ezekiel, and before that Babylonian zodiac symbols (Werner, 1969). The early Christians adopted these to represent the four evangelists – they appeared, for example, in the fourth century in the mosaics of Santa Pudenziana in Rome. The idea of using an isolated animal, without evangelist portrait (as in the case of Durrow) probably originated in a Syrian or Egyptian model. The absence of wings and attributes have led to the suggestion that in the case of the Book of Durrow, the model may have been east Mediterranean (Nordenfalk, 1968). As with other symbolism in the Celtic world, the four evangelist symbols set in angles of a cross that appear in manuscripts contain inner

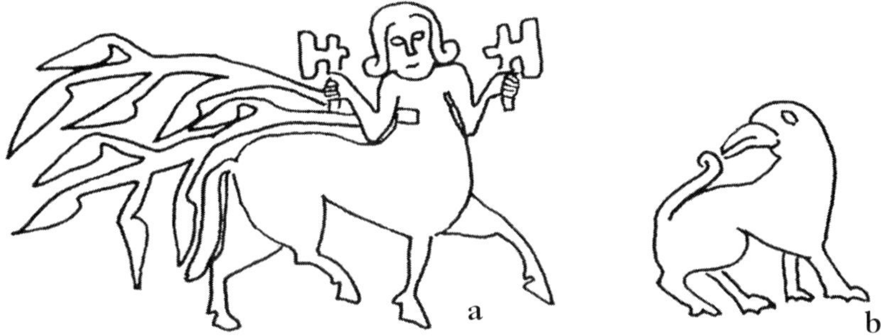

7.3 Pictish centaur and griffin. a: Aberlemno 3, Angus; b: St Vigeans 19, Perths.

symbolism. The four creatures symbolize the four gospels, united by one spirit, represented by the cross (Cronin, 1995).

Of the other symbols, the centaur figured in the *Physiologus*, where it was described as half man, half ass (as opposed to horse in Classical sources). Along with the siren, it represented demonic force, or the conflict between good and evil (between the human and animal elements in its body). It figures in Pictish relief sculpture, such as at Rhynie, Golspie and Glamis Manse. On the Aberlemno Roadside and the Glamis Manse cross-slabs, there is in image – a centaur holding a branch – which seems to have been derived from Anglo-Saxon sources, notably a version of the *Marvels of the East*, where the branch became a symbol of healing (Hicks, 1993a, 145). The Centaur also appears in Pictland and Ireland with a bow, a zodiac symbol of Eastern origin. By the eleventh to twelfth centuries the arrow's flight was seen as symbolic of the flight of the soul. It may well already have had this connotation in early Christian Celtic art (Hicks, 1993a, 147). Some Celtic centaurs appear to be equipped with axes, as for example on the fragmentary cross at Tibberaghny, Co. Kilkenny, and in Pictland on Aberlemno 3 and Glamis Manse, Angus (Laing, 2001b, fig. 13) (fig. 7.3).

The griffin was a symbol of the dual nature of Christ, and may also represent the bread and wine of the Eucharist. It represented Christ as lord over the heaven (the eagle) and the earth (the lion) (Harbison, 2007, 223). It originated in the Antique world, where it was one of the creatures that carried off the souls of the dead, and in early Christian art it can represent the Devil carrying off sinners. Its use was widespread in early medieval Europe, occurring in particular on Burgundian buckles. It seems to have been used sometimes in Daniel scenes (Ryan, 1993, 156–7). In

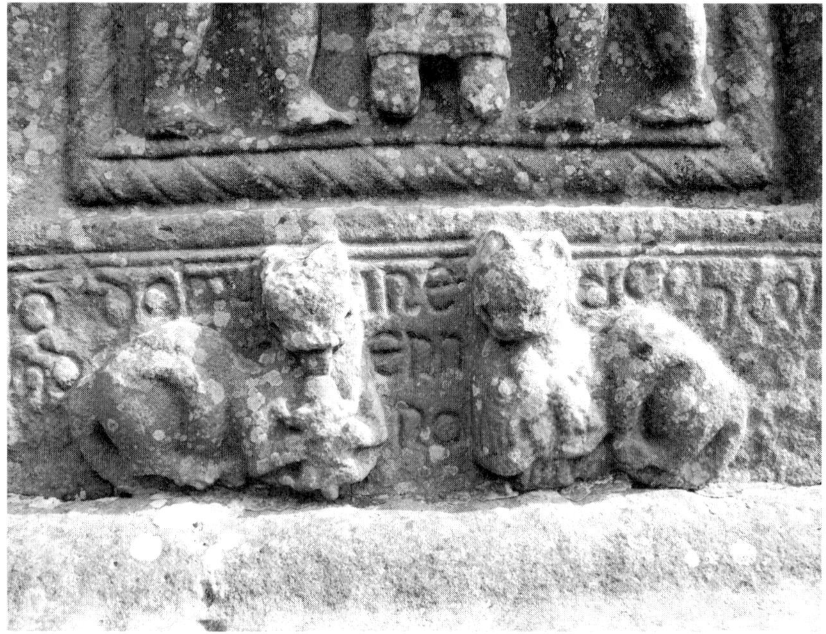

7.4 Cats, Cross of Muiredach, Monasterboice (photo: Casandra Masse).

metalwork, the griffin appears, arguably, on the Derrynaflan Chalice, and it features prominently in both Irish and Pictish sculpture. In Ireland, the symbol appears on the Tall Cross at Monasterboice; on the north face of the base of the Cross of the Scriptures at Clonmacnois, and on the cross at Duleek, Co. Meath (Harbison, 2007, 223–4). In Pictish sculpture, it occurs on a broken cross shaft at Meigle, and on the St Andrews Sarcophagus (Henderson, 1996, 26) (fig.7.3).

Cats figure relatively rarely. A pair appear at the bottom of the west face of the Cross of Muiredach at Monasterboice, where one is about to eat a bird, and the other is holding what has been seen as a kitten (though a frog has also been suggested) between its paws (fig. 7.4). This scene has been interpreted as symbolic of life and death, and as relating to the Crucifixion higher up the cross (Harbison 2007, 222). Another pair of cats on the east face appear to be fighting, and may symbolize the fight between good and evil.

HUMAN FIGURES AND THEIR ATTRIBUTES

Individual human figures and more particularly human heads can carry their own symbolism in addition to their their symbolic value as part of

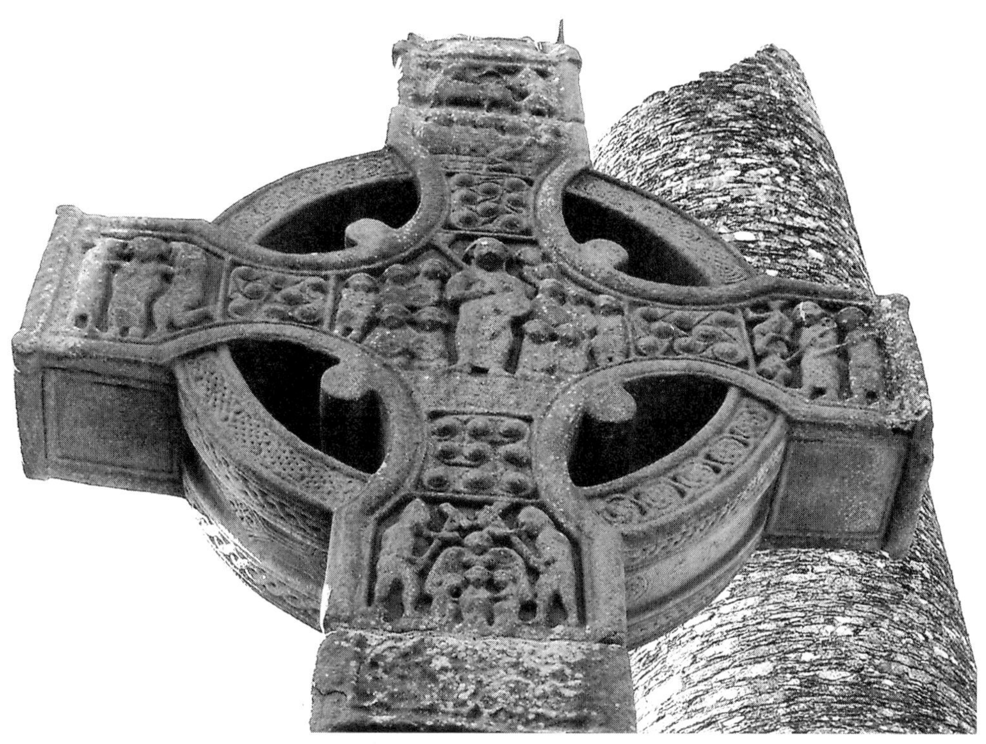

7.5 Head of the Tall Cross, Monasterboice.

scenes. Heads with long tangled hair were a mark of superfluous thoughts and shame (possibly following a suggestion by St Paul in 1 Corinthians II:14), while entangled figures represent those who fail to hear the word of God (Pulliam, 2007, 267). Beard-pulling figures may have been a symbol of confusion or discord (Harbison, 2007, 221), but it has also been suggested that they may convey sin and are sexual in content, symbolic of lust (Henderson, 1996, 47; Hall et al., 1998; Pulliam, 2007, 267). Human heads were used in the Book of Kells to indicate the proper reception of Christ's teaching. Twenty-two of the twenty-nine initials with heads in the Book of Kells, appear in passages relating to the acknowledgment or rejection of Christ's identity (Pulliam, 2007, 259). Heads were often represented within the monogram of Christ and were intended as glimpses of eternal life.

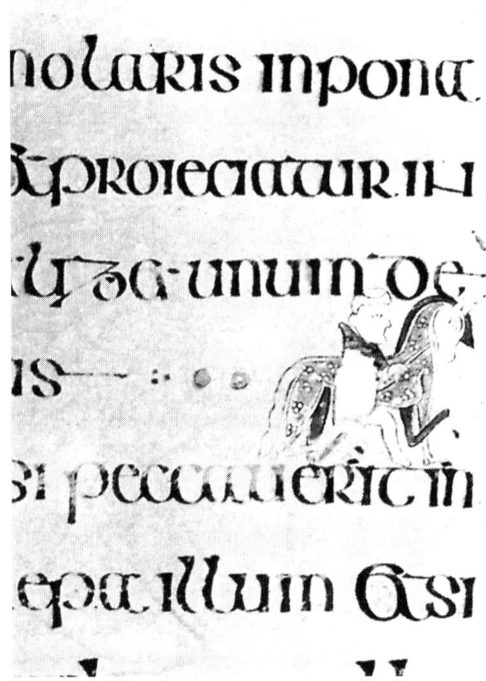

7.6 Kells, fo. 255v: riding monk (The Board of Trinity College, Dublin).

In the Book of Kells, a bearded warrior holds a shield and spear on fo. 200r. His penis is inked in and outlined with red dots, just below and parallel to his spear. It has been suggested that as the page deals with the genealogy of Christ, perhaps it is an allusion to procreation and death, the spear being a prediction of the Crucifixion (Meehan, 1994, 64).

The image of a man between beasts, or, in some cases merely a head between two beasts, is usually interpreted in early Christian art as representing Daniel in the Lions' Den. However, there are three different designs in which a human figure is flanked by animals. One group comprises a figure flanked by confronted upright animals which seem to be whispering in his ears. A second group shows the central figure flanked by human figures with animal features. In the third group, the composition has been discarded – all that remains is a human figure with animal attributes (usually an animal head), frequently armed, and positioned either to the side of a cross on a cross-shaft or in a Crucifixion scene (Roe, 1945, 3) (fig. 7.5).

On the Tall Cross at Monasterboice, the subject matter of the head relates to the way in which God protects those who have faith. One of the two figures on the left arm of the east face is animal-headed and holds a human in a long robe (fig. 7.5). The figures appear to be whispering in his ears, and the scene is usually taken to represent the Temptation of St Anthony. On the opposite arm, two figures, one with a crook, overcome a naked and inverted figure, which has been interpreted as either Paul and Anthony overcoming the Devil, or Peter and Paul defeating Simon Magus, who attempted to fly (Pulliam, 206, 166). Inverted figures symbolize the damned, and the shepherd's crook is a symbol of good clerics (Pulliam, 2006, 166). A figure on the Market Cross at Kells also uses a crook to poke the eye of an inverted figure, while a similar subject appears on the Cross of Muiredach, Monasterboice.

A tonsured monk in the Book of Kells is probably a symbol of pride, since the foot is associated with pride (fig. 7.6) and his foot is placed on the word *peccaverit* ('he has sinned'). The use of a mounted figure here may relate to St Augustine's comparison of those on horseback with those who are inattentive. The riding monk should also be viewed in the context of the initial letter to the line, which shows a man entwined in a beast. This probably relates to the moral confusion of the sinner (Pulliam, 2006, 162).

Figures with books abound in the Book of Kells. A depiction of a book was symbolic of the medium which carried the message of Christ, and had talismanic properties. There are thirty representations of books in the Book of Kells – some with figures that have been identified as deacons, who were responsible for the altar and its furnishing, and also read the gospel at Mass (Farr, 1995, 142).

BIBLICAL SYMBOLISM

Biblical symbolism is most apparent in the sculptural scenes on Irish High Crosses and in illuminated manuscripts. The High Crosses are themselves symbolic of the Cross of the Crucifixion scene and further aspects of Christian belief.

SYMBOLISM ON IRISH HIGH CROSSES

Crucifixes (that is, effigies of Christ upon the Cross) are comparatively rare, and are usually late in both Irish and Pictish sculpture. For the early Christian Celts, the cross was in itself the symbol of the person of Christ (Richardson & Scarry, 1990, 11) and the cult of the Cross originated with Constantine.

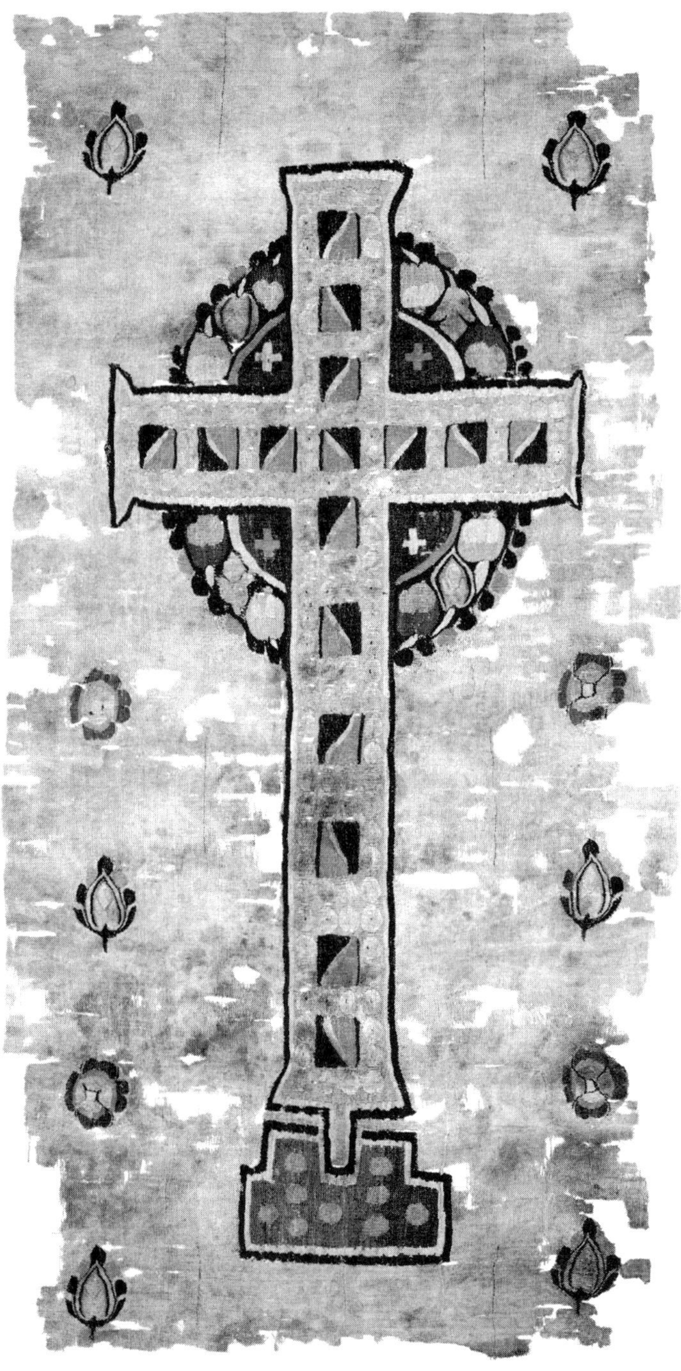

7.7 Coptic textile sanctuary curtain, sixth century (Minneapolis Institute of Arts, The Centennial Fund: Aimee Mott Butler Charitable Trust, Mr and Mrs John F. Donovan, Estate of Margaret B. Hawks, Eleanor Weld Reid).

Origins of the free-standing cross

Free-standing stone crosses are rare except in Britain, Ireland and the eastern areas of the Christian world, especially Armenia and Georgia (Richardson, 1987). It has been suggested that the characteristic ring on Irish High Crosses is derived from the laurel wreath which was attached to the victor's standard after a successful battle. It may also represent Christ's halo (Richardson & Scarry, 1990, 24). Certainly, there is good reason to believe that the ringed cross was established in the east Mediterranean long before its first appearance in the Celtic world, since a surviving Coptic textile of sixth-century date depicts a jewelled, ringed cross, apparently tenoned into a stepped base (Werner, 1990a; Stack, 1991) (fig. 7.7).

The form of the Irish High Cross is in itself an allusion to the jewelled, canopied cross erected at Golgotha. It was depicted on ampullae (flasks of holy water) brought back by pilgrims from the sixth century onwards (Richardson, 1995). A description of it was provided by Adomnán in the late seventh century in his *De Locis Sanctis* – where he mentions the church which stood 'on the site which in Hebrew is called Golgotha. From the roof hangs a large bronze wheel for lamps, and below it stands a great silver cross, fixed in the same socket as the wooden cross on which the Saviour of mankind once suffered'. It is probable that the house-shaped capstone on many High Crosses was intended to represent the shrine built by Constantine to mark the site of the Resurrection. The bun-shaped capstone on some crosses, such as those at Ahenny, was possibly modelled on the canopy over the cross in the Church of the Holy Sepulchre, Jerusalem (Richardson, 1984b).

The earliest free-standing stone crosses in the Celtic world have generally been assumed to be those on Iona (Stevenson, 1956), where the ringed head has been seen as a response to the need to strengthen that on St John's Cross after a fall. The presumed earlier St Oran's Cross was without a ring (Fisher, 2001, 15). It also pre-supposes that the prototypes were wooden crosses. However, these need not have been the only inspiration. Metal altar crosses and processional crosses can be seen as possible models for the design of some of the earliest stone crosses in Ireland. The rope-mouldings on the shafts of the Ahenny crosses apparently copy a feature of metalwork, which employed corner binding strips. Bosses found in both Ireland and Scotland have also been seen as inspired by metalwork (Edwards, 1983, 31–2) (fig. 7.8). A model for the design of St John's Cross has been seen in the metal Rupertus Cross (now in Salzburg), which was made by an Anglo-Saxon for an Iona monk, Vergil

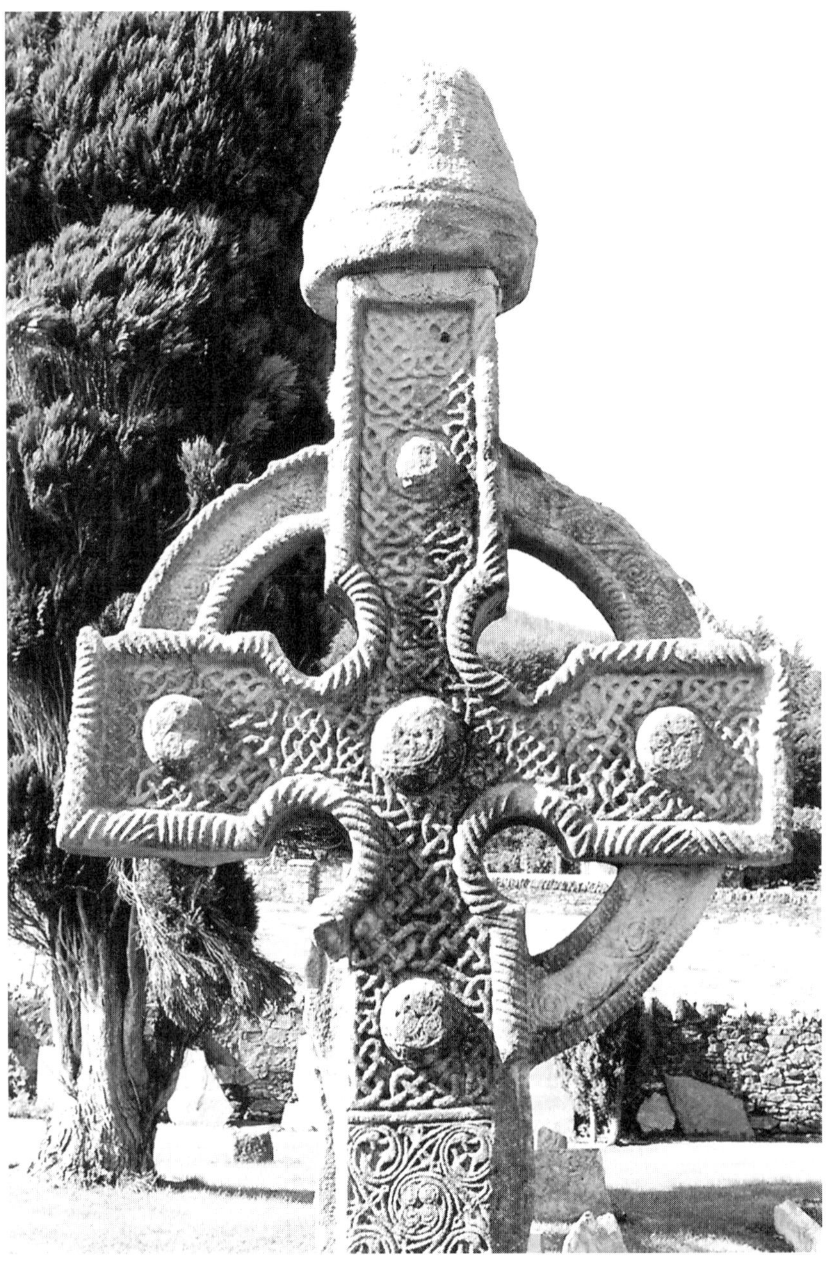

7.8 Ahenny, South Cross, Co. Tipperary, showing mouldings (photo: Gavin Williams).

(Fisher, 2001, 15). The discovery of the Tully Lough Cross in 1986 shows that metal models were available in the Celtic arena in the eighth to early ninth century (Kelly, 2000). Many stone crosses display features of metalwork models (Harbison 1993, 346–7).

The influence of Anglo-Saxon free-standing crosses on the transition to stone should not be underestimated, however, and it has to be stressed that the Ruthwell and Bewcastle Crosses (if Bewcastle was a cross and not a column) in Northumbria are probably at least half a century earlier than the earliest four-sided free-standing Celtic crosses.

Models in wood and metal were available in the Celtic world long before the first stone free-standing crosses. The inspiration for the appearance at Iona of the stone monument known as the High Cross, which was decorated on four faces, came from Northumbria. It is also the case that the cross at Kilnave on Islay (Fisher, 2000, no. 374), possibly of mid-eighth-century date, shows the inspiration of an earlier type of Northumbrian flat stone (undecorated) cross known at Whitby. Merovingian influence has been seen in this (Cramp, 1993, 69; Bailey, 1996a, 50–1), and there is an undecorated parallel for it at Inchnadamph, Argyll (Fisher, 2001, no. 23). In this context, the cross at Toureen Peacaun, Co. Tipperary, is significant, since it follows wooden constructional techniques and bears an inscription in geometric capitals that appears to name an Anglo-Saxon woman, Osgyd (Charles-Edwards, 2003). Although seriously damaged and broken in pieces, the Toureen Peacaun cross shows stylistic links with St Oran's Cross on Iona, and more particularly with the cross at A'Chill, on Canna (Kelly, 1993, 224). It is possible that under Anglo-Saxon influence the High Cross was developed in western Ireland, taken to Dál Riata, which then played an important part in the dissemination of the form in Ireland, through the daughter houses of Iona. The snake-boss ornament of the Iona crosses, which may have originated in Pictland, was certainly also taken up in Iona's daughter houses, such as at Dromiskin, Co. Louth, and Boho, Co. Fermanagh (Kelly, 1993, 225).

It would appear that, with certain exceptions, High Crosses were erected facing west, following patristic tradition, expressed by Sedulius in the *Carmen Paschale*, that Christ faced west on the cross (Ó Carragáin, 1987, 120). In some instances, the scenes were intended to be read by moving sunwise (or following one's right hand), round the cross. The importance of *dessel* (the Irish word for this process), was emphasized by early Irish writers (O'Rahilly, 1946, 296–7). The Cross at Moone, for instance, can only be understood by starting in the east and then moving to the south, west and north sides (Henry, 1964, 39–41). The reading of the monuments is also often intended to be done from the bottom upwards.

Symbolism on High Crosses

The arrangement of scenes on the Irish High Crosses and to a less obvious extent on Pictish relief cross-slabs, was devised deliberately to make particular points, mostly concerning salvation and the sacraments. One favoured device was the juxtaposition of Old and New Testament scenes to make the point that events in one heralded events in the other. Paired episodes of this type (known as Types and Antitypes), are widespread in Christian art. Thus, the Fall of Man was seen as the start of a series of events which necessitated Christ dying for mankind, and Adam and Eve and the Crucifixion are often found in close relationship, for example on the crosses at Tihilly and Castledermot, Ireland (Harbison, 1992, 330).

Salvation is another important theme which was illustrated by such scenes as the sacrifice of Isaac; Noah's ark; Daniel in the Lions' Den; Moses Smiting Water from the Rock; the Judgment of Solomon; the Children in the Fiery Furnace (where the child is saved) and Samson Rending the Pillars of the House (Harbison, 1992, 330). It may be that these were a visual response to the text of the *Commendatio Animae*, which was a prayer asking for the saving of the dying, as certain Old Testament personages had been saved (Flower, 1954, 91–2). It is increasingly apparent, however, that the individual scenes were not merely intended to be seen in isolation, but in the context of the entire composition.

The subject matter on the Moone High Cross, for example, is concerned very much with life in the desert, and has a Eucharistic significance, which is one of the meanings to be read in the popular themes of, for example, the Desert Fathers (Paul and Anthony) and the Flight into Egypt. Thus, on Moone, the Eucharist is alluded to in the scene depicting the Loaves and Fishes, which are flanked by two serpent-like monsters which refer, in all probability, to the Eucharistic bread being Christ (Ó Carragáin, 1987, 119) (fig. 7.9).

The arrangement of the scenes on High Crosses is very much concerned with the history of the Old Testament world seen in a structured sequence, from a theological viewpoint. Thus, the scenes on Moone start with Adam and Eve, followed by the Sacrifice of Isaac, and Daniel in the Lions' Den, all of which were scenes which the patristic writings associated with the first, third and fifth ages of the world (Ó Carragáin, 1987, 119).

The Cross of Muiredach at Monasterboice has much more complex imagery. On the east side, in reverse order, are Adam and Eve, and Cain

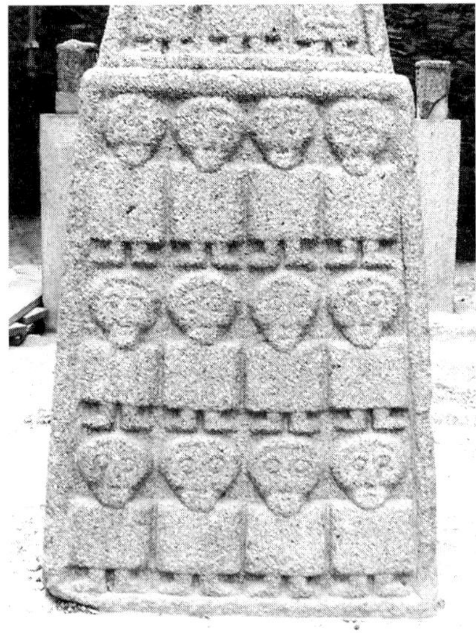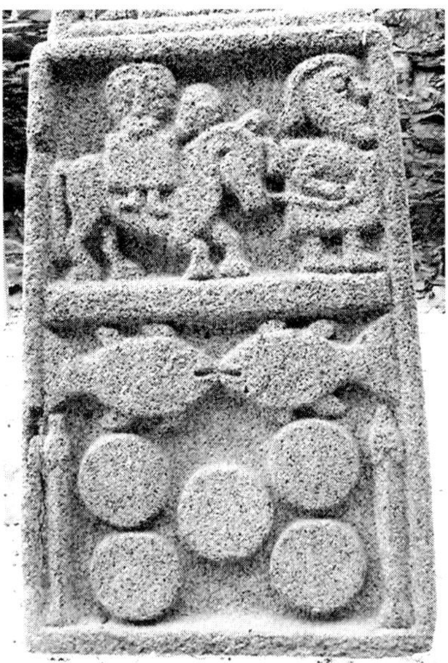

7.9 Moone High Cross, Co. Kildare: panels with apostles and loaves and fishes
(photos: Jim Fitzpatrick).

and Abel juxtaposed with David and Goliath, and Saul and Jonathan: Loss
of Paradise and the First Murder are matched with the establishment of
the kingdom of Israel and the death of the champion of her enemy.
History is then reversed, for above David is Moses striking the rock and
Mary showing Christ to the Three Kings. This is an allusion to I
Corinthians 10:4, where St Paul identifies the rock which Moses strikes, as
Christ, which signified how the sacraments flow from Christ to all
Christians. The juxtaposing of Mary showing Christ to the Gentiles was
trying to make a parallel example of the sacraments flowing from Christ.
This prepares the viewer for the Last Judgment, at the top of the cross on
this side (Ó Carragáin, 1987, 120). The same idea of Christ as the fountain
of the sacraments is employed in a different way in the Chi-Rho page in
the Book of Kells.

The Broken Cross at Kells has been clearly demonstrated as showing
the relationship between the subjects of the panels on different faces of the
cross (Harbison 1992, 334) (fig. 7.10). The west face is given over to scenes
from the Old Testament, the east face to scenes from the New. The Old
Testament scenes are arranged in chronological order, three scenes
depicting the liberation of the Israelites. The New Testament scenes are
not arranged in chronological order, but to provide parallels with those in
the Old Testament, with the most important scenes at the bottom. Thus,

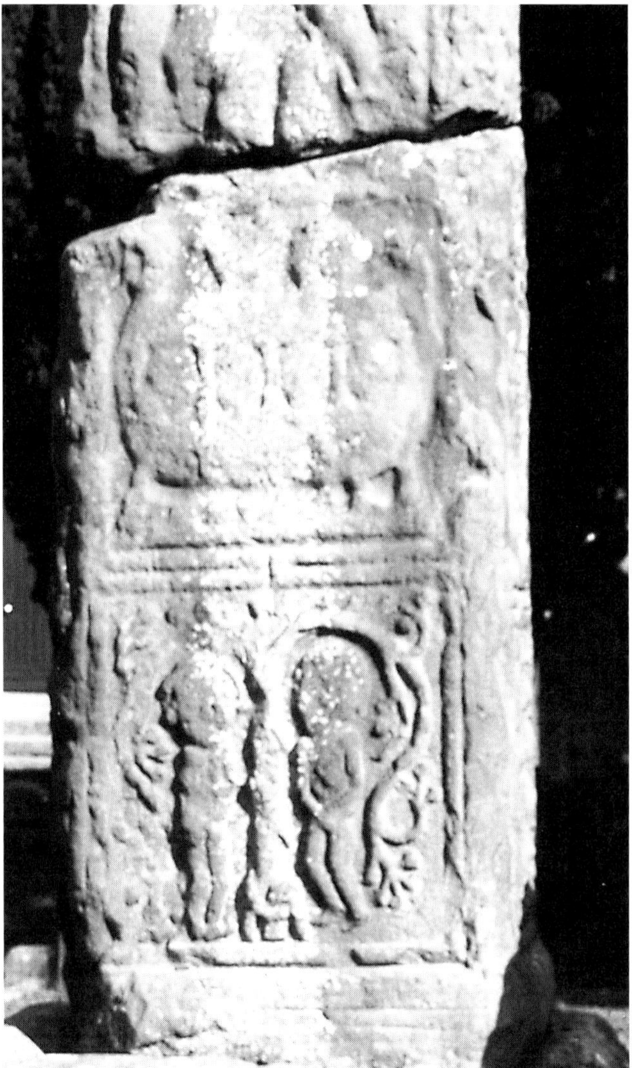

7.10 Kells, Co. Meath, Broken Cross, Adam and Eve.

at the top, the Crossing of the Dead Sea is matched with Christ's Entry in Jerusalem. Both scenes involve horses, but the Israelites in the Old Testament scene are riding to destruction, whereas Christ in the New Testament scene is riding to triumph. In the next pair there is the Pillar of Fire and the Wise Men questioning Herod (both scenes involving a supernatural light leading the way to Salvation, though the light is not shown in the panel). In the third pair, Moses is turning the waters of Egypt into blood, which is a foretelling of the Miracle at Cana, which appears on the New Testament side, though not directly opposite, where there is a miracle; probably Christ healing the Lame Man at Bethesda. Beneath these is Noah's Ark and at the bottom on the west face Adam and Eve, with the Baptism of Christ at the bottom on the New Testament side. Many of the scenes involve water, which relates to the theme of baptism. In fact, many of the scenes have a baptismal connotation, and the primary function of the cross should be read as connected with baptism.

The Tall Cross at Monasterboice similarly separates Old and New Testament scenes on different faces, though not in chronological order. With the exception of one baptism scene, the theme of the cross seems to be the Passion and Resurrection. This is also the theme of the Cross of Muiredach at Monasterboice, the Durrow Cross and the Cross of the Scriptures at Clonmacnois (Harbison, 1992, 340).

Other themes that were particularly favoured involved the hermit SS Paul and Anthony, and John the Baptist. St Jerome mentions John the Baptist and Elijah as the models for the life of an eremitical monk, and the writings of St Ambrose also associated Elijah with baptism. It is therefore not surprising that these saints appear alongside the depiction of the Baptism of Christ and the sinking of St Peter (a subject with a baptismal connotation) on the Tall Cross at Monasterboice, where there were also scenes from the early life of John the Baptist (Harbison, 1992, 331). SS Paul and Anthony were particularly favoured in Celtic art, though they are not common subjects in early medieval art generally. As founders of the eremitic life, they were deemed particularly appropriate for monastic sculpture, and they had significance in terms of the Eucharist. For this reason, they are frequently shown receiving bread from a raven, and sometimes with a chalice between them. They occur in both Ireland and Pictland.

MANUSCRIPTS

It is in the Book of Kells that the full complexity of early Christian symbolism can be seen. The book has virtually the full range of ornament to be found in early medieval manuscripts: twenty-four full-page images and over two thousand decorated initials, mostly containing human or zoomorphic designs (Pulliam, 2006, 14). One theme which appears to run through the book is the Eucharist. In folio 34, the object between the mice is Eucharistic bread (it is marked with a cross); the fish in the mouth of an otter is Christ, and the object between the moths or butterflies at the top represents a chrysalis, a symbol of rebirth (Lewis, 1980, 140) (fig. 7.11). The whole of folio 34 is a clear example of symbolism within symbolism. The butterflies and angels can be seen to represent air; the cats and mice

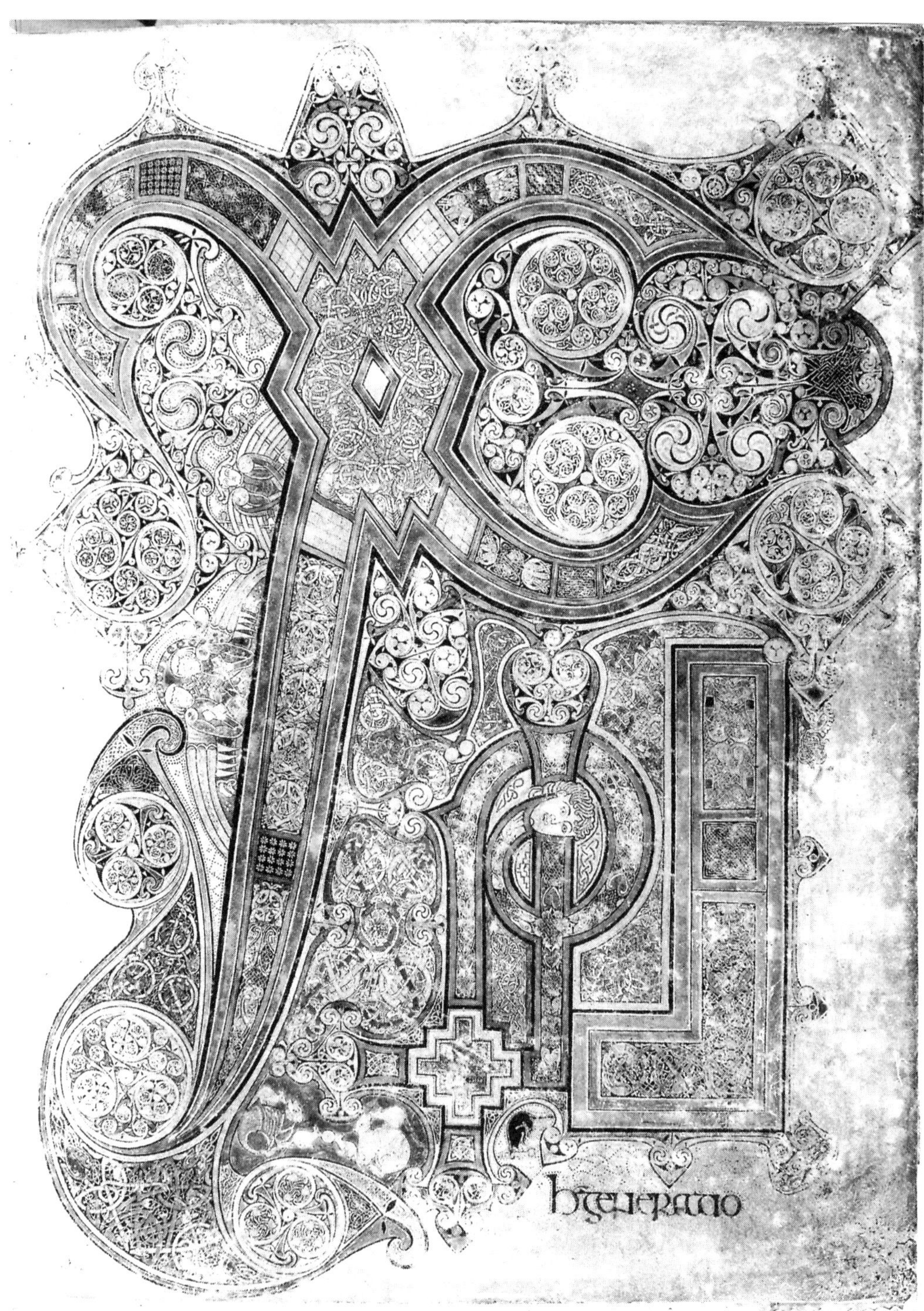

7.11 Book of Kells, fo. 34r (The Board of Trinity College, Dublin).

7.12 Book of Kells, fo. 48r (The Board of Trinity College, Dublin).

represent land, and the otter and fish represent water; thus symbolizing the dimensions through which Christ reigned. The Chi-Rho, which is the central theme of the page, is Christ, and his head is represented on the loop of the rho. The context of this is explained by a text of St Jerome's relating to the four rivers of the Virtues which flow out of one bright and health-giving paradise, irrigating the whole breadth of the Christian Church (cited by the Anglo-Saxon monk Alcuin – Henderson, 1987, 161).

The Host (the communion bread) is depicted as a circle with a cross on it and reappears in a number of other contexts, such as in the mouth of a lion in folio 29r, and on the leg of the calf symbol on folio 27v. On folio 48r, a cat chases a rat that is holding a Host, and the text below it seems to relate to it 'what man is there among you, of whom his son shall ask bread, will he reach him a stone?' (Matthew, 7:9) (Lewis, 1980) (fig. 7.12). Meehan has suggested that the images of a rodent eating the Host may have prompted a consideration of the problem of how a mouse could partake of the body of Christ (Meehan, 1994, 44). Depictions of grapes being eaten or figures drinking from a chalice taking place both abound, and may again be Eucharistic allusions, as are representations of flabella, which were originally used to keep flies off the Host (see above, p. 85) (Meehan, 1994, 45, 48). It has been suggested that the page usually interpreted as the Arrest of Christ (fo. 114r), which is now more commonly agreed to represent the Passion, has Eucharistic connotations, represented by the urns sprouting vines (Christ being the vine) above Christ's head (O'Reilly,

1993). The pose of Christ in this scene is that of an orant, which is also the sign of the cross. The scene was for contemplation on Holy Thursday and seems to allude to the blessing of the oils, a particular ceremony (Farr, 1997, 134). The Temptation Page (fo. 202v) in Kells is equally complex, representing both the Temptation and also the Baptism and Genealogy of Christ (O'Reilly, 1994, 345–90; Henderson, 1987, 168–74; Farr, 1997, 86).

The Book of Kells embodies all that is European in Celtic Christian art. From the pagan Roman world has come much of the abstract, curvilinear ornament that is so apparent in its carpet pages and in the individual embellishments of some of the letters. From a pagan European source too, has come interlace and animal ornament derived from the art of the Germanic Migration Period – some originating in the far north, in Scandinavia – which was blended into the same carpet pages.

But, although the ornament comes from a pagan European past, it was reworked to express Christian symbolic values that are Christian, which originate in thinking developed in the Mediterranean. Elsewhere, the pictorial pages of Kells seem to draw upon artistic traditions that in some cases originate in the East, but which also draw upon European art which was separately occidental in conception. Indeed, all the figural work may be said to owe a debt to late Roman art – itself subject to or even born of, considerable Eastern influence. The concept of a bound book was itself an introduction from the Mediterranean, since none existed in the pre-Christian Celtic world Christianity. However, although it is possible to point to antecedents for virtually everything in the Book of Kells that were not native to Irish culture, the artistic fusion assuredly was. It was what the Celts made of the disparate elements they found elsewhere that created the phenomenon that people faultlessly recognize, but can rarely define.

POSTSCRIPT – THE ACHIEVEMENTS OF CELTIC ART

Like Joseph Anderson, one of the major figures of nineteenth-century archaeology in Scotland, I see clearly that the achievement of the Celts lay not in their isolation but in their openness to the cultural trends of the rest of Europe. They had good trade and cultural links by sea, north and south, as well as across the Irish Sea, eastwards. The distances they travelled are indicative of their readiness to assimilate ideas from all their European neighbours. The artworks they revered or created are the tangible proof of it.

Writing about art in Early Christian Scotland in 1881, Anderson showed clear awareness, as we have today, that artists do not flourish in insolation:

> While it is manifest therefore, that a national system of art like this of the Scottish monuments is described in correct terms by saying that in all the essential features of its individuality it differs from every other, it does not necessarily follow that its essential elements must have originated in Scotland or Ireland.
>
> (Joseph Anderson, *Scotland in Early Christian Times*, 2nd Ser., 1881, 110–11).

I hope that in this book I have enabled the general public and students to find pathways through the myriad confusions that have become the study of Celtic art.

Modern technology and approaches have made sense of much that was, half a century ago, a frustration that led to much emotional rather than intellectual discussion. This is not to say that I believe there is any one way to view the Celts and their art. Quite the opposite: I hope that readers will find stimulus to take their own studies, researches and analyses along new routes to insights, approaches and conclusions.

The intellectual routes that beg to be explored remain tantalizingly exotic – Roman, Byzantine, Saxon, Frankish, Armenian, Coptic Egyptian and Norse are all influences discernible in the formation of Celtic Christian art. The diversity of inspiration is awesome, but the distinctiveness of the fusion is unique.

Bibliography

Abdy, R. 2006. 'In the pay of the Emperor: coins from the Beaurains (Arras) (Oise)', *Gallia*, 44, 29–53.

Alcock, L. 1963. *Dinas Powys: an Iron Age, Dark Age and Medieval settlement in Glamorgan*, Cardiff.

Alcock, L. 1998. 'From realism to caricature: reflections on Insular depictions of animals and people', *PSAS*, 128, 495–513.

Alexander, J.J.G. 1978. *Insular manuscripts, 6th to the 9th century*, London.

Allen, J.R. & Anderson, J. 1903. *The Early Christian monuments of Scotland*, Edinburgh.

Allen, J.R. 1887. *Early Christian symbolism in Great Britain and Ireland*, London.

Allen, J.R. 1899. *Celtic crosses of Wales* (repr.), Llanerch.

Allen, J.R. 1904. *Celtic art*, London.

Armstrong, E.C.R. & Macallister, R.A.S. 1920. 'Wooden block with leaves indented and waxed found at Springmount Bog, Co. Antrim', *JRSAI*, 1, 160–6.

Arnold, B. & Gibson, D.B. (eds). 1995. *Celtic chiefdom, Celtic state*, Cambridge.

Arrhenius, B. 1979. 'Ein Goldschmildegrab von Havgaradsberg, Vendel, Uppland, Sweden', *Frümittelalterische Studien*, 13, 393–414.

Backhouse, J. 1981. *The Lindisfarne Gospels*, London.

Bailey, R. & Cramp, R. 1988. *Cumberland, Westmorland and Lancashire North-of-the-Sands, corpus of Anglo-Saxon sculpture*, II, Oxford.

Bailey, R. 1980. *Viking Age sculpture*, London.

Bailey, R. 1996a. *England's earliest sculptors*, Toronto.

Bailey, R. 1996b. *Ambiguous birds and beasts: three sculptural puzzles in south-west Scotland*, Whithorn.

Bakka, E. 1965. 'Some decorated Anglo-Saxon and Irish metalwork in Norwegian Viking graves' in Small, A. (ed.), *The Fourth Viking Congress*, Torshavn, 39–40.

Ball, M. & Fife, J. (eds). 1993. *The Celtic languages*, London.

Barber, J.W. 1981. 'Excavations on Iona, 1979', *PSAS*, 111, 282–380.

Bateson, J.D. 1973. 'Roman material from Ireland: a reconsideration', *PRIA*, 73C, 21–97.

Bateson, J.D. 1976. 'Further finds of Roman material from Ireland', *PRIA*, 76C, 171–80.

Bateson, J.D. 1981. *Enamel-working in Iron Age, Roman and sub-Roman Britain*, BAR British Series, 93, Oxford.

Berger, L. 1956. 'Die Thekenbeschlage des Gemellianus von Baden-Aquae Helveticae', *Funfundvierzigstes Jahrbuch der Schweizerischen Gesellschaft für Urgeschichte 1956*, 24–39.

Berger, P. 1979. 'The Ardagh Chalice, numerology and the Stowe Missal', *Eire-Ireland*, 14:3, 6–16.

Biddle, M. & Biddle, B. 1985. 'The Repton Stone', *Anglo-Saxon England*, 14, 233–92.

Bieler, L. (ed. & trans.). 1979. *The Patrician texts in the Book of Armagh*, Dublin.

Binchy, D.A. (ed.). 1978. *Corpus Iuris Hibernici*, 5 vols, Dublin.

Bitel, L.M. 1990. *Isle of the saints: monastic settlement and Christian community in early Ireland*, Ithaca.

Blindheim, M. 1984. 'A house-shaped Irish-Scots reliquary in Bologna, and its place among the other reliquaries', *Acta Archaeologica*, 55, 1–53.

Böhme, H.W. 1974. *Germanische Grabfunde des 4 bis 5 Jahrhunerts. Zwiischen unterer Elbe und Loire*, Munich.

Böhme, H.W. 1986. 'Das Ende der Römerherrschaft in Britannien und die angelsachsische Besiedlung Englands im 5. Jahrhundert', *Jahrbuch des Römische-Germanischen Zentralmuseums*, 33, 469–574.

Bourke, C. (ed.). 1995a. *From the Isles of the north: Early Medieval art in Ireland and Britain*, Belfast.

Bourke, C. 1995b. 'The chronology of Irish crucifixion plaques' in Bourke (ed.), 168–74.

Bradley, J. 1991. 'Excavations at Moynagh Lough, Co. Meath', *JRSAI*, 111, 5–26.

Bradley, J. 1993. 'Moynagh Lough: an insular workshop of the second quarter of the eighth century' in Spearman & Higgitt (eds), 74–81.

Braun, J. 1940. *Die Reliquiare des christlichen Kultes und ihre Entwicklung*, Freiburg im Breisgau.

Brenan, J. 1991. *Hanging bowls and their contexts*, BAR British Series, Oxford.

Brogan, O. 1953. *Roman Gaul*, London.

Brown, J. 1984. 'The oldest Irish manuscripts and their late antique background' in Ní Chatháin, P. & Richter, M. (eds), *Irland und Europa: Die Kirche im Frümittelaalter/ Ireland and Europe: the early church*, Stuttgart, 311–27.

Brown, M. 1993. '"Paten and purpose": the Derrynaflan Paten inscriptions' in Spearman & Higgitt (eds), 162–7.

Brown, M. 2003. *The Lindisfarne Gospels: society, spirituality and the scribe*, London.

Brown, P.D.C. & Schweizer, F. 1973. 'X-ray fluorescent analysis of Anglo-Saxon jewellery', *Archaeometry*, 15:2, 175–92.

Brown, S.A. & Herren, M.W. 2001. 'Neo-Pelagianism, early Insular religious art, and the image of Christ' in Redknap et al. (eds), 61–71.

Bruce-Mitford, R.L.S. 1974. *Aspects of Anglo-Saxon archaeology: Sutton Hoo and other discoveries*, London.

Bruce-Mitford, R.L.S. 2005. *A corpus of Late Celtic hanging bowls*, Oxford.

Brulet, R. 1966. 'Tournai, fouille d'une nécropole des Bas-Empire', *Archeologia*, 145, 55–9.

Bu'lock, J.D. 1972. *Pre-Conquest Cheshire, 383–1066*, Chester.

Budny, M. 2001. 'Deciphering the art of interlace' in Hourihane (ed.), 183–210.

Bushe-Fox, J.P. 1949. *Fourth report on the excavations at Richborough, Kent* (=Society of Antiquaries of London Research Report, 16).

Byrne, F.J. 1973. *Irish kings and high kings*, London.

Campbell, E. & Lane, A. 1993. 'Celtic and Germanic Interaction in Dalriada: the 7th-century metalworking site of Dunadd' in Spearman & Higgitt (eds), 52–63.

Campbell, E. 1992. 'The post-Roman pottery' in Edwards & Lane (eds), 124–38.

Campbell, E. 1996. 'The archaeological evidence for external contacts: imports, trade and economy in Celtic Britain, AD400–800' in Dark (ed.), 83–96.

Carrington, A. 1996. 'The horseman and the falcon: mounted falconers in Pictish sculpture', *PSAS*, 126, 459–68.

Carroll, J. 1995. 'Millefiori in the development of Early Irish enamelling' in Bourke (ed.), 49–57.

Carver, M. & Spall, C. 2004. 'Excavating a parchmenerie: archaeological correlates of making parchment at the Pictish monastery at Portmahomack, Easter Ross', *PSAS*, 134, 183–200.

Carver, M. 1982. *Sutton Hoo: burial ground of Kings*, London.

Carver, M. 2008. *Portmahomack: monastery of the Picts*, Edinburgh.

Chadwick, S.C. 1958. 'The Anglo-Saxon cemetery at Finglesham, Kent', *Med. Arch.*, 2, 1–71.

Charles-Edwards, G. 2003. 'The East Cross inscription from Toureen Peacaun: letterform analysis and a suggested reading', *Archaeology Ireland* (spring 2003), 13–15.

Charles-Edwards, T.M. 1993. *Early Irish and Welsh kinship*, Oxford.

Charles-Edwards, T.M. 2000. *Early Christian Ireland*, Cambridge.

Child, H. & Colles, D. 1971. *Christian symbols, ancient & modern: a handbook for students*, London.

Christie, N. 2005. 'Charlemagne and the renewal of Rome' in Story (ed.), 167–82.

Clancy, T.O. 1993. 'The Drosten stone: a new reading', *PSAS*, 123, 345–53.

Clarke, H.B., Ní Mhaonaigh, M. & Ó Floinn, R. (eds). 1998. *Ireland and Scandinavia in the early Viking Age*, Dublin.

Close-Brooks, J. 1986. 'Excavations at Clatchard Craig, Fife', *PSAS*, 116, 117–84.

Coatsworth, E. & Pinder, M. 2002. *The art of the Anglo-Saxon goldsmith: fine metalwork in Anglo-Saxon England, practice and practitioners*, Woodbridge.

Cocke, T. & Kidson, P. 1993. *Salisbury Cathedral: perspectives on the architectural history*, London.

Coffey, G. 1909. *Guide to the Celtic antiquities of the Christian period in the National Museum, Dublin*, Dublin.

Comber, M. 2004. *Native evidence of non-ferrous metalworking in early historic Ireland*, BAR International Series, 1296, Oxford.

Connolly, S. & Picard, J-M. 1987. 'Cogitosus: Life of St Brigit', *JRSAI*, 117, 11–27.

Cool, H. 1986. 'A Romano-British gold workshop of the second century', *Britannia*, 17, 231–7.

Cool, H. 1990. 'Roman metal hair pins from southern Britain', *Archaeol. J.*, 147, 148–82.

Cool, H. 2000. 'The parts left over: material culture into the fifth century AD' in Willmott, T. & Wilson, P. (eds), *The Late Roman transition in the North*, BAR British Series, Oxford, 47–65.

Coulson, J.C. & Phillips, E.J. 1988. *Hadrian's Wall west of the North Tyne and Carlisle*, *Corpus Signorum Imperii Romani*: Great Britain, 1, fas. 6, Oxford.

Court, A. 1985. *Puck of the Droms*, Berkeley.

Craig, D. 1991. 'Pre-Norman sculpture in Galloway: some territorial implications' in Oram, R. & Stell, G.P. (eds), *Galloway: land and lordship*, Edinburgh, 45–62.

Craig, D. 1997. 'The sculptured stones' in Hill (ed.), 433–41.

Cramp, R. 1978. 'The Anglian tradition in the ninth century' in Lang, J. (ed.), 1–21.

Cramp, R. 1993. 'A reconsideration of the monastic site of Whitby' in Spearman & Higgitt (eds), 64–73.

Crawford, B. (ed.). 1994. *Scotland in Dark Age Europe*, St Andrews.

Crawford, B. 1987. *Scandinavian Scotland*, Leicester.

Crawford, O.G.S. 1937. 'The vine scroll in Scotland', *Antiquity*, 11, 469–73.

Cronin, J. 1995. 'The evangelist symbols as pictorial exegesis' in Bourke (ed.), 111–17.

Cruikshank, G. 1999. *The Battle of Dunnichen*, Balgavies.

Cubbon, A.M. 1983. 'The archaeology of the Vikings in the Isle of Man' in Fell et al. (eds), 13–26.

Curle, A.O. 1923. *The Traprain Treasure*, Glasgow.

Curle, C.L. 1940. 'The chronology of the Early Christian monuments of Scotland', *PSAS*, 74 (1939–40), 60–116.

Curle, C.L. 1975. 'An engraved lead disc from the Brough of Birsay, Orkney', *PSAS*, 105, 301–06.

Curle, C.L. 1982. *Pictish and Norse finds from the Brough of Birsay, 1934–74*, *Society of Antiquities of Scotland Research Reports*, 1, Edinburgh.

Curtis, N. & Hunter, F. 2006. 'An unusual pair of Roman bronze vessels from Stoneywood, Aberdeen and other Roman finds from north-east Scotland', *PSAS*, 136, 199–214.

Cust, A.M.E. 1902. *The ivory-workers of the Middle Ages*, London.

Davidson, H.E. & Webster, L. 1967. 'The Anglo-Saxon burial at Coombe (Woodnesborough), Kent', *Med. Arch.*, 11, 1–41.

Davies, W. 1982. *Wales in the early Middle Ages*, Leicester.

Davies, W. 1992. 'The myth of the Celtic church' in Edwards & Lane (eds), Oxford, 12–21.

Davis, M. & Gwilt, A. 2008. 'Material, style and identity in first century AD metalwork, with particular reference to the Seven Sisters Hoard' in Garrow et al. (eds), 146–184.

Davis-Weyer, C. 1971. *Early Medieval art, 300–1150*, New Jersey.

DeCaens, J. 1971. 'Un nouveau cimetière du haut moyen age en Normandie, Hérouvillette (Calvados)', *Archéologie Médiévale*, 1, 1–125.

Denison, S. 2000. 'Gemstone evidence for late Roman survival', *British Archaeology*, 52, 4.

Di Martino, V. 2003. *Roman Ireland*, Cork.

Dodwell, C.R. 1982. *Anglo-Saxon art: a new perspective*, Manchester.

Dodwell, C.R. 1993. *The pictorial arts of the West, 800–1200*, New Haven & London.

Doherty, C. 1980. 'Exchange and trade in early medieval Ireland', *JRSAI*, 110, 67–89.

Doherty, C. 1984. 'The use of relics in early Ireland' in Ní Chatháin, P. & Richter, M. (eds), *Ireland and Europe*, Stuttgart, 89–104.

Doherty, C. 1985. 'The monastic town in early medieval Ireland' in Clarke, H. & Simms, A. (eds), *The comparative history of urban origins in non-Roman Europe*, Oxford, 45–75.

Doherty, C. 1998. 'The Vikings in Ireland: a review' in Clarke et al., 288–330.

Driscoll, S.T. 1988. 'The relationship between history and archaeology: artefacts, documents and power' in Driscoll, S.T. & Nieke, M. (eds), *Power and politics in Early Medieval Britain and Ireland*, Edinburgh, 162–87.

Driscoll, S.T., O'Grady, O. & Forsyth, K. 2005. 'The Govan School revisited: searching for meaning in the Early Medieval sculpture of Strathclyde' in Foster, S. (ed.), 135–57.

Dungworth, D. 1996. 'The production of copper-alloys in Iron Age Britain', *PPS*, 62, 399–421.

Duval, P-M. 1977. *Les Celtes*, Paris.

Eagles, B. 1979. *The Anglo-Saxon settlement of Humberside*, BAR British Series, 68, Oxford.

Edwards, N. & Lane, A. 1992. *The early church in Wales and the West*, Oxford.

Edwards, N. 1983. 'An early group of crosses from the kingdom of Ossory', *JRSAI*, 113, 5–46.

Edwards, N. 1986. 'The South Cross, Clonmacnois (with an appendix on the incidence of vine-scroll on Irish sculpture' in Higgitt (ed.), 23–36.

Edwards, N. 1990. *The archaeology of Early Medieval Ireland*, London.

Edwards, N. 1995. 'Eleventh-century Welsh illuminated manuscripts: the nature of the Irish connection' in Bourke (ed.), 147–55.

Edwards, N. 2001. 'Early Medieval inscribed stones and stone sculpture in Wales: context and function', *Med. Arch.*, 45, 15–40.

Edwards, N. 2007a. *A corpus of Early Medieval inscribed stones and stone sculpture in Wales, II: south-west Wales*, Cardiff.

Edwards, N. 2007b. 'Early Medieval sculpture in south-west Wales: the Irish Sea connection' in Moss (ed.), 184–97.

Elbern, V.H. 1963. *Der Eucharistiche Kelch im Frühen Mitteralter: Zeitschrift des Deutchen Vereins für Kunstwissenschaft*, 17, 1–76 & 117–88.

Elbern, V.H. 1965. 'Eine Gruppe Insularter Kelche' in Schlegel, U. & von Manteuffel, Z. (eds), *Festschrift für Peter Metz*, Berlin, 115–23.

Erdrich, M., Gianotta, K.M. & Hanson, W.S. 2000. 'Traprain Law: native and Roman on the frontier', *PSAS*, 130, 441–56.

Etchingham, C. & Swift, C. 2004. 'English and Pictish terms for brooch in an eighth-century Irish law text', *Med. Arch.*, 48, 31–50.

Evans, A.C. 1994. *The Sutton Hoo ship burial*, rev. ed., London.

Evans, S. 1997. *Lords of Battle*, Woodbridge.

Evison, V. 1968. 'Quoit brooch style buckles', *Antiq. J.*, 35, 231–49.

Fanning, T. & ÓhÉailidhe, P. 1980. 'Some cross-incised slabs from the Irish midlands' in Murtagh, H. (ed.), *Irish Midland studies: essays in commemoration of N.W. English*, Athlone, 5–23.

Fanning, T. 1981. 'Excavation on an Early Christian cemetery and settlement at Reask, Co. Kerry', *PRIA*, 81C, 67–172.

Farr, C. 1995. 'History and mnemonic in Insular gospel book decoration' in Bourke (ed.), 137–46.

Farr, C. 1997. *The Book of Kells: its function and audience*, London.

Feachem, R.W. 1951. 'Dragonesque fibulae', *Antiq. J.*, 31, 32–44.

Fell, C., Foote, P., Graham-Campbell, J. & Thomson, R. (eds). 1983. *The Viking Age in the Isle of Man*, London.

Fellows-Jensen, G. 1983. 'Scandinavian settlement in the Isle of Man and north-west England: the place-name evidence' in Fell et al. (eds), 37–52.

Finlay, I. 1973. *Celtic art*, London.

Fisher, I. & Greenhill, F.A. 1974. 'Two unrecorded carved stones at Tower of Lethendy, Perthshire', *PSAS*, 104 (1971–2), 238–41.

Fisher, I. 2001. *Early Medieval sculpture in the West Highlands and Islands*, Edinburgh.

Flower, R. 1954. 'Irish High Crosses', *J Warburg & Courtauld Institutes*, 87–97.

Forsyth, K. 1995. 'The inscriptions on the Dupplin Cross' in Bourke (ed.), 237–44.

Forsyth, K. 2006. '*Hic Memoria Perpetua*: the Early inscribed stones of southern Scotland in context' in Foster (ed.), 113–32.

Foster, J. 1977. *Bronze boar figurines in Iron Age and Roman Britain*, BAR British Series, 39, Oxford.

Foster, J. 1986. *The Lexden Tumulus: a re-appraisal of an Iron Age burial from Colchester, Essex*, BAR British Series, 156, Oxford.

Foster, S. (ed.). 1998. *The St Andrews Sarcophagus: a Pictish masterpiece and its international connections*, Dublin.

Foster, S. (ed.). 2005. *Able minds and practiced hands*, London.

Fowler, E. 1960. 'The origins and development of the penannular brooch in Europe', *PPS*, 26, 149–77.

Fowler, E. 1963. 'Celtic metalwork of the fifth and sixth centuries AD', *Archaeol. J.*, 120, 98–160.

Fowler, E. 1968. 'Hanging bowls' in Coles, J. & Simpson, D.D.A. (eds), *Studies in ancient Europe*, Leicester, 287–310.

Fowler, E. 1981. 'A fragment of an enamelled bronze bowl from Bradley Hill, Somerton, Somerset' in O'Connor& Clarke (eds), 237–42.

Fowler, E. 1983. 'Penannular brooches' in Crummy, N. (ed.), *Colchester archaeological report, 2: the Roman small finds from excavations in Colchester, 1971–9*, Colchester, 18–19.

Fox, C. 1958. *Pattern and purpose: a survey of early Celtic art in Britain*, Cardiff.

Fraser, J. 2004. 'The Iona Chronicle, the descendants of Aedan mac Gabrain and the "principal kindreds of Dal Riata"', *Northern Studies*, 38, 77–96.

Friend, A.M. 1939. 'The canon tables in the Book of Kells' in Koehler, W. (ed.), *Medieval studies in memory of A. Kingsley Porter, II*, Cambridge, Mass, 611–66.

Fuchs, R. & Oltrogger, D. 1994. 'Colour material and painting techniques in the Book of Kells' in O'Mahoney (ed.), 133–71.

Fuglesang, S.H. 1980. *Some aspects of the Ringerike Style: a phase of 11th century Scandinavian Art*, Medieval Scandinavia (Supplement), Odense.

Fulford, M. & Peacock, D. 1984. *Excavations at Carthage: the British Mission, vol. 1:2: the Avenue du President Habib Bourguiba, Salammbo: the pottery and other ceramic objects from the site*, Sheffield.

Fulford, M. 1989. 'Byzantium and Britain: a Mediterranean perspective on post-Roman Mediterranean imports in western Britain and Ireland', *Med. Arch.*, 33, 1–6.

Gameson, R. 1995. *The role of art in the late Anglo-Saxon church*, Oxford.

Garrow, D. 2008. 'The time and space of Celtic art: interrogating the "Technologies of Enchantment" database' in Garrow et al. (eds), 15–39.

Garrow, D., Gosden, C. & Hill, J.D. (eds). 2008. *Rethinking Celtic art*, Oxford.

Gaskell-Brown, C. & Harper, A.E.T. 1984. 'Excavations on Cathedral Hill, Armagh, 1968', *UJA*, 47, 109–61.

Geake, H. 1999. 'When were hanging bowls deposited in Anglo-Saxon graves?', *Med. Arch.*, 43, 1–8.

Gelly, M.A. 1995. 'The Irish High Cross: methods of design' in Bourke (ed.), 157–66.

Gibson, D.B. 1995. 'Chiefdoms, confederacies and statehood in early Ireland' in Arnold & Gibson (eds), 116–28.

Gillies, W. 1981. 'The craftsman in early Celtic literature', *Scottish Archaeological Forum*, 11, 70–85.

Gillies, W. 1993. 'Scottish Gaelic' in Ball & Fife (eds), 145–227.

Gogan, L. 1932. *The Ardagh Chalice*, Dublin.

Gondek, M. 2006. 'Investing in sculpture: power in early historic Scotland', *Med. Arch.*, 50, 105–42.

Gough, M. 1961. *The Early Christians*, London.

Gough, M. 1973. *The origins of Christian art*, London.

Graham-Campbell, J. & Batey, C. 1998. *Vikings in Scotland: an archaeological survey*, Edinburgh.

Graham-Campbell, J. 1973. 'A fragment of a decorated bronze strap-end, of Viking-Age date, from the Udal excavations, North Uist', *Med. Arch.*, 17, 130–3.

Graham-Campbell, J. 1981. 'The finds' in Reece, R. (ed.), *Excavations in Iona, 1964–1974*, London, 23–6.

Graham-Campbell, J. 1987. 'From Scandinavia to the Irish Sea: Viking art reviewed' in Ryan, M. (ed.), 144–52.

Graham-Campbell, J. 1991. 'Dinas Powys metalwork and the dating of enamelled zoomorphic penannular brooches', *Bulletin of the Board of Celtic Studies*, 38, 220–32.

Graham-Campbell, J. 2003. *Pictish silver: status and symbol*, Chadwick Memorial Lectures, 13, Cambridge.

Granger-Taylor, H. & Pritchard, F. 2001. 'A fine quality Insular embroidery from Llan-Gors crannog, near Brecon' in Redknap et al. (eds), 91–100.

Greene, D. & O'Connor, F. 1967. *A golden treasury of Irish poetry*, London.

Hall, M. et al. 1998. 'A sculptured fragment from Pittensorn Farm, Gellyburn, Perthshire', *Tayside and Fife Archaeological Journal*, 4, 129–44.

Hamlin, A. 1972. 'A Chi-Rho carved stone at Drumaqueran, Co. Antrim', *UJA*, 35, 22–8.

Hamlin, A. 1982. 'Early Irish stone-carving: content and context' in Pearce, S. (ed.), *The early church in western Britain and Ireland*, BAR British Series, 102, Oxford, 283–96.

Harbison, P. 1981. 'The date of the Moylough Belt-Shrine' in Ó Corráin, D. (ed.), *Irish antiquity: essays and studies presented to Professor M.J. O'Kelly*, Cork, 231–9.

Harbison, P. 1984. 'The bronze crucifixion plaque said to be from St John's (Rinnagan) near Athlone', *JIA*, 2, 1–17.

Harbison, P. 1985. 'Three miniatures in the Book of Kells', *PRIA*, 85C, 181–94.

Harbison, P. 1987. 'The Carolingian contribution to Irish sculpture' in Ryan, M. (ed.), 105–10.

Harbison, P. 1988. 'Exotic ninth- to tenth-century cross-decorated stones from Clonmore, Co. Carlow and Begerin, Co. Wexford' in Mac Niocaill, G. & Wallace, P.F. (eds), *Keimelia: studies in Medieval archaeology and history in memory of Tom Delaney*, Galway, 59–66.

Harbison, P. 1992. *The High Crosses of Ireland*, 3 vols, Bonn.

Harbison, P. 1994a. *Irish High Crosses with the figure sculpture explained*, Drogheda.

Harbison, P. 1994b. 'The extent of royal patronage on Irish High Crosses', *Studia Celtica Japonica*, 6, 77–105.

Harbison, P. 2007. 'Classical animals on Irish High Crosses' in Moss (ed.), 215–27.

Harden, J. 1995. 'A potential archaeological context for the Early Christian sculptured stones from Tarbat, Easter Ross' in Bourke (ed.), 221–7.

Harding, D.W. 2007. *The archaeology of Celtic art*, London.

Harris, J. 2003. *Byzantium, Britain and the West: the archaeology of cultural identity, AD400–650*, Stroud, Gloucestershire.

Hartley, E., Hawkes, J., Henig, M. & Mee, F. (eds). 2006. *Constantine the Great, York's Roman Emperor*, York.

Haseloff, G. 1950. *Die Tassilokelch*, Munich.

Haseloff, G. 1974. 'Salin's Style 1', *Med. Arch.*, 18, 1–13.

Haseloff, G. 1981. *Die germanische Tierornamentik der Volkerwanerungszeit. Studien zu Salin's Stil 1*, 3 vols, Berlin.

Hassall, M. & Rhodes, J. 1974. 'Excavations at the New Market Hall, Gloucester, 1966–67', *Transactions of the Bristol and Gloucestershire Archaeological Society*, 92, 15–100.

Hattatt, R. 1982. *Ancient and Romano-British brooches*, Sherborne.

Hattatt, R. 1985. *Iron Age and Roman brooches*, Sherborne.

Hawkes, J. 2005. 'Figuring salvation: an excursus into the iconography of the Iona crosses' in Foster (ed.), 259–74.

Hawkes, J. 2006. 'The legacy of Constantine in Anglo-Saxon England' in Hartley et al. (eds), 104–15.

Hawkes, S. & Dunning, G.C. 1961. 'Soldiers and settlers in Britain, fourth to fifth century', *Med. Arch.*, 5, 1–70.

Hawkes, S.C., Merrick, J.M. & Metcalf, D.M. 1966. 'X-ray fluorescent analysis of some Dark Age coins and jewellery', *Archaeometry*, 9, 98–138.

Hay Fleming, D. 1931. *St Andrews Cathedral Museum*, Edinburgh.

Helms, M.W. 1993. *Craft and the kingly ideal*, Austin.

Hemphill, S. 1911–12. 'The gospels of MacRegol of Birr: a study in Celtic illumination', *PRIA*, 29C, 1–10.

Hencken, H.O'N. 1936. 'Balinderry 1 Crannog', *PRIA*, 43C, 103–226.

Hencken, H.O'N. 1942. 'Balinderry 2 Crannog', *PRIA*, 47C, 1–75.

Hencken, H.O'N. 1950. 'Lagore, a royal residence of the seventh to tenth centuries AD', *PRIA*, 53C, 1–247.

Henderson, G. & Henderson, I. 2004. *The art of the Picts: sculpture and metalwork in Early Medieval Scotland*, London.

Henderson, G. 1987. *From Durrow to Kells, the Insular gospel books, 650–800*, London.

Henderson, G. 1999. *Vision and image in Early Christian England*, Cambridge.

Henderson, I. 1967. *The Picts*, London.

Henderson, I. 1978. 'Pictish vine-scroll ornament' in O'Connor & Clarke (eds), 243–66.

Henderson, I. 1978. 'Sculpture north of the Forth after the takeover by the Scots' in Lang, J. (ed.), 47–59.

Henderson, I. 1982. 'Pictish art and the Book of Kells' in Whitelock, D., McKitterick, R. & Dumville, D. (eds), *Ireland in Early Medieval Europe: studies in memory of Kathleen Hughes*, Cambridge, 79–105.

Henderson, I. 1983. 'Pictish vine-scroll ornament' in O'Connor & Clarke (eds), 243–68.

Henderson, I. 1986. 'The 'David Cycle' in Pictish art' in Higgitt (ed.), 87–113.

Henderson, I. 1987. 'The Book of Kells and the snake-boss motif on Pictish cross-slabs and the Iona crosses' in Ryan, M. (ed.), 56–65.

Henderson, I. 1990. *The art and function of Rosemarkie's Pictish monuments*, Rosemarkie.

Henderson, I. 1996. *Pictish monsters: symbol, text and image*, Chadwick Memorial Lectures, 7, Cambridge.

Henderson, I. 1997. 'Variations on an old theme: panelled zoomorphic ornament on Pictish sculpture at Nigg, Easter Ross, and St Andrews, Fife, and the Book of Kells' in Karkov, C.E., Ryan, M. & Farrell, R.T. (eds), *The Insular tradition*, New York, 143–66.

Henderson, I. 1998. '*Primus inter pares*: the St Andrews Sarcophagus and Pictish sculpture' in Foster (ed.), 97–167.

Henderson, I. 1987. 'Early Christian monuments of Scotland displaying crosses but no other ornament' in Small, A. (ed.), *The Picts: a new look at old problems*, Dundee, 45–58.

Henig, M. 1995. *The art of Roman Britain*, London.

Henry, D. (ed.). 1996. *The worm, the germ and the thorn*, Balgavies.

Henry, F. & Marsh-Micheli, G.L. 1932. 'A century of Irish illumination, 1070–1170', *PRIA*, 32C, 101–65.

Henry, F. 1936. 'Hanging bowls', *JRSAI*, 66, 209–46.

Henry, F. 1940. *Irish art in the Early Christian period*, London.

Henry, F. 1964. *Irish High Crosses*, Dublin.

Henry, F. 1965. *Irish art in the Early Christian period to AD800*, London.

Henry, F. 1967. *Irish art during the Viking invasions, 800–1020AD*, London.

Henry, F. 1970. *Irish art in the Romanesque period, 1020–1170AD*, London.

Henry, F. 1974. *The Book of Kells*, London.

Hicks, C. 1980. 'A Clonmacnois workshop in stone', *JRSAI*, 110, 1–35.

Hicks, C. 1993a. *Animals in Early Medieval art*, Edinburgh.

Hicks, C. 1993b. 'Pictish Class 1 animals' in Spearman & Higgitt (eds), 196–202.

Higgitt, J. (ed.). 1986a. *Early Medieval sculpture in Britain and Ireland*, BAR British Series, 152, Oxford.

Higgitt, J. 1986b. 'Words and crosses: the inscribed stone cross in Early Medieval Britain and Ireland' in Higgitt (ed.), 125–52.

Higham, N. (ed.). 2007. *Britons in Anglo-Saxon England*, Woodbridge.

Hill, P. et al. 1997. *Whithorn and St Ninian: the excavation of a monastic town, 1984–91*, Stroud, Gloucestershire.

Hillgarth, J.N. 1963. 'Visigothic Spain and Early Christian Ireland', *PRIA*, 62, 167–94.

Hills, C. 1981. *The Anglo-Saxon cemetery at Spong Hill, North Elmham, Part II*, East Anglian Archaeological Report, 11, Norwich.

Hines, J. 1992. 'The Scandinavian character of Anglo-Saxon England: an update' in Carver, M. (ed.), *The Age of Sutton Hoo*, Woodbridge, 315–30.

Hinton, D. 1998. *Anglo-Saxon smiths and myths*, Manchester.

Holmes, N. & Hunter, F. 2001. 'Roman counterfeiters: moulds from Scotland', *PSAS*, 131, 167–76.

Hopper, V.F. 1969. *Medieval number symbolism*, New York.

Hourihane, C. (ed.). 2001. *From Ireland coming*, Princeton.

Hourihane, C. (ed.). 2004. *Irish art historical studies in honour of Peter Harbison*, Dublin.

Hughes, K. 1966. *The church in early Irish society*, London.

Hughes, K. 1972. *Early Christian Ireland: introduction to the sources*, London.

Hunt, J. 1956. 'On two D-shaped objects in the Saint-Germain Museum', *PRIA*, 57, 153–7.

Hunter, F. 2002. 'Birnie: buying peace on the northern frontier', *Current Archaeology*, 181, 12–16.

Hunter, F. 2006. 'New light on Iron Age massive armlets', *PSAS*, 136, 135–60.

Hunter, F. 2008. 'Celtic art in Roman Britain' in Garrow et al. (eds), 129–45.

Hunter, J. 1997. *A persona for the northern Picts*, Rosemarkie.

Inker, P. 2000. 'Technology as active material culture: the quoit brooch style', *Med. Arch.*, 44, 25–52.

Ivens, R.J. 1984. 'Movilla Abbey, Newtonards, Co. Down: excavations 1981', *UJA*, 47, 71–108.

Ivens, R.J. 1987. 'The Early Christian monastic enclosure at Tullylish, Co. Down', *UJA*, 50, 55–121.

Jacobsthal, P. 1944. *Early Celtic art*, Oxford.

James, E. 1977. *The Merovingian archaeology of south-west Gaul*, BAR International Series, 27, Oxford.

James, E. 1982. 'Ireland and western Gaul in the Merovingian period' in Whitelock, D., McKitterrick, R. & Dumville, D. (eds), *Ireland in Early Medieval Europe*, Cambridge, 362–86.

James, E. 1988. *The Franks*, Oxford.

James, E. 2001. *Britain in the first millennium*, London.

James, H. 2005. 'Pictish cross slabs: an examination of their original archaeological context' in Foster (ed.), 95–112.

James, S. 1999. *The Atlantic Celts: ancient people or modern invention?*, London.

Janes, D. 1996. 'The golden clasp of the late Roman state', *Early Medieval Europe*, 5:2, 127–53.

Jarman, A.O.H. 1988. *Aneurin: Y Gododdin, Britain's oldest heroic poem*, Llandysul.

Jensen, R.M. 2000. *Understanding Early Christian art*, London.

Johns, C.M. 1996. *The jewellery of Roman Britain: Classical and Celtic traditions*, London.

Johnson, R. 1990. 'Ballinderry Crannog, no. 1: a reconsideration', *PRIA*, 99C, 23–71.

Jope, E.M. 2000. *Early Celtic art in the British Isles*, Oxford.

Karkov, C. 1993. 'The chalice and cross in Insular art' in Spearman & Higgitt (eds), 237–44.

Kelly, D. 1991. 'The heart of the matter: models for Irish High Crosses', *JRSAI*, 121, 105–45.

Kelly, D. 1993. 'The relationships of the crosses of Argyll: the evidence of form' in Spearman & Higgitt (eds), 219–29.

Kelly, D. 1996. 'A sense of proportion: the metrical and design characteristics of some Columban High Crosses', *JRSAI*, 126, 108–46.

Kelly, E.P. 2000. 'Tully Lough Cross', *Archaeology Ireland*, 17:2, 9–10.

Kelly, E.P. 2001. 'The Hillquarter, Co. Westmeath, mounts: an Early Medieval saddle from Ireland' in Redknap et al. (eds), 261–74.

Kelly, F. 1988. *A guide to early Irish law*, Dublin.

Kelly, F. 1997. *Early Irish farming*, Dublin.

Kemble, J.M., Franks, A.W. & Latham, R.G. 1863. *Horae ferales, or studies in the archaeology of the northern nations*, London.

Kendrick, T.D. 1932. 'British hanging bowls', *Antiquity*, 6, 161–84.

Kendrick, T.D. 1949. *Late Saxon and Viking art*, London.

Kennett, D.H. 1968. 'The Irchester bowls', *Journal of the Northampton Museum and Gallery*, 4, 5–39.

Kennett, D.H. 1971. 'Late Roman bronze vessel hoards in Britain', *Jahrbuch des Romische-Germanischen Zentalmuseums*, 16, Mainz, 123–46.

Kenney, J.F. 1929. *The sources for the early history of Ireland, I: ecclesiastical*, New York.

Kent, J.P.C. & Painter, K. (eds). 1977. *Wealth of the Roman world*, London.

Keppie, L.G.F. & Arnold, B.J. 1984. *Scotland, Corpus Signorum Imperii Romani: Great Britain*, 1, fas. 4, Oxford.

Kermode, P.M.C. 1907. *Manx crosses*, Douglas.

Kilbride-Jones, H.E. 1980a. *Zoomorphic penannular brooches* (=Society of Antiquaries of London Research Report). London.

Kilbride-Jones, H.E. 1980b. *Celtic craftsmanship in bronze*, London.

King, H. 1992. 'Excavations at Clonmacnoise', *Archaeology Ireland*, 6:3, 12–14.

King, H. (ed.). 2003. *Clonmacnoise studies, 2: seminar papers 1998*, Dublin.

Kitzinger, E. 1956. 'The coffin-reliquary' in Battiscombe, E. (ed.), *The relics of St Cuthbert*, Durham, 202–304.

Kitzinger, E. 1977. *Byzantine art in the making: main lines of stylistic development in Mediterranean art, 3rd–7th century*, London.

Kitzinger, E. 1993. 'Interlace and icons: form and function in early Insular art' in Spearman & Higgitt (eds), 3–15.

Knight, J. 1981. 'In tempore Iustini Consulis: contacts between the British and Gaulish churches before Augustine' in Detsicas, A. (ed.), *Collectanea Historica: essays in memory of Stuart Rigold*, Maidstone, 109–20.

Knight, J. 1999. *The end of Antiquity: archaeology, society and religion, AD235–700*, Stroud, Gloucestershire.

Knight, J. 1996. 'Seasoned with salt: Insular-Gallic contacts in the early memorial stones and cross-slabs' in Dark, K. (ed.), *External contacts and the economy of Roman and post-Roman Britain*, Woodbridge, 109–20.

Knight, J. 1992. 'The Early Christian Latin inscriptions of Britain and Gaul: chronology and context' in Edwards & Lane (eds), 45–50.

Kunzl, E. 2008. 'Celtic art and tourist knick-knacks', *Current Archaeology*, 222, 22–7.

La Neice, S. & Stapleton, C. 1993. 'Niello and enamel on Irish metalwork', *Antiq. J.*, 73, 148–51.

La Neice, S. 1983. 'Niello: an historical and technical survey', *Antiq. J.*, 70, 279–97.

Laing, J. 1997. *Art and society in Roman Britain*, Stroud, Gloucestershire.

Laing, J. 2000. *Warriors of the Dark Ages*, Stroud, Gloucestershire.

Laing, L. & Laing, J. 1984a. 'The date and origin of the Pictish symbols', *PSAS*, 114, 261–76.

Laing, L. & Laing, J. 1984b. 'Archaeological notes on some Scottish Early Christian sculptures', *PSAS*, 114, 277–87.

Laing, L. & Laing, J. 1990. *Celtic Britain and Ireland, c.AD200–800: the myth of the Dark Ages*, Dublin.

Laing, L. & Laing, J. 1992. *The art of the Celts*, London.

Laing, L. & Laing, J. 1993. *Ancient art: the challenge to modern thought*, Dublin.

Laing, L., Laing, J. & Longley, D. 1998. 'The Early Christian and later medieval ecclesiastical site at Kingarth, Bute', *PSAS*, 128, 551–65.

Laing, L. & Longley, D. 2006. *The Mote of Mark, a Dark Age hillfort in south-west Scotland*, Oxford.

Laing, L. 1972–4. 'Picts, Saxons and Celtic metalwork', *PSAS*, 105, 189–99.

Laing, L. 1990. 'The hoard of Pictish silver from Norrie's Law, Fife', *Studia Celtica*, 28, 11–38.

Laing, L. 1993a. *A catalogue of Celtic ornamental metalwork in the British Isles, c.AD400–1200*, BAR British Series, 229, Oxford.

Laing, L. 1994. 'The Norrie's Law hoard of Pictish silver', *Studia Celtica*, 27, 11–38.

Laing, L. 1996. 'Alternative Celtic art: Early Medieval non-Pictish sketches on stone in Britain', *Studia Celtica*, 30, 127–46.

Laing, L. 1998. 'The Early Medieval sculptures from St Blane's, Kingarth Bute', *Pictish Arts Society Journal*, 12, 19–23.

Laing, L. 1999. 'The Bradwell Mount and the uses of millefiori in post-Roman Britain', *Studia Celtica*, 33, 137–53.

Laing, L. 2000a. 'The chronology and context of Pictish relief sculpture', *Med. Arch.*, 44, 81–114.

Laing, L. 2001a. 'The date of the Aberlemno churchyard stone' in Redknap et al. (eds), 241–52.

Laing, L. 2001b. 'The date and context of the Glamis, Angus, carved Pictish stones', *PSAS*, 131, 223–39.

Laing, L. 2005a. 'The Roman origins of Celtic Christian art', *Archaeol. J.*, 162, 146–76.

Laing, L. 2005b. 'Some Anglo-Saxon artefacts from Nottinghamshire' in Semple, S. (ed.), *Anglo-Saxon studies in archaeology and history*, 13, 80–96.

Laing, L. 2006. *The archaeology of Celtic Britain and Ireland, c.AD 400–1200*, Cambridge.

Laing, L. 2007. 'Romano-British metalworking and the Anglo-Saxons' in Higham, N. (ed.), *Britons in Anglo-Saxon England*, 42–56.

Lane, A. & Campbell, E. 2000. *Dunadd, an early Dalriadic capital*, Oxford.

Lane, A. 1994. 'Trade, gifts and cultural exchange in Dark-Age western Scotland' in Crawford, B. (ed.), 105–15.

Lang, J. 1972–4. 'Hogback monuments in Scotland', *PRSAS*, 105, 206–35.

Lang, J. (ed.). 1978. *Anglo-Saxon and Viking Age sculpture*, BAR British Series, 49, Oxford.

Lang, J. 1984. 'The compilation of design in colonial Viking sculpture' in *Universitets Oldsaksamlings Skrifter*, 5, 125–37.

Lang, J. 1986. 'Principles of design in free-style carving in the Irish Sea province: *c.*800 to *c.* 950' in Higgitt (ed.), 153–74.

Lang, J. 1987. 'Eleventh-century style in decorated wood from Dublin' in Ryan, M. (ed.), 174–8.

Lang, J. 1991a. *York and Eastern Yorkshire: corpus of Anglo-Saxon stone sculpture, 3*, Oxford.

Lang, J. 1991b. 'Survival and revival in Insular art: some principles' in Karkov, C. & Farrell, T. (eds), *Studies in Insular art and archaeology*, Oxford, Ohio, 63–77.

Lang, J. 2000. 'Monuments from Yorkshire in the age of Alcuin' in Geake, H. & Kenny, J. (eds), *Early Deira: archaeological studies of the East Riding in the fourth to ninth centuries AD*, Oxford, 109–120.

Lang, J. 2001. *Northern Yorkshire: corpus of Anglo-Saxon stone sculpture, 6*, Oxford.

Lapidge, M. (ed.). 1997. *Columbanus: studies in the Latin writings*, Woodbridge.

Larsen, A-C. (ed.). 2001. *The Vikings in Ireland*, Dublin.

Lasko, P. 1971. *The kingdom of the Franks*, London.

Lasko, P. 1972. *Ars sacra, 800–1200*, Harmondsworth.

Lawlor, H.C. 1925. *The monastery of St Mochaoi at Nendrum*, Belfast.

Lawson, G. 1981. 'An Anglo-Saxon harp and lyre of the ninth century' in Widdess, D.R. & Wolpert, R.F. (eds), *Music and tradition: essays on Asian and other musics presented to Lawrence Picken*, Cambridge, 229–44.

Leeds, E.T. 1933. *Early Celtic ornament in the British Isles*, Oxford.

Leeds, E.T. 1945. 'The distribution of the Angles and Saxons archaeologically considered', *Archaeologia*, 91, 1–106.

Lewis, S. 1980. 'Sacred calligraphy: the Chi-Rho page in the Book of Kells', *Traditio*, 36, 139–59.

Lionard, P. 1961. 'Early Irish grave-slabs', *PRIA*, 61C, 95–169.

Lowe, E.A. (ed.). 1935–72. *Codices Latinae antiquores: a palaeographical guide to Latin manuscripts prior to the ninth century*, 12 vols, Oxford.

MacCready, S. & Thompson, F.H. (eds). 1984. *Cross-channel trade between Gaul and Britain in the pre-Roman Iron Age*, London.

MacDermott, M. 1955. 'The Kells Crozier', *Archaeologia*, 96, 59–113.

MacLean, D. 1993. 'Snake-bosses and redemption at Iona and in Pictland' in Spearman & Higgitt (eds), 245–53.

MacLean, D. 1995a. 'Technique and contact: carpentry-constructed Insular stone crosses' in Bourke (ed.), 167–75.

MacLean, D. 1995b. 'The status of the sculptor in Old-Irish law and the evidence of the crosses', *Peritia*, 9, 125–55.

Mahr, A. & Raftery, J. 1932–41. *Christian art in ancient Ireland* (1, ed. Mahr, 1932; 2 ed. Raftery, 1941), Dublin.

Margeson, S. 1983. 'On the iconography of the Manx crosses' in Fell, C, Foote, P, Graham-Campbell, J. & Thomson, R. (eds), *The Viking Age in the Isle of Man*, London, 95–106.

Mathews, T.F. 1993. *The clash of the gods: a reinterpretation of Early Christian art*, Princeton.

Mayr-Harting, H. 1972. *The coming of Christianity to Anglo-Saxon England*, London.

McKitterick, R. 1979. 'Town and monastery in the Carolingian period' in Baker, J. (ed.), *Studies in church history XVI: the church in town and countryside*, Oxford, 93–102.

McKitterick, R. 2005. 'The Carolingian renaissance of culture and learning' in Story, J. (ed.), *Charlemagne, empire and society*, Manchester, 151–66.

Meehan, B. 1994. *The Book of Kells*, London.

Megaw, R. & Megaw, J.V.S. 1989. *Celtic art from its beginnings to the Book of Kells*, London.

Megaw, V. & Megaw, R. 2008. 'A Celtic mystery: some thoughts on the genesis of insular Celtic art' in Garrow et al. (eds), 40–58.

Meid, W. 1967. *Táin Bó Fraich*, Dublin.

Meyer, K. 2005. 'Bird, beast or fish? Problems of identification and interpretation of the iconography carved on the Tarbat peninsula cross-slabs' in Foster (ed.), 243–57.

Michelli, P. 1996. 'The inscriptions on pre-Norman Irish reliquaries', *PRIA*, 96C, 1–48.

Miller, S. & Ruckley, N.A. 2005. 'The role of geological analysis of monuments: a case study from St Vigeans and related sites' in Foster (ed.), 277–92.

Moller, J. 1987. *Katalog der Grabfunde uas Vokerwanderungsund Merowingerzeit im sudmainischen Hessen (Starkenburg)*, Wiesbaden.

Moore, C.N. 1978. 'An enamelled skillet-handle from Brough-on-Fosse and the distribution of similar vessels', *Britannia*, 9, 319–27.

Moss, R. (ed.). 2007. *Making and meaning in Insular art*, Dublin.

Mowbray, C.L. 1936. 'Eastern influence on carvings at St Andrews and Nigg, Scotland', *Antiquity*, 10, 428–40.

Murray, R. 2007. 'Iron-masters of the Caledonians', *Current Archaeology*, 212, 20–5.

Nash-Williams, V.E. 1950. *Early Christian monuments of Wales*, Cardiff.

Neal, D.S. 1996. *Excavation of the Roman Villa at Beadlam, Yorkshire*, Yorkshire Archaeological Reports, 2, York.

Nees, L. 2007. 'Words and images, texts and commentaries' in Moss (ed.), 47–69.

Netzer, N. 1994. 'The origin of the beast canon tables reconsidered' in O'Mahony (ed.), 322–32.

Neuman de Vegvar, C. 1984. *Northumbrian renaissance*, Princeton.

Neuman de Vegvar, C. 2007. 'Remembering Jerusalem: architecture and meaning in Insular canon table arcades' in Moss (ed.), 242–56.

Newman, C. & Walsh, N. 2007. 'Iconographical analysis of the Marigold Stone, Carndonagh, Inishowen, Co. Donegal' in Moss (ed.), 167–83.

Newman, C. 1995. 'The Iron Age to Early Christian transition: the evidence from dress fasteners' in Bourke (ed.), 17–25.

Newman, C. 2006. 'St Matthew's cloak, Durrow fol. 21v' in Condit, T. & Corlett, C. (eds), *Above and beyond: essays in memory of Leo Swan*, Dublin, 219–25.

Ní Brolcháin, M. 1986. 'Mael Iosa Brolcháin: an assessment', *Seanchus Ard Mhacha*, 12, 43–67.

Nieke, M. 1993. Penannular and related brooches: secular ornament or symbol in action?' in Spearman & Higgitt (eds), 128–34.

Nordenfalk, C. 1947. 'Before the Book of Durrow', *Acta Archaeologica*, 18, 141–74.

Nordenfalk, C. 1963. 'The apostolic canon tables', *Gazette des Beaux Arts*, 6:62, 17–34.

Nordenfalk, C. 1968. 'An illustrated Diatesseron', *Art Bulletin*, 50, 119–40.

Nordenfalk, C. 1973. 'The Persian Diatesseron once more', *Art Bulletin*, 55, 532–46.

Nordenfalk, C. 1987. 'One hundred and fifty years of varying views on the early Insular gospel books' in Ryan (ed.), 1–6.

O'Brien, E. 1993. 'Contacts between Ireland and Anglo-Saxon England in the seventh century', *Anglo-Saxon Studies in Archaeology and History*, 6, 93–102.

O'Brien, E. 1999. *Post-Roman Britain to Anglo-Saxon England: burial practices reviewed*, BAR British Series, 289, Oxford.

O'Brien, W. 2004. *Ross Island: mining, metal and society in early Ireland*, National University of Ireland Bronze Age Studies, 6, Galway.

Ó Carragáin, E. 1987. 'The Ruthwell Cross and Irish High Crosses: some points of comparison and contrast' in Ryan (ed.), 118–28.

Ó Carragáin, E. 1994. '"*Traditio evangeliorum*" and "*sustentatio*": the relevance of liturgical ceremonies to the Book of Kells' in O'Mahoney (ed.), 398–436.

O'Connor, A. & Clarke, D. (eds), *From the atone age to the 'forty-five*, Edinburgh.

Ó Cróinín, D. 1995. *Early Medieval Ireland, 400–1200*, London.

O'Connor, N. 1983. 'Cross-slab' in Ryan (ed.), 142–3.

Ó Floinn, R. 1983. 'Viking and Romanesque influence, 1000AD–1169AD' in Ryan (ed.), *Treasures of Ireland: Irish art, 3000BC–1500AD*, Dublin, 58–69.

Ó Floinn, R. 1987. 'Schools of metalworking in eleventh- and twelfth-century Ireland' in Ryan (ed.), 179–86.

Ó Floinn, R. 1989. 'Secular metalwork in the eighth and ninth centuries' in Youngs, S. (ed.), 72–91.

Ó Floinn, R. 1994. *Irish shrines and reliquaries of the Middle Ages*, Dublin.

Ó Floinn, R. 1995. 'Clonmacnoise: art and patronage in the Early Medieval period' in Bourke (ed.), 251–60.

Ó Floinn, R. 2001. 'Patrons and politics, art, artefacts and methodology' in Redknap et al. (eds), 1–14.

Okasha, E. 1993. *Corpus of Early Christian inscribed stones of south-west Britain*, Leicester.

O'Kelly, M.J. 1961. 'The Cork horns, the Petrie Crown and the Bann Disc: the technique of their ornamentation', *JCHAS*, 66, 1–12.

O'Kelly, M.J. 1963. 'The excavation of two earthen ringforts at Garryduff, Co. Cork', *PRIA*, 63C, 17–124.

Oldenstein, J. 1976. 'Zu Austrustung romischer Auxiliareinheiten', *Bericht Rom.-Germa Komm.*, 57, 49–284.

O'Loughlin, R. 2001a. 'Monasteries and manuscripts: the transmission of Latin learning in Early Medieval Ireland' in Morgan, H. (ed.), *Media and power through the ages*, Dublin, 46–64.

O'Loughlin, T. 2000. 'The plan of the New Jerusalem in the Book of Armagh', *Cambrian Medieval Celtic Studies*, 39, 23–38.

O'Loughlin, T. 2001b. 'Irish preaching before the end of the ninth century: assessing the extent of the evidence' in Fletcher, A. & Gillespie, R. (eds), *Irish preaching, 700–1700*, Dublin, 18–39.

O'Mahoney, C. (ed.). 1994. *The Book of Kells: proceedings of a conference at Trinity College Dublin, 6th–9th September 1992*, Dublin.

O'Meadhra, U. 1987a. 'Irish, Insular, Saxon and Scandinavian elements in the motif-pieces from Ireland' in Ryan (ed.), 159–65.

O'Meadhra, U. 1987b. *Early Christian, Viking and Romanesque art: motif pieces from Ireland, 2: a discussion*, Stockholm.

O'Meadhra, U. 1993. 'Viking-age sketches and motif-pieces from the northern earldoms' in Batey, C.E., Jesch, J. & Morris, C.D. (eds), *The Viking Age in Caithness, Orkney and the North Atlantic*, Edinburgh, 423–40.

O'Meara, J.J. 1969. *Eriugena*, Cork.

O'Rahilly, T.F. 1946. *Early Irish history and mythology*, Dublin.

O'Reilly, J. 1993. 'The Book of Kells, folio 114r: a mystery revealed yet concealed' in Spearman & Higgitt (eds), 106–14.

O'Reilly, J. 1994. 'Exegesis and the Book of Kells: the Lucan Genealogy' in O'Mahony, F. (ed.), 344–97.

Ó Ríordáin, S.P. 1942. 'The excavation of a large earthen ring-fort at Garranes, Co. Cork', *PRIA*, 47C, 77–150.

Ó Ríordáin, S.P. 1947. 'Roman material in Ireland', *PRIA*, 51C, 35–82.

Painter, K.S. 2005. 'A note on the Water Newton hanging-bowl and other Roman hanging vessels' in Bruce-Mitford (ed.), 2005, 81.

Patterson, N.T. 1991. *Cattle-lords and clansmen: kinship and rank in early Ireland*, New York & London.

Patterson, N.T. 1995. 'Clans are not primordial: pre-Viking Irish society and the modelling of pre-Roman societies in Europe' in Arnold & Gibson (eds), 129–36.

Pearce, S. 2004. *South-west Britain in the Early Middle Ages*, Leicester.

Perkins, A. 1976. *The art of Dura Europos*, London.

Phillips, E.J. 1977. *Corbridge: Hadrian's Wall east of the Tyne, Corpus Signorum Imperii Romani*: Great Britain, I, Fas. 1, Oxford.

Pirotte, E. 2001. 'Hidden order, order revealed: new light on carpet pages' in Redknap et al. (eds), 2001, 203–7.

Proudfoot, E. & Aliaga-Kelly, C. 1996. 'Towards an interpretation of anomalous finds and place-names of Anglo-Saxon origin in Scotland', *Anglo-Saxon Studies in Archaeology and History*, 9, 1–13.

Proudfoot, E. 1997. 'Abernethy and Mugdrum: towards reassessment' in Henry, D. (ed.), *The worm, the germ and the thorn*, Balgavies, 47–63.

Pulliam, H. 2006. *Word and image in the Book of Kells*, Dublin.

Pulliam, H. 2007. 'Therefore do I speak to them in parables': meaning in the margins of the Book of Kells' in Moss (ed.), 257–67.

Raftery, B. 1983. *A catalogue of Irish Iron Age antiquities*, Marburg.

Raftery, B. 1984. *La Tène in Ireland: problems of origins and chronology*, Marburg.

Raftery, B. 1987. 'La Tène Art in Ireland' in Ryan (ed.), 12–18.

Raftery, B. 1994. *Pagan Celtic Ireland*, London.

Rance, P. 2001. 'Attacotti, Dési and Magnus Maximus: the case for Irish federates in lat Roman Britain', *Britannia*, 32, 243–70.

Redknap, M. & Lewis, J.M. 2007. *A corpus of Early Medieval inscribed stones and stone sculpture in Wales, I, Breconshire, Glamorgan, Monmouthshire, Radnorshire and geographically contiguous areas of Herefordshire and Shropshire*, Cardiff.

Redknap, M. 1991. *The Christian Celts: treasures of late Celtic Wales*, Cardiff.

Redknap, M. 2000. *Vikings in Wales: an archaeological quest*, Cardiff.

Redknap, M., Edwards, N., Youngs, S., Lane, A. & Knight, J. (eds). 2001. *Pattern and purpose in Insular art*, Oxford.

Richards, M. 1954. *The laws of Hywel Dda*, Cambridge.

Richardson, H. 1984a. 'Number and symbol in Early Christian Irish art', *JRSAI*, 114, 28–47.

Richardson, H. 1984b. 'The concept of the High Cross' in Ní Chatháin, P. & Richter, M. (eds), *Ireland and Europe: the early church*, Stuttgart, 127–34.

Richardson, H. 1987a. 'Ireland, Georgia and Armenia' in Ryan (ed.), 128–37.

Richardson, H. 1987b. 'Observations on Christian art in early Ireland, Georgia and Armenia' in Ryan (ed.), 129–37.

Richardson, H. 1990. *An introduction to Irish High Crosses*, Cork.

Richardson, H. 1993. 'Remarks on the liturgical fan, flabellum or rhipidion' in Spearman & Higgitt (eds), 27–44.

Richardson, H. 1995. 'The jewelled cross and its canopy' in Bourke (ed.), 177–86.

Richter, M. 1999. *Ireland and her neighbours in the seventh century*, Dublin.

Ritchie, A. 1989. *The Picts*, Edinburgh.

Ritchie, A. (ed.), 1994. *Govan and its Early Medieval sculptures*, Stroud, Gloucestershire.

Ritchie, A. 1995. 'Meigle and lay patronage in Tayside in the 9th and 10th centuries AD', *Tayside and Fife Archaeological Journal*, 1, 1–10.

Ritchie, A. 1997a. *Iona*, London.

Ritchie, A. 1997b. *Meigle Museum: Pictish carved stones*, Edinburgh.

Ritchie, J.N.G. & Ritchie, A. 1984. 'Pictish stones from Lindfores and Westfield Farm, Fife', *PSAS*, 112, 563–4.

Roe, H. 1945. 'The interpretation of certain symbolic sculptures in Early Christian Ireland', *JRSAI*, 75, 1–23.

Roe, H. 1958. *The High Crosses of Western Ossory*, Kilkenny.

Roe, H. 1965. 'The Irish High Cross: morphology and iconography', *JRSAI*, 95, 213–26.

Roe, H. 1981. *Monasterboice and its monuments*, Dundalk.

Roe, H.M. 1949. 'The "David Cycle" in early Irish Art', *JRSAI*, 79, 39–59.

Roth, H. 1986. *Kunst und Handwerk in frühen Mittelalter*, Stuttgart.

RCAHMS. 1982. *Argyll: an inventory of the monuments, IV, Iona*, Edinburgh.

RCAHMS. 1994. *South-east Perth: an archaeological landscape*, Edinburgh.

Ryan, M. (ed.). 1983. *Treasures of Ireland: Irish art, 3000BC–1500AD*, Dublin.

Ryan, M. (ed.). 1987a. *Ireland and Insular art, AD500–1200*, Dublin.

Ryan, M. 1982. 'Some archaeological comments on the occurrence and use of silver in pre-Viking Ireland' in Anon, *Ireland 800BC–800AD: essays in honour of M.V. Duignan*, Belfast, 45–50.

Ryan, M. 1983. 'The significance of the hoard' in Ryan, M. (ed.), *The Derrynaflan Hoard, I: a preliminary account*, Dublin, 17–30.

Ryan, M. 1984. 'The Derrynaflan and other early Irish eucharistic chalices: some speculations' in Richter & Ní Chatháin (eds), 135–48.

Ryan, M. 1987b. 'Some aspects of sequence and style in the metal-work of eighth- and ninth-century Ireland' in Ryan (ed.), 66–74.

Ryan, M. 1987c. 'A suggested origin for the figure representations on the Derrynaflan Paten' in Rynne, E. (ed.), *Figures from the past: studies in honour of Helen M. Roe*, Dublin, 62–72.

Ryan, M. 1987d. 'The Donore Hoard: Early Medieval metalwork from Moynalty, near Kells, Ireland', *Antiquity* (March 1987), 57–63.

Ryan, M. 1989. 'Fine metalworking and Early Irish monasteries: the archaeological evidence' in Bradley, J. (ed.), *Settlement and society in Medieval Ireland*, Dublin, 33–48.

Ryan, M. 1990a. 'The formal relationships of Insular Early Medieval eucharistic chalices', *PRIA*, 90C, 281–356.

Ryan, M. 1990b. 'Decorated metalwork in the Museo dell'Abbazia, Bobbio, Italy', *JRSAI*, 120, 102–11.

Ryan, M. 1991. 'Links between Anglo-Saxon and Irish Early Medieval art: some evidence of metalwork' in Farrell, R. & Karkov, C. (eds), *Studies in Insular art and archaeology: American Early Medieval Studies, I*, Oxford, Ohio, 117–26.

Ryan, M. 1993. 'The menagerie of the Derrynaflan Chalice' in Spearman & Higgitt (eds), 151–67.

Ryan, M. 1995. 'The decoration of the Donore Discs' in Bourke (ed.), 27–35.

Ryan, M. 2002. *Studies in Medieval Irish metalwork*, London.

Salin, B. 1904. *Altgermanische Thierornamentik*, Berlin.

Salin, E. 1952. *La civilisation Mérovingienne*, II: *les sépultures*, Paris.

Savory, H.N. 1960. 'Excavations at Dinas Emrys, Beddgellert, Caernarvonshire, 1954–6', *Archaeologia Cambrensis*, 109, 13–77.

Scheller, R.W. 1963. *A survey of Medieval model books*, Harlem.

Schwind, F. 1984. 'Zu karolingerzeitlichen Klostern als Wirtschafts-Organiismen und Statten handwerklicher Tätigeit' in Fenske, L., Rosner, W. & Zotz, T. (eds), *Instituionen Kultur und Gesellschaft im Mitteralter, Festchrift für Josef Fleckenstein*, Suigmaringen, 101–23.

Sharpe, R. 1984. 'Some problems concerning the organization of the church in Early Medieval Ireland', *Peritia*, 3, 230–70.

Sheehan, J. 1994. 'A Merovingian background for the Ardmoneel Stone?', *JCHAS*, 99, 23–31.

Sheehy, J. 1980. *The rediscovery of Ireland's past: the Celtic revival, 1830–1930*, London.

Sirat, J. 1966. 'Les stèles Mérovingiennes du Vexin français', *Bulletin archéologique du Vexin français*, 2, 73–83.

Small, A., Thomas, C. & Wilson, D.M. 1973. *St Ninian's Isle and its treasure*, Oxford.

Smith, I. 1996. 'The origins and development of Christianity in north Britain and southern Pictland' in Blair, J. & Pyrah, C. (eds), *Church archaeology: research directions for the future*, CBA Research Report, 140, London, 19–37.

Smyth, A. 1974. *Warlords and holy men*, London.

Speake, G. 1980. *Anglo-Saxon animal ornament*, Oxford.

Speake, G. 1989. *An Anglo-Saxon bed-burial at Swallowcliffe Down*, English Heritage Archaeological Report, 10, London.

Spearman, M. & Higgitt, J. (eds). 1993. *The age of migrating ideas*, Edinburgh.

Spearman, R.M. 1990. 'The Helmsdale bowls: a re-assessment', *PSAS*, 120, 63–77.

Spearman, R.M. 1994. 'The Govan Sarcophagus: an enigmatic monument' in Ritchie, A. (ed.), 33–45.

Stack, I. 1991. 'A Coptic textile: iconography and function', *Minneapolis Institute of Arts Bulletin, 1983–86*, 66, 97–104.

Stalley, R. 1990. 'European art and the Irish High Crosses', *PRIA*, 90C, 135–58.

Stalley, R. 1997. 'The Tower Cross at Kells' in Karkov, C.E., Ryan, M. & Farrell, R.T. (eds), *The Insular tradition*, New York, 115–41.

Stalley, R. 2007. 'Artistic identity and the Irish scripture crosses' in Moss (ed.), 153–66.

Stapleton, C.P., Freestone, I.C., & Bowman, S.G.E., 1999. 'Composition and origin of Early Medieval opaque red enamel from Britain and Ireland', *Journal of Archaeological Science*, 26, 913–21.

Stead, I.M. 1985a. *The Battersea Shield*, London.

Stead, I.M. 1985b. *Celtic art*, London.

Stevenson, R.B.K. 1954–6. 'Pictish chain, Roman silver and bauxite beads', *PSAS*, 88, 208–21.

Stevenson, R.B.K. & Emery, J. 1963–4. 'The Gaulcross hoard of Pictish silver', *PSAS*, 97, 206–11.

Stevenson, R.B.K. 1956. 'The chronology and relationship of some Irish and Scottish crosses', *JRSAI*, 85, 84–96.

Stevenson, R.B.K. 1974. 'The Hunterston Brooch and its significance', *Med. Arch.*, 18, 16–42.

Stevenson, R.B.K. 1981–2. 'Aspects of ambiguity in crosses and interlace', *UJA*, 44–5, 1–27.

Stevenson, R.B.K. 1989. 'The Celtic brooch from Westness, Orkney, and hinged pins' in Niclasen, B. (ed.), *The fifth Viking congress*, Torshavn, 25–31.

Stevick, R. 1994a. *The earliest Irish and English bookarts: visual and poetic forms before AD1000*, Philadelphia.

Stevick, R. 1994b. 'Page design of some illuminations in the Book of Kells' in O'Mahony, F. (ed.), 243–56.

Stevick, R. 1999. 'Shapes of early sculptured crosses of Ireland', *Gesta*, 38, 3–21.

Stevick, R. 2001. 'High Cross design' in Redknap et al. (eds), 221–31.

Stokes, W. (ed.). 1905. *The Martyrology of Angus*, London.

Suzuki, S. 2000. *The quoit brooch style and Anglo-Saxon settlement*, Woodbridge.

Swan, L. 1965. 'Fine metalwork from the Early Christian site at Kilpatrick, Co. Westmeath' in Bourke (ed.), 75–80.

Swan, L. 1994–5. 'Excavations at Kilpatrick, Killucan, Co. Westmeath', *Ríocht na Midhe*, 9:1, 1–21.

Swift, C. 2001. 'Irish monumental sculpture: the dating evidence provided by linguistic forms' in Redknap et al. (eds), 49–60.

Swift, C. 2003. 'Sculptors and their customers: a study of Clonmacnoise grave-slabs' in King, H. (ed.), *Clonmacnoise Studies*, 2, 105–24.

Talbot Rice, D. 1963. *Art of the Byzantine era*, London.

Thomas, C. 1963. 'The interpretation of the Pictish symbols', *Archaeol. J.*, 120, 31–97.

Thomas, C. 1971. *The Early Christian archaeology of north Britain*, Oxford.

Thomas, C. 1981. *Christianity in Roman Britain to AD500*, London.

Thomas, C. 1987. 'The earliest Christian art in Ireland and Britain' in Ryan (ed.), 7–11.

Thomas, A.C. 1992. *Whithorn's Christian beginnings*, Whithorn.

Thomas, C. 1998. *Christian Celts, messages and images*, Stroud, Gloucestershire.

Thomas, G. 2001. 'Strap-ends and the identification of regional patterns in the production and circulation of ornamental metalwork in late Anglo-Saxon and Viking-Age Britain' in Redknap et al. (eds), 39–48.

Thompson, F.H. 1968. 'The zoomorphic pelta in Romano-British art', *Antiq. J.*, 48, 47–58.

Todd, M. 1985. 'The Falkirk hoard of denarii: trade or subsidy?', *PSAS*, 115, 229–32.

Tommasini, A.M. 1937. *Irish saints in Italy*, London.

Trench-Jellicoe, R. 1998. 'The Skeith Stone, Upper Kilrenny, Fife, in its context', *PSAS*, 128, 495–513.

Trench-Jellicoe, R. 1999a. 'A missing figure on slab fragment no. 2 from Monifieth, Angus, the a'Chill Cross, Canna, and some implications of the development of a variant form of the Virgin's hairstyle in early medieval Scotland', *PSAS*, 129, 597–647.

Trench-Jellicoe, R. 1999b. 'Messages on a monument: iconography on a late Manx fragment recently recovered from Bishopscourt' in Davey, P.J. (ed.), *Recent archaeological research on the Isle of Man*, BAR British Series, 278, Oxford, 183–98.

Tweddle, D. 1984. *The Coppergate Helmet*, York.

Van der Meer, F. & Mohrmann, C. 1958. *Atlas of the Early Christian world*, London.

Van Es, W.A. 1967. 'Late Roman pins from Xanten/Dodewaard and Asselt', *Bericht van de Rijksdienst voor het Oudheikundig Bodemonderzoek*, 17, 121–8.

Veelenturf, K. 2001. 'Irish High Crosses and Continental art: shades of iconographical ambiguity' in Hourihane (ed.), 83–103.

Verkerk, D.H. 2001. 'Pilgrimage *ad Limina Apostolorum* in Rome: Irish crosses and Early Christian sarcophagi' in Hourihane (ed.), 9–26.

Verzone, P. 1967. *From Theodoric to Charlemagne*, London.

Vierck, H. 1970. 'Cortina Triripodis: zu Aufhangung und Gebrauch Subrömischer Hangebecken aus Britannien und Irland', *Frümitteralterliche Studien*, 4, 8–52.

Wadell, J. & Clyne, M. 1995. 'M.V. Duignan's excavations at Kiltiernan, Co. Galway, 1950–1953', *Journal of the Galway Archaeological and Historical Society*, 47, 149–204.

Wallace, P. & Ó Floinn, R. (eds). 2002. *Treasures of the National Museum of Ireland: Irish antiquities*, Dublin.

Warner, R.B. 1979. 'The Clogher yellow layer', *Medieval Ceramics*, 3, 37–40.

Warner, R.B. 1987. 'Ireland and the origins of escutcheon art' in Ryan, M. (ed.), *Ireland and Insular art, AD500–1200*, Dublin, 19–22.

Warner, R.B. 1994. 'The earliest history of Ireland' in Ryan, M. (ed.), *Irish archaeology illustrated*, Dublin, 112–16.

Warner, R.B. 1995. 'Tuathal Techtmhar: a myth or ancient literary evidence for a Roman invasion?', *Emania*, 13, 23–32.

Waterman, D. 1951. 'Excavations at Dundrum Castle, 1950', *UJA*, 14, 15–29.

Webster, L. & Backhouse, J. (eds). 1991. *The making of England: Anglo-Saxon art and culture, AD600–900*, London.

Webster, L. 1982. 'Stylistic aspects of the Franks Casket' in Farrell, R.T. (ed.), *The Vikings*, London, 20–32.

Werckmeister, O.-K., 1967. *Irische-northumbrische Buchmalerei des 8. Jahrhunderts und monastische Spiritualität*, Berlin.

Werner, J. 1964. 'Frankish royal tombs in the cathedrals of Cologne and St Denis', *Antiquity*, 38, 201–16.

Werner, J. 1979. *Spätes Kelentum zwischen Rom und Germanien*, Munich.

Werner, J. 1987. 'Jonas in Helgö', *Bonner Jahrbücher*, 178, 519–30.

Werner, M. 1969. 'The four evangelist symbols page in the Book of Durrow', *Gesta*, 8, 3–15.

Werner, M. 1972. 'The Virgin and Child miniatures in the Book of Kells', *Art Bulletin*, 54, pp 1–23, 129–39.

Werner, M. 1990a. 'On the origin of the form of the Irish High Cross', *Gesta*, 29:1, 98–110.

Werner, M. 1990b. 'The cross-carpet page in the Book of Durrow: the cult of the true cross, Adomnán and Iona', *Art Bulletin*, 72, 174–229.

Werner, M. 1994. '*Crucifixi, sepulti, suscitati*: remarks on the decoration of the Book of Kells' in Mahoney (ed.), 450–88.

Whitfield, N. 1987. 'Motifs and techniques of Celtic filigree: are they original?' in Ryan, M. (ed.), 75–84.

Whitfield, N. 1993. 'The filigree of the "Tara" and Hunterston Brooches' in Spearman & Higgit (eds), 115–27.

Whitfield, N. 1995. 'Formal conventions in the depictions of animals in Celtic metalwork' in Bourke (ed.), 89–104.

Whitfield, N. 1996. 'Brooch or cross? The lozenge on the shoulder of the Virgin in the Book of Kells', *Archaeology Ireland*, 10:1, 20–3.

Whitfield, N. 1999. 'Design and units of measure on the Hunterston Brooch' in Hawkes, J. & Mills, S. (eds), *Northumbria's Golden Age*, Stroud, Gloucestershire, 296–314.

Whitfield, N. 2001a. 'The "Tara" Brooch: an Irish emblem of status in its European context' in Hourihane (ed.), 211–47.

Whitfield, N. 2001b. 'The earliest filigree from Ireland' in Redknap et al. (eds), 141–54.

Whitfield, N. 2004. 'More thoughts on the wearing of brooches in Early Medieval Ireland' in Hourihane (ed.), 70–108.

Whitfield, N. 2006. 'Gold wire coil' in Laing & Longley (eds), 40.

Whitfield, N. 2007. 'Motifs and techniques in Early Medieval Celtic filigree: their ultimate origins' in Moss (ed.), 18–39.

Williams, I. 1938. *Canu Aneirin*, Cardiff.

Wilson, D. & Blunt, C.E. 1961. 'The Trewhiddle Hoard', *Archaeologia*, 98, 75–122.

Wilson, D. & Klindt-Jensen, O. 1966. *Viking art*, London.

Wilson, D. 1973. 'The treasure' in Small et al., 45–148.

Wilson, D.M. 1976. 'The Borre style in the British Isles' in Vilhjalmsson, B. (ed.), *Minjasr og Menntir*, Reykjavik, 502–9.

Wilson, D.M. 1983. 'The art of the Manx crosses in the Viking Age' in Fell, C. et al. (eds), 175–85.

Wooding, J.M. 1996. *Communication and commerce along the western Sea-lanes, AD400–800*, BAR International Series, 654, Oxford.

Woods, D. 2002. 'Arculf's luggage: the sources for Adomnán's *De Locis Sanctis*', *Ériu*, 52, 25–52.

Wormald, P. 1996. 'The emergence of the Regnum Scottorum: a Carolingian hegemony?' in Crawford, B. (ed.), *Scotland in Dark Age Britain*, St Andrews, 131–53.

Youngs, S. (ed.). 1989. *The work of angels: masterpieces of Celtic metalwork 6th–9th centuries AD*, London.

Youngs, S. 1993. 'Two medieval Celtic enamelled buckles from Leicestershire', *Transacrions of the Leicestershire Archaeological and Historical Society*, 67, 15–22.

Youngs, S. 2007. 'Britain, Wales and Ireland: holding things together' in Jankulak, K. & Wooding, J.M. (eds), *Ireland and Wales in the Middle Ages*, Dublin, 80–100.

Zimmer, H. 1902. *Keltische Kirche in Britannien und Irland', Realencyclopädie fur Protestantische Theologie und Kirche*, Leipzig.

Zimmer, H. 1909–10. 'Über direkte Handelsverbinungen Westgalliens mit Irland im Alterum und frühen Mittelalter', *Sitzungberichte der königlich preussischen Akademie der Wissenschaften*.

Index